T0361234

ROUTLEDGE LIBRARY EDITIONS:
DEVELOPMENT

WEST AFRICAN TRADE

WEST AFRICAN TRADE

A Study of Competition, Oligopoly and Monopoly in a Changing Economy

P. T. BAUER

Volume 28

Routledge
Taylor & Francis Group

LONDON AND NEW YORK

First published in 1954 by The Cambridge University Press
Reissued with a new preface in 1963 by Routledge & Kegan Paul Ltd

This edition first published in 2011
by Routledge
2 Park Square, Milton Park, Abingdon, Oxon, OX14 4RN

Simultaneously published in the USA and Canada
by Routledge
270 Madison Avenue, New York, NY 10016

Routledge is an imprint of the Taylor & Francis Group, an informa business

© 1963 P.T. Bauer

British Library Cataloguing in Publication Data
A catalogue record for this book is available from the British Library

ISBN 13: 978-0-415-58414-2 (Set)
eISBN 13: 978-0-203-84035-1 (Set)
ISBN 13: 978-0-415-59383-0 (Volume 28)
eISBN 13: 978-0-203-83855-6 (Volume 28)

Publisher's Note
The publisher has gone to great lengths to ensure the quality of this reprint but
points out that some imperfections in the original copies may be apparent.

Disclaimer
The publisher has made every effort to trace copyright holders and welcomes
correspondence from those they have been unable to contact.

FRENCH WEST

SENEGAL

R. Senegal

Cape
Verde

R. Gambia

Bathurst

GAMBIA

PORTUGUESE
GUINEA

FRENCH GUINEA

Timbuktu

R. Niger

Black Volta

NORT
TERR

GOL
COA

AS

Marampa
Makeni

Freetown

SIERRA

Pendembu

LEONE

LIBERIA

IVORY COAST

GOLD CO
COLO

Ta

ATLANTIC OCEAN

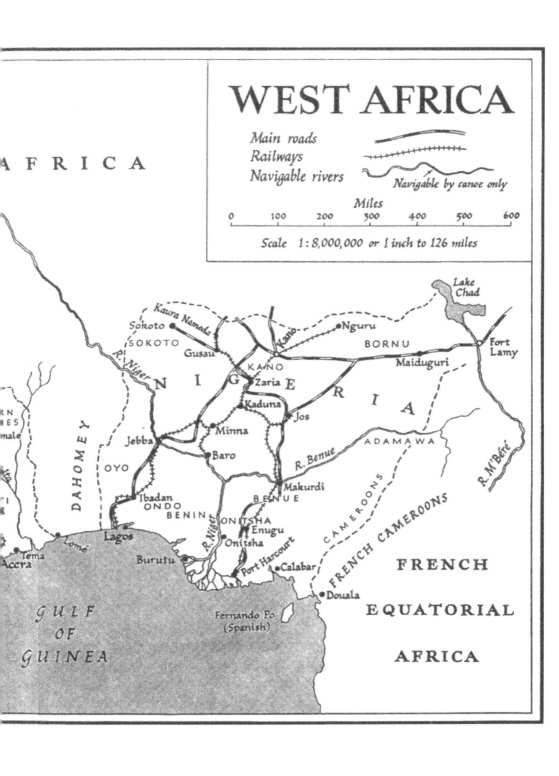

WEST AFRICA

Main roads
Railways
Navigable rivers

Navigable by canoe only

Miles

0   100   200   300   400   500   600

Scale   1 : 8,000,000 or 1 inch to 126 miles

AFRICA

Lake
Chad

Kaura Namada

Sokoto

SOKOTO   Gusau

Nguru

Kano

BORNU   Fort
Lamy

R. Niger   KANO   Maiduguri

N   I   G   Zaria   E

Kaduna   R   I   A

Minna   Jos

Jebba   Baro   ADAMAWA

R. Benue   R. M'Bére

OYO

DAHOMEY   Makurdi

Ibadan   BENUE

ONDO   BENIN   CAMEROONS

Lomé   Lagos   ONITSHA   Enugu   FRENCH CAMEROONS

Tema   Burutu   Onitsha

Accra   Port Harcourt   Calabar   FRENCH

Douala

GULF   EQUATORIAL

OF   Fernando Po
(Spanish)

GUINEA   AFRICA

R. Niger

WEST AFRICAN TRADE

A Study of Competition, Oligopoly and Monopoly in a Changing Economy

P. T. BAUER

University Lecturer in Economics, Fellow and Lecturer
of Gonville and Caius College, Cambridge

ROUTLEDGE & KEGAN PAUL LTD
BROADWAY HOUSE, 68-74 CARTER LANE
LONDON, E.C.4

First published in 1954
by The Cambridge University Press
Reissued, with a new preface
by Routledge & Kegan Paul Ltd
Broadway House, 68-74 Carter Lane
London, E.C.4
Printed in Great Britain
by Lowe & Brydone (Printers) Ltd
London, N.W.10

© 1963 P. T. Bauer

CONTENTS

Part 1

GENERAL ASPECTS OF THE WEST AFRICAN ECONOMIES AND OF THE ROLE OF TRADE

Part 2

THE IMPORT TRADE

A*

Part 5

THE STATUTORY MARKETING BOARDS
AND THEIR POLICIES

Part 6

THE ECONOMICS OF MARKETING REFORM

Part 7

INTERNAL TRADE

APPENDICES

LIST OF TABLES

LIST OF CHARTS

MAPS

West Africa, showing main roads, railways and navigable rivers

PREFACE

The work for this study began as an investigation into the structure of West African trade and especially of monopolistic tendencies, undertaken at the request of the Colonial Office. For reasons stated in the introduction, its scope had to be extended substantially beyond the topics usually covered under these headings, and it broadened into a detailed study of West African trade and of those aspects of the West African economies which bear on trade. It was conducted under the auspices of the Colonial Economic Research Committee, which recommended to the Secretary of the State for the Colonies that it should be financed by a grant from Colonial Development and Welfare funds. The views expressed are not those of any government authority.

The collection and analysis of the material for this study were undertaken between the early part of 1949 and the latter part of 1952. The book deals mostly with basic factors and aspects of the West African economies largely unaffected by the political and economic developments of the last few years. But important changes have occurred in a number of subjects reviewed, notably such matters as the administration of trade controls and the policies of the marketing boards. It has not been possible to bring up to date the material beyond about the middle of 1952, and it should be remembered that the discussion refers to conditions at that time, and to policies pursued up to that time.

I have received much liberal help from both official and private sources. I was given free access to the relevant files of the Colonial Office, of the local governments and of the marketing boards. Moreover, not only was this material placed at my disposal, but much information was specially collected and tabulated by the authorities for the purpose of this inquiry. Both in Nigeria and in the Gold Coast the executives of the marketing boards have been of the greatest help in making information available. I have also had much assistance from the Department of Commerce and from the Department of Statistics both in Nigeria and in the Gold Coast.

The attitude adopted by the commercial firms has also been very liberal. I have been greatly assisted in my work by European, Levantine and African firms and merchants. I received much confidential information from the firms of John Holt and Company Ltd., A. G. Leventis and Company Ltd., and the United Africa Company Ltd.

The help I have received from the United Africa Company was especially generous. The Company made available to me much confidential information, and the material was given to me without restriction on its use. As well as adopting this very liberal attitude, directors and officers of the Company gave me freely of their time for discussion of problems of West African trade.

In the writing of this book I have had great assistance from Mr B. S. Yamey. I assembled the material, but in the greater part of the book our collaboration was so close that the analysis and presentation are his as much as mine, and I am very much indebted to him indeed. In the analysis of the problems of the statutory marketing boards I have benefited greatly from collaboration with Professor F. W. Paish. Those familiar with contemporary economic literature will realize how fortunate I have been in my collaborators. I am also obliged for helpful criticisms of earlier drafts of this book to Professors E. A. G. Robinson and S. Herbert Frankel.

In the collection, analysis and presentation of statistics I was greatly helped by Mr G. L. Unsworth, formerly of the Colonial Office and at present with the Board of Trade, and Miss S. Y. Mallett, Statistical Assistant in Research, Cambridge University. In the closing stages of the work a very heavy burden was borne by Miss Mallett in the preparation and presentation of the tables and diagrams. Her helpfulness and efficiency made it possible to extend all the time series to the end of 1951.

Some of the material in this book has appeared at various times (or will appear shortly) usually in a somewhat different form, in *Economica*, the *Journal of the Royal Statistical Society*, the *Business History Review* (Harvard) and the *South African Journal of Economics*. I am obliged to the editors of these journals for permission to use it again.

I am also grateful to my publishers, the Cambridge University Press, and to their staff, for unfailing efficiency, courtesy and forbearance at various stages in the production of the book. Lastly, I should like to thank Miss S. D. Lyman who has borne the burden of the secretarial work in the preparation of this book, and whose efficiency and patience have been of great help.

P. T. BAUER

GONVILLE AND CAIUS COLLEGE
CAMBRIDGE
March 1954

PREFACE TO THE 1963 REISSUE

The reissue of a book long out of print is always gratifying to an author, particularly when, as in this instance, it represents several years of work in his special field of study.

I think that the shortcomings which a revision would need to rectify are those of omission rather than of commission. The major subjects treated represent either examination of dominant features of the West African economies and analysis of their implications, or description and discussion of topics or policies of some general interest. This applies, for instance, to the rapid progress of the West African economies over the last half-century; the multiplicity of traders and the role and productivity of trade; the operation of restrictive tendencies in emerging economies; the high degree of concentration in the private sector of external trade; the factors influencing new entry and the prospects of entrants; the operation of private market sharing agreements, and the relation between these and official controls; the effect of buying competition on the terms of trade of producers; the main features of internal trade; the problems of price and income stabilization; the operation of official export monopolies; the special problems of official controls in underdeveloped countries; and the implications of the immigration policy.

These topics were chosen because they seemed of more than ephemeral significance in West Africa, or because they raised issues of some general interest, or because they reflected the operation of forces at work elsewhere also and thrown into unusually clear relief in West Africa. The statistics presented are all designed to illustrate one or other of these topics, and in this sense are still relevant. I hope, therefore, though this is necessarily only an expression of hope, that much of the book, including the statistics, is not out of date.

The familiar problem of the need for revision arises acutely because of the far reaching political and social changes in West Africa, which were already apparent when the book was completed about ten years ago, as is recognized in its sub-title. If I were to re-write this book now, or if I had the opportunity to revise it extensively, I would have to discuss at length certain important developments which have taken place in West Africa during the last decade, and which are relevant to the trading situation and methods there. Perhaps the most important of these are the expansion of the market; the development of local manufacturing activity; the increase in the numbers of officially sponsored or controlled industrial and trading organizations; and the decision of some of the major expatriate merchant firms to abandon or curtail produce buying and the retailing or semi-whole-saling of important branches of merchandise.

The expansion of the market is the result of several factors, notably the secular advance of these economies, especially through the progress of the exchange economy, the running down of the reserves of official boards, notably the former West African Currency Board and the marketing boards, and the injection into these ecomomies of substantial external aid. The expansion of the market and the development of local manufacturers, in part spontaneous, in part officially sponsored, have considerably reduced the effective dominance in the market of the larger expatriate firms.

The larger size of the market has been particularly important, since it has increased its attraction to overseas manufacturers, many of whom have set up sales organizations, agencies and depots outside the control of the larger established merchants. The recovery and expansion of some of the West European economies, especially those of West Germany and Italy, and the greater interest in West Africa of various East European countries, have increased actual and potential competition in the merchandise trade, and they have greatly reduced the scope and significance of exclusive agencies. In Nigeria at any rate, a wider market seems to have more than offset the inhibiting effects of political uncertainties and official restrictions on the entry and activities of expatriate merchants, inhibiting effects which tend to strengthen the relative position of established firms. The increase in the number of official and semi-official industrial organizations are the result partly of familiar forces and influences at work in many underdeveloped countries, and partly the result of the search for outlets for the very large funds accumulated by the marketing boards. The withdrawal of some of the larger firms from produce buying and from certain branches of the merchandise trade is the result partly of various forms of political pressure and of the operation of the immigration regulations; partly of the unremunerative level of the margins prescribed by the marketing boards to the licensed private buying agents; and partly the development of personnel and capital into more profitable directions.

Some of these results are implicitly covered by the discussion, especially those which represent acceleration of tendencies already at work when the book was written. But the absence of explicit and systematic discussion of these topics is undoubtedly a serious, though unavoidable, defect of omission

I stand by the argument of the book. The discussion of price stabilization and of the operation of the marketing boards aroused much controversy at the time, but the analysis and conclusions are no longer disputed. In particular, the contention that the operation of the system is simply a method of taxation is today no longer questioned, and is indeed officially recognized in such measures as the imposition of a governmentally prescribed price for cocoa in Ghana, and the effective diversion to the Government of practically the entire difference between the market price and this fixed price; and in the directive in Nigeria by the Northern Regional Government to its Marketing Board not to concern itself with stabilization but fixed producer prices so as to ensure a surplus each year.

There is one topic where I think a change of emphasis is perhaps necessary. In view of the extended discussion of the high degree of concentration in the private sector of external trade, more emphasis might have been placed on the relative unimportance of the barriers to entry (in the absence of official restrictions on the establishment or progress of new enterprises), and on the consequent limitation on the scope for abnormal returns, or monopoly or quasi-monopoly profits. Although these points are made in the book, I think that greater and more explicit stress might have been placed on the distinction between natural or inevitable scarcities on one hand, and contrived scarcities on the other, the former representing the limitation of the total supply of certain types of scarce resources, and the latter the withholding from the market of part of the total supply, through various restrictive devices. During the war and early post-war years, contrived scarcities, generally the result of the operation of official controls and of private market sharing agreements, buttressed by such controls, considerably inflated the profits of the 'expatriate merchants. But generally the contribution of contrived scarcities to trading profits has been negligible, even before the results of the expansion of the market have weakened the dominant position of the large expatriate firms; the trading profits represent very largely the returns for the provision of capital, skills, experience and risk taking, effectively under long term competitive conditions. This should be emphasized, since so much of the discussion of the operation of the private sector covers the war and early post-war years.

December 1962   P. T. B.

INTRODUCTION

SCOPE AND METHOD OF THE STUDY

I. OUTLINE OF THE SCOPE OF THE STUDY

This study began as an inquiry into the structure of West African external trade with special reference to monopolistic tendencies. As it is generally interpreted, a study of the structure of trade involves an inquiry into the role of different classes of trading intermediary, the quantitative significance of each class, and the shares of the trade handled by one or more of the largest firms. Where the emphasis is on monopolistic tendencies, the share of trade handled by large firms and by groups of firms acting together deserves special attention; in addition, the nature and effects of various marketing practices which influence the extent of concentration also require more detailed investigation. Some of these topics have been prominent in the emphatic and acrimonious, though generally imprecise and uncritical, discussions on West African trade in recent decades.

These matters are discussed at some length in this study. It gradually became clear, however, that proper discussion of the original subject-matter of the inquiry postulated analysis and review of the forces influencing economic power and the extent of concentration in trade. Some of these varied and diverse forces are in turn so closely interwoven with certain general characteristics of the West African economies that it has been necessary to examine these also. A lengthy treatment thus became inevitable once the study extended beyond the confines of the structure of trade.

2. LIMITATIONS ON THE SCOPE OF THE STUDY

The British West African colonies have about one-half of the population of the colonial Empire; indeed, the population of Nigeria, which by now may be not far short of 30 million, is itself almost one-half of the total. The external trade of these colonies is about one-fifth of the total of the colonial Empire. The proportion would be larger if entrepôt trade were excluded; and it would be larger still if the prices received by the producers of export crops were nearer their commercial values than they are at present. The total value of the merchandise trade of these territories in recent years is shown in Table 1.

A measure of selection has been necessary to reduce to manageable proportions a survey of the trade of the large and diverse territories and economies of the British colonies in West Africa. Thus there is no special consideration of Sierra Leone and the Gambia. I visited Sierra Leone in the course of my inquiries, and collected some interesting material which has helped to clarify some of the arguments; this material is largely incorporated in this study. In general, however, the two smaller colonies have had to be omitted from the discussion in the interests of brevity; the study concentrates on the economies of Nigeria and the Gold Coast. These two colonies comprise well over 90 % of the population of the four West African territories, and their external trade is over 95 % of that of British West Africa.

This study is primarily concerned with trade; therefore the economic problems of manufacturing industry and of transport and banking are discussed only in so far as they bear closely on trading activities.

Table 1. *External trade of Nigeria and the Gold Coast, 1948–51*

Note. The figures refer to visible trade, excluding specie and currency.

	Nigeria			Gold Coast		
	Exports (f.o.b.) £ m.	Imports (c.i.f.) £ m.	Total £ m.	Exports (f.o.b.) £ m.	Imports (c.i.f.) £ m.	Total £ m.
1948	62·3	41·2	103·5	55·6	30·1	85·7
1949	80·2	57·5	137·7	49·6	44·4	94·0
1950	87·2	60·0	147·2	76·4	48·0	124·4
1951	128·4	84·0	212·4	91·3	63·4	154·7

3. DIVERSITY AND CONTRAST IN WEST AFRICA

The heterogeneity of the population and of the physical structure of the country is a feature of all four British West African colonies. The vast area of Nigeria, though to some extent administered as one country, contains three regions, whose populations differ in history, social organization, outlook and language quite as much as the British differ from the French or the Germans. Within each region there are other major groups, tribes or races with widely different institutions and languages. This diversity extends even to very small areas and communities. It bears on this survey at many points; and it is relevant to the conduct and organization of trade as well as to issues of official policy.

In addition to this heterogeneity, there are instances of extreme contrasts such as can be found in very few other countries. Some examples may be useful here. In Port Harcourt several African wholesale merchants operate on a large scale. Among them there is an African lady whose annual turnover with one of the big European trading firms runs into six figures. Her business methods are essentially those of a modern wholesale trader. Thirty miles away there are markets in which the sale of meat without the hide is prohibited to ensure that no human flesh is sold for human consumption.

The Oni of Ife, the spiritual head of the Yoruba in western Nigeria, is a member of the Cocoa Marketing Board and a director of the Nigeria Produce Marketing Company; in this capacity he is concerned with the marketing of produce which at present has an annual value of about £100 million. But as spiritual head of the Yoruba he is considered responsible for the regulation of the supply of rainfall in Nigeria.

In Onitsha I witnessed a remarkable transaction in which the three partners of an African trading firm (all women) bought on credit over £9000 worth of tobacco from a European trading house; the informal elegance and dignity of the proceedings and the obvious mutual respect and confidence could not have been excelled in the most select trading circles of London and Amsterdam. The same day in the vicinity I visited a fair-sized market close to a large number of the crudest ju-ju shrines; some of the adult participants in the market were without a shred of clothing.

The United Africa Company is a giant concern operating enterprises employing the most up-to-date equipment. Yet a year or two ago five night watchmen employed by the company were found guilty of having murdered two men and having eaten their fingers in order to acquire greater strength. At about the same time in a native court two men were tried for tying up the rain and preventing it from falling. They pleaded guilty (it is not known whether from conviction or from shrewd business motives), and were fined £5.

There are also extreme contrasts in the size of transactions. The big merchant firms may import merchandise in lots of hundreds of cases or bales and resell at times in units of scores of cases or bales. At the other extreme cheap imported scent is sometimes sold by the drop; for a half-penny two dabs of scent can be bought.

These contrasts reflect the fact that certain sectors of the economies have reached an advanced and in some cases even a sophisticated stage, while others are only a few decades removed from a barbarous and savage state, or have not as yet fully emerged from it. The factors underlying these contrasts and extremes themselves present difficult problems for economic policy and its administration. They are central to an understanding of the functioning of these economies.

In a meaningful description and analysis of such economies it is necessary to restrict abstraction rather severely, and to investigate factors and influences which are often regarded in modern studies in economics as institutional elements (or as data given to the economist). This survey therefore includes a review of some factors which are normally omitted from most modern text-books on economics, and even from some of those professedly dealing with applied economics.

PART 1

GENERAL ASPECTS OF THE WEST AFRICAN ECONOMIES AND OF THE ROLE OF TRADE

CHAPTER 1

UNDERLYING FORCES AND INFLUENCES

This chapter treats of certain underlying forces and influences in the West African economies of special relevance to this study. The selected aspects are the impact of the money economy and of its recent and rapid growth; the imperfect specialization of economic activity; the low level of certain productive resources, especially of capital; and the unemployment of unskilled general workers. These have been chosen because an understanding of the phenomena is fundamental to an appreciation of the trading situation in West Africa.

1. DIFFICULTIES OF ADJUSTMENT TO A MONEY ECONOMY

Although by Western standards the real income of the population of the West African colonies is still low, and very low in some territories, these economies are not stagnant. In fact, many of their problems arise from the very rapid and necessarily uneven development which has taken place, and especially from the impact and progress of a money and exchange economy. There has been trade between Europe and the west coast of Africa since the sixteenth century, but its character, composition and volume have changed fundamentally during the last few decades. Until about fifty years ago there were no exports of cocoa, groundnuts, hides and skins or timber, and the export of palm products was only a fraction of what it is today. The Ibo, who today play an important part in Nigerian trade, were in an almost savage state as recently as 1910. It would call for anthropologists and sociologists to analyse many facets of the progress and the effects of this rapid transition. But those which bear closely on the present study require discussion here.

The comparatively recent emergence of a money economy explains the presence of institutions and attitudes which are largely unsuited to its requirements. The family system is an example.[1] In West Africa a reasonably prosperous man is frequently obliged to support even

[1] The term 'family' includes many more distant relatives and kinsmen than in Europe. The brief discussion of the family system in the text is intended only as a rough outline of those of its features which bear on the structure of West African trade. The information is based on numerous discussions with Europeans and Africans, and on some personal observations of the system and of its results. This seems sufficient for the brief analysis of its effects on the structure of trade, but comprehensive discussion would, of course, require the methods and the training of an anthropologist, by whose standards and for whose purposes the discussion presented here is necessarily amateurish.

distant kinsmen and relatives. A moderately successful man may find that a score or more relatives descend on him, expecting to live off his bounty. Some of the successful Africans probably enjoy the status and sense of power attaching to the support of their relatives, but many admit in private discussion that they dread these extensive obligations.

The system is not without redeeming features. It exhibits elements of real charity and generosity. Moreover, it often results in the pooling of family resources for such purposes as the education of promising children or the setting up of a member of the family in trade or in a profession. In such circumstances it amounts to a circulation of capital within the family. Persons supporting a number of needy kinsmen may themselves have been supported by distant relatives a few years earlier.

The principal weakness seems to be the comparative absence of discrimination in its exercise. Relatives who might be able to support themselves qualify for assistance on much the same basis as those who cannot find employment. Quite clearly the system is largely the legacy of a subsistence economy.[1] Excessive and indiscriminate hospitality is a feature of subsistence economies where surpluses cannot be marketed, and where it is therefore expected that these should be used for charity, and in particular for liberal entertainment of kinsmen, friends and visitors.

The excessive hospitality and the indiscriminate maintenance of distant relatives are likely to diminish in West Africa as economic and social life increasingly sheds the habits and institutions of subsistence economies. Meantime capital formation and economic development are retarded; thrift, enterprise and initiative and the productive use of accumulated savings are discouraged, and an incidental premium is placed upon idleness. The fear of the obligations of the family system is partly responsible for the widespread use of textiles and trinkets as outlets for savings, in preference to more productive forms of investment which are more likely to attract the attention of relatives.[2]

The comparatively slow spread of banking in parts of the Gold Coast and Nigeria may also be partly attributed to the family system. Africans often mistrust the bank clerks, fearing that they may disclose the size of their accounts to members of their families. They therefore prefer to keep their savings under the fireplace or buried in the ground.[3] An

[1] The widespread unemployment of unskilled workers is possibly a secondary reason. But the system is so indiscriminate as to make it certain that this is not a major reason.

[2] There are other reasons as well, mostly connected with imperfect adjustment to the requirements of a market economy.

[3] It appears that the fear of disclosure to relatives is as yet more important than the fear of disclosure to the authorities, which is the reason for similar practices in more advanced economies.

educated African chief told a bank manager in the Gold Coast that were it not for this particular suspicion the banking habit among Africans would spread very rapidly. The failure of some prosperous traders to keep bank accounts makes it more difficult for them to secure bank advances, since bankers do not like lending to customers who do not pass all their transactions through the bank.

The complexities of African land tenure, which are connected with the family and the tribal systems, require only brief mention here. Both in Nigeria and in the Gold Coast family and tribal rights in rural land are often so complex that land is an unsatisfactory security for loans. This obstructs the flow and application of capital to certain uses of high return, which in turn retards the growth of income and hence of accumulation.

The people often exhibit a pronounced ignorance of the operations of an exchange and market economy, again partly because of its novelty. The profit margins of the European firms and of the Levantine[1] and African intermediaries are believed to depend solely or largely on their own decisions, which are only remotely connected with such academic matters as supply and demand. Accumulated wealth is thought to have been earned solely by the impoverishment of customers or competitors. It is a widespread article of faith that the wealth of the mercantile firms has been extracted from the Africans and has in no way been created by the activities of the merchants.

Unfortunately, many of these fallacies have now become respectable doctrine in more sophisticated countries, and are often explicitly supported by members of the European community in West Africa. This has an important practical corollary: even the cruder notions current in West Africa are not effectively refuted, because the underlying fallacies are not discerned. Consequently certain unreasonable African demands are not resisted, even where a little analysis would show that the proposed measures would not only be harmful but would also defeat their own ends. It is by no means a foregone conclusion that the Africans would be unable or unwilling to understand the confused and self-frustrating character of some of their demands if this were clearly shown to them, but this must remain an open question for the time being.

This imperfect understanding of the operation of market forces is also evident in the widespread complaint of Africans that whenever they attempt to establish themselves in business, especially in the direct importing of commodities from overseas, the European merchant firms deliberately reduce prices to put them out of business. As we shall see

[1] Throughout this study the term 'Levantine' includes Lebanese, Syrians, Greeks, Cypriots, Tripolitanians and Arabs; Lebanese are numerically the most important in West Africa.

later there may have been instances where firms have engaged in localized or temporary underselling with the deliberate intention of destroying a competitor. But Africans are apt to regard any fall in prices as evidence of a deliberate attempt to put them out of business.

The smaller African importers and traders have great difficulty in understanding the various government regulations affecting them. Some government departments, especially the Department of Commerce and Industries in Nigeria, attempt to give wide publicity in simple language to the various licensing regulations, especially to those relating to import control, and they have obtained some measure of success. But there are still many *bona fide* traders who do not understand the operation of these and of other regulations. There is a steady increase in direct government control and direction of economic life. The administration of these regulations, especially the compulsory inspection of export produce, opens the door to corruption, graft and oppression. This is only to be expected where the regulations are not understood by the majority of those affected by them, and where those who are injured are unable or unwilling to protest effectively.

Many African traders, especially importers, are not always meticulous in honouring commercial contracts. This naturally makes commercial intercourse between foreign firms and African traders more difficult, and slows down economic development in West Africa, as well as the Africanization of commerce and industry. Many examples of African commercial dishonesty stem from the period of imperfect import and price control during and after the war. Quick and almost riskless profits were open to those traders who were able to obtain short-supply merchandise at controlled prices or who were allotted the necessary import permits. The trade attracted many *ad hoc* traders (including schoolboys), who, because they regarded their activities as isolated and discontinuous ventures, were not averse to breaking contracts if owing to changes in market conditions their fulfilment was no longer advantageous. In 1949 the warehouses of Lagos and Accra were stacked with consignments addressed to African importers on firm orders which they had refused to accept, either because the market had turned against them, or because they hoped that the goods would eventually have to be auctioned and that they would thus obtain them direct, or through nominees, at prices well below the contract terms. But this weakness should properly be associated with conditions which make for episodic commercial relationships, when lapses from commercial standards of honesty are likely to be frequent in all trading communities in Africa or elsewhere. In fairness it should be stated that some overseas suppliers of African customers are also apt to follow standards very different from those prevailing in Britain and Western Europe.

Africans in the import trade may sometimes appear to be dishonest when they fail to meet their obligations. Often the failure is not due to dishonesty or even to irresponsible risk-taking, but to a combination of small capital, severe price fluctuations, and a tendency to overtrade which is often encouraged by European exporters eager to secure business.

These differences in the trading methods of Europeans and Africans arise from social, institutional and political factors. The comparatively recent emergence of a money economy has, however, also played a part, since the importance of continuity in business relationships, and of integrity as a condition of this continuity, has not yet come to be generally appreciated. But the observer cannot fail to be impressed by the numerous examples testifying to the commercial trustworthiness of African traders and intermediaries. Continuous business relationships, often of long duration, exist between parties in produce buying and in the distribution of imported merchandise. European merchant houses grant substantial trade credit to African customers or make advances to Africans to finance produce buying. There are also extensive credit transactions between Levantines and Africans. Loans are often outstanding for considerable periods on conditions which require much mutual trust.

2. IMPERFECT SPECIALIZATION

The economic activities of large sections of the population of West Africa are still partly or largely unspecialized. The preponderance of a few staple exports is compatible with a low degree of economic specialization. Many farmers produce a number of products on a very small scale.[1] Even in northern Nigeria and in the Northern Territories of the Gold Coast many farmers spend a substantial part of their time in non-agricultural activities, or in activities away from their home as migrant labourers or traders. In other parts of these countries, especially in southern Nigeria and the colony area of the Gold Coast, the great bulk of the population has other occupations, generally some form of trading, in addition to their main activity. The lack of specialization becomes more apparent when the economic activities of wives and children are taken into account. Africans frequently do not regard trade as an occupation (especially when carried on by dependants), and would not refer to it as such. They regard it as part of existence and not as a distinct occupation.[2]

[1] The cocoa farmers are probably more specialized than the rest of the farming population.
[2] In general the wives and children are independent economic agents as much as dependent relatives. They almost invariably take part in trade, and participate to

The lack of specialization which affects a large section of West African economic life derives from narrow markets which are an aspect of the low level of the local economy. In turn it impedes efficiency and retards economic progress. Thus it is both a symptom and a cause of the low standard of living.

This imperfect specialization and the importance of secondary activities carried on by members of the household greatly diminish the value and relevance of the conventional occupational classifications of statistical compilations. This fact has not been sufficiently recognized. Official reports and standard works state, for example, that five-sixths of the population is engaged in agriculture,[1] and they rarely mention trade among the lists of the economic activities of the population.[2] In fact, in many of these so-called agricultural households the head of the family trades part-time even during the normally short farming season, and more actively outside the season, whilst members of his family trade intermittently throughout the year. It is misleading to ignore these trading activities and to imply that the great bulk of the population is engaged in farming only.

The fluidity of activity extends to personal relations where they bear closely on economic life. A prominent African trader in Lagos, whose children are being educated at expensive residential schools and universities in Britain, told me that his wife was one of his principal customers, and that she bought goods from him both on cash and on credit terms. He did not consider this unusual; indeed, it is not so, as similar commercial relations exist between other prominent Africans and their wives and children. It is not unusual for wives to sue their husbands for commercial debts.

It is well known that many African doctors and lawyers have extensive trading interests. Government employees are also frequently part-time traders. Every servant or driver who worked for me on my two visits to Nigeria was either in trade or asked for my assistance in finding

some extent in the economic life of the country. The wife is expected to make some contribution to the family income. This is no doubt partly because there is very little for her to do in the house. In parts of Nigeria and the Gold Coast a man expects his wife to trade, and he is likely to regard the bride price (which is in fact a dowry in reverse and not a sign of the low social status of women) partly as an investment in a trading concern. In certain parts of the Gold Coast a husband can divorce his wife if she fails more than twice as a trader. On the other hand, women often trade in order to save enough money to return the bride price and thus to be able to divorce their husbands. The children also generally trade, as there are few adequate schools and there is little else to occupy them.

[1] Cf. the statistics quoted, apparently with approval, in *An African Survey*, 2nd edition, pp. 1425–6.

[2] The official annual reports on Nigeria and the Gold Coast provide examples.

trading contacts for him. Many of these requests were simply advanced to obtain either free samples or else so-called short-supply goods at controlled prices for re-sale at easy and immediate profit. But at least one of my drivers, a full-time employee of a government department, displayed an excellent knowledge of market prices and of market conditions for provisions throughout southern Nigeria, and acted upon it.[1]

Quite apart from this imperfect occupational specialization there is still widespread lack of specialization in trading operations both horizontally (by type of commodity handled) and vertically (by successive stages of distribution). These will be considered when the import trade comes to be reviewed.

3. THE LOW LEVEL OF PRODUCTIVE RESOURCES

West Africa is generally poor in disclosed and accessible natural economic resources, acquired capital and technical and administrative skills. It is preferable to speak of the low level of capital rather than of its scarcity. The comparative lack of local technical and administrative skill aggravates the effects of the scarcity of equipment; it is not lack of capital alone which retards development. For this reason indiscriminate import of capital, or even substantial capital accumulation in the hands of public organizations, alone would not necessarily improve the situation.

The African communities are very poor in acquired reserves of fertile soil, in accumulated plant, buildings, roads and railways, as well as in stocks of working capital and in liquid assets with which external capital can be obtained. Though the measurement of capital raises conceptual difficulties, it is quite easy to illustrate its low level in West Africa. Nigeria may be taken as an example. The territory has an area of approximately 372,000 sq. miles and a population of about 30 millions. The f.o.b. value of its exports is at present over £100 m. a year. Two of its major export crops originate in the north, 700–1000 miles from the sea. The bulk of the meat supply also comes from that area or even farther north. The volume of the shipborne cargo handled in the ports of Nigeria in 1949 was almost 2½ m. tons. The capital equipment sustaining this very large trade is extremely small. At the end of 1949 the total track mileage of the Nigerian railway was 1900 miles. There were only

---

[1] The following episode is characteristic of several aspects of economic life and of trade in Nigeria. This driver, when on tour with me, ascertained in Ibadan (112 miles from Lagos) that the price of tins of Horlicks was lower there than in Lagos, where they were originally landed. The difference was 6d. a tin. He decided to buy a dozen tins, gave a deposit of 5s. and on our return to Lagos a few days later sent a relative to collect the goods. The return fare of the relative was 3s. and the gross profit on the transaction was 6s.; the net profit was divided between the driver and the relative.

900 miles of bituminous roads in the country. There were about 11,000 commercial vehicles, almost one-half of which were over ten years old, and the poor roads and inadequate maintenance reduce their effectiveness. There were less than 900 telephone subscribers and about 8000 instruments.

The low level of fixed capital increases the working capital requirements of the economy by tying up large quantities of resources in the form of stocks and goods in transit. The large accumulation of unrailed groundnuts in Kano is well known, but it is only one instance of a general problem. Part of the Benue, the principal tributary of the Niger, is open for navigation during two months of the year only, and the annual requirements of the substantial hinterland of the upper Benue have to be transported within that short period. Considerable quantities of export produce are evacuated by the Benue, and if they are not shipped in time they may have to wait for almost another year before they can be removed. Similar difficulties also arise in the movement of palm produce from certain areas of the Eastern Provinces. In short, owing to the dearth of fixed capital much larger stocks are required to sustain an even flow of goods than would otherwise be necessary.

The low level of technical knowledge reduces both the life and the efficiency of available capital. Lack of spare parts combined with inadequate repairs result in rapid deterioration of machinery and equipment. The difficulties are aggravated by restrictions on imports from North America; British transport equipment does not stand up to local conditions as successfully as American.

Some financial data also illustrate the low level of capital. Deposits in the Nigerian Post Office Savings Bank increased fifteen-fold between 1934 and 1951, but still totalled only about £3 m. The total currency in circulation in Nigeria in March 1951 was about £40 m., and this included money held for business transactions and for current expenditure on consumption, as well as for savings accumulated over a period. The total volume of bank deposits outstanding was about £18 m., and these were largely business and government deposits.

In a subsistence economy the low level of capital may be regarded as inherent in the situation. The very rapid progress of the West African colonies beyond the subsistence stage has been so recent that there has been no time to accumulate much capital. The general poverty of these territories, the backward state of very large sections of the population, the social and institutional organization and the rapid growth of population have all enhanced the difficulty of capital accumulation. The substantial increase in the volume of trade and general activity in these territories over the last few decades has greatly strained the stock of capital. Lorries are in service twenty-four hours a day for seven days a week and are generally tightly packed with passengers and freight. The railway is barely able to move the traffic which is offering. By the middle of June 1950 some of the groundnut crop of 1948–9 had not yet been railed, fifteen months after the close of the season; and if the 1949–50 crop had not been a comparative failure an appreciable part of that would also have remained unrailed.

There are in West Africa a number of wealthy Africans, many more than before the war. But there is no substantial local capitalist class comparable to the Chinese and Indians in south-east Asia and in the territories bordering on the Indian Ocean. There were substantial African traders operating in West Africa in the nineteenth century, but their resources and methods were inadequate to meet the great expansion of trade over the last half-century or so, with its increased capital requirements brought about by larger turnover, the extension of trade into the interior and the gradual emergence of cash payments for the services of employees.

The absence of a strong local capitalist class helps to explain certain features of the West African trade. The activities of the European trading firms spread into small-scale wholesaling partly because there were too few local merchants able to handle imported commodities in wholesale quantities.[1] The firms were compelled to carry stocks and take them up-country to their own stores because the local African merchants were unable to undertake the task. The large firms still experience difficulties in finding Africans willing and able to buy readily and regularly on a wholesale basis.

The extension of the activities of the firms into local selling, as distinct from importing or wholesaling only at ports and central towns, has greatly raised the capital requirements of trading in West Africa compared with, for example, the Far East or South America, where generally speaking the British import merchants are able to turn their capital over fairly rapidly. The long distances, the backward communications, the shortage of equipment and the absence of a local capitalist class have thrown a greater burden on the capital resources of the importer. This in turn has served to strengthen the position of the large firms.

The low level of local capital is reflected in the much-discussed practice by which non-African firms make advances to middlemen (often Africans) for the purchase of export produce on their behalf. The merchant firms frequently advance substantial sums of money for weeks and occasionally even for months for the purchase of a

---

[1] This was not the only reason for the development of vertically integrated organizations; considerations of market strategy have contributed towards this development. This is discussed in Chapter 9 below.

particular crop. Although the risks are often exaggerated[1] much capital is used in this way.[2]

The system has been much criticized in recent years, often without appreciation of the conditions which have brought it about. In essence the system of advances uses foreign capital to assist in the harvesting and movement of local crops. It has grown up largely[3] as a result of the absence of a substantial capitalist class, and it has continued even after the elements of such a class have emerged. These advances are generally given by the firms to middlemen and distributed by them to their sub-buyers, through whom they reach the producers. Sometimes the funds are advanced well before the purchase of the produce; the intermediary often uses the money for the temporary financing of other projects such as the purchase of transport equipment. He may secure such a substantial return on this outlay that he may be able to repay much of his loan before his obligation to deliver produce has matured. Thus here again European capital finances local enterprises. Advances are generally intended for the movement and transport of crops already harvested. Where they reach producers before the harvest, the advances from the firms may serve partially to finance the collection or harvesting of the crop.

These transactions are somewhat different from advances and loans given by brokers and other intermediaries to the producers early in the season, which may be used to finance the planting and growing of the crop or the personal consumption of the borrower until after the harvest. But the extent of such pre-harvest loans from brokers to producers is increased because brokers realize that later in the season they are likely to receive advances from the European firms.

The low level of capital has been one of the factors militating against the development of small locally owned estates or larger peasant holdings. It is true that some cocoa farmers have acquired several scattered holdings, but this has been exceptional. The absence of such enterprises has retarded the growth of locally owned capital, especially in the agricultural sector of the economy.

[1] Many of these advances are not really a credit risk as the firms may hold sufficient security; in other instances the advances really represent moneys entrusted to semi-independent employees who are advantageously placed for the purchase of produce. In accounting language it would be difficult to decide whether to call these advances 'cash' or 'debtors' balances'.

[2] The system differs from that prevailing generally in the Far East where the trading firms buy rubber and copra at prices ruling at the time of delivery from intermediaries who provide their own finance.

[3] But it may be connected with motives of market strategy of the type discussed in Part 3 below. It is in some respects analogous with vertical integration which is a feature of the organization of the large merchant firms.

The curious practice known in Lagos and the Western Provinces of Nigeria as 'gold-coasting' also illustrates the low level of local capital. This is the use of merchandise obtained from the importing firms for the purpose of raising short-term funds for trade or money-lending. An established customer of an importing house buys standard lines of merchandise on credit at the beginning of the month, promptly sells these (if necessary, even at a loss), and uses the proceeds to finance internal trade or money-lending. The practice is widespread, and 'to gold-coast' has become a recognized expression. Thus imported cigarettes are frequently gold-coasted; they are bought from the firms at £130 a case, immediately resold at £128 or £129 and the funds so received are used as short-term capital. It is frequently possible to lend the money at a rate of interest of 6d. in the pound from market day to market day, which in Yoruba country is generally every fifth day. At even much lower rates than this the gold-coaster can recover his loss and make a substantial profit, as he is expected to settle his account with the firm only at the end of the month. By this process European capital is used for financing trade in local foodstuffs and in the petty retailing of imported merchandise.

With the rapid but very uneven expansion of activity in recent years the low level of capital has made itself increasingly felt. One outward manifestation is the very high rate of interest paid even by sound and indeed financially strong African enterprises for loans of all kinds. In Lagos respectable money-lending institutions can obtain 12–18 % on first-class mortgages on unencumbered property, the sale of which in Lagos is not subject to the same restrictions as it is elsewhere. The real return on capital under suitable management in internal trade and transport is so high that borrowers can afford to pay these high rates, while the meagre supply of capital forces them to do so.

This insistent demand for credit is a sign not only of the poverty and improvidence of the local population, but also of the high real return to be obtained locally from the use of capital when directed with a small measure of skill and competence. This raises the obvious question why more foreign capital has not been attracted by the favourable rates of return.

Of course large amounts of capital have been invested in West Africa, and this process has played a major part in the development of these colonies. Part of this capital was imported and part was accumulated by non-Africans who saved part of the incomes they created. Nevertheless, certain obstacles have impeded a heavier inflow of capital. Though the low level of local capital leads to attractive rates of return, it also increases the difficulties of the foreign firm establishing itself in West Africa. The initial capital requirements and risks are high, particularly in view of the necessity of granting advances to African intermediaries, of establishing business contacts and of setting up premises and stores up-country, where capital is turned over slowly. In recent years the difficulties have been increased by the high cost of buildings and the presence of various shortages and controls, which again raise capital requirements. The severe restrictions upon the immigration of non-Africans (especially Levantines) and the refusal to alienate land to them act as important deterrents to the inflow and internal creation of capital. Immigration policy has been a particularly serious obstacle. These and other difficulties of entry provide some security for firms already established, and reduce the pressure on them to seek out and exhaust all profitable opportunities, particularly those provided by medium- and small-scale activities. This in turn also retards the influx, growth and application of capital.

4. LACK OF EMPLOYMENT

In West Africa, as in many other comparatively undeveloped countries, there is widespread involuntary unemployment of unskilled or poorly skilled manual and clerical workers resulting from lack of resources, and especially capital, to set it to work. Unskilled or poorly skilled labour is unemployed owing to lack of other factors of production to co-operate with it in the productive process. The term 'unemployment' is now generally used to refer to another type of unemployment, that is, unemployment of labour in industrialized societies resulting not so much from lack of co-operating factors of production as from deficiency of aggregate demand and from various other influences discouraging investment and enterprise. This study is concerned only with the unemployment which results from lack of resources.[1]

Although its presence in West Africa is occasionally denied, there can be no doubt of the prevalence of unemployment in Nigeria, in Sierra Leone and in parts of the Gold Coast. There is no dearth of general evidence. Notices of 'no vacancies' are ubiquitous. A constant

---

[1] Although it is an aspect of the low level of co-operant factors of production, this type of unemployment and under-employment in under-developed countries is aggravated by the comparatively high rates (high by comparison with what can be earned in other occupations) at which wages for hired labour are maintained in certain occupations in these countries. It is a striking feature of many under-developed countries that money wages are maintained at high levels by institutional arrangements (such as international pressure, governmental measures or trade union action), while large numbers are seeking but unable to find work. This discourages the growth of activities relying on hired labour and encourages (or actually enforces on a certain section of the population) the pursuit of activities which do not use hired labour, or in which these high wages are not enforced, notably self-employment in agriculture, petty trading and domestic service.

stream of applications for employment reaches the mercantile firms, and this increases several times over when it becomes known that a definite vacancy has occurred or that an extension of activities can be expected. The inclination to trade even when only a few pence a day can be earned, the large internal migrations in both Nigeria and the Gold Coast (which are only partly seasonal), the frequent applications addressed to European visitors by their servants to find employment for friends and relatives and the short notice at which these applicants make their appearance—all these point in the same direction and suggest a widespread lack of opportunities for unskilled or poorly skilled people seeking employment at current wages.

I inquired specifically into this question, partly because of its great importance and serious implications for policy, and partly because its existence has been denied. Here are a few random examples of the results. I asked the manager of the tobacco factory of the Nigerian Tobacco Company (a subsidiary of the British-American Tobacco Company) in Ibadan whether he could expand his labour force without raising wages if he wished to do so. He replied that his only problem would be to control the mob of applicants. Very much the same opinion was expressed by the Kano district agent of the firm of John Holt and Company in respect of their tannery. In December 1949 a firm of produce buyers in Kano dismissed two clerks and within two days received between fifty and sixty applications for the posts without having publicized the vacancies. The same firm proposed to erect a groundnut crushing plant. By June 1950 machinery had not yet been installed; but without having advertised a vacancy it had already received about seven hundred letters asking for employment. The larger commercial firms in Kano usually receive about five or six written applications daily for employment, and in the groundnut season this might rise to twenty or more a day. The figures of applications are much larger in the south. I did not think it necessary to collect further detailed information, though I learnt that the European-owned brewery and the recently established manufacturers of stationery constantly receive shoals of applications for employment.[1]

Some of these applications are duplications, the same person applying for several posts; others presumably come from people already employed who want to improve their position; but this does not affect the general picture. Similarly, it is not immediately relevant how far these offers of labour are the result of lack of opportunity, and how far they reflect dissatisfaction with the emptiness of life in the bush. In Nigeria and

[1] This unemployment has not, of course, been caused by economic advance in West Africa, but it has been brought into the open by it. In a purely subsistence economy idleness tends to be regarded as part of the nature of things.

probably in the Northern Territories of the Gold Coast the former is certainly a major factor. The Ibo are greatly attached to their country and would not migrate to distant parts if they had opportunities in their native provinces.

The general lack of employment opportunities is not caused everywhere by the absence or shortage of the same type of resources. In the Eastern Provinces of Nigeria there is an insufficiency of suitable land; in northern Nigeria there is ample land but a dearth of capital and of local technical and clerical skill. Not only are physical resources unequally distributed throughout these territories, but the aptitudes of the different sections of the population differ markedly. In Nigeria the southerners have the advantage in enterprise, thrift, resourcefulness, literacy and ability to perceive economic opportunity; the northerners display greater sense of discipline, endurance and perhaps greater discrimination in the choice or acceptance of leaders. Whatever may be the reasons for these differences they are certain to persist for years and they may even become more pronounced.

This uneven scarcity of suitable productive agents has important corollaries. When internal trade and migration are restricted these scarcities are thereby made more acute and the lack of employment becomes more severe. When the activities of southern clerks and traders are openly or covertly restricted in northern Nigeria, the growth of employment, the formation of capital and the general development of that area are retarded for want of skill and enterprise, while the underemployment and overcrowding in the south are also aggravated.

There is a strong tendency towards fragmentation in the West African colonies, both in Nigeria and in the Gold Coast. It is partly the result of xenophobia and partly the result of clamour by interested parties. There is an increasing number of restrictions on the movement and employment of people and on the movement of commodities. The reasons for the increasing effectiveness of the pressure for these restrictions are analysed at some length in Chapter 3 below. Fragmentation of West African economies is certain to aggravate the lack of employment.

The controversial matter of immigration policy is also relevant to the lack of employment. The low level of capital and of technical and administrative skill can only be rectified satisfactorily at present by the introduction of foreign capital and personnel, both European (and possibly American) and Levantine. The former can supply a larger volume of capital and a higher level of skill; the latter can subsist at a much lower cost and on a lower turnover, and they can thus widen the market in the remote areas in which the former cannot operate. Immigrant capital and personnel are likely to be seen in a different light when it is realized that they provide work for the unemployed.

The political implications of this want of employment are far-reaching. The semi-literate or barely literate unemployed are the most inflammable political material. They have nothing to lose in a general disorder, either in the way of property or of employment. They are apt to be undiscriminating as well as poor. Those who are literate have much time available for the reading of inflammatory literature, spelling it out slowly. These are considerations of the greatest importance for official policy covering *inter alia* the framing and administration of immigration policy and the control of internal trade and migration.

CHAPTER 2

THE MULTIPLICITY OF TRADERS AND THE PRODUCTIVITY OF TRADE

I. NUMBER AND DIVERSITY OF INTERMEDIARIES IN WEST AFRICA

The remarkable number of traders selling imported merchandise, frequently in very small quantities, is a conspicuous feature of the West African economies. A large number of intermediaries is also to be found in the handling of produce, though here they are not quite so numerous and conspicuous. It is often said by administrators that in the southern parts of Nigeria and the Gold Coast everybody is engaged in trade, and this is scarcely an exaggeration.

The large number of intermediaries and the diversity of conditions in which they operate result in great differences in individual status and volume of trading. The large European merchant firms stand in a class by themselves with trading turnovers of several million pounds a year. They act as import and export merchants and are also engaged in a variety of other activities which, in the case of the largest firms, include the operation of industrial and transport enterprises, shipping lines, timber concessions and estates. Much the largest is the United Africa Company, which, together with its subsidiaries and associates, conducts a business in West Africa and elsewhere totalling between £200 and £300 m. annually. There are African traders with annual turnovers amounting to several hundred thousand pounds. They often operate in streets in which children sell a few empty bottles or cigarettes. Similar contrasts can be found in produce buying.

The number and variety of intermediaries have been much criticized by official and unofficial observers. They are condemned as wasteful and are said to be responsible for wide distributive margins both in the sale of merchandise and the purchase of produce. These criticisms rest on a misunderstanding. The system is a logical adaptation to certain fundamental factors in the West African economies which will persist for many years to come. So far from being wasteful, it is highly economic in saving and salvaging those resources which are particularly scarce in West Africa (above all, real capital) by using the resources which are largely redundant and for which there is very little demand; and thus it is productive by any rational economic criteria.

2. THE TASK OF BULKING AND OF BREAKING BULK IN PRODUCE BUYING AND IN THE SELLING OF MERCHANDISE

West African agricultural exports are produced by tens of thousands of Africans operating on a very small scale and often widely dispersed. They almost entirely lack suitable storage facilities, and they have no, or only very small, cash reserves. Accordingly they produce on a small scale and have to sell on an even smaller scale. The large number and the long line of intermediaries in the purchase of export produce essentially derive from the economies to be obtained from bulking very large numbers of small parcels. If each of five farmers situated twenty miles from the nearest village or town himself marketed his own very small weekly output, this would require five return journeys of forty miles each. If, however, one middleman (who may in fact be one of the farmers acting for the others) intervenes and carries the produce to the market, the number of journeys is reduced by four-fifths, saving scarce and valuable capital (in the form of animal or lorry transport) as well as labour. This last economy may also be important, since, in spite of the general surplus of labour, the harvesting of produce has to be accomplished within a given short period so that at times the farmer cannot afford to leave his holding. The same principle applies at the next stage; if each small middleman carried his purchases direct to the large markets the number of journeys would be greater than if another intermediary stepped in and carried the purchases of several traders; and so on all along the line.[1] In produce marketing the first link in the chain may be the purchase, hundreds of miles from Kano, of a few pounds of groundnuts, which after several stages of bulking arrive there as part of a wagon or lorry load of several tons.

The task of bulking cannot be avoided. So long as there is competitive entry into trade the producer is not affected whether the performer of the service of bulking and transport is remunerated by salary or by the profits of trade. If the farmers formed themselves into a co-operative society these services would be undertaken by the servants of the co-operative society, whose time and effort would still have to be paid for.

The arrangements for the purchasing of palm produce in Nigeria illustrate the economies of bulking small quantities and the saving to be

---

[1] Although the wastefulness of the long chain of intermediaries is a constant theme of critics of produce marketing in backward countries, and is usually combined with proposals for a reduction in the number of links in the distributive chain, the proposals have not yet been carried to their logical conclusion. It has not yet been suggested that each groundnut producer, for instance, should deal direct with the crushing mills in England.

obtained by leaving the task to independent traders. In eastern Nigeria it is quite usual to see African traders sitting just outside the produce-buying stations of the European firms (or even inside their compounds); they buy produce from smaller traders, who bring in palm oil and palm kernels in small quantities, and after cleaning and blending re-sell these to the firms. It pays the firms not to buy direct from the small traders but to allow dealers to carry out the bulking and blending of small parcels, as their margins of profit are less than would be the cost of supervising and maintaining a staff of salaried employees engaged in the same work. From this example it should also be obvious that the number of links in the distributive chain could nominally be reduced by simple changes in terminology or in financial arrangements without in any way saving labour or capital; the reverse would actually happen.

The same principles apply in the sale of imported merchandise. The intermediaries break bulk and economize resources at all stages between the first seller and the final buyer. Imported merchandise arrives in very large consignments and needs to be distributed over large areas to the final consumer who, in West Africa, has to buy in extremely small quantities because of his poverty. In the absence of intermediaries the consumers would have to buy in wholesale quantities, and they might have neither the financial resources nor the storage facilities to do so. The intermediary intervenes, breaks bulk and makes the commodity available in small quantities.

The activities of intermediaries thus enable consumers to enjoy commodities which would otherwise be outside their reach.[1] They also save working capital by bringing about a more effective geographical distribution of merchandise stocks than would be the case if consumers (or small retailers) had to deal directly with the importing firms. Their

---

[1] This was clearly set out by Adam Smith: 'Unless a capital was employed in breaking and dividing certain portions either of the rude or manufactured produce, into such small parcels as suit the occasional demands of those who want them, every man would be obliged to purchase a greater quantity of the goods he wanted, than his immediate occasions required. If there was no such trade as a butcher, for example, every man would be obliged to purchase a whole ox or a whole sheep at a time. This would generally be inconvenient to the rich, and much more so to the poor. If a poor workman was obliged to purchase a month's or six months' provisions at a time, a great part of the stock which he employs as a capital in the instruments of his trade, or in the furniture of his shop, and which yields him a revenue, he would be forced to place in that part of his stock which is reserved for immediate consumption, and which yields him no revenue. Nothing can be more convenient for such a person than to be able to purchase his subsistence from day to day, or even from hour to hour, as he wants it. He is thereby enabled to employ almost his whole stock as a capital. He is thus enabled to furnish work to a greater value, and the profit which he makes by it in this way, much more than compensates the additional price which the profit of the retailer imposes upon the goods' (*Wealth of Nations*, Book II, Chapter v).

operations result in a faster turnover of total stocks and therefore in a more intensive utilization of both the foreign and African-owned working capital sustaining the local economy. They also assist the importing firms by maintaining contact with consumers and petty traders and ascertaining their requirements; their knowledge of local conditions equips them for these tasks. Thus their labour and activities replace both capital and salaried personnel and expensive European supervision. They reduce the cost of imported merchandise to the consumer and serve to bring it within the reach of wider sections of the population.

The organization of retail selling in Ibadan (and elsewhere) exemplifies the services rendered by petty traders both to suppliers and to consumers. Here there is no convenient central market, and it is usual to see petty traders sitting with their wares at the entrances to the stores of the European merchant firms. The petty traders sell largely the same commodities as the stores, but in much smaller quantities. It does not pay the European-owned stores to deal in these smaller quantities on the terms on which the petty traders are prepared to handle this business. On the other hand, consumers find it preferable to deal with the petty traders rather than to buy in less convenient quantities from the adjacent stores.[1]

The low level of capital affects the situation in various ways. The lack of telephones increases the difficulty of maintaining contact with customers and discovering their wants. The poor state of transport enhances the difficulty of maintaining contact with customers and increases the capital required for a given rate of consumption. Moreover, as most of the intermediaries have very little capital they can each handle only comparatively small quantities. This greatly increases the required number of intermediaries both horizontally and vertically: at each stage more middlemen are required, and the number of successive stages is increased as some of the final purchases take place in extremely small units, which may be a single drop of perfume, half a cigarette or a small bundle of ten matches. The number of different stages in the process of breaking bulk and of finding customers will be

---

[1] Another reason for this system of trading was also present during the war, and may have been present to a very limited extent in recent years since the war. The breaking of bulk made it easier to evade price-control regulations, which generally did not apply and certainly could not be enforced in respect of very small quantities. The profits of evasion, which accrued largely to the petty traders, nevertheless also served to benefit the suppliers and their executives, partly through conditional sales, and partly by enabling them to strengthen the position of some of their customers and also their own hold over them. However, this aspect did not account for the prevalence of this method of trading, which was practised before the war and which in 1949–50 was not confined to the very few remaining price-controlled commodities in short supply.

readily appreciated when it is remembered that these commodities are imported in consignments of scores or hundreds of cases.

The extensive trade in empty containers such as kerosene, cigarette and soup tins, flour, salt, sugar and cement bags and beer bottles, presents a revealing example of the operation of these forces. Some types of container are turned into various household articles or other commodities. Cigarette and soup tins become small oil lamps, and salt bags are made into shirts or tunics. But more usually the containers are used again in the storage and movement of goods. Those who seek out, purchase, carry and distribute second-hand containers maintain the stock of capital. They prevent the destruction of the containers, usually improve their condition, distribute them to where they can best be used, and so extend their usefulness, the intensity of their use, and their effective life. The activities of the traders represent a substitution of labour for capital. Most of the entrepreneurs in the container trade are women or children. The substitution is economic so long as six or eight hours of their time are less valuable (in view of the lack of desirable alternatives) than the small profit to be made from the sale of a few empty containers. So far from the system being wasteful it is highly economic in substituting superabundant for scarce resources; within the limits of available technical skill nothing is wasted in West Africa.

3. THE RATIONALE OF THE MULTIPLICITY OF TRADERS

The large number of intermediaries and links in the chain of distribution accords with expectations; and it is the result of basic underlying circumstances.

There is an extensive demand for the services of intermediaries both in the marketing of agricultural produce, whether for export or for local consumption, and in the distribution of imported merchandise. There are many people available to perform these services at a low supply price in terms of daily earnings. Few other profitable channels of employment exist, because of the relative scarcity of suitable land, technical skill and, above all, capital; and not much skill or experience is required for the simpler trading operations. Moreover, women and children are generally unoccupied because, in the towns at any rate, there are few household duties and few schools; they are thus available to act as intermediaries even for very low earnings.

The intermediaries are productive as they conserve real resources, especially capital, substituting for it semi-skilled and unskilled labour, which is abundant, stimulate production, and provide employment. Their trading methods are economic in that they use resources which are redundant, and economize in the use of capital and supervisory staff for which there is a keen demand and for which there are more valuable alternative uses.

These considerations dispose of the belief that the value of agricultural or manufacturing output could be increased by compulsory reduction in the number of traders. Such measures would only serve to add to the numbers of redundant unemployed or under-employed unskilled Africans (especially women and children), and to aggravate the low level of capital and the lack of employment opportunities. The volume of production would not be increased, since the resources set free would be of the type already redundant, while the enforced adoption of uneconomic trading methods would absorb resources (notably capital) in distribution which would otherwise be available for use in agriculture and industry.

Thus it is clear that the large number of traders, and more especially the large number of stages in the distributive process, are not simply redundant. If the traders were superfluous, and their services unnecessary, the customers would by-pass them to save the price of their services, that is, the profit margin of the intermediaries.

The criticisms which neglect these considerations possibly derive from a confusion between technical and economic efficiency. It is true that marketing arrangements in West Africa are primitive technically when compared with those in industrialized societies. But, given the vastly different economic features of West Africa, any attempt to force marketing arrangements more closely into line with those in other societies is certain to waste resources. A set of arrangements which are economically efficient in one society will not be economically efficient in another in which the availability of resources is different. The criticisms may also partly stem from a widespread and influential desire for tidy and controllable economic arrangements; those who share this desire regard the existing unorganized and *seemingly* chaotic arrangements as irrational.

4. INADEQUACY OF A FAMILIAR ECONOMIC GENERALIZATION

The existence of numerous intermediaries and traders in West Africa conflicts with the widely held generalization in economics that a large proportion of the population engaged in the distributive trade and other service industries is associated with a high standard of living and that this proportion tends to increase with economic progress. The generalization is based on the following reasoning. Agriculture supplies the primary necessities of life, and at an early stage of development it necessarily dominates economic activity. Resources are available for manufacturing industry or trade only when a surplus has emerged over primary necessities. In particular, labour can be spared for trade only when agricultural production is more than sufficient to satisfy food requirements; with economic progress resources can be increasingly diverted into secondary and tertiary activity. This general reasoning is said to be corroborated by the available occupational statistics of many countries; those of under-developed countries purport to show that almost their entire population is engaged in agriculture.

It is clear from West African experience that the empirical generalization is invalid, since trade is a very large proportion of total activity, though this fact is obscured in the official statistics. The analytical reasoning is defective *inter alia* because it does not recognize sufficiently that certain distributive tasks are essential in the early development of an exchange economy, and that in such circumstances they tend to be expensive in terms of available resources. It also neglects the possibility of mass substitution of labour for capital in the performance of these distributive tasks.[1]

There is at least a possibility that the proportion of people engaged in trade in West Africa may actually decline with economic progress. But it is incorrect to suppose that progress could be accelerated by compulsory limitation of the number of traders; so long as trade is productive and so long as no more productive alternative employments are available for those engaged in trade, it would be wasteful to attempt to reduce their numbers.

5. STATIC AND DYNAMIC PRODUCTIVITY OF TRADE

In West Africa as elsewhere it is often believed, especially in official circles, that trade is in an important sense less productive than agriculture or industry. Even when it is conceded that some trading activity is necessary, it is frequently suggested that trading takes up too many resources, especially labour, with a consequential avoidable loss to the community. Examination of the West African economies and analysis of the role of trade do not bear out these views.

Trade is productive in what may be termed a static as well as a dynamic sense. Statically, trade conduces to the most economic deployment of available resources. In under-developed economies such as West Africa this is a difficult task, as capital (notably transport equipment and storage capacity) is scarce, distances are great, communications poor, and individual requirements and supplies are small in quantity and dispersed geographically.

Trade is also productive dynamically, that is, it promotes the growth

---

[1] The relation between economic progress and occupational distribution is considered at greater length in an article in the *Economic Journal*, December 1951, by Mr B. S. Yamey and the present writer.

of resources. It does so in several directions, all of which are of special importance in under-developed economies. It widens markets and thus promotes specialization and increases production, both of export crops and of produce for local consumption. It serves to bring new commodities to the notice and within the reach of actual or potential producers of cash crops, making it worth their while to produce for sale, and, at the same time, providing a market for these products. This process encourages production and the extension of capacity, more especially the extension of the acreage under cash crops. Consumers of local produce have access to larger volumes of supplies from more numerous sources, and this tends to reduce the cost of living and the severity of price fluctuations.

The accumulation of capital and its productive employment are stimulated. The larger volume of production is likely to improve the real return on capital. It also creates a surplus for accumulation. Trade also brings into prominence and influence a type of trader-entrepreneur accustomed to the ways of an exchange economy, notably the habitual and systematic use of money. These trader-entrepreneurs are more likely to accumulate savings and place them in productive employment than are other sections of the population. The services of alien traders are likely to be of particular value, because they usually possess some special managerial or technical skills, and are generally more industrious and frugal than the people among whom they work.

So ingrained is the view that trade is unproductive that no pride is taken either by the government or by the population in the development of several large centres of trade which have grown up in the last few decades under the protection of law and order. Onitsha on the Niger is a very large entrepôt market, probably the largest in West Africa. There, as elsewhere in southern Nigeria, probably the entire population is engaged in trade on at least a part-time basis; in its two large markets alone there are probably more than 6000 traders, including petty traders. In Aba the number of traders in the central market is probably of the order of 7000 or 8000. These towns are in areas which forty or fifty years ago were very backward and almost savage. A very large volume of trade passes through these centres; and this has provided inducements to many producers in the Eastern Provinces to expand the production of palm oil and palm kernels. The process has been accomplished solely by the successful establishment of law and order without any other direct intervention on the part of the administration.

6. TRADER-ENTREPRENEURS IN WEST AFRICA

The rapacious and unproductive middleman in primary producing countries is often unfavourably contrasted with the allegedly more deserving farmer. This contrast is misleading. It neglects the fact that as long as entry is free the middleman is unlikely to secure an excessive income since this would quickly attract competitors. Perhaps more important, the dichotomy is a false one. More often than not the real distinction is not between the producer and the middleman, but between unenterprising, indolent, unambitious and perhaps thriftless individuals, and others more venturesome, energetic, resourceful and frugal. The small-scale produce buyer or village trader is quite often the farmer who thinks the effort worth while to collect and market his neighbours' produce or to cater for their simple requirements. These intermediaries are generally members or former members of the agricultural community (or are at least closely connected with it), who have improved their position through their effort, enterprise and thrift.

I have discussed their careers with many successful African traders in different parts of Nigeria and the Gold Coast. The general impression I formed was always the same: exceptional effort, foresight, resourcefulness, thrift and ability to perceive economic opportunity. A Hausa trader, who now operates on a large scale, when a child walked with his mother from northern Nigeria to the Gold Coast, where he spent some years peddling from the Northern Territories to Accra. After saving some money he engaged in the cattle trade and exported cattle from the Gold Coast to Lagos. He returned to Nigeria in 1910, and was in the north when the railway was extended to Kano. He realized that this revolutionized the prospects of the groundnut industry, for he had seen the influence of the railway on the development of the cocoa industry in the Gold Coast. He decided to set up as a groundnut buyer with an organization of sub-buyers through which he reached producers over large parts of northern Nigeria. He provided his intermediaries with cotton piece goods partly as a means for immediate purchase of groundnuts, but also to serve as inducement goods for the cultivation of groundnuts for sale. His organization has played a valuable part in the spread of the industry. Another prominent Hausa trader gave me an account of his early trading experience, and it was a remarkable story of endurance and patience, peddling and trading over enormous areas of West Africa from the French Cameroons to Sierra Leone and the French Sudan, much of it on foot.

In the Ibo country thrift, resourcefulness and foresight were the

[1] These are the traders to whom reference was made in Chapter 1, § 3, above.

principal themes. I met in Onitsha three African ladies who have been in partnership as traders for twenty-five years.[1] Two of them had been at school together and had attended Y.W.C.A. sewing classes. In their spare time they sewed, sold cloth, saved their earnings and with their savings bought palm kernels which they sold to a European firm. Subsequently they bought merchandise, mainly textiles, from the same firm, thus trading both in produce and in merchandise. Later they withdrew from produce buying and began to deal exclusively in imported merchandise. Today their annual turnover exceeds £100,000. Several Ibo traders told me how they began trading with a few shillings or even a few pence derived from the sale of agricultural or jungle produce. They generally turned to petty trading in imported merchandise and gradually increased their capital; at the same time they slightly enlarged their still very small scale of operations. They then proceeded to rent part of a stall in Onitsha market. At the next stage they invested in a journey to Port Harcourt, Sapele, or Warri, or even Lagos, where they bought suitable merchandise, sometimes on credit, returned with it to Onitsha, and gradually increased the size and perhaps the range of their activities. With the improvement in communications between Lagos and Onitsha the more enterprising of them were able at times to turn over their capital twice a week. In practically all cases they were members of farming families.

In Lagos I met the managing proprietor of a large firm of bicycle traders, who started life as a bicycle repairer and built up his business from his savings. Another large-scale African trader who is now at the head of a substantial trading enterprise, which includes a small manufacturing subsidiary, started as a petty trader twenty years ago, reinvested most of his profits and was a man of considerable substance already by 1939. Another prominent African business man, who started his career as a trader, now controls a transport enterprise with over thirty lorries.[1]

7. SOURCES OF TRADING INCOMES

The African community is apt to believe that the wealth of the merchant firms and individual expatriate traders in West Africa has been taken or extracted from the Africans; at times this view is also shared by some administrators, at least by implication. The opinion derives superficial plausibility from the fact that many traders began operations in West

---

[1] The rise of these African trader-entrepreneurs is likely to promote development in the widest sense: 'The habits besides, of order, economy, and attention, to which mercantile business naturally forms a merchant, render him much fitter to execute, with profit and success, any project of improvement' (*Wealth of Nations*, Book III, Chapter IV). The importance of this in West Africa is obvious.

Africa with little or no capital, so that the increase in their capital and their prosperity have been obvious. However, this belief is fallacious because it ignores the productivity of trade. The wealth of the traders has not been taken or extorted from the Africans but has been created by their trading activities. It was not previously in existence and available for appropriation either by Africans or by expatriates; this wealth emerged in the course of, and as a result of, trading operations and the economic development following in their train. Wealth has been brought into being by the application of effort and skill and by the accumulation and use of capital. These activities have played a major part in the economic development and growth of West Africa, and they have been of great economic benefit to the African population.

The expatriate firms and individual merchants have not consumed the whole of their incomes; they have saved part of it and re-invested it. This has served further to increase the total wealth they have created, as well as the absolute size of their incomes. The savings re-invested in the business have taken a tangible or visible form; and to Africans they have become ever-present objects of suspicion tinged with envy, more particularly as Africans on the whole have been less disposed to save and to re-invest part of their share of the wealth created. Moreover, the African beneficiaries of the activities of traders and of the growth of trade have been numerous and dispersed; the benefits have thus been widely but thinly spread over a period of time. The benefits to the expatriate traders have been concentrated and easily identifiable, whereas the diffused benefits to African consumers and producers have tended to escape notice. This lack of balance has been aggravated by the fact that the misfortunes of individual African traders in competition with expatriate firms have been specific and noticeable.

Thus the mistaken belief that the wealth of expatriate traders has been gained at the expense of Africans seems to derive from two sources: the failure to appreciate that trade is productive and that it creates income and wealth; and the fact that there is unmistakable visible evidence of the prosperity of a small number of expatriate traders, whereas the benefits to large numbers of Africans are less evident.

The incomes of expatriate traders provide proof that they render services desired by their African customers on terms which the latter find economic and acceptable. If this were not so their customers would dispense with the services altogether or develop more economic methods for the provision of these services. So long as the services of the traders are used at all, this indicates that their activities are economic and productive.

Nevertheless, there may be a more substantial argument than those implicit in the usual allegations. The services of traders may be performed at an excessive price and traders may earn profits greater than those necessary to call forth these services. This can arise if prospective competitors who are willing to perform the services at a lower price are barred from entry or expansion either by government action or by restrictive devices of the established traders. Even in such circumstances the activities of traders are productive; but their customers are being deprived of the advantages which would result if trade were competitive and unrestrained.[1] The examination of the presence and significance of the restraints upon competition in trade is a principal topic of this study. Anticipating some of the conclusions, it may be said that such restraints have been and still are fairly widely operative in West Africa, as a result both of government action and of private arrangements and activities; on the other hand, their total adverse effects are not such as to warrant the view that a great part of the traders' wealth has in any significant sense been extorted or appropriated from the Africans. It must be stated at once that this latter conclusion is not capable of formal proof or statistical measurement. To a considerable extent it is a judgement based principally on consideration of the nature of the obstacles to entry.

The very large and easy profits of traders during and immediately after the war, and the special circumstances in which they were earned, provide something of an exception to the preceding general conclusion. During the period of trade controls profits were much larger than were necessary to secure the services of the traders. Over this period of great prosperity the effective bar to the entry of new firms reserved the very large profits for those already in the trade. A large part of their earnings was the result of the system of import licences and export quotas, the administration of which by statute barred entrants and/or restricted competition among established traders. To that extent profits represented unearned incomes to the licensees and quota-holders. This unearned income would have been shared differently and more widely had there been no bar to competition and to the entry of additional firms.

---

[1] Excessive gross profit margins may arise even where entry into trade is un-restricted but where there are arrangements for resale or retail price maintenance. Where such arrangements are effective they may result in excessive and assured distributive margins, the extra profits of which are competed away when entry into the relevant stage of trade is possible. Distributive net profits are not excessive, but costs, gross profit margins and prices are higher than they would have been in the absence of price maintenance. Such arrangements are widespread in Britain and elsewhere, but are not important in West Africa. Re-sale price maintenance as an influence inflating gross profit margins is unimportant in West Africa because of its limited scope. Even in the narrow field in which it is nominally operative it is not practically enforceable at the retail stage proper.

8. SOME IMPLICATIONS OF THE PRODUCTIVITY OF TRADE

Much of the analysis of this chapter bears on official policy on trading activities. The principal implications are discussed elsewhere in this study; but two points, closely relevant to current issues of policy, may be mentioned here.

First, it is often believed in West Africa, as elsewhere, that the amount of trade to be performed in a country is fixed so that a new entrant reduces the volume of trade available to others. Although under conditions of widespread licensing this view has some foundation, as a general proposition it is nevertheless erroneous. Neither trading activity as such, nor income from trade, nor employment in trade, is fixed in quantity. It is therefore not the case that the entry of new and additional traders is harmful to the economy and to the African population generally.[1] This is particularly relevant to the framing and administration of immigration policy, and to certain measures restricting the movement and activities even of indigenous traders.

Secondly, under the various development schemes and plans loans are made available to farmers and manufacturers but not to traders, at least not to traders other than co-operative societies. Possibly this practice merely reflects the difficulties of administration, since it is much easier to grant loans from official funds for the establishment of new industries than to grant them to some traders, who would thereby secure unfair advantages over competitors who were not in receipt of officially provided capital. Loans to traders are often also difficult and expensive to administer and supervise as traders tend to be more scattered and mobile than other entrepreneurs. But more probably the policy reflects the view that trade is unproductive. (It was formally stated by a responsible official to an applicant for a development loan that while farmers and manufacturers benefit the country the trader benefits only himself.)

---

[1] Additional competition may naturally harm the interests of some existing traders. The relations between sectional interests and the interests of the economy as a whole are analysed in Chapter 3.

CHAPTER 3

THE GROWTH OF RESTRICTIVE TENDENCIES

I. RESTRICTIVE TENDENCIES IN EMERGING ECONOMIES

A serious result of the rapid growth and sudden impact of a money economy in West Africa is a marked tendency towards economic restrictionism drawing strength from two distinct sources: xenophobia and the pressure of sectional economic interests. In West Africa the two sources seem to operate simultaneously, whereas elsewhere they have often been separated by considerable periods of time.

Xenophobia is found in societies near the tribal level, much as elsewhere. It is directed not only against those who are of different colour or who are racially far removed, but also frequently against members of neighbouring tribes and of related races. This sentiment leads to an exclusion of strangers and restriction of trade with them.

There is a strong restrictive tendency in societies based on specialization and the division of labour. In such a society each specialized group can improve its relative position (and up to a point also its real income) by restricting its numbers and thereby increasing the scarcity value of its services. Restriction can be achieved openly by obstructing entry into a trade, or indirectly by a multitude of devices. Such measures are widespread in modern economic society, and the promotion of the public welfare is generally advanced in their support. The nature, motivation and effects of this type of restrictionism deserve analysis in some detail, since public acceptance of restrictive measures is connected with the underlying motives of this restrictionism.

2. RESTRICTIVE TENDENCIES IN SPECIALIZED ECONOMIES

An increase in the supply of a particular commodity or service is likely to affect numerous consumers and producers. But these effects will differ in direction and extent. Generally, the benefits tend to be diffused over a large number of people so that each benefits slightly; moreover, the benefits may be indirect in the sense that they are partly enjoyed by producers and consumers not directly concerned with the market for the particular commodity or service. On the other hand, the adverse consequences tend to be concentrated upon a small number of people so that each is more seriously affected; again, the adverse effects tend to be directly felt in the market for the particular commodity or service. Thus there is a tendency for the gains to be less noticeable than the losses.

Further, the changes in the real income of those affected by the increase in supply are compounded of benefits and losses; changes generally are net results, being on balance either an excess of gain over loss, or vice versa. And as the losses tend to be more concentrated and obvious than the gains, the offsetting (and perhaps preponderant) gains tend to be ignored. It follows, in general, that in public discussions the losses will be more clearly perceived and vigorously stressed than the benefits. This goes a long way towards explaining the frequent and effective political pressure for restriction of supplies and for the erection of barriers to the entry of new suppliers, and the weakness of the opposition it encounters.

Ultimately this asymmetry is intimately connected with the fact that in a specialized economy each individual earns his income from a single activity (or a narrow range of activities), and spends only a small part of his income on each of a large number and variety of commodities and services.[1] He is thus sensitive to competitive activity and increased supplies in the market in which he sells his services, and less concerned with these influences as they affect some or other of the many things he buys.[2]

In specialized economies the only persistent and occasionally effective resistance to particular restrictive practices, notably control of entry, is offered by individuals or groups who, *as sellers*, suffer because they are excluded or their expansion is controlled. Potential entrants are the most vocal protestants against restrictive acts, since they are most immediately and evidently affected.[3] Restriction of entry is apt to inflict greater hardship on individual would-be entrants than on individual consumers. The former are excluded from a trade or occupation they wish to enter and have to content themselves with a less preferred occupation even if they do not remain unemployed; the harm to consumers through the higher prices of individual commodities is more diffused and less keenly felt.

As the demands of would-be entrants for freedom of entry are clearly connected with their desire to improve their position, especially their income, their views are frequently suspect and are easily discredited as

---

[1] Some reasons for the effectiveness of restrictive tendencies are analysed on a somewhat technical level in the note to this chapter.

[2] An obvious exception to this is a sharp rise in the prices of necessities or other important items of expenditure. However, this does not generally result from the operation of restrictive tendencies but from various other factors. The effects of restriction on costs and prices tend to be gradual and blurred by other influences and are therefore not easily identifiable.

[3] Generally their opposition to particular restrictive practices ceases once they are no longer excluded. Low-cost sellers who are members of cartels, especially of statutory cartels, are also at times vigorous opponents of restrictive practices, especially the more extreme forms.

being those of interested parties. Those sheltering behind the barriers are able to parade their own social and civic virtues, and to make specious appeals for the maintenance of these barriers in the name of stability, security, order, good conditions of employment, quality of service, high standards of conduct, co-operation within the trade and, perhaps more telling, co-operation with the administration and with organized labour (or capital). In particular, appeals to the administrative convenience of government departments to deal only with well-established firms and organizations seem to be generally effective. Where the would-be entrants are of different colour, race, nationality or tribe, the demand for their exclusion assumes an additional stridency and gains in political effectiveness.

3. NET LOSS TO SOCIETY FROM RESTRICTIVE TENDENCIES

It can be shown formally, and it might be clear on reflexion, that, considering only the economic aspect of the matter, an increase in the number or activities of a particular group or class (i.e. an enlarged supply of a product or service) must always benefit the rest of society taken as a whole. There is an increase in the total national income.[1] This may be accompanied by a fall (sometimes real and often imaginary) in the remuneration secured by members of certain groups or classes, but the benefits to the rest of society are greater than the losses of those members of the groups or classes (or of closely related groups or classes) who suffer any disadvantage.

Restrictions on the number of participants or on the volume of economic activity of particular groups bring about a reduction in the national income per head of population. Moreover, they bring this about not only by hindering the most economic use of available resources, but also by retarding the growth and the development of the economy. Restrictions tend to retard the accumulation of capital and the exchange of knowledge and of skills. These various adverse effects are cumulative.

In practical affairs it is necessary to note that the application of the foregoing analysis is subject to some limitations because an increase in national income per head is not a decisive criterion of economic policy. It is possible that the improvement of the economic position of certain groups in a population may take precedence as a goal over the raising of the national income; and as a corollary, measures may be advocated to achieve the former even at the expense of a reduction of the national

---

[1] There are certain exceptions to this proposition. If the increase in the number of a group reflects an increase in the total population it may be responsible for a deterioration in the terms of trade, or an acceleration in the rate of depletion of natural resources, or the emergence of external diseconomies. These exceptions are of no significance in West Africa today.

C

income. However, in practice it is unlikely that restrictive measures reducing the supply of particular goods and services will result in a net benefit to large sections of the population. It is plainly improbable that the real income of any large group can be improved by measures which tend to diminish the total output of goods and services. In any event the real cost of such measures remains the same and needs to be clearly realized and stated, and to be set against the advantages claimed for these measures on grounds of distributive justice. Moreover, there is a strong presumption that the desired alleviation of the position of the selected groups could be achieved by other measures which are less deleterious to the economy as a whole.

Again, in many societies (though by no means all), economic groups or individual members of the society may be more concerned with their relative position than with their absolute standard of living. Thus they may resent the progress of another group even though their own standard of living improves as a result of it. A particular group with these sentiments may be thought to deserve special consideration or sympathy; the feelings of a native population towards alien residents or immigrants provide an obvious illustration. The weight to be attached to such sentiments would seem to depend largely on the prevailing and prospective standard of living of the community, and to be greater in a prosperous society than in one where the standard of living is low.

Political considerations obviously need to be taken into account when the enlargement of the economy takes place as a result of an influx of aliens. The increase in real income and the growth of the economy may be thought less important than the political and social complications which may result from the influx. In assessing this it is appropriate to consider the number of aliens already in the economy, and the nature and extent of their contribution towards economic development, in particular, the accumulation of capital and of skills and the consequential enlargement of employment opportunities. Another consideration of practical importance is the depth, the extent and the sincerity of the opposition to their activities. These may often differ considerably from what might be inferred from the sentiments expressed by a vocal and possibly interested section of the population.

An unformulated argument or assumption seems sometimes to underlie measures restricting the immigration or the activities of non-natives in the colonies, even where their activities would clearly conduce to economic development and growth. This is the assumption that a particular territory can support only a given number of people (i.e. that there is a ceiling to the growth of the national income), and that this income is likely to be reached by the native population sooner or later even without the co-operant activities of the non-natives. It is felt that some delay in reaching this maximum income is a small price to pay for the maintenance of a homogeneous population and the consequent avoidance of the complications of a plural society. But the underlying assumption that the level of resources, or the ultimate level of development, is unaffected by the nature or the activities of the population is unrealistic. They are clearly affected by the amount of capital and the level of administrative, technical and entrepreneurial skill in the economy, all of which in turn are much influenced by the outlook, industry, thrift and abilities of the population.

4. XENOPHOBIA AND RESTRICTIONISM

In modern communities the tendency towards restriction has gone very far and restrictionism is highly effective. Sectional interests are better organized than in the past and, with the increasing variety of issues which concern public opinion, their influence in particular directions is less strongly resisted. They frequently gain that administrative and political support which, more often than not, is a necessary condition for the effectiveness and maintenance of restrictive measures. Increasing official control and intervention in economic life thus greatly reinforce the scope and effectiveness of these restrictive tendencies. But the economies of advanced countries have generally reached a measure of prosperity, and generally they have in the past enjoyed a considerable period without much effective restriction, so that they are in a better position to afford the costs of these practices.

In West Africa restrictions originating in tribal and racial xenophobia may merge into the more modern type of restrictive measures without a sufficient period of unhampered economic development. The results may be costly in terms of economic progress. For many reasons the restrictive tendencies are particularly strong in West Africa. The transition has been rapid from tribal and subsistence economies to partially specialized and individualistic money and exchange economies. There is thus a dangerous coincidence of restrictive arrangements which derive from xenophobia and those which arise in a specialized economic society.

The hostility to strangers frequently comes from economic motives rather than from simple xenophobia. Agitation against new entrants into districts or trades is provoked irrespective of the racial origin of the likely entrants. As is well known, there is in West Africa a vocal and politically influential opposition to the immigration of non-Africans. It is less well known that there is frequently equally vehement opposition to the entry or activities of Africans from other tribes or regions within the same colony. An important instance is the opposition in northern

Nigeria to migrants from southern Nigeria. This finds expression in public statements of the Hausa spokesmen and in various local restrictions on the establishment and activities of the southerners. Should they extend, these restrictions will have serious adverse effects on the development of northern Nigeria. There is also hostility and opposition to the Ibo, not only in the Hausa regions of northern Nigeria but also in the Yoruba country in the south-west. In Kumasi in the Gold Coast there is opposition from Ashanti traders to the Gao migrants, and farther south by the Fanti to the Kwahu, as well as to the Yoruba from Nigeria. Somewhat similar tendencies can be seen in Sierra Leone, where in the Protectorate area there is now a noticeable hostility to the Creoles[1] from Freetown and the Colony.

An instructive instance is provided by the vocal opposition in the Oyo and Ondo provinces of western Nigeria to the operations of produce buyers from Ijebu-Ode. For some years past Jebu traders from Ijebu-Ode have been operating in the neighbouring districts of Oyo and Ondo purchasing cocoa and palm kernels. The Jebus are racially closely related to the population of Oyo and Ondo; ethnically and linguistically they are almost identical; moreover, the Jebus frequently engage local agents and lorry drivers to act on their behalf. These traders have secured supplies by outbidding the local produce buyers, and their activities have aroused opposition which is led by certain influential Yoruba chiefs. It is clearly unconnected with racial animosity and is a straightforward attempt by the local produce buyers to curtail competition which obviously benefits the local farmers. This is a particularly clear-cut example of the economic basis of ostensible xenophobia.

Frequently the hostility towards strangers, including African strangers, is not confined to the expression of disapproval and dislike. In many cases it has official support, and is embodied in various restrictive measures of which the immigration regulations and the various restrictions on the activities of expatriates are obvious examples. But such measures also include restrictions on the granting of trading plots or market-stalls to Africans from other districts or tribes, restrictions on the leasing or alienation of land even where it is amply available, and restrictions on the employment of strangers and on the movement of commodities.

[1] In West Africa the term Creole refers largely to descendants of freed slaves settled in Freetown and its vicinity in the late eighteenth and early nineteenth centuries. They are not mulattoes.

5. SPECIALLY HARMFUL EFFECTS IN WEST AFRICA

The underlying reasons for the strength of restrictive tendencies in specialized economies spring from fear of the possible consequences of changes which are beneficial to the economy as a whole but which may injure sectional interests. In countries with populations as heterogeneous as those of West Africa there is a real danger that restrictive tendencies may result in widespread fragmentation of the economies. There are scores of different linguistic and ethnic groups among the African population both in Nigeria and in the Gold Coast. In Nigeria there is the familiar geographical division of the country into three major regions with widely different ethnic composition; it appears from the 1931 census (the latest available at the time of writing), that there are at least a dozen major distinct ethnic groups, besides many smaller groups. In the Gold Coast the 1948 census lists some sixty different and distinct tribes.

In West Africa the restrictive and disruptive tendencies have been reinforced by a variety of factors. These include the trading interests of the traditional political leaders of the African population. Almost every prominent Yoruba, Ashanti and Fanti chief has widespread trading interests, and so have many Hausa emirs. In many instances the official attitude has also failed to check, and has at times encouraged, the restrictive aims of sectional interests, possibly for reasons of administrative convenience and because of fear of political unsettlement.[1] Sectional pressures also gain in effectiveness from a fairly general failure to appreciate the effects of restrictionism on African interests, and from an inadequate realization of the divergence of economic interests between different sections of the native population. African spokesmen are apt to imply that there is no such divergence, while there is a cleavage between African and expatriate economic interests, and this opinion seems to be accepted at least by implication even in more responsible discussions of West African economic problems. It should be clear from the analysis of the present and preceding chapters that this view is facile.

Obstacles to the movement of people and of commodities aggravate the incidence of local scarcities of productive resources and thus increase unemployment. Obstacles to internal movement and trade tend to discourage the expansion of local food production by narrowing markets, and to increase the frequency and severity of local food shortages. As a corollary they increase the severity of price fluctuations and the width of inter-district differences in prices. They also strengthen the position of local monopolies. Taking a wider view, the

[1] Instances include some official support for the restrictions on the operations of Gao traders in Ashanti, on the activity of southerners in the Northern Provinces of Nigeria and of the Jebu in parts of western Nigeria.

constriction of internal trade and migration, as well as of immigration, narrows the economic horizons of those affected, slows down the spread of ideas and new techniques and retards the growth of national income and capital. In the political sphere it leads to the growth of pressure groups and of warring economic and political forces.

6. SIMILARITIES UNDERLYING APPARENT DIVERSITIES

The discussion may be concluded by indicating the diverse expressions of economic restrictionism in West Africa. When in 1949 a group of European firms enlisted the support of a section of the Nigerian administration to ban the entry of a highly respected, old-established and wealthy English firm from groundnut buying, they acted from the same motive as that of the Fish Market Women's Union in Lagos which a few years ago endeavoured to bar the wives of fishermen from selling in the Lagos markets. But whereas the European firms and administration questioned whether the would-be entrant had complied with the conditions imposed on licensed buying agents, the Yoruba fishwives simply said that they did not want to have more competition in their markets.

NOTE TO CHAPTER 3

Analysis of some influences strengthening restrictive tendencies in specialized economies

In § 2 of this chapter it is suggested that the familiar restrictive tendencies in specialized economies are ultimately connected with the fact that in such economies individuals earn their incomes in a narrow range of activities but spend them on a wide variety of goods and services. The propositions of the text can be elaborated by tracing the consequences for different categories of consumers and producers of an increase in the supply of a particular commodity.

The final consumers of the product obviously benefit because it is cheaper. Consumers rarely appreciate this since they spend only a small part of their income on any one commodity or service. Moreover, prices are affected by so many factors that the operation of one particular cause is difficult to observe and to identify.[1] Manufacturers or processors who buy the product as raw material for their activities benefit from an increase in its supply. They will generally be aware of this benefit, and of the consequent enlargement of the market for their products.[2] But they are likely to overlook the benefits

---

[1] This is the usual difficulty of appreciating a functional relationship when a situation is affected by a multiplicity of factors and influences.

[2] In some cases these benefits may be offset by losses on the stocks manufacturers hold.

they derive from the indirect enlargement of these markets which may come about in various ways. Thus when other goods and services become cheaper, consumers may be left with more purchasing power to spend on the products of these processors or manufacturers. Again, these producers may also benefit from the expansion of other industries brought about by the cheapening of productive resources used in them.

An increase in the supply of a commodity may come about in a variety of ways. Where it is brought about by an enlargement of the industry, the prices of certain commodities and services may rise, and their consumers (including manufacturer-consumers) may suffer from these higher prices. But whereas the consumers of the products of the industry who benefit from its expansion are likely to be dispersed, those encountering the competing demands of the expanding industry are likely to be geographically concentrated or occupationally specialized.[1]

An increase in supply is likely to reduce the incomes of some established suppliers of the particular commodity or service and of other closely similar products. In fact, the loss is somewhat mitigated by the fact that they gain as consumers of the product or service. But these gains do not outweigh their loss of incomes as producers; moreover, in practice the gains are likely to be small (as part of their incomes), and are rarely related by the recipients to their sources. The various gains partly offsetting the losses of suppliers are likely to be unperceived. Even when they in fact benefit on balance from increases in the supply of particular commodities or services, many suppliers (including employees and workers) are likely to believe that their interests are damaged.

The participants in a specialized economy are thus anxious to restrict supply and activity not only in their own sphere of activities, but also in those related to it. And since they underestimate the benefit and exaggerate the loss they suffer from the expansion of supply and increase in activity in these directions, they are apt to carry these tendencies so far that they themselves are harmed, as well as the rest of the community; and this may be so even apart from the retaliatory and cumulative effects and results of restrictive tendencies.

Even those who would most clearly gain as consumers are not likely to resist restrictive tendencies. Their own gains are not obvious to them and seldom loom large in their calculations, chiefly because their expenditure on the products of any one trade is likely to be a small part of their total expenditure. Moreover, for most people any tendency or desire to combat restrictions in other grades is tempered by a natural sympathy for those who

---

[1] Though this adverse effect may be more vividly perceived by the smaller number of geographically (or in some cases even occupationally) concentrated consumers than are the more dispersed benefits, it is nonetheless not likely to be as important as the losses to particular groups in their capacities as producers; and this is particularly true for the response it evokes in the form of pressure for restriction. This is so for the usual reason that the proportion of income spent on one commodity or service is generally small, while a large part of personal income is derived from one source or one economic activity.

suffer from greater abundance, and by fear of the possibility that a similar fate may some day afflict their own trade. These sympathies and attitudes are not confined to conditions of general unemployment. They are reinforced by such conditions, but the real element of conflict and its widespread exaggeration (which arises from the advantage to be secured by any group by increasing its scarcity value) are inherent in an exchange economy.[1]

Once restrictionism has made headway various factors serve to extend and to strengthen its influence. Widespread control over entry into trades and occupations increases the difficulty of finding alternative employment if one's own is in jeopardy. Hence it intensifies the desire to secure one's own position against the intrusion of competitors. Moreover, the real or supposed beneficiaries of restrictive practices are not likely to resist similar developments in other trades and occupations for fear of directing attention to themselves.

---

[1] Economists will recognize that the argument deals with the relationship between different agents of production, and it suggests that the participants in economic life are generally apt to emphasize the competitive (substitutive) relationship to the neglect of the complementary relationship. There are instances where the relationship is obviously complementary, as, for instance, when the product of one group is sold direct to another, but in general the relationship is a net result of elements of complementarity and substitution (rivalry), and the latter are more readily perceived than the former.

PART 2

THE IMPORT TRADE

CHAPTER 4

OUTLINE OF THE COMPOSITION OF IMPORTS AND OF THEIR METHOD OF DISTRIBUTION

I. GROWTH AND COMPOSITION OF THE IMPORT TRADE

The import trade of West Africa has expanded rapidly in the last half-century or so, although it has been subject to marked fluctuations. There are numerous defects and gaps in the trade statistics, which are not always strictly comparable; but the general trend revealed in Table 2 is unmistakably one of rapid growth.

Table 2. *Imports of certain commodities into Nigeria and the Gold Coast, 1899–1951*

	1899–1901	1909–1911	1919–1921	1929–1931	1935–1937	1951
Nigeria						
Cotton piece goods (£000's)	322	1,188	3,913	2,634	3,371	14,744
(m. sq.yd.)	27	77	68	89	151	121
Wheat flour (000's cwt.)	—	32	27	78	57	272
Sugar (000's tons)	0·2	—	0·7	4·7	9·8	11·0
Cigarettes, estimated consumption (m.)	—	—	156	298	417	1,700
Cement (000's tons)	—	16	15	48	51	261
Motor fuel (000's tons)	—	—	—	16	25	167
Kerosene (000's tons)	—	9	8	11	11	43
Gold Coast						
Cotton piece goods (£000's)	289	471	2,121	1,142	1,726	10,787
(m. sq.yd.)	16	22	25	31	65	83
Wheat flour (000's cwt.)	27	49	58	205	154	501
Sugar (000's tons)	0·8	1·6	1·5	4·8	6·2	14·7
Cigarettes (m.)	—	20	125	159	214	811
Cement, including lime (000's tons)	—	—	19	43	64	222
Motor fuel (000's tons)	—	—	4	20	23	75
Kerosene (000's tons)	2	3	5	11	11	23

Note. Some of the figures for the earlier years are estimated, chiefly from value figures on the basis of export prices from the supplying countries.

It is evident from the table that these economies were not stagnant, but were growing rapidly in the decades before the war. For all practical purposes the figures in Table 2 can serve as consumption indices; and they indicate a rapid increase in consumption. Total imports into Nigeria (excluding bullion, specie and currency) were about £750,000 in 1900 against £84 m. in 1951; for the Gold Coast the corresponding figures were £1·1 m. and £63 m. Even allowing for the rise in prices there was over this period a very large increase in the volume of imports, as is clear from the figures in Table 2.

The great increase in the volume of the import trade has been accompanied by important changes in its composition. Half a century ago, imports of petroleum products, of artificial silk manufactures and of machinery and technical goods (including motor-cars and bicycles) were negligible; and there were hardly any imports of cement, wheat flour, sugar, high-grade apparel and higher quality provisions. Today all these are important items, as will be seen from Tables 3 and 4 below.

There has also been a general improvement in the quality of imported

Table 3. *Principal imports into Nigeria, 1949–51*

Item	Average, 1949–51		1951	
	£000's	% of total imports	£000's	% of total imports
Cotton manufactures	16,862	25·0	16,353	19·7
Artificial silk manufactures	4,592	6·8	7,672	9·2
Petroleum products	3,506	5·2	4,985	6·0
Machinery	2,874	4·3	3,906	4·7
Corrugated iron sheets	1,800	2·7	2,553	3·1
Footwear and other apparel	1,648	2·4	2,157	2·6
Cement	1,560	2·3	2,562	3·1
Jute bags and sacks	1,311	1·9	1,466	1·8
Motor-cars and parts	1,248	1·8	1,799	2·2
Cycles and tricycles	1,246	1·8	1,401	1·7
Ale, beer, stout and porter	1,170	1·7	1,768	2·1
Salt	1,029	1·5	1,453	1·7
Unmanufactured tobacco	1,092	1·6	1,362	1·6
Chassis with engines and fitted tyres	1,018	1·5	1,092	1·3
Medicines and drugs	942	1·4	1,228	1·5
Railway locomotives and parts	840	1·2	437	0·5
Ships and boats	681	1·0	597	0·7
Wheat flour	642	1·0	811	1·0
Sugar	637	0·9	833	1·0
Cigarettes	619	0·9	362	0·4
Total of above	45,317	67·1	54,797	65·8
All others	22,219	32·9	28,404	34·2
Total imports (excluding bullion)	67,536	100·0	83,201	100·0

merchandise. On the whole this kind of change cannot be measured easily, especially in view of the imperfect West African trade statistics in the earlier years. Proportionately the share of staple lines of low unit value, particularly such articles as salt and low-grade textiles, has tended to decline. In the main there has been a *relative* decline in the importance of the more uniform and standardized lines of merchandise; cigarettes, petroleum products, cement, sugar and wheat flour are probably the most important exceptions.

Table 4. *Principal imports into the Gold Coast, 1949–51*

Item	Average, 1949–51		1951	
	£000's	% of total imports	£000's	% of total imports
Cotton manufactures	11,052	21·3	11,970	18·9
Machinery	2,932	5·6	3,254	5·1
Petroleum products	2,505	4·8	3,234	5·1
Artificial silk piece goods	1,846	3·6	2,282	3·6
Cement	1,440	2·8	2,200	3·5
Commercial vehicles and parts	1,273	2·5	1,375	2·2
Wheat flour	1,223	2·4	1,541	2·4
Footwear and other apparel	1,126	2·2	1,565	2·5
Fish	1,013	2·0	1,412	2·2
Corrugated iron sheets	992	1·9	1,454	2·3
Cigarettes	933	1·8	1,068	.1·7
Sugar	900	1·7	1,139	1·8
Private cars and parts	831	1·6	1,146	1·8
Road-vehicle chassis with engines and fitted tyres	783	1·5	832	1·3
Bags and sacks	734	1·4	767	1·2
Unmanufactured tobacco	352	0·7	431	0·7
Total of above	29,935	57·7	35,670	56·3
All others	21,973	42·3	27,652	43·7
Total imports (excluding bullion and specie)	51,908	100·0	63,322	100·0

The introduction and growth of many types of imported merchandise are evidence of the great expansion of the West African economies in recent decades. These imports have also contributed to economic growth since they have served to stimulate the expansion of local production both for export and for internal consumption. The value of imported consumer goods as incentives for the production of cash crops is familiar; and so is the significance of imports of transport and of agricultural equipment in the promotion of production for export. Less well known is the part played by imported merchandise in the promotion of increased production of local foodstuffs. For instance, imports of net cord, sail-cloth and fish-hooks have radically altered the methods of West African fishermen over the last half-century or so and have greatly increased the output of locally caught fish.

2. PRINCIPAL IMPORTS INTO WEST AFRICA IN 1951

Tables 3 and 4 show the broad outlines of the merchandise composition of the import trade of Nigeria and the Gold Coast in 1951.

Although cotton manufactures (almost entirely cotton piece goods)[1] stand out, for various reasons the figures substantially understate their importance in the West African merchandise trade since the war, and especially in consumer expenditure on imports in recent years. First, in 1950 and 1951 textile stocks were being run down, chiefly because of disappointing sales. Moreover, there is some evidence of a long-period decline in the relative importance of cotton manufactures (especially of the lower grades) with the growth of other imports, especially of durable goods. For the period 1947–51 cotton manufactures were 28 % of all imports in Nigeria and 22 % in the Gold Coast.[2] Again, total imports include government imports, which in 1950 were about one-seventh of total imports in Nigeria and about one-tenth of total imports in the Gold Coast.[3] Government imports include hardly any textiles, and accordingly the percentage of textiles in commercial imports is correspondingly greater. Lastly, a large proportion of imported merchandise, even apart from government imports, is represented by commodities not destined for consumption by the local population, such as capital goods, mining supplies, containers for export crops and provisions for the expatriate population.

The importance of cigarettes is also somewhat understated in these tables. The figures exclude the substantial output of locally manufactured cigarettes in Nigeria produced by the Nigerian Tobacco Company, which now exceeds the quantity of cigarettes imported.

[1] According to the trade returns, imports of cotton piece goods are about 90 % of imports of all cotton manufactures. This, however, understates the true proportion. The classes of cotton piece goods listed exclude velveteens, which seem to be included under other cotton manufactures. Velveteens are, however, clearly piece goods, and their inclusion would raise to about 95 % the proportion of cotton piece goods in imports of all cotton manufactures.

[2] For the period 1940–51 (that is, effectively from the outbreak of war till the end of 1951), the figures are 33 and 23 %.

[3] This information was not available for 1951 at the time of writing.

Again, cigarettes attract duty at high rates. Therefore the proportion of consumer expenditure on this product is raised further.

The broad categories in Tables 3 and 4 naturally cannot do justice to the diversity of the imports. Administrators and merchants, Europeans and Africans alike, emphasize the great improvement in quality and the growing diversity which has taken place in recent decades, both in the trade as a whole and within the broad categories.

3. LEVEL OF CONSUMPTION OF IMPORTED MERCHANDISE

In spite of the rapid increase in imports (which serve as consumption indices for these types of merchandise) the level of consumption of most of these commodities is still very low, not only by Western standards but also by those of other colonial areas. Thus the annual consumption of cigarettes per head is about sixty in Nigeria, which is less than one-third of the figure in the Gold Coast, the Belgian Congo, or East Africa and about one-twelfth of that in Malaya. It is a very low level, even allowing for the social habits of the moslem North. Cigarette consumption has, however, increased very substantially in recent years, and further increases are certain.

The comparison with Malaya is of some interest, since the Federation of Malaya and the West African colonies are by far the most important producers of export crops in the British Colonial Empire. The population of Malaya is somewhat larger than that of the Gold Coast (about 5 million against 4¼ million), but it is only about one-sixth of that of Nigeria. In 1950 imports of sugar into Malaya were 140,000 tons against 11,000 tons for Nigeria and 13,000 tons for the Gold Coast; imports of flour 70,000 tons against 21,000 tons and 12,000 tons for Nigeria and the Gold Coast respectively; and in Malaya there were also very heavy imports of rice. Imports of petroleum products into Malaya were about 470,000 tons against 65,000 tons in Nigeria, the area of which is about seven times as large. The Nigerian figure is particularly low for such a large area transacting a large volume of external and internal trade and with a poorly developed railway system. These are striking differences, even allowing for imports for the military in Malaya.

Consumption of textiles in Nigeria (which is met by imports with the exception of a comparatively small quantity of locally woven cloth of a special type) is also low. In 1950 imports were about 150 m. sq.yd., which represents about 5 yd. per head of population. A large part of imports was bafts, shirtings and other lower grade textiles. In the Gold Coast, on the other hand, the consumption of textiles is much larger; for that year imports (85 m. sq.yd., mostly of printed cotton goods) were about 20 sq.yd. per head of population, which is quite a striking figure when it is remembered that the population includes infants and children, many of whom go about naked.[1]

4. CATEGORIES OF IMPORTERS

Imported commercial supplies reach the country through European, Levantine, Indian and African import merchants. Certain overseas suppliers and manufacturers maintain local depots through which supplies in wholesale quantities are released to the merchant firms. The most important of these depots are those of the Nigerian Tobacco Company and the bulk installations of the oil companies operating in West Africa. These special arrangements underline the need for care in assessing the importance of the leading merchant houses in the trade in imported merchandise; they handle the bulk of the trade in cigarettes, for example, even though they do not appear as direct importers. Similar arrangements obtain for the distribution of the output of local manufacturing enterprises operated by expatriate firms. The cigarette factory of the Nigerian Tobacco Company at Ibadan is by far the most important of these; there are also, for example, two breweries, two or three soap factories and a firm of manufacturing stationers.

There are a few manufacturers' representatives in West Africa. They do not themselves carry stocks, and orders placed with them are executed by the overseas principals as direct shipments to the importers. Certain enterprises of a specialized nature, such as building contractors and transport operators, import their requirements either direct or through the trading firms.

The large European import houses are vertically integrated; that is, besides importing they also operate wholesale and retail establishments. But not all their imports reach the consumer through subsequent stages of their own organizations. They also sell to independent middlemen, both wholesalers and retailers. Thus not infrequently a retail store of a large import house may compete with independent retailer customers who have obtained their merchandise from a wholesale store of the same firm, or from an independent wholesale firm which had bought wholesale quantities from that same firm.[2]

---

[1] The figure in Malaya is of the same order, but imports of silk and artificial silk textiles into that country are several times larger than for Nigeria or the Gold Coast.

[2] An account of the system of merchandise distribution is presented in the *Statistical and Economic Review* of the United Africa Company, no. 6, September 1950. The system of distribution of that company is set out as follows:

(1) Goods are received at the ports.

(2) They are either (*a*) sent on direct to the branch destination; or (*b*) received

The great majority of non-European import merchants confine their distributing activities to the ports of entry or at most to a few principal commercial centres. In some cases African importers engage runners who penetrate into the country selling partly on their own account and partly on behalf of their employers. However, the organizations of the non-European importing firms are not as extensive geographically or as elaborately integrated as those of the principal European firms.

5. ABSENCE OF CLEAR SEPARATION OF STAGES IN TRADING ACTIVITIES

There is in these countries no clear-cut division between successive stages of the distributive process. The same European or African trader may import direct, and also sell by wholesale, semi-wholesale and retail methods (and African traders sell by petty retail as well). In these circumstances the distinction between wholesale and retail is difficult to draw, and it is thus inappropriate to define a particular trader as purely a wholesaler, or semi-wholesaler or retailer.[1]

As a result of the absence of specialization by stages of distribution, the same firm, or even the same branch of a firm, may transact business in units of widely different size. The larger merchant houses import merchandise in very large consignments, and sell it in transactions of any scale with the exception of the pettiest retail sale. In general, all those engaged in a particular stage of distribution are also likely to participate in subsequent stages.

The size of the transaction does not necessarily indicate whether the purchaser is the final consumer or user rather than a reseller. A cocoa farmer or a successful African trader may buy in one transaction four or five pieces of cotton cloth of 10 or 12 yd. each for his or her own

at a distribution centre in the port, where bulk packages are broken down and sorted into smaller parcels for dispatch to branches.

(3) At the branches—which are wholesale stores—the goods are either (a) sold to wholesale customers or middlemen; or (b) sent on to the Company's retail stores.

(4) The wholesale customer and the retail store then sell partly to the African public and partly to the African petty trader and market storekeeper.

(5) The petty trader and market storekeeper sell to African consumers.

[1] The following example serves to illustrate both the imperfect specialization by stages of distribution, and also the close connexion between family and commercial relations. In Warri a stall was noticed at which an African and two of his wives were selling sugar. The husband sold by the bag of 100 lb. or by the carton of 56 packets of 1 lb. each; one of the wives sold largely by the packet, but occasionally by the cube; while the other wife sold by the cube, or granulated sugar by the cigarette tin. The wives had bought their supplies from the husband.

present or future use. Individual cocoa farmers have also been known to purchase entire brass bands. On the other hand, the purchaser of a single cotton print of 6–12 yd. often cuts it up into pieces of 2 yd. with a view to resale.[1] The purchase of a box of matches worth 1½d. to 2d. and containing about 70 matches may be a wholesale transaction, as in eastern Nigeria the buyers frequently break bulk and resell the matches in bundles of 10–15 each. Purchasers of single packets of cigarettes are also often traders reselling by the single cigarette or even the half-cigarette. The sale of a packet of sugar containing 96 cubes, and costing about 10d., is again likely to be a wholesale transaction, as the buyer may resell in lots of three or six cubes at a halfpenny or a penny.

The terms wholesale and retail are used in West Africa in a sense different from their ordinary meaning elsewhere. In Great Britain and Western Europe wholesale transactions mean sales to resellers, and retail transactions mean sales to consumers or users. In West Africa wholesale transactions refer to direct importing and to sales by importers to resellers without breaking bulk of units of shipment or of individual containers. Transactions subsequent to this stage are frequently termed retail transactions, and they are almost invariably thus referred to officially, even though the transactions may be in substantial units, and the merchandise may have to pass through the hands of several resellers before reaching the consumers. Even sales of scores of pieces of cloth are referred to as retail or at the most as semi-wholesale transactions. A large part even of the sales in the so-called retail stores of the merchant firms are in fact wholesale transactions in the usual meaning of the term. The purchasers resell, possibly to other resellers in smaller quantities, and so on for several stages.[2]

It is usual to portray channels of distribution schematically by means of a type of flow chart, and it would be possible to prepare such a diagram for West African trade in imported merchandise. This, however, would be inappropriate, since such charts are apt to imply and suggest a rigid separation of distributive functions and stages and stability of trading relationships which are absent in West Africa. The lack of clear-cut and stable lines of division between stages in the distributive chain after importation and the extent of vertical integration in particular firms are important aspects of the unspecialized nature of commercial activities in West Africa.

[1] This is not necessarily undertaken with a view to reselling the cloth in small pieces. The ultimate consumer may wish to buy 8 yd. and not the 6, 10 or 12 yd. in which the pieces are imported.
[2] Although the distinction between wholesale and retail in West Africa is so evidently nebulous, it has nevertheless been adopted as an important criterion in the operation of immigration policy in West Africa. This is discussed in Chapter 12 below.

For these reasons it is not possible for the firms themselves to ascertain what proportion of their sales is to consumers. It is safe to say that the great bulk of the sales of the European import merchants is to resellers; and this would apply largely to sales even through the so-called retail-stores.[1] Similarly, it is not possible to determine the share of different firms, groups of firms, or firms of different nationalities in the trade in any particular stage subsequent to importation. In fact, the final consumer almost invariably buys from Africans who form the last link in the usually long chain of resellers and in most instances themselves purchase their merchandise from Africans. At the other end of the chain the bulk of the imports are handled in the first place by European firms, whose first sales to independent dealers are very largely to African middlemen; when sales are made to non-African intermediaries these in turn subsequently deal largely with African resellers. In short the African consumer is connected with the overseas supplier by a series of successive stages of distributive activity. The stage furthest removed from him is almost entirely conducted by non-African firms. The extent of African participation is already high in the second furthest stage and increases progressively until the final stages nearest the consumer are almost wholly in African hands. Altogether most imported merchandise passes through one or more African trader before reaching the African consumer.

It is certain that the aggregate value and volume of trade in imported commodities handled by African merchants is at present many times greater than it was 40 or 50 years ago; and it is probable that the quantities they import direct are also much larger. It is worth emphasizing this point, since Africans are apt to suggest that their trade has suffered as a result of the activities of expatriate merchants, and that their trade is now less than it had been half a century ago.

The African consumers generally buy in small quantities in the markets or from itinerant traders, hawkers and street vendors. These rather than shops are the final links in distribution. In rural areas markets are held at regular intervals, usually four days in eastern Nigeria and five days in western Nigeria. Markets tend to be permanent in larger communities and, with the improvement of communications,

[1] In the Gold Coast, but not in Nigeria, the United Africa Company operates certain stores which it calls 'central cash wholesale stores' in which wholesale customers can buy a variety of goods on a cash basis. In 1948–9 two-fifths of the company's sales in the Gold Coast (excluding technical goods) were made through these; just over one-quarter was sold to wholesale credit customers and about one-third through stores in charge of African storekeepers, the so-called retail stores. These proportions do not indicate the proportion of sales to ultimate consumers, but they make it clear that the great bulk is to resellers. Cf. United Africa Company, *Statistical and Economic Review*, no. 6, September 1950.

the larger ones tend to supplant the smaller. This is apparent through-out southern Nigeria. Several administrators drew my attention to this development by which some markets originally held every four days have now become permanent; in one or two instances it was possible to observe the change. With the improvement of communications people find it worth their while to frequent more distant markets, both to obtain their supplies and to sell their produce, and a gradual con-centration takes place.

6. EUROPEAN PARTICIPATION IN WHOLESALE AND SEMI-WHOLESALE TRADING

The integrated organization of the large merchant firms is to some extent peculiar to West Africa. The participation of large importing houses in smaller-scale trade is rarely found, for example, in the Far Eastern, Indian, South African or South American trade. In West Africa this participation exists because the gap caused by the absence of a substantial local capitalist class had to be filled by European enterprise, and there were also important strategic advantages which prompted the importing firms to extend their activities vertically.[1]

In recent years the major importing firms have tended to withdraw gradually from small-scale trading. They have done this for several reasons. There has been political pressure, both from official sources and from Africans, to leave this type of activity (the so-called retail trade) to African enterprise. But there have been commercial reasons as well. The cost of supervision and control of the small trading stations and stores tends to be rather high and the rate of turnover in these establishments tends to be slow. Moreover, these stations and stores have very frequently competed against the wholesale customers of the firms, a situation which has caused complaints by the latter and has often been used in arguments about prices. The strategic disadvantages of withdrawal from the later stages of distribution have been reduced by other developments which have strengthened the position of the importing firms, who have also been able to retain a large measure of indirect control over the activities of these small stores even after formal ownership and control has been surrendered.[2] In pursuance of the policy of withdrawal some of the firms have granted increasing inde-pendence to some of their African storekeepers, and have changed them from employees into credit customers trading on their own account and continuing to operate the stores largely as outlets for merchandise of their former employers.

[1] The considerations of market strategy are discussed in greater length in Chapter 9 below.
[2] Cf. Chapter 9, § 4.

In some areas, especially in northern and eastern Nigeria, the firms have found it more difficult to carry out this policy than was anticipated. The main reason has been the absence of an established capitalist class interested in and capable of financing regular trading. Such a class is slowly emerging, but it is as yet of little importance.

7. EXTENT OF SPECIALIZATION IN MERCHANDISE TRADE

Trade in West Africa is still largely unspecialized by types of commodity. This lack of specialization partly reflects the maxim that the division of labour depends on the extent of the market. The long distances, poor communications and the low level of capital, including the insufficient storage capacity in outlying areas, tend to narrow the market and to restrict the division of labour in trading operations.

The general stall, shop or store is still the predominant type of selling point, and even small-scale importers and wholesale traders frequently turn from one assortment of commodities to another of quite different composition. A child carrying an enamel basin or a calabash with an assortment of goods, or sitting behind a similar assortment placed on the ground, constitutes a retail outlet. The assortment is often very varied and may comprise twenty or thirty commodities, including sugar, cigarettes, empty bottles, sardines, combs, hardware and many others. Even in Lagos it is usual to see quite small shops or stalls selling an assortment of goods such as palm wine, textiles, bicycles and haberdashery.

The up-country retail and semi-wholesale stores of the European firms are also unspecialized. This is largely the result of the narrowness of dispersed markets (which similarly explains the position of the village general store throughout the world). The European firms tend to be universal providers in their capacities as importers and wholesalers, partly in order to supply their own outlets and to serve the requirements of their numerous unspecialized customers.

It is probable that considerations of market strategy have partly influenced the large firms to stock a very wide range of goods; in this way it is made more difficult for new independent importers or wholesalers to develop in the West African market by supplying the semi-wholesale and retail trades.

The narrowness of markets also contributes to the unspecialized nature of much trading activity in West Africa in a less obvious way. In narrow and dispersed markets opportunities for profit in trade occur frequently and unpredictably, and there is thus a premium on readiness and ability rapidly to recognize a new opportunity and to take advantage of it. In these circumstances there is less incentive for traders to specialize on a limited range of merchandise or even in a particular locality. This is connected with the ease with which large numbers can participate in trade on a part-time or casual basis and with the readiness with which the African turns from petty trading to direct importing and back again, or from clerical work to driving and trading.

Nevertheless, there is clear evidence of the emergence of specialization. In the markets there are now separate sections for the principal types of commodities sold. The European firms are developing separate departments in the principal types of merchandise. There are specialized establishments for the sale of motor-cars and accessories, machinery and other technical goods, building materials, certain types of apparel, especially footwear, medicines and drugs, and bicycles and accessories. The trading activities of Levantine traders are generally more specialized; they are largely confined to dealing in textiles, motor accessories and certain high-grade provisions.

8. TRADING MARGINS

An attempt at detailed statistical discussion of selling margins in West African trade would be unrewarding. To begin with, the size of margins is apt to create a misleading impression, since very wide margins may represent a low return on invested capital if the turnover is slow; while, conversely, low margins may represent a generous return on capital when the rate of turnover is high. Wide margins without abnormal returns on capital are a familiar feature the world over in the trade in certain types of durable commodities of a semi-luxury type. Again, unless it is stated very precisely what items are included in the cost on which selling margins are calculated the figures are of only very limited meaning. As all the larger firms engage in a variety of activities, operate in a number of territories, and also maintain head offices or buying offices elsewhere, the allocation of overheads presents a particularly intractable problem.

In West Africa the meaning of the figures is also affected by credit terms and by price fluctuations in the different stages and phases of the flow of transactions, and in some cases by the practice of gold-coasting,[1] in which case the merchandise transaction is inseparably linked with the main purpose of obtaining and granting credit. Lastly, as the trade in West Africa is undifferentiated vertically, profit margins are an amalgam of wholesale and retail margins, which much affects the meaning of any statistics.

In the broadest terms, the gross margins of most European firms in 1950 were about 20–25 % of the duty-paid landed cost. The margins differed greatly on different types of merchandise, and they also fluctu-

---

[1] See above, Chapter 1, § 3.

ated substantially with changes in trading conditions. In view of the very limited significance of the figures they are not shown here in any detail.[1]

It is not possible to present in a meaningful fashion a structure of margins for wholesale and retail stages (i.e. the stages between importation and consumption) for the simple reason that no such definite structure of margins exists. However, it has been possible to collect some data on the price structure for certain standardized commodities in particular areas in the summer of 1950.

Table 5 summarizes the approximate price structure of matches in the town of Aba in eastern Nigeria in July 1950. The prices are only approximate, but are certain to be reasonably close to those at which the bulk of transactions took place in this standardized commodity on cash terms or on short-period credit terms. The prices are largely derived from the records of a well-informed manager of one of the trading firms, supplemented and checked by the figures collected directly by myself and by my African driver.

Table 5. *Price structure of matches in Aba, Nigeria, July 1950*

		Approximate equivalent per case
	One case of 7200 boxes	£47. 10s. 0d.
Each case contains	6 zincs selling approximately at £8. 2s. 6d.	£48. 15s. 0d.
Each zinc contains	10 large packets of 120 boxes selling at 17s. 6d. a packet	£52. 10s. 0d.
Each large packet contains	12 packets of 10 boxes each selling at 1s. 7d.	£57. 0s. 0d.
Each packet contains	10 boxes selling at 2d. per box	£60. 0s. 0d.
Each box contains	70–80 matches selling at ½d. for 12–15 matches	£75 to £105

There were variations in prices at all stages. At the time the prices for zincs and individual boxes were reasonably clear, but those in between were rather fluid. In one or two instances it was possible to obtain as many as seventeen matches for a halfpenny, which gave a case equivalent of about £65.

[1] According to figures presented in the *Statistical and Economic Review* of the United Africa Company, March 1948, appreciably higher average gross margins appear to have been earned by that company in the Gold Coast in 1945–6. The figures suggest that for the year 1945–6 gross margins (i.e. the difference between landed cost (including duty) and selling prices) were on the average around 50% of landed cost. These figures refer to wholly abnormal conditions and would certainly be appreciably lower today.

It was possible to secure a fair amount of information about sugar prices. The market for this commodity was firm and the market prices substantially exceeded those charged by the large firms, which were fixed on the basis of an understanding with the authorities. Accordingly there was a fair amount of conditional selling (that is, customers had to accept other merchandise as well as the desired commodity), which meant that resellers' true margins were lower than the figures indicate. Throughout southern Nigeria large firms were selling sugar at 42s. 6d. for a carton of 56 packets of 1 lb. each. Each packet contained 96 lumps of the standard cube generally purchased in West Africa. The packet was being sold in the market at prices ranging from 10d. to 1s. 2d., equal to 47s. to 65s. per carton; in the petty retail stage sugar was sold at three cubes for a halfpenny, which equalled about 75s. a carton.

Cigarettes present an interesting case because they are the principal commodity used in the practice of gold-coasting. This was clearly reflected in the price quotations ruling in southern Nigeria in the summer of 1950 which are summarized in Table 6.

Table 6. *Price structure of 'Guinea Gold' cigarettes in southern Nigeria, July 1950*

		Approximate equivalent per case
	1 case of 'Guinea Gold' cigarettes	£130. 0s. 0d.
Each case contains	40 dozen tins selling at 63s. to 65s. a dozen	£126 to £130
Each dozen lot contains	12 tins selling at 5s. 5d. to 5s. 6d. a tin	£130 to £132
Each tin contains	50 cigarettes selling at 1¼d. to 1½d. each	£125 to £150

These prices differed from those stipulated by the Nigerian Tobacco Company, which attempts to maintain prescribed resale prices down to the petty retail stage. The Company's prices, however, were not observed, except by the first sellers who rarely sold at less than £130 a case.

Very much the same general impression of moderate margins emerged from information on the structure of prices of standardized commodities such as cabin bread, bafts and shirtings, locally manufactured cigarettes and kerosene collected during several months in Nigeria in 1950. In two places, Ibadan and Benin, the resellers appeared to be making no profit at all on kerosene until I realized that their profit was represented by the empty tin; the standard four-gallon tin, which, full, was selling for about 15s. or 16s. had a market value of 1s. 6d.

In general, this information does not suggest exorbitant charges for the services of intermediaries. This is as expected, since it is unlikely that highly profitable margins should persist in view of the ease of entry into trading. The entry of competitors would compress margins either by bidding up prices at the earlier stage and/or reducing them at the subsequent stage.

9. CREDIT IN MERCHANDISE TRADING

A substantial proportion of the trade of the importing firms is conducted on a credit basis. The exact proportion is difficult to assess. The bulk of what the firms designate as wholesale trade is with credit customers. The trade of the stores in charge of African storekeepers is also frequently conducted on a credit basis, but this credit is granted by the storekeeper, who is responsible for making up any defaults.

The transactions of the so-called credit customers are not always on credit terms. Often they are covered by some security such as a mortgage or a surety or even, strangely enough, partially or wholly by a cash deposit. In the latter case the true credit is only the difference between the nominal credit limit and the cash deposit. Many credit customers would more appropriately be referred to as registered or regular customers who have ledger accounts with the firm. Thus the total volume of transactions with credit customers is no indication either of the credit risk taken by the firms, or of the volume of credit trading. In general, however, it is safe to say that expatriate capital finances a fair proportion of the trade in imported merchandise after first importation.

In recent years the period of credit has generally been shortened in view of the greater capital requirements of the firms themselves, the generally stronger position of sellers at present than in pre-war years, and the stronger financial position of some of their larger African customers.

Although the volume of credit business is substantial, the credit risk is not so great as might appear, since usually the firms grant credit only to those customers whom they know well and with whom they have had long trading connexions. The head office representative of one of the firms estimated that before the war a charge of $\frac{1}{2}\%$ on turnover would have covered the bad debts on merchandise trading while at present $\frac{1}{4}\%$ is ample. During and since the war, with extensive price control and official and unofficial rationing at the wholesale level, it has always been possible to recover bad debts by allocating scarce commodities to doubtful debtors on the understanding that the proceeds would be used to redeem their obligations.

There is also extensive credit trading among the Africans in the stages of the trade between the importing firms and the ultimate consumer. Credit terms of between a week and six months appear to be quite common. It is usual for a trader to hand over goods to agents or runners or clients and obtain payment either at the end of a fixed period or more probably on the re-sale of the goods. The traders may send their agents from Kano to Lake Chad and beyond, or northwards almost into the desert. In the south the agents or customers of an Ibo trader in Onitsha or Port Harcourt may operate from Ibadan to Calabar. Some of these work as agents, others as principals, but in general they deal on credit.

Elements of credit trading often extend down to the petty retail stage. Market women frequently sell food and cigarettes to manual workers on credit. It is usual to see market women congregating around the offices of government departments or mercantile firms on pay day to collect their accounts from the clerks and the workers.[1]

Ultimately, the structure is to a considerable extent founded on credit furnished by expatriate enterprises; the large firms act to a certain extent as bankers in transmitting European capital for the financing of African trade.

10. CONSUMER PREFERENCES

The African consumer is a selective and discriminating buyer. This is well known to those in the trade, but is less often appreciated by those who are apt to equate illiteracy and poverty with carelessness and gullibility in economic activities. Africans are frequently very sensitive to price differences, and they may spend much time in ascertaining whether price differences exist and in taking advantage of their presence. This presumably is the result of comparatively low incomes and of the low value set on time relatively to money.

There is much evidence that Africans are generally sensitive to differences in quality and design. Their standards of taste and their judgement may of course differ from those adopted elsewhere, but they are apt to insist on preferred designs, styles and qualities. This again is partly the result of the time available for shopping, comparing and choosing.[2] This does not mean that the taste and preferences of African consumers are not liable to change; they evidently do change quite often. But at any given time African consumers are likely to have clearly marked preferences which the trade refers to as 'choosiness'.[3]

[1] Most of the petty traders are illiterate and have to rely solely on their memories in the administration of their credit dealings. They appear to do so quite successfully.

[2] For branded goods it is also often the result of preference for a supplier known to the customer, or believed to be reliable. This is discussed in subsequent paragraphs of this section.

[3] An interesting account of this characteristic is presented in the *Statistical and Economic Review* of the United Africa Company, nos. 5 and 6, March and September 1950.

While African consumers undoubtedly prefer certain brands this preference is often neither irrational nor invariable. Very generally these preferences rest on a solid foundation, even where at first sight they may appear to be irrational. There is a distinct preference in West Africa for one or two particular makes of bicycle. Educated Africans are emphatic that these makes have a stronger resistance to the poor roads and paths and in general a higher mechanical efficiency than others. This appears to be confirmed by the fact that the two most popular makes are manufactured by the same firm in England, although this is not generally known in West Africa, where they are distributed by different firms.

Brand preference for durable goods often seems related to superior durability which is also reflected in higher secondhand values. Moreover, the existence of brand preference is apt to give the brand some 'snob value', which is important in durable consumer goods such as bicycles.

Other apparently irrational instances of brand preference also appear on examination to have (or at least to have had) a rational foundation. There is a preference for a particular brand of corned beef. The fat content of this particular brand is higher than that of most of its competitors and the Africans like this. There is also a preference for a particular brand of sardines. The supplier of this brand was the first in the West African market to pack four large sardines to a tin instead of a larger number of smaller sardines. This was preferred by the African consumer who eats sardines as a whole fish rather than as an ingredient of a sandwich or snack. The preference for American as distinct from Canadian flour has also a sound basis in West African conditions, partly because it bakes into a larger and lighter loaf, and partly because its keeping qualities in West Africa are better. Again, in Nigeria, especially in the north, English salt seems to be strongly preferred. In northern Nigeria and the neighbouring territories salt is essential on long journeys, including caravan journeys in the Sahara, and is more easily carried and divided when baked into slabs or loaves. Consumers and traders find that light and fluffy factory-filled 'light Lagos' salt of British orgin is best for the purpose. In northern Nigeria the salt marketed by a particular merchant firm commands a slight premium over the same salt marketed by other firms. The salt comes from the same British factory, but the firms supply their own sacks, and those of this particular firm are of slightly heavier material and therefore ultimately make a better shirt.

In other instances brand preference is simply a recognition of the reliability of quality from a particular source. The African consumer has no easy means of testing and comparing the different products and therefore frequently prefers the brand or the trading firm with which he has had a satisfactory trading experience. The preference for dealing with a source of supply which has proved reliable in the past is not peculiar to West Africa, nor is it in any way irrational. The West African retailer or consumer has, however, particular difficulties in obtaining redress for defective merchandise from the overseas producers. This makes for greater reliance on the trusted merchant and the brands he handles.

There have been several instances in recent years of the successful establishment of new brands. One British bicycle has become very popular and is practically as readily acceptable as older-established makes. In the Gold Coast a new brand of beer has come to occupy a leading position a year or two after its introduction. A few years ago a brand of cigarettes declined considerably in popularity until it practically disappeared from the market. Thus consumer preferences in West Africa are not obviously more invariable or static than elsewhere.

CHAPTER 5

SHARES OF RACIAL GROUPS AND OF FIRMS IN THE IMPORT TRADE

I. SHARES OF RACIAL GROUPS IN DIRECT IMPORTING

In West Africa the first stage in the import trade, that is, direct importing, is largely in non-African hands. From information extracted by the Department of Statistics in Nigeria from customs records it appears that in 1949 about 85 % of the import trade of that country was handled by European firms, about 10 % by Levantine and Indian firms, and about 5 % by African firms. Since then the African share has probably increased slightly, partly as a result of preferential treatment in the allocation of import licences in the commodities affected by specific licensing.

The information available for the Gold Coast is less comprehensive than for Nigeria, but as will be suggested subsequently in this chapter it is sufficient to show that the general pattern of the participation of different groups in the import trade is similar to that in Nigeria. The share of African traders is probably somewhat larger as a result of more marked discrimination in their favour in the administration of import licensing. But as in recent years (especially in 1949 and 1950) specific licensing covered only a comparatively small part of all imports it did not affect the general picture greatly. It is probable that if the statistics for the Gold Coast were available in the same detail as for Nigeria they would show a somewhat larger proportion of importing in Indian and Levantine hands.

2. PROBLEMS OF PRESENTATION OF THE SHARES OF FIRMS IN THE TRADE IN IMPORTED MERCHANDISE

Africans frequently maintain that their small participation in direct importing proves that the import trade is in the nature of a monopoly. This is misleading, since a trade can be highly competitive even if all the traders are members of the same expatriate community. In the West African import trade there is in fact a substantial measure of concentration,[1] a large share of the trade being handled by a small number of firms. In view of the political and social importance of this question it seems worth while to investigate the degree of concentration

---

[1] Which, however, does not necessarily indicate or measure monopoly power; cf. Chapter 7 below.

quantitatively in some detail. Some points of presentation need to be clarified before summarizing the results.

In computing the share of a firm in the import trade, all financially linked and associated firms have been included with the parent firm. This is the proper course in an examination of the degree of concentration in the import trade.

A special problem arises in the presentation of the shares of the merchant firms in the distribution of petroleum products and cigarettes. With few exceptions petroleum products are imported by the oil companies but are released by them through the merchant firms. Broadly the same applies to a substantial part of the supplies of imported cigarettes for which the leading manufacturer acts as an importer but releases supplies through the merchant firms. In assessing the shares of the merchant firms in the trade in imported merchandise their shares in the sale of these products need to be added to their shares in mercantile imports.

Somewhat similar complications arise for a few other commodities manufactured locally, partly from imported materials, by expatriate enterprises. These are not sufficiently important to justify adjustments in the calculations.

Except for a few commodities it would make little difference whether the shares of individual firms were calculated on the basis of c.i.f. values of imports or of duty-paid[1] landed cost of imports. The principal exceptions are petroleum products, cigarettes and spirits. These products attract duty at heavy rates and their distribution does not conform to the general pattern, as the share of the largest firms is appreciably greater than it is in the general range of merchandise. Where necessary the differences between the participation of the firms in the import trade calculated on the basis of c.i.f. values or on the basis of landed costs will be indicated in the text.

There is another matter of presentation, or rather of terminology, which needs to be mentioned. With few exceptions the leading European merchant firms are members of the Association of West African Merchants (A.W.A.M.), a trade association of West African merchant firms which have their offices in Europe. During the war this Association included various temporary or *ad hoc* members. But it is only some of the permanent members who, collectively, are generally referred to in West Africa as the A.W.A.M. group. At various times some of these firms have acted in concert in the import trade, though when they did so they were not strictly speaking acting as members of A.W.A.M. These firms were members of the Staple Lines Agreement and the Merchandise Agreement, market-sharing arrangements in operation

---

[1] Including excise duty on locally produced manufactures.

before and during the war; and they are parties to various agreements with suppliers. Although these firms are colloquially generally referred to as the A.W.A.M. group, they are more properly termed the Merchandise Agreement group, as these were the participants in that agreement. This will be the term generally used in this study. It is in no way intended as a term of abuse or criticism, but simply as a convenient collective noun for a distinct group of old-established European firms. Except where the contrary is specifically indicated it does not even imply the existence of concerted action by the group of firms.

The composition of this group of firms is well known.[1] In Nigeria it comprises the following: The United Africa Company Ltd. and all subsidiaries, including G. B. Ollivant Ltd. and G. Gottschalk and Co. Ltd.; John Holt and Co. (Liverpool) Ltd.; Compagnie Française de L'Afrique Occidentale; Société Commerciale de L'Ouest Africain; Paterson, Zochonis and Co. Ltd.; and the Union Trading Company Ltd.[2] In the Gold Coast it comprises the same firms with the addition of the Commonwealth Trust Ltd., a special trust which in its trading activities operates as any other concern.[3]

3. SHARES OF INDIVIDUAL FIRMS IN THE IMPORT TRADE IN NIGERIA

The information to be presented on the shares of firms in the import trade is derived partly from official and partly from private sources or calculated from data so obtained. This section discusses the information available on the import trade of Nigeria; the corresponding statistics for the Gold Coast are reviewed in § 5 below.

For Nigeria much of the material was provided by the information on the shares of particular firms in the importation of different commodities assembled from customs records by the Departments of Statistics and of Commerce and Industry. This has been supplemented by information supplied by private sources. Information on the releases of petroleum products and cigarettes was obtained partly

[1] Its composition was discussed in the Sachs Report published in the Gold Coast in 1948; for this report see Chapter 6, § 4, below.

[2] For certain purposes some importers of motor-cars and accessories are also full members of A.W.A.M. In the trade in export produce there are certain substantial non-importing firms who are also members of the Association.

[3] Certain German missionary societies financed themselves before 1914 by taking part in trade. At the outbreak of war in 1914 their trading interests in West Africa were taken over by the Custodian of Enemy Property. Eventually they were placed in charge of a special trust, which functions to this day. It conducts an extensive and profitable trading business, and the profits are largely reserved for educational and religious purposes.

from the Department of Commerce and Industry and partly from private sources. For most of the data the information was made available both from official and from private sources, and in every instance the figures provided independently by these sources agreed very closely, which confirms the reliability of those data derived from one type of source only.

The information from official sources was largely collected for this inquiry by the departments concerned; it was not available previously. The absence of any official information on this subject before this present inquiry has one important implication. From about 1940 to 1947 the extensive official import control system was administered on the basis of importers' shares in imports in certain pre-war years; this was popularly known as the system of past performance. Yet with negligible exceptions none of the appropriate government departments possessed independently compiled information about the past performance of the importing firms.

The distribution of the import trade in Nigeria among the direct importers is shown in Table 7. The firms A to F[1] are the members of the Merchandise Agreement group. The residual item Z includes all firms importing individually less than 1 % of all merchandise. It also includes imports of petroleum and tobacco products by those importers who are not merchant firms. If these imports are divided among the merchant firms on the basis of commercial releases made to them, the shares of the largest firms in the sale of imported merchandise are raised quite considerably. The share of A becomes about 40 %, and that of the

Table 7. *Shares of principal importers in commercial merchandise imports into Nigeria, 1949*

Firm	Percentage of value
A	34 ⎫
B	8 ⎪
C	7 ⎬ 58
D	4 ⎪
E	3 ⎪
F	2 ⎭
H	3
I	2
Z (aggregate of all other importers)	37

---

[1] The code letters are used consistently throughout the book to denote the same firms; for code letter G see Table 9, below.

Merchandise Agreement group as a whole is raised from 58 to about 66 %.

The data presented in Table 7 and the figures just quoted refer to the shares of firms in all commercial merchandise imports. This total includes many items such as mining equipment and supplies, marine and river vessels, ships' and aircraft stores and so forth which are not trade goods in the usual sense of the term. Mining equipment and supplies are imported largely by the mining companies themselves, and ships, boats, stores and supplies by the shipping lines and by the British Overseas Airways Corporation. If these items are excluded, the share of the Merchandise Agreement group of firms in the sales of imported trade goods in Nigeria in 1949 becomes about 70 % or slightly more.[1]

In short, in 1949 in Nigeria members of this group imported just under three-fifths of total commercial imports; they handled about two-thirds of the first sales of all imported merchandise, and between two-thirds and three-quarters of the first sales of imported trade goods. The largest single firm and its associates imported about one-third of all commercial merchandise imports, handled about two-fifths or slightly more of the total sales of all commercial imports and a slightly larger fraction of the sales of all imported trade goods.

The shares of firms in the aggregate imports of all commercial merchandise is information which is of limited meaning only. Not only do such figures include imports which are not trade goods and which are not handled by merchant firms at all; but they also obscure the wide differences in the shares of firms and in the degree of concentration in the import of different commodities.[2] For these reasons quantitative information on the proportionate shares of the firms in individual commodities is in some ways of greater significance and interest than their shares in total imports. Table 8 presents this information for Nigeria

[1] This estimate also allows broadly for the higher rates of duty on cigarettes, petroleum products and spirits. The share of this group in the distribution of these products is much greater than in merchandise imports as a whole; as the share of these firms is larger in those commodities which are liable to heavy duty, their share in the sale of all imported merchandise at market prices is necessarily somewhat higher than their share in imports which are valued at c.i.f.; the difference is of the general order of around 2–3 %. Cigarettes manufactured locally by the Nigerian Tobacco Company are included with imports in these calculations.

[2] Information on the degree of concentration in the import trade of different commodities needs also to be presented for another reason. A high degree of concentration in the trade in individual commodities would be compatible with a much lower degree of concentration in the import trade as a whole, if the leading firms in different branches of the trade were not the same. To obtain a reasonably complete and meaningful picture it is necessary to show the degree of concentration in the import trade as a whole, as well as separately for at least some of the major branches of the trade.

D

for twenty-three commodities or commodity groups; in recent years these commodities have represented about three-fifths of the value of all merchandise imports.

As will be clear from Table 8, there are wide differences in the degree of concentration in different commodities which are of some practical interest.

In the absence of licensing the degree of concentration tends to be specially high in standardized bulk staple lines, such as flour, cement, salt, cabin bread and the other items in columns 2–9 in Table 8. This result is as expected, since the economies of large-scale purchasing and bulk handling, transport and storage in these commodities are marked; moreover, they offer few opportunities for the judicious gauging of the requirements of the consumer and the other advantages which flow from close contact with suppliers and with customers.

Flour and sugar imports in 1949 were subject to specific licensing, and this also applied to corrugated iron sheets from certain sources. For reasons of policy, preferential treatment was granted to African importers in the allocation of import licences. It is certain that without this the share of the small firms (included in Z in the tables) would have been appreciably smaller. As direct importing requires considerable capital and skill, this particular type of assistance to African merchants is apt to be costly in real terms, particularly when applied in a sphere of trading where small-scale operations tend to be inappropriate.[1]

The tendency for the degree of concentration to be higher in standardized lower-grade merchandise emerges quite strikingly in the trade in textiles. The share of the largest firm is greatest in the import of bleached and unbleached textiles and becomes progressively smaller for those categories in which variety, design and colour are of greater importance, such as for printed cotton piece goods and rayon piece goods.

The table also provides quantitative information on another proposition which seems plausible on general grounds. A large measure of concentration among overseas suppliers conduces to concentration among importers. This is an instance of the general tendency of a high degree of concentration at one stage of production or distribution leading to similar conditions at subsequent stages. The influence towards concentration in distribution is especially strong where a product is standardized and the overseas supply is largely concentrated. In the West African merchandise trade petroleum products, cigarettes, salt and sewing thread provide obvious examples.[2]

---

[1] This tendency has been carried much further in the Gold Coast than in Nigeria (cf. Table 10 below).

[2] Most of the imports of sewing thread are derived from the United Kingdom, where one producer holds a dominant position both in the home and the export trade.

Table 8. Shares of merchant firms in the import or distribution of certain commodities or commodity groups in Nigeria, 1949 (percentages of values)

Firms	1 All commercial imports	2 Cabin bread	3 Cement	4 Corrugated iron sheets	5 Dried fish	6 Matches	7 Salt	8 Sugar	9 Wheat flour	10 All cotton piece goods	11 White bleached cotton piece goods	12 Unbleached cotton piece goods	13 Dyed cotton piece goods	14 Coloured cotton piece goods	15 Printed cotton piece goods	16 Mixed rayon piece goods	17 Pure rayon piece goods	18 Sewing thread	19 Motor vehicles	20 Bicycles	21 Cigarettes	22 Petrol	23 Kerosene
A	34	52	48	39	52	44	58	43	46	33	41	32	33	32	30	30	16	31	28	43	74	58	59
B	8	16	11	18	4	11	6	10	16	8	11	9	11	5	7	5	2	14	12	7	1	12	14
C	7	17	16	12	9	12	20	11	9	7	11	10	4	3	5	3	...	13	...	11	13	12	14
D	4	3	3	2	3	7	4	2	5	5	4	4	7	3	6	2	...	8	20	4	3	5	6
E	3	9	2	2	5	7	3	3	5	5	6	7	4	3	5	...	2	13	...	2	...	6	3
F	2	...	3	3	...	...	...	1	3	1	...	2	1	...	1	2	...	3	12	...	1	1	2
	58	97	83	76	73	81	91	70	84	59	73	64	60	46	54	42	20	82	72	67	92	94	98
H	3	...	2	3	...	12	...	2	5	6	3	7	2	9	7	4	5	...	2	1	...	3	1
I	2	...	1	...	...	...	...	2	4	4	1	2	2	12	2	1	2	...	...	...	...	...	...
Z (all others)	37	3	14	21	27	7	9	26	7	31	23	27	36	33	37	53	73	18	26	32	8	3	1
	100	100	100	100	100	100	100	100	100	100	100	100	100	100	100	100	100	100	100	100	100	100	100

Notes. 1. The symbol ... is used to indicate shares of less than 1%.

2. Columns 1 to 20 refer to percentage shares of imports effected directly by the listed firms.

3. For cigarettes (column 21) the figures refer to the shares of the merchant firms in the sales of all cigarettes; the figures in this particular column include a very small element of estimate.

4. In columns 22 and 23 the figures refer to the shares of the distributors in the trade of petroleum products released by the oil companies from their bulk installations. About one-half to three-fifths of the total supply is handled by one oil company, approximately one-third about equally by two companies, and the balance by the smallest supplier.

There is also a comparatively high degree of concentration in the import trade in complex durable goods, especially technical goods. The handling of these requires considerable capital and skill, often engineering skill which may also be necessary for post-sales services. Partly for these reasons, the sole agencies frequently granted to distributors of these commodities are also largely concentrated in the hands of the leading firms, though not necessarily in the hands of the largest firm. The sole agent often undertakes not to handle other types or brands of the same commodity, and this necessarily leads to a certain spreading of these agencies among the larger firms. The operation of these forces can be seen in the comparatively high degree of concentration in the import trade in motor vehicles and bicycles shown in Table 8. This runs counter to the general proposition that the degree of concentration tends to be highest in standardized staples. However, for the reasons just mentioned the comparatively high degree of concentration in these lines also accords with expectations.

4. SHARES OF INDIVIDUAL FIRMS IN THE IMPORT TRADE IN THE GOLD COAST

The information on the structure of the import trade in the Gold Coast is not available in quite such a comprehensive and convenient form as it is in Nigeria. The material is presented in Tables 9 and 10.

Table 9 refers to 1949 and is based partly on the records of the Director of Supplies and partly on information derived from private sources. The information is not quite comprehensive because in some cases the records of the Director of Supplies covered only those imports which were subject to specific licensing, which applied to imports from certain sources only.

Table 10 is based largely on the records of the Customs Department. It shows the shares of firms in the imports of certain commodities into the Gold Coast for the nine months May–August 1950 and January–May 1951, i.e. nine months out of the thirteen months May 1950–May 1951.

The incomplete coverage of these two tables affects the figures to a small extent. The figures in Table 9 seem somewhat to understate the combined share of B–F in the import of cotton manufactures, while Table 10 certainly overstates both the share of A and the combined shares of A–G in the import of this commodity. The residual groups include one or two firms whose share in total imports may exceed 1 %. Again, the fact that Table 10 does not refer to twelve consecutive months also affects to some extent the shares of the different groups in the imports of sugar and flour. It is almost certain that for various technical

Table 9. *Shares of merchant firms in the import or distribution of certain commodities or commodity groups in the Gold Coast, 1949 (percentages of values)*

Firms	Sugar	Flour	Cotton manufactures	Cigarettes
A	31	40	40	57
B C D E F G (a)	36	20	18	32
H	12	8	10	3
Z (all others)	21	32	32	7

(a) G refers to a member of the Merchandise Agreement group not established in Nigeria.

Note. The figures in the last column differ slightly from those presented in *Economica*, November 1953. The figures in the article referred to the distribution of cigarettes imported in the first instance by the British-American Tobacco Company (over 90% of the total). Those shown here also include cigarettes imported direct by some merchant firms.

Table 10. *Shares of merchant firms in the import of certain commodities into the Gold Coast, May–August 1950 and January–May 1951 (9 months) (percentages of values)*

Firms	Cement	Corrugated iron sheets	Sugar	Wheat flour	Cotton manufactures	Cycles and tricycles	Canned fish	Unmanufactured tobacco
A	49	28	12	30	45	43	36	39
B	7	7	3	5	9	4	15	12
C	5	2	2	3	3	12	8	—
D	4	16	3	5	6	—	5	14
E	1	6	1	1	3	1	4	7
F	2	11	2	4	5	—	6	8
G	—	8	2	2	1	11	6	7
	68	78	25	50	72	71	80	87
H	4	8	4	5	6	1	3	3
Z (all others)	28	14	71	45	22	28	17	10
	100	100	100	100	100	100	100	100

Note. For cement and corrugated iron sheets Z may include a few local authorities and certain government departments; for the remaining items it refers to commercial imports only.

reasons connected with the issue and expiry of licences and with the trading methods of African importers, Table 10 somewhat overstates the share of the residual group (Z) in the imports of sugar and flour. If statistics were available for twelve consecutive months, it is probable that the share of Z in the import of sugar in 1951 would be about 60–65 % and of flour about 40 %, instead of 71 and 45 % as shown in the table.

But in spite of these imperfections in the data, they show that the broad pattern of participation of the firms in the import trade in the Gold Coast is very similar to that shown for Nigeria in Tables 7 and 8. African participation is larger in the Gold Coast than in Nigeria in the staples subject to specific licensing; and the share of Levantines and of Indians in the imports of certain commodities, especially textiles, is probably larger in the Gold Coast than in Nigeria; lastly, there are considerable differences in the relative positions of firms B–F in the external trade of the two colonies. But these differences do not affect substantially the general picture of the participation of the large firms in the merchandise trade of the two colonies.[1]

The large share of Z in the imports of sugar and flour reflects the strong discrimination in favour of Africans in the administration of specific licensing which applied to these commodities. This discrimination became much more marked in 1950 and 1951, as is obvious from a comparison of their shares in the imports of these commodities as shown in Tables 9 and 10, the former of which refers to 1949 and the latter to 1950–1. In the absence of this discrimination the African share in the direct importation of these commodities would be small; this is evident from the small share of the residual importers (Z) in those staple imports in Nigeria which are not subject to specific licensing.

5. REGIONAL TRADING REPRESENTATION

The participation of the firms in the import trade of a territory does not measure the degree of concentration in merchandise trade in different parts of that territory. The measure of overall concentration does not necessarily indicate the number of alternative sources of supply open to the population of a particular region. This needs to be discussed in terms

[1] This broad similarity of the shares of the firms in the import trade of the two colonies is confirmed by other evidence. The records and the Report of the Sachs Commission (a commission of inquiry in the Gold Coast in 1947–8) estimate that the share of the Merchandise Agreement group in the import trade of the Gold Coast was then about two-thirds, which was practically the same as in Nigeria. The structure of the export trade also offers indirect confirmation of this similarity. Both the wartime export quotas and the participation of these firms in the export trade of the two colonies (as shown in Table 11 below) show a closely similar degree of concentration.

of the district or regional trading representation, that is, in terms of the number of firms operating in areas or regions rather than in a particular country or territory. However, this question is less important than in the past, in view of the slow but steady improvement of communications in Nigeria and the Gold Coast, which is likely to continue.

In general, it would appear that throughout most of Nigeria and the Gold Coast consumers have reasonable access to the stores, or at least to the wholesale customers, of at least three or four different importers. This is suggested by information from various sources.

In both Nigeria and the Gold Coast reliable information is available on the number of produce-buying firms (whether acting as agents of the marketing boards or as independent shippers) in different districts. This suggests that the great bulk of producers of export crops have access to four or more buyers of their produce. Generally speaking the consumers of merchandise have access to more alternatives than the sellers of produce. There are more selling points of imported merchandise than buying points of export produce, and merchandise is generally easier to transport than the bulky export produce.[1]

There are large numbers of itinerant traders as well as agents and runners of African traders selling imported merchandise. They are in the aggregate an important channel of distribution in the retail and petty retail trade. Through them the merchandise stores of the importing firms exert influence outside the places in which they are established.

The mobility of traders, which is a consequence of improved means of communication, may be illustrated by an example. In June 1950 a visit to the village of Garko in the vicinity of Kano disclosed that a trader there sold textiles which he had originally bought from one of the trading firms in Lagos 700 miles away. They were being offered more cheaply than in the stores of the firms in Kano, about 40 miles away. The trader had visited Lagos some months previously on private business and had brought back the merchandise as his own luggage, and thus it was not debited with the cost of transport.

In certain extensive sparsely populated areas in Nigeria the population has access to few alternative sources of merchandise. These are the Middle Belt or Rivers area of Nigeria (generally speaking the area of the middle Niger and the Benue), certain regions on both sides of the lower Niger, and the Cross river area of south-eastern Nigeria. Over most of these areas only two firms operate, and they own the power-driven river transport on the Niger and the Benue. There are generally

---

[1] Information relating to the distribution of merchandise during the war with details of the trading points maintained by the largest firms confirms this general picture.

informal zoning arrangements between these firms. In the aggregate the population affected is not very large. Most of these regions are thinly populated, which is the principal reason why more firms are not established. A third merchant firm has, however, recently established itself on the Benue; the opening of one or two new stores by other merchant firms can also be expected on the middle Niger, as well as in some of the districts in south-eastern Nigeria where at present only one or two firms are represented.

CHAPTER 6

SOME TOPICS IN THE RECENT HISTORY
OF THE IMPORT TRADE

I. SUMMARY OF THE DEGREE OF CONCENTRATION IN WEST AFRICAN MERCHANDISE TRADE

The degree of concentration in the import trade in West Africa has been illustrated in the preceding chapter (Tables 7–10). The tables show that one firm is dominant in the (economic and statistical) sense of handling a significantly large share of the total; and it therefore substantially influences the market. However, it would not be correct to infer from this alone that the firm is able to coerce other firms or customers, or to dictate the volume, range and prices of merchandise imports into West Africa. The term 'dominant' is used in this study in the indicated technical sense only.

In addition to the dominant position of one firm a (comparatively) small group of firms (including the dominant firm) is seen to import and distribute merchandise imports of the order of two-thirds of the total, and an even larger proportion of the principal staples of West African trade. This broad pattern of concentration appears to have come into being by the early 1930's. There is evidence that the dominant firm lost ground in the 1930's in certain directions. This was slightly more than compensated for by its acquisition of several previously independent firms.

2. MARKET-SHARING ARRANGEMENTS IN WEST AFRICA

In markets in which there is a high degree of concentration firms are likely to have formal or informal market-sharing agreements. In the import trade the most important market-sharing agreements in recent years were the Staple Lines Agreement operative from 1934 to 1937, and the Merchandise Agreement which operated with some modification from 1937 until after the war. These were agreements between a group of firms on familiar cartel lines. The Staple Lines Agreement was limited to certain staples such as corrugated iron sheets, cement, sugar, flour, salt and so forth. It divided up the trade in these commodities on a percentage basis. The Merchandise Agreement was more ambitious and covered practically the entire range of merchandise trade. Its principle of operation was similar to that of the earlier agreement; for non-standardized merchandise the percentage shares were calculated for broader classes of merchandise instead of for individual lines.

Participating firms which imported more than their share had to pay penalities to those who had fallen short of their agreed shares. The penalties were calculated on the basis of the estimated gross profits on their excess imports. Minimum prices were also occasionally fixed. The operation of these agreements was facilitated by agreements with suppliers who granted preferential and sometimes exclusive terms to the participating firms.

In spite of fairly stringent control measures the agreements were frequently broken locally; in particular, the price-fixing provisions were difficult to enforce. Local executives were frequently remunerated by commission on turnover and were anxious to increase sales, often by covert evasion of minimum prices or other provisions of the agreements.[1] Moreover, the market-sharing agreements could not prevent the growth of outside firms or the emergence of new competitors. Indeed, by helping to raise prices the agreements provided shelter to the smaller non-participating firms and also encouraged the entry of new firms.

The collaboration of the parties to the Merchandise Agreement was strengthened during the war. Shortly after the outbreak of war the firms informed their coast executives, as well as the authorities, that they would henceforth act in close consultation and collaboration; and in particular that they would share the trade in accordance with their own quotas based on past trading experience. These arrangements were recognised by the authorities in West Africa. Thus the authorities selected their advisers on commercial matters, in particular on the principles and administration of trade controls, from among the participants in the Merchandise Agreement; and for purposes of import licensing the licences issued to these firms were regarded as interchangeable within the group.

These comprehensive market-sharing arrangements appear to have been terminated a year or two after the end of the war. At present they seem to be confined to certain lines of merchandise where the group of firms have special arrangements with suppliers. There is also a general understanding among the firms that there will be no significant departure from their relative trading positions prevailing at the end of the previous formal agreements. No formal agreement appears to exist at

---

[1] Evasion was possible in the sales even of standardized staples. For instance, the price-fixing arrangements stipulated different sale prices for different quantities of flour, providing for quantity discounts. It was impossible for headquarters to check the units in which a given total of flour imports had been re-sold, and hence the sales proceeds which should have been received in terms of the agreed prices; quantity discounts could be allowed on smaller sales than provided for in the agreement. For unstandardized merchandise, such as textile prints, the difficulties of enforcing price agreements were naturally much greater.

present, and there is no system of penalties. In general, the understanding seems to be that departures from the agreed standard percentages will be resisted competitively unless special circumstances are recognized by the participants. Liquidation of heavy stocks, or the entry of one of the firms into a new region, would probably be accepted as legitimate reasons for alterations in relative positions.

On a local basis there are periodic agreements on prices. In recent years there appear to have been agreements for maintaining minimum selling prices of certain staple lines, including salt and bleached and grey cotton piece goods, in northern Nigeria.

3. THE RISE OF A NEWCOMER: ESTABLISHMENT AND GROWTH OF THE FIRM OF A. G. LEVENTIS AND COMPANY, LTD.

The possibility of the entry of new firms is the most potent limitation on the establishment of monopolies and the exercise of their powers. The rise of the firm of A. G. Leventis and Company Ltd. in recent years has been one of the most remarkable developments in West African trade for many years past. Although there have been other successful new entrants into West African trade in the course of the last decade or two, and, indeed, within the last few years, this firm has been by far the largest and most successful.[1] The circumstances of its rise bear on the argument of this study at many points; in particular, they are closely relevant to an assessment of the possibilities of new entry, the growth of new firms and the obstacles in their way. They well reflect the characteristics of trade rivalry in oligopolistic conditions, that is, a situation in which a few firms share the bulk of the trade, and in which they are intensely preoccupied with the position and conduct of particular individual competitors.[2] Incidents in the history of the firm also illustrate exceptionally well the effects of the operation of trade controls on the

[1] This is the firm referred to in the United Africa Company's *Statistical and Economic Review*, March 1950: 'At least one new entrant in the last fifteen years has worked up from modest beginnings to a position of eminence in the West African merchandise trade.'

[2] The terms 'oligopoly' (as noun or adjective) or 'oligopolistic' (as adjective) are frequently used in this study. As these expressions have not yet found their way into dictionaries they require some explanation here. They are very useful technical terms used in contemporary economic literature to refer to industries, trades and market situations in which there is a high degree of concentration in the sense that a small number of firms (but more than one firm) handles a large proportion of the trade or output. In such a situation the behaviour of firms tends to exhibit certain characteristics which differentiate it from situations in which there is either only one firm on the one hand, or a large number of firms on the other. The main special characteristics are discussed in Chapter 7.

trading situation and, beyond that, their possible effects on general political developments.[1]

Mr A. G. Leventis, the founder, managing director and controlling shareholder of the firm, was formerly general manager in the Gold Coast of the firm of G. B. Ollivant Ltd., which is financially linked with and ultimately controlled by the United Africa Company. He left their service in 1937, and at the beginning of 1938 established his own business to engage in both the import and the export trades in the Gold Coast. From the outset his firm enjoyed the financial backing of a highly respected and old-established English firm of cotton manufacturers and merchants, as well as of a large British bank.

The firm was established at a time when the tendency towards concentration and market-sharing agreements in West African trade appeared to be very strong, and when the prospects of newcomers seemed singularly unpromising. The large firms felt in a sufficiently powerful position to extend their market-sharing arrangements in the import trade from staple lines to the whole range of imported merchandise; the Staple Lines Agreement was converted into the Merchandise Agreement at the end of 1937. In the export trade the participants of the cocoa-buying agreement of 1937 handled almost the entire trade. Moreover, the parties to the Staple Lines Agreement and the Merchandise Agreement had as a group entered into preferential or exclusive supplying arrangements with overseas suppliers of many important products, which restricted the opportunities of new entrants.[2] The concerted action of a group of firms implied a further danger to the prospects of new competitors, the threat that suppliers, acting under pressure from this group, might refuse to supply new firms. In conditions of relatively depressed trade such pressure was more likely to be effective.

Moreover, trading conditions and developments in the Gold Coast were especially unfavourable in the cocoa season of 1937-8. The year 1938 was one of exceptional depression in West Africa; and in the Gold Coast conditions were aggravated, and indeed trade brought almost to a standstill, by the cocoa hold-up from November 1937 till the spring of 1938. When the hold-up came to an end in April 1938 the authorities were anxious to avoid the rapid shipment of accumulated supplies and consequent depression of the price of cocoa. A system of export quotas was instituted largely on the basis of the past performance of the exporters.

---

[1] Only those aspects and incidents of the career of the firm are reviewed here which shed light on matters germane to this study. The discussion implies no assessment of its prospects, nor does it provide a comprehensive history of its rise.

[2] On the other hand, the market-sharing agreements tended to make trading more profitable and thus more attractive to newcomers, a usual result of such arrangements when unaccompanied by a bar on entry.

In spite of all these difficulties the rise of the firm was meteoric. During the 1938–9 season, its first complete season of operation, the firm was already the fifth largest cocoa exporter;[1] by November 1939, when the wartime controls began, it had moved to the third or fourth position. In the import trade its rise was even more spectacular; by about 1941, before the imposition of comprehensive import controls, it had become about the third largest importer in the Gold Coast. Thus it reached its position of eminence in both the export and import trades before the imposition of widespread controls. The success of the firm seems to have been the result largely of the ability, initiative, hard work and independence of action of its principals.

4. ASPECTS AND CONSEQUENCES OF THE RIVALRY BETWEEN THIS FIRM AND ITS COMPETITORS

During the war the rivalry between the members of the Association of West African Merchants, especially the leading members of the Merchandise Agreement group, and the firm of Leventis grew in bitterness and led to developments which came greatly to influence the subsequent history of the Gold Coast.[2] From the early days of the war the principals of the firm and its supporters severely criticized the operation of the trade controls and the influence of the Association of West African Merchants (very largely of the Merchandise Agreement group) on their establishment and administration. Conversely, these firms accused their rival of improper action in obtaining privileges in the allocation of licences, supplies and foreign exchange.[3] In 1946 an official commission of inquiry was appointed in the Gold Coast, largely to examine specific charges against this firm by its principal competitors; this was the

[1] Not only was this the first season in which it was able to operate, but it had the difficulty, which it shared with all shippers who were not parties to the cocoa-buying agreement, that it did not know when and on what conditions the export quotas introduced at the end of the hold-up would be lifted. This hampered its preparations for the season. The quotas were lifted at the end of September 1938. In these circumstances it was a remarkable feat for a newcomer to become the fifth largest exporter in 1938–9.

[2] The struggle between these firms and A. G. Leventis and Co. Ltd. is an outstanding example of the bitterness of commercial rivalry and of the intensity of preoccupation with the activities of individual competitors characteristic of a situation (oligopoly) when several participants each have an appreciable share of the trade and the policies of each obviously influence the fortunes of the others.

[3] For obvious reasons some of the local executives of the large firms would tend to ascribe the success of a new competitor to alleged malpractices rather than to superior efficiency. This would add to the difficulty of the overseas head offices of these firms in assessing the real factors influencing the changing position of their firms.

Martindale Commission, presided over by a judge of the Supreme Court, which published its report in 1947.[1]

The leading members of the Merchandise Agreement group submitted formal complaints before this Commission, alleging that for some years past the controls of imports, supplies and foreign exchange had been misconducted, and had been administered contrary to declared policy so as to favour certain firms, particularly the firm of Leventis. The Commission found that these allegations were justified, and special favours had been granted by the licensing authorities to some firms, of which A. G. Leventis and Co. was by far the most important,[2] and that this preferential treatment had been on such a large scale that the control of imports as a whole was vitiated by these favours, which were almost certainly corruptly secured.

There followed an extremely bitter press campaign in the course of which documents were published which were calculated to discredit members of the Association of West African Merchants as well as the Martindale Report. Memoranda were also submitted to the administration by persons whose conduct was impugned. These denied the charges and maintained that the proceedings of the Martindale Commission had been irregular. After months of agitation another Commission was appointed with Mr Eric Sachs, K.C., Bencher of the Middle Temple, as sole commissioner. This Commission was to review the findings of its predecessor. Its report was published in 1948.[3]

The Sachs Commission found that the proceedings of the Martindale Commission had been improper; and that this report contained

a number of misstatements of fact of a type far transcending those incidental errors which almost inevitably creep into a lengthy report. They were indeed so fundamental as to strike at the roots of the general reliability of the report itself[4]... it followed that the findings of the (Martindale)

[1] *Report of the Commission of Inquiry into the Conduct and Management of the Supplies and Customs Departments*, Accra, 1947.

[2] The Commission went out of its way to accuse Levantine firms. 'This course [evasion of controls] was permitted to a small group of importers, none of whom notably was of race other than Greek or Asiatic.'

[3] *Report of Commission of Enquiry into the Representations made by W. E. Conway, Esq., A. D. W. Allen, Esq., A. G. Leventis, Esq., A. G. Leventis and Co., Ltd., repudiating Allegations in the Report of the Commission of Enquiry into the Conduct and Management of the Supplies and Customs Departments*, Accra, 1948.

[4] Thus, to take only one instance, the Martindale Report stated that the firm of A. G. Leventis and Company received highly preferential treatment in the granting of import licences for quicklime, and that as a result their imports for the particular year were far in excess of their entitlement on the basis of past performance; and that in particular they had secured an unwarranted preference over one of their competitors. In actual fact over the relevant period imports of quicklime were unrestricted.

Report could not reasonably be regarded for the purposes of the present proceedings as of quasi-judicial status or prima-facie evidence of the facts therein stated.[1]

The Sachs Commission substantially reversed the findings of the Martindale Commission. In particular, it established that the share of the firm of Leventis in restricted imports over these years was no greater than it would have been entitled to under a policy of past performance uniformly and fairly applied.[2]

The Sachs Commission did find that over a comparatively short period from May 1944 to the beginning of 1946 the firm of A. G. Leventis and Company had improperly secured certain advantages. So far from subverting the machinery of import control and defeating government policy, these favours offset only partly the preferential treatment of the Merchandise Agreement group from 1939 to 1944. The Sachs Commission emphasized that the preferential treatment of these firms had been proceeding for four years before any preferential treatment was accorded to A. G. Leventis and Company; and that the method of control adopted was largely responsible for this result.[3] Thus, preferential treatment by the licensing authorities was certainly not a factor in the success of the enterprise.

The bitter and specific press campaign against the government and the Merchandise Agreement firms took place in 1947–8, when many types of imported merchandise were very scarce and profit margins very high. It exacerbated an already highly charged atmosphere. The widely publicized evidence before the Sachs Commission, notably on the operation of trade controls and on the proceedings of the Martindale Commission, served to discredit the administration, the Association of West African Merchants and even the judiciary. These factors contributed to the events which led to the Accra riots of 1948 which in turn directly influenced the political development of the Gold Coast.

[1] Sachs Report, paras. 21 and 22.
[2] The Commissioner investigated several but not all of the representations made by the firm. On the basis of its inquiries it became clear that the firm had not received in total more than its due entitlement. As this already disposed of the principal finding of the Martindale Commission, the Commissioner did not proceed to inquire into certain other representations of the firm (Sachs Report, paras. 101, 102).
[3] In this connexion the findings of the Commission might well have been far more emphatic if Mr Sachs had not taken for granted that all the restrictions imposed were required by the war, and had considered the possibility of shifting commodities from the unrestricted to the restricted class for other reasons. This matter is considered in Chapters 11 and 19 below.

5. COMMERCIAL AND OFFICIAL OBSTACLES TO THE RISE
AND GROWTH OF A NEW ENTRANT

Comprehensive official trade controls inevitably tend to restrain the growth of newly established firms. They tend to maintain the previously existing distribution of trade among firms to the detriment of expanding firms; this is true for most types of trade controls, but particularly for those based on past performance. In practice these inherent disadvantages may be reinforced by the interpretation of broad objectives of policy (such as the maintenance of the *status quo*) which are inherently ambiguous and vague. Firms not connected with the framing and administration of trade controls may find themselves at a particular disadvantage through varying applications and interpretations of vague and general policies; and their inherent disadvantage under a system of trade controls may become a crushing disability. Some well-documented instances of the operation of trade controls in West Africa in relation to A. G. Leventis and Co. illustrate this theme exceptionally clearly.

The most obvious example is provided by the operation of the cocoa export quotas established in the Gold Coast in 1939 which affected this firm particularly adversely. This instance is of special interest as an example of the imposition of a control which was clearly unnecessary as the market was unlimited in view of an official British undertaking to purchase the entire exportable crop.[1]

In the import trade it is less easy to find such unambiguous examples of the shifting of commodities into the restricted class not required by the exigencies of war. But the tendency seems to have operated also in the import trade. Thus the imposition of severe restrictions on imports from South Africa into the Gold Coast from 1943 in fact involved a drastic re-allocation of that trade against the interests of the firm of Lenventis and in favour of the Merchandise Agreement group. This came about by applying to imports from South Africa a licensing system based on the shares of the firms in pre-war years in the total trade in the relevant commodities. The South African trade had been largely developed during the war by A. G. Leventis and Co., and at the time it had a very large share in it. As a result of the restrictions the imports of this firm from South Africa were reduced by over 90 % from 1943 to 1944. The necessity for this restriction could not be taken for granted, since South Africa was in the sterling area, while shipping space was available in ships coming in ballast from the Middle East to load manganese at Takoradi.[2]

---

[1] This example is only mentioned here; the operation of the quota system is examined in some detail in Chapter 19 below.

[2] There might have been a case for imposing these restrictions on various other grounds. But it is certainly not self-evident that the restrictions were necessary and

Another example of the incidence of import restrictions may be taken from the textile trade. This instance also illustrates the interaction of different sets of controls operating simultaneously, but on different bases, in the supplying and in the receiving countries. From 1940 exports of textiles from the United Kingdom to West Africa as a whole were controlled on the basis of past performance of exporters in certain previous years. In February 1943 the Cotton Control in the United Kingdom announced that with immediate effect quotas would be calculated separately for each colony, and no longer on a global basis for West Africa. The Gold Coast quota was fixed at 22 %, the Nigerian quota at 70 %, with the balance available for Sierra Leone and the Gambia. This amounted to an increase in the share of Nigeria and a substantial reduction in the share of the Gold Coast. The new quotas applied in effect retroactively so far as licences already issued were concerned, and exporters were not permitted to use their existing licences to rush textiles to the Gold Coast.[1] The reason for this drastic measure was said to be the desperate need for oilseeds from Nigeria. It was hoped to improve the production by increasing the supply of textiles to act as an inducement to producers of oilseeds. Yet the same oilseeds were at the time bought on a strict quota basis with rigid exclusion of new buyers.

The decision adversely affected all those firms which operated exclusively or principally in the Gold Coast. Of these by far the most important was A. G. Leventis and Company, which was established only in the Gold Coast. The firm therefore decided to establish a branch in Nigeria to use its licence there. An application to the authorities to establish itself in Nigeria was at first rejected on unspecified grounds, but the firm was subsequently permitted to open a branch. This was a costly palliative, since there were heavy expenses of establishment and the textile trade in Nigeria is quite different from that of the Gold Coast. However, the use of the textile export quotas was of such importance that the firm had to establish itself there.

In 1944 substantial quantities of American army drill were allocated to Nigeria from the United States. The United Kingdom agents of A. G. Leventis and Company were advised by the Cotton Board that the firm should approach the delegate of the Association of West African Merchants to the Nigerian Supply Board (i.e. a private individual in the service of their principal competitor) for a share in the allocation of this army drill. The firm refused and applied direct to the authorities. The application was, however, rejected on the ground that the firm had no past performance in Nigeria. Yet there was no legislation in force

desirable; and the manner of the imposition and the allocation of the restricted trade were open to criticism.

[1] From this it was clear that they were badly needed there.

stipulating past performance as a condition for textile imports into Nigeria from the United States.[1]

More examples could be given of major instances where the administration of trade controls affected this firm adversely, far beyond the inevitable disadvantages which controls based on past performance tend to have for growing firms. Its exclusion from the administration of control also brought it about that it was neither in a position to assess the necessity for the imposition of these restrictions, nor to modify their general effects by securing concessions for accepting particular hardships.

The firm now participates substantially in all principal branches of the import and export trades.[2] It has achieved this in spite of the setback it suffered from the operation of wartime controls. Moreover, it has had to operate in an atmosphere in which damaging accusations and allegations were widely broadcast which could not fail to influence at least some suppliers.

In the main the firm has found that government policy, in particular the framing and administration of trade controls, has proved to be a much more serious limitation upon its opportunities and growth than has been the existence of preferential or tying arrangements between some suppliers and its principal competitors. The latter rarely proved to be absolute barriers to the firm's development. Their inhibiting effects proved to be temporary and generally left undisturbed a large part of the import trade, including the highly important textile trade. The firm, moreover, was able to assess the situation and frame its policy confidently on that basis. On the other hand, the controls until about 1947 or 1948 embraced the bulk of the import trade; they were rigid and could not be circumvented by the development of substitute sources; they were at times subject to influence by the principal competitors of the firm; and they were subject to unpredictable and often unannounced changes. It is thus not surprising that the firm should have found these controls far more serious obstacles to its development than the private marketing arrangements and the commercial power of even its most formidable competitors.[3]

---

[1] At that time textiles were restricted by means of export quotas from the supplying countries and not by import quotas in the receiving countries; it was precisely because of this that the firm had established itself in Nigeria. In fact, export quotas to West Africa from the United Kingdom were slightly reduced at the time, because these American supplies became available.

[2] These remarks do not of course imply an assessment of the prospects of this (or of any other) firm; cf. Chapter 8, § 8, below.

[3] The foregoing sections are intended purely as a factual account of certain aspects and results of the wartime controls in the West African import trade. There is no suggestion that those who devised or administered the machinery of control intended to use it consciously to influence the course of commercial rivalry or to destroy a particular competitor.

MONOPOLISTIC AND COMPETITIVE INFLUENCES IN WEST AFRICAN EXTERNAL TRADE

CHAPTER 7

CRITERIA, CHARACTERISTICS AND
BASES OF MONOPOLY

Part 3 of this study[1] reviews certain factors in the degree of concentration in West African trade, in the emergence of monopoly and oligopoly, and in the limitations on the exercise of monopoly and oligopoly power. These matters bear on both branches of external trade. But they are discussed here immediately after the import trade, and in the general context of that trade, because the export trade is dominated by the statutory marketing boards. The monopoly power of these organizations is of a different order from that of even the largest private firm or concerted group of firms in West Africa, because they are the only buyers in their respective fields (which together cover almost all agricultural exports) and the barriers to new entry are erected by statute. For this reason, as well as for the quantitative importance of the statutory monopolies, the marketing boards are discussed separately in Part 5.

This part of the book covers a wide and diverse range of topics. It may help the reader if the order in which they are treated is set out here.

The criteria and characteristics of monopoly and oligopoly and of a high degree of concentration are considered in this chapter and the appended note. Some underlying factors in these economies favouring concentration in external trade are reviewed in Chapter 8. This is followed by an examination of the importance and limitations of some self-perpetuating influences engendered by a high degree of concentration, especially through certain types of marketing arrangements (Chapters 9 and 10). The importance of official attitudes and policies in creating barriers to the entry and expansion of newcomers and smaller firms are discussed in Chapters 11–13. Chapter 14 deals with the effects on the trading situation of the comparatively high degree of concentration in the provision of certain important ancillary services.

1. CRITERIA AND CHARACTERISTICS OF MONOPOLY

Allegations of monopoly are frequent and widespread in West Africa. On closer examination it is found that the term 'monopoly' covers a variety of different sets of circumstances or situations, and some of its

[1] The discussion of this part of the study is in places more technical than that of the other parts. The reader more interested in a description of the principal aspects of West African trade rather than in an analysis of underlying factors can pass straight to Part 4.

uses are not only different but contradictory. It is an omnibus expression which is apt to be used loosely elsewhere too, but in West Africa it is at times bandied about so indiscriminately as to be devoid of precise meaning, though not of political significance. This, of course, in no way implies the absence of monopoly in West Africa; but before any useful examination is possible of its presence, strength and extent, its meaning must be analysed and defined.

The essence of monopoly is the absence of alternatives or a severe restriction on their number. Monopoly is present where those dealing either as buyers or as sellers with a firm or concerted group of firms cannot obtain the same commodity or service from other independent sources (or where such sources are quantitatively unimportant), and where there are no close substitutes for the commodity or service. Monopoly is therefore essentially a matter of degree, because there generally are some substitutes for most commodities. A monopoly situation is significant when there is a distinct gap in the chain of substitutes or the range of alternatives open to those who deal with the monopolist; here the term monopoly or quasi-monopoly is used only where such a gap exists.[1]

It is inherent in such a situation that the sole seller (or buyer) is able substantially to influence the price of the commodity or service in which he deals. Thus the monopolist may be able to secure a rate of return or other advantages in excess of what is necessary to call forth the required capital, skill, effort and enterprise. The possibility of exceptional returns is likely to depend chiefly on the barriers to the entry and expansion of competitors rather than on the proportion of the trade handled by a firm or group of firms.

Such an exceptional return is usually conceived of as additional profits; but in practice it may often take the form of inflated costs, the subsidizing of unprofitable activities and extensions, and the weakening of enterprise and effort generally. The inflation of costs may enable executives or employees to secure higher earnings than would be necessary to secure their services. These considerations provide one reason (though by no means the only one) why the level of profits is an imperfect indicator of either the presence or the use of monopoly power.

A monopoly situation by definition implies a high degree of depen-

---

[1] Much of the analysis of this section applies broadly also to a situation in which a small number of firms handles the bulk of a particular trade. This situation, known in technical economic language as an oligopoly, is examined in some detail in the following section. As with monopoly, the term will be used only where there is a significant gap in the chain of substitutes between the commodity or service in question and its closest substitute.

dence on the part of those who sell to or buy from the monopolists and quasi-monopolists. This is an important aspect of the limited range of alternatives which is of the essence of monopoly, and it is largely independent of the active exercise of monopoly power.

The foregoing reasoning suggests that certain corollaries of monopoly are independent of the active exploitation of monopoly situations. The monopolist necessarily influences price by his action (or inaction); to a considerable extent he 'makes the market' whether he wishes it or not. This remains true even if he is reluctant to take full advantage of the situation, and even if he can maintain price at a level securing returns much in excess of that necessary to call forth the supply. The power to influence prices is likely to breed resentment at all times, particularly so in the politically highly charged atmosphere often found in multi-racial societies.

2. CRITERIA AND CHARACTERISTICS OF OLIGOPOLY

Outside the admittedly important field of statutory organizations, instances of pure monopoly (sole buyer or seller of a product or service without close substitutes) are rare, particularly in the provision of trading services. A more prevalent form of market situation is one in which there is a small number of buyers or sellers, each of whom handles a large share of the total supply and therefore has certain attributes of monopoly and monopoly power. Such a situation of economic concentration is often referred to as oligopoly. For a study of monopoly in general and of West African trade in particular the similarities of pure monopoly and oligopoly, as well as the differences between them, are relevant and important.

The most important point of similarity is that the oligopolist, as well as the true monopolist, necessarily influences price (i.e. to some extent makes the market) within certain limits. The range within which each oligopolist can independently influence prices is, however, narrower than where there is a pure monopoly, for he has to take into account not only the availability of substitutes (as does a pure monopolist as well), but also the likely actions of his principal competitors in his own market.

In all circumstances price changes are likely to affect adversely the interests of certain participants in the market. Increases in price naturally are harmful to consumers, while decreases injure the interests of producers and of some traders. In monopoly and oligopoly situations the power of firms to influence prices, coupled with a high degree of dependence on these firms, tend to provoke allegations that all price changes are deliberately engineered to injure certain interests. Consumers, producers or rival traders may consider that they have been specially and deliberately injured by the actions of the monopolist or oligopolists, and may ascribe market changes to their intentional activities. Plausibility is lent to these views because in these situations the firms can undoubtedly influence the market; indeed, they cannot help doing so. It is therefore impossible conclusively or convincingly to refute allegations of profiteering, of destructive underselling to eliminate particular competitors, of deliberate depression of producer prices, or of wasteful inflation of costs.

An important and distinctive characteristic of oligopoly is the realization by each firm that its fortunes depend very closely upon the actions of the others in the same market. Their behaviour is necessarily influenced by the realization of mutual interdependence. Each firm appreciates that in initiating price changes it must expect the other firms to react to these changes, and that in assessing the net effects of a price change it must take account of the probable reaction of others. In deciding on price changes each firm considers not only the general market situation and its own financial and stock position, but also the probable conduct of its principal competitors.

Firms recognizing their mutual interdependence may find it convenient and profitable to co-ordinate their policies and to act together, and co-operation is made easier because the numbers are comparatively small. An oligopolistic situation is frequently accompanied by market-sharing arrangements between a number of producers or firms. This is particularly likely in the supply of standardized products or services, where these price-fixing agreements may be effective and stable even without formal market-sharing arrangements; banking and shipping provide familiar examples in the United States, in Britain and in Western Europe. Where the product is largely unstandardized, agreements are less often concluded, and, moreover, tend to be unstable; the motor industry seems to be a convenient example.

Co-operation is, however, by no means the inevitable outcome of oligopoly. Individual firms may decide to try their strength and to enlarge their share in the market by active competition. Moreover, when new entry is possible, or when some firms do not participate in group activity, the cohesion within the co-operating group tends to be weakened, as differences are likely to arise over the appropriate price and marketing policy to be pursued in the light of the actual or potential outside competition. There are likely to be recurrent phases of intense competition alternating with formal or informal market-sharing arrangements. As each contestant is as much preoccupied with the actual or prospective position and conduct of a few firms as with the general market situation, the competition between the firms is at times likely to assume an almost personal character. The severity and bitterness of the struggle are likely to be enhanced when the risks of trade are considerable, whether as a result of market fluctuations or heavy capital requirements or other factors.

The most obvious difference between oligopoly and monopoly is that under oligopoly buyers and sellers are confronted with at least one more firm, possibly several more, so that the dependence upon any one firm is reduced; the reduced dependence is an important advantage to customers which is present to a limited extent even when firms act in concert on major issues of business policy.

When the principal firms act together, either informally or in terms of written agreements, the results approximate more or less closely to the results of pure monopoly. The power to influence prices is increased and the number of independent alternatives open to customers is reduced; nevertheless, for reasons already mentioned, the concerted action is unlikely to be as effective as where there is a single monopolist. A measure of peripheral competition, which may take the form either of covert price concessions or of the provision of extra services and benefits, is likely to exist even during the currency of the market-sharing arrangements. The mere presence of several firms in independent ownership itself may lessen both the reality and the sense of dependence of customers.[1]

However, when the principal firms do not act together, either informally or in terms of formal agreements, the market struggles and manoeuvres tend to differentiate oligopoly sharply from pure monopoly. In the course of such struggles valuable concessions, particularly price concessions, are made to customers. At the same time prices are likely to be unstable and, at times, to show erratic and discontinuous movements. The market warfare may have political consequences affecting the community as a whole, and the government may be drawn into the struggle. Moreover, although customers are likely to receive considerable advantages in the course of the struggle, these may be partly offset by the extra risks of loss in an unstable market situation and their reactions may again have political repercussions.[2]

The difference between monopoly and oligopoly may also affect the cost of producing the commodity and providing the service in question. It is not possible on *a priori* grounds to say whether it will be higher in

---

[1] This is largely true whether or not the other firms are participants in market-sharing arrangements.

[2] The disadvantages of unstable prices are most likely to affect adversely the trading customers of the oligopolists. They may suffer heavy losses on the stocks they hold if prices fall drastically during a spell of price war. In West Africa, for instance, African re-sellers are one of the most vocal sections of public opinion, and are much more vocal than producers or consumers. In this way the political repercussions of the instability of oligopoly are magnified, while the benefits of price concessions are obscured and underrated.

one case than in the other. For a number of reasons the costs of a monopoly may be inflated. The spur of competition is absent or less keen; and monopoly advantages may be reflected in the form of higher costs rather than of higher profits. Conversely, oligopoly may lead to the under-utilization of duplicated facilities. Some of these ostensible duplications may confer genuine advantages on customers; others may be largely redundant. Genuine redundancy is likely to be less important in the provision of trading services in which fixed capital plays a relatively minor part. However, even if average costs are greater under oligopoly than under monopoly, the price of the commodity or service is likely to be more favourable to customers in conditions of oligopoly.[1]

In general, oligopoly is an attenuated form of monopoly; compared with the latter it results in reduced dependence on individual firms, less complete control of the market by any one firm, and more favourable prices to buyers and sellers. On the other hand, prices may be subject to more rapid and erratic changes under oligopoly.

3. BARRIERS TO ENTRY AS A KEY ELEMENT IN MONOPOLY AND OLIGOPOLY

Both in monopoly and oligopoly situations the firms concerned necessarily have the power to influence market prices, which, however, does not imply that the price can be set at a level which will secure a return to the firms, or remuneration to their management or employees, above the level which could be secured in trades or employment of similar risk and complexity elsewhere. The establishment and continued maintenance of such a price postulates not only a monopoly or oligopoly situation, but also appreciable and lasting obstacles to the entry of new firms.[2]

The duration and extent of the power to influence prices, and the likelihood that it will be exercised to secure additional profits and advantages, depend primarily on the nature of the obstacles which impede the provision of additional independent sources of supplies and additional suitable substitutes. The nature of the obstacles also conditions

---

[1] The influence of numbers of traders on prices is examined in Chapter 18. It is conceivable that prices may be more favourable under monopoly than under oligopoly. This exceptional case requires very special conditions of cost and entry which are not relevant to the provision of trading services, and for this reason is not pursued here.

[2] In many oligopoly situations there may be several small firms which in the aggregate handle a small share of the total supply. Their expansion affects the position of the larger firm or firms in exactly the same way as the appearance of entirely new firms. For this reason the expansion of small fringe firms is not specifically mentioned in the text.

with the degree of concentration, and is likely to be independent of both the real extent of dependence (which is governed in part by the factors thus listed) and the active exercise of monopoly of power.

With very few exceptions the dependence is greater for sellers who are confronted by a monopolistic buyer of their products or services than for buyers who are confronted by monopolistic sellers. This follows from the functioning of a specialized economy in which incomes are earned by individuals by selling a specialized service or its products (or at most a few specialized services or their products), and in which they spend their incomes on a wide range of commodities. Dependence on a monopoly buyer of one product or service greatly affects the livelihood of all who supply it; dependence on a selling monopoly covering one product or service normally affects only a small proportion of individual expenditure.

Thus by themselves statistics of the degree of concentration cannot serve as reliable indices of the extent of monopoly and of the degree of monopoly power. Such quantitative treatment is unable to convey certain essential elements in the situation. For instance, it cannot indicate the reasons for the limited number of alternatives, nor can it fully convey the reality of the limitation. It cannot distinguish a situation in which the entry of additional firms is effectively barred from one in which entry is free but not profitable because the existing firms are efficient and charge competitive prices.

In general the strength, character, permanence and profitability of monopolistic or oligopolistic situations depend on factors which cannot usually be expressed quantitatively in a meaningful sense and cannot be summarized in a simple formula. Such factors include the effectiveness of co-operation among participants, the closeness of substitutes and the ease of entry; and these can be assessed only by qualitative analysis and discussion.

6. OLIGOPOLY AS A CHARACTERISTIC OF WEST AFRICAN TRADE

In West Africa a small number of firms handle a large proportion of the import trade as well as the purchase of produce for export. Six or seven firms handle between two-thirds and three-quarters of a large and varied trade. In trading activities so high a degree of concentration is exceptional for such an extensive and diverse market as that of the West African territories, which at present engage in an external trade of between £300 and £400 m. a year, ranging over manufactures, processed foodstuffs, raw materials, agricultural crops and forest products.[1]

[1] The extent of oligopoly in industry today is difficult to assess and has been a topic of some controversy. It is, however, certainly a somewhat unusual situation in

This degree of concentration would be high even if the firms were of approximately equal size and always acted independently. In an important sense it is even higher in West African trade. First, there is one dominant firm; and secondly, most of the large firms have often acted in concert. Moreover, with very few exceptions the same large firms participate in the import trade and in the purchase of export produce more or less in the same proportions. The degree of concentration is therefore greater than would be suggested by the shares of the largest firms in the import or export trades separately.

For many years oligopoly has been present in a large part of West African trade. Indeed, some of the most characteristic features and methods of West African trade are the expected accompaniments of oligopoly. Firms have been intensely preoccupied with the activities and conduct of individual competitors; they have acted in the knowledge that a price change initiated by one of their number was likely to bring about retaliation on the part of others; there have been recurrent phases of intense competition followed by market-sharing arrangements; and there have been occasional spectacular attempts to keep out or destroy particular competitors. The wide range of merchandise handled by the large firms and the forward integration of the importing firms into the semi-wholesale and retail trade are partly the results of oligopoly structure, even though they may originally have been adopted for quite different reasons.

Oligopoly in West African trade has had widespread effects on business conduct. Until quite recently local executives of several firms bribed members of the postal staff to obtain copies of the telegrams or summaries of the telephone conversations of their rivals (with whom they may at the same time have had market-sharing arrangements) in order to secure information about their stock position and prospective selling and price policies. In the absence of oligopoly such conduct is pointless, as the position and prospective policies of one or two firms would not provide a valuable guide to market prospects. The oligopolistic and occasionally monopolistic nature of West African trade has also exerted considerable influence on political life and events. The Gold Coast cocoa hold-up of 1937–8, the Martindale and Sachs commissions of inquiry after the war, and the Gold Coast disturbances of 1948 were all connected with this particular economic feature.

Distrust of middlemen and traders is widespread in most societies and foreigners are also generally the objects of misgiving; expatriate traders attract hostility for both these reasons. A large measure of concentration

wholesale trade, especially in the foreign trade of large territories. The extent of concentration and the resulting oligopoly in trade in Nigeria and the Gold Coast seem exceptional for such large markets.

implies a substantial measure of economic dependence which is likely to be felt and resented particularly keenly where the predominant firms act both as buyers and sellers and are powerful expatriate merchant houses. Where prices of imports or exports are liable to frequent and marked fluctuations, feelings of dependence and resentment lead the native population to ascribe any adverse price changes to the malice of foreign firms pursuing their selfish ends. The high degree of concentration, especially the large share of the total trade handled by one firm, also brings it about that a strike against one firm may paralyse the economic life of trading areas. Thus without necessarily securing monopoly profits to the firms (such profits postulate lasting obstacles to entry which may or may not accompany an oligopolistic situation), the high degree of concentration has embarrassing results.

7. BARRIERS TO ENTRY AS A PRINCIPAL TOPIC OF PART 3 OF THIS STUDY

The remainder of Part 3 is confined to those sectors of West African trade which are conducted by private firms, and deals principally with barriers to entry, which are of great importance in a study of monopoly and oligopoly. It is necessary to discuss these barriers in some detail, and the length of the discussion may create a false impression of their magnitude. To correct this in advance some general conclusions need be stated here. The obstacles deriving from natural scarcities or from private marketing arrangements are certainly not insuperable; the difficulties of new entrants derive at least equally from political and administrative measures. Even in combination the various obstacles have not prevented the emergence of substantial new competitors.[1]

NOTE TO CHAPTER 7

Misleading criteria of monopoly

This note reviews some of the various meanings attached to the term 'monopoly', especially in West Africa. It will be suggested that some uses of the term, frequently met with in official usage and in serious discussions influencing public opinion and policy, are not only misleading and contradictory, but are likely to result in measures calculated to restrict entry, reduce the alternatives open to the customers of the traders, and to secure exceptional profits to the latter. In such circumstances the loose use of the term tends in effect to promote monopoly or quasi-monopoly situations, and little is to

---

[1] Examples include the rise of A. G. Leventis and Co. Ltd., and the growth of Mr S. Raccah's enterprise in groundnut buying. The picturesque example of the successful competition of the Kakanda tribesmen in the groundnut trade is described in Chapter 18 below.

be gained by using it to cover a variety of situations widely different in their causes and effects. At present its misuse is a symptom of confusion, while it also serves as an expression of dislike and abuse.

The term monopoly is used, for instance, to describe a situation where members of one tribe, race or nationality occupy a prominent position in any one trade. Thus it is said that Lebanese monopolize the textile trade of parts of West Africa, or that the Gao traders monopolize the wholesale food trade in Kumasi. These traders do not act in concert and are in fact highly competitive; and entry into the trade is free. Thus this popular use of the term is particularly misleading, and frequently gives rise to demands for measures to limit entry which, if accepted, are likely to endow those in the trade with some degree of monopoly.

The prevalence of a high gross margin between selling price and cost is sometimes referred to as proof of the presence of monopoly, or at least as a symptom of monopoly. This again is misleading, since there are trades in which these margins are always very high, while yielding only a small or moderate return on capital. Thus the margin of profit on sales in the furniture or jewellery trades is always high, but since the rate of stock turnover is low the rate of return on capital need not be high.

Successful accumulation of wealth by individuals or firms is often regarded axiomatically as the fruits of successful monopoly. Profits made from the holding of stocks of agricultural produce between successive harvests are often stigmatized as the result of monopoly.

In general, high prices, wide profit margins, or generous rates of return on capital are imperfect and misleading guides to the existence and extent of monopoly. High prices are meaningless unless related to cost of production, to the prices of other commodities and to general economic conditions. High gross profit margins may co-exist with low returns on capital even under competitive conditions, as well as in certain monopoly situations. A favourable market situation may result in a very high return on capital in an industry which comprises a multiplicity of small independent units. Conversely, a concern possessing a very large degree of monopoly may make comparatively small profits owing to inefficiency, uneconomic extensions, the payment of inflated rewards to its management or staff, or the subsidizing of unprofitable activities.

Even if the rate of return on capital in particular activities could be accurately and objectively ascertained, the results would be of very limited usefulness as indices of monopoly. In fact, accurate and objective measurement is altogether impossible, and effort expended on the task would be unrewarding. Changing price levels make it difficult to compare current proceeds with corresponding investments made at different dates in the past. Moreover, it is impossible to discover the amount of investment in particular activities because of amalgamation of firms, discontinuation of certain activities and expenditure covering several different activities. Because of these difficulties any calculation of the rate of return on capital is largely arbitrary even in apparently simple cases. The conceptual and accounting difficulties in the way of significant calculation are exceptionally intractable in West

Africa, where there have been many instances of amalgamation, liquidation, adjustment of capital values and dissolution of firms into smaller independent parts. These changes have taken place at widely different price levels and in some cases over a very long period. Moreover, the leading firms are engaged in a remarkably wide range of activities geographically and functionally. Those of the United Africa Company range from the operation of an ocean shipping line to the maintenance of small stores and produce-buying stations in remote villages, and from the management of huge estates in Central Africa and elsewhere to the purchase of dates in Iraq, the operation of a department store in Istanbul, and the maintenance of buying offices in numerous cities all over the world. In short, for present purposes it would be of little value to examine rates of return on capital for particular firms as a whole, and this applies much more to an attempt to estimate the return on capital invested in particular activities.

Indeed, it seems that statistical, quantitative data are insufficient and at times even misleading indices of monopoly, and it is for this reason that no attempt is made in this study to measure the degree of monopoly (in any of its meanings) or the extent of monopoly profits in West African trade. But this does not mean that systematic analysis of monopoly is not possible. As the absence of alternatives, or the paucity of their number, is the essence of monopoly or oligopoly, the principal element in the investigation of such situations is an assessment of the nature and number of accessible alternatives and an inquiry into the forces influencing these. Such factors, in particular the possibilities of new entry, require qualitative analysis and discussion.

The most informative quantitative data relevant to monopoly or oligopoly seem to be the statistics of concentration (especially under West African conditions where the rate of return on capital invested can hardly be assessed objectively). These describe the proportion of a clearly defined trade or industry handled by a specified small number of large firms. This information is of interest only where the trade or industry is clearly defined and distinct, and where there are no very close substitutes for its products. This condition of an appreciable gap in the chain of substitutes is clearly satisfied in the import and export merchanting activities in West Africa. This is obvious where the total import or export trade is under consideration; but this condition is also present in the trade in those staple import and export products for which statistics of the degree of concentration have been presented in earlier chapters. However, as already stated, even this information is not a complete or reliable index of monopoly power.

CHAPTER 8

THE ADVANTAGES OF CAPITAL AND SIZE

1. ADVANTAGES OF FINANCIAL STRENGTH
IN TROPICAL TRADE

Assured access to substantial capital is everywhere a source of commercial strength, and this is more pronounced in some trading activities than in others. The advantages conferred by access to supplies of capital appear to be very marked in foreign trade with tropical or subtropical countries exporting primary products, and they provide the principal explanation for the successive waves of amalgamation of firms in the West African trade and the resulting emergence of a few large predominant firms.

Although the extent of concentration in West African trade is unusually high for such a large market, a fairly high degree of concentration is a feature of the external trade of many of the so-called under-developed areas. While in some instances fortuitous circumstances have served to promote concentration (for instance, administration of certain territories in the past by chartered companies), the principal reason for the predominance of a comparatively small number of large firms seems to be the advantages offered by the possession of large capital.

The most obvious factor responsible for the heavy capital requirements is the long period over which merchants have to finance stocks in many branches of tropical trade. In the import trade there is often a long time between the placing of orders and the ultimate disposal of the merchandise, a considerable period may also elapse between the purchase of produce up-country and its eventual sale. Although bank credit is sometimes available for some of these operations, the capital requirements of the merchants are heavy.

Moreover, the capital is exposed to considerable risk, which tends to increase with the length of time over which commitments are undertaken and stocks held; this also places a premium on the possession of capital resources. The wide fluctuations in the prices of their principal exports, and the resulting variations in local purchasing power, are apt to increase the risks of trading in under-developed countries well beyond the normal commercial risks in more advanced territories. A fall in incomes is likely to bring about losses on stocks of merchandise, indeed, stocks may at times become unsaleable. Firms short of liquid resources may be unable to weather temporary adversity, or to develop stable and continuous relationships with overseas suppliers. Wide fluctuations in the prices of export produce may also result in losses on stocks and consequent financial embarrassment unless reserves are ample.

Merchants in tropical trade often find it difficult to raise loans and loan capital, particularly in times of strain; assets in foreign countries are not readily acceptable as security; certain types of lender, especially the British banks, prefer to lend to customers of whose activities they have fairly detailed information which tropical traders find it difficult to furnish; and lenders are aware of the general hazards of this type of enterprise. On the other hand firms with large capital of their own, are likely to survive the frequent fluctuations in trade without severing established contacts. They are likely to be in a position to buy up the assets and/or the organization of firms in financial difficulties; indeed, at times they may almost be compelled to do so to prevent the demoralization of the market by distress selling of stocks.

Other advantages also accrue from the possession of large capital. There are generally few independently owned warehouses or blocks of residential or office buildings, and the fixed investment in these facilities has to be provided by the merchants. Moreover, important ancillary services, especially warehousing and local transport, are poorly developed, and firms able to operate these are at an important advantage.

Possession of liquid resources also enables traders to take early advantage of new economic opportunities thrown up in a developing economy. Outstanding opportunities are in this way frequently presented to the merchants in these territories, and developed and exploited by them both in the general interest and to their own advantage. A well-known example is the part played by the East India merchants in the development of the rubber and tea industries. In West Africa the activities of the merchants in promoting the rapid growth of groundnut exports and in the development of the timber trade are examples that come to mind. Similarly, established merchants are well placed to handle the introduction and distribution of new lines of merchandise, particularly those requiring considerable capital in their movement, storage and handling.

In practice it is often difficult to distinguish between the advantages arising from the possession of capital and the mere size of the enterprise and those accruing to firms already well established in the field. Both types of advantage are clearly important; the former appear to be specially weighty in the earlier stages of economic development and before the establishment of law and order.

Developments since the outbreak of the Second World War have enhanced capital requirements in external trade in many parts of the world. Trade and exchange controls, periodic shortages of shipping, and other interruptions of access to convenient or customary sources of supply, have forced traders to turn to more distant sources, which tends to slow down the rate of turnover of capital and thus increases capital requirements. Longer delays in deliveries produce a similar result. These factors are likely to be influential in long-distance trade, such as the external trade of many tropical countries.

Under conditions of full employment in the overseas supplying countries, sellers show a particularly marked preference for dealing with firms able to place large orders, quite apart from their preference for confining available supplies to established customers. This incidental by-product of full employment, especially of over-full employment, may act as a substantial influence on the trading situation and on the prospects of different classes of trader. With the rising costs of all types of labour and equipment, suppliers are likely to demand increased charges for handling small orders, even when they are prepared to accept them.

2. CAPITAL REQUIREMENTS IN WEST AFRICAN TRADE

In the external trade of West Africa local conditions tend particularly to favour firms with large capital resources. Especially in Nigeria, the long distances, poor communications and wide dispersal and small scale of individual production and consumption, postulate a relatively large volume of stock in storage and transit to sustain a given volume of trade. The storage and movement of the stocks in turn call for larger fixed investment and more European supervisory and technical personnel.

The absence of a local capitalist class comparable to the Chinese or the Indians in the Eastern trade has also affected the capital requirements of the merchant firms. They have not been able to dispose of imports in wholesale quantities to local intermediaries financing their own activities. They have found it necessary to finance many of their customers, and they have also been drawn into small-scale semi-wholesale or retail trade in widely dispersed establishments. Thus directly or indirectly the firms have had to carry large stocks to secure a given volume of trade. The same forces have operated in the purchase of local produce for export; it has had to be bought at up-country establishments frequently in small quantities, and financed by means of advances prior to purchase which increases both the capital required and the risk involved. For many years past the granting of advances has been an important prerequisite of successful entry into produce buying, especially in the purchase of cocoa and groundnuts.

Various factors increasing capital requirements in recent years have also operated in West African trade. Import restrictions and foreign exchange control have forced traders to draw supplies from more distant sources than they had to formerly. In West Africa itself the transport system, including port facilities, has not expanded at the same rate as have the demands on it. This is partly due to the rapid growth of trade, partly to difficulties in obtaining equipment and replacements, and partly to emphasis on general development plans instead of more specific and less spectacular attacks on bottlenecks. In consequence, traders have had to lock up much larger amounts of capital in the form both of stocks and of storage facilities, including the provision of larger warehouses. All these difficulties do not mean, of course, that trading operations are less profitable than they would be otherwise; but they strengthen the position of firms with access to large funds.

Higher price-levels have increased the cost of the essential minimum assets and expenses necessary for the establishment of a firm (or for the enlargement of an existing firm). The rise in building costs has been particularly onerous. In the most important commercial centres, notably Lagos, they have increased more than the general level of import and export prices. For various reasons new firms find it necessary to set up business and residential establishments in areas recognized for this purpose, in which costs are very high. In recent years the shortage of transport equipment has been an added reason for choosing sites in central, recognized business and residential districts. Moreover, in many trading centres no sites (or only very poor sites) are available except at high prices, either because the suitable sites are occupied, or because for reasons of policy the government is not now prepared to make available further urban sites for non-African firms. The small firm (and the newcomer) has little or no opportunity for economizing on this heavy item of initial expenditure. The cost of recruiting and employing European personnel has also increased greatly, and this is another item on which economies are often difficult.

3. AMALGAMATIONS IN WEST AFRICAN TRADE

In common with the trade of other tropical regions the external trade of West Africa has been subject to wide fluctuations of fortune, and, as we have seen, capital requirements in West Africa are especially heavy. There are therefore certain underlying influences making for a high degree of concentration, and in recent decades certain fortuitous circumstances have also played their part in promoting this.

In 1886 a royal charter was granted to the Niger Company conferring upon it powers of government in the colony of Nigeria. This charter was withdrawn in 1900, but the Company's authority as the government of the largest West African colony over the previous period of fourteen years conferred a long-term advantage on it and on its eventual successor, the United Africa Company. The acquisition of the Niger Company by Lever Brothers in 1930 was again partly fortuitous, as it was a by-product of the endeavours of the first Lord Leverhulme to establish plantations in West Africa.

The two most important instances of amalgamation since 1920 were both precipitated by chance events. The amalgamation of the Niger Company and the African and Eastern Trade Corporation in 1929 to form the United Africa Company was brought about partly by heavy losses incurred by the African and Eastern Trade Corporation through unsuccessful cocoa speculations and the incomplete observance of a market-sharing agreement by one important participant. The absorption of the substantial firm of G. B. Ollivant by Lever Brothers (the parent company of the United Africa Company) was also partly fortuitous. The firm had for some years been financed by a shipping company which encountered difficulties, partly because the United Africa Company withdrew much of its custom from it following a dispute, and partly because it suffered losses as a result of the Royal Mail frauds. The shipping company was forced to withdraw the funds it had provided, and which this trading firm was unable to replace at short notice. The Unilever group was prepared to take over the firm (partly to forestall distress selling of stocks), but this of course resulted in its loss of financial independence.

It is possible, indeed probable, that the progress of amalgamation has been accelerated by the aim of executives of the largest organizations to secure a measure of monopoly power and to acquire the prestige associated with a dominant position. Such ambitions were much assisted in the case of the United Africa Company by the ability to draw on the large capital resources of the Unilever organization.

The above events were in a sense chance occurrences, but they promoted concentration only because advantage was taken of them by organizations with large capital.

4. CAPITAL REQUIREMENTS OF NEW ENTRANTS

For generally familiar reasons insufficient capital is likely to hamper particularly the activities and the progress of new entrants. Weakness in capital is likely to affect the ability of a new firm to carry its organization during the long period of establishing and developing trade contacts. This period of initial development is likely to be longer where the scale of operations is restricted by the insufficiency of capital and consequent inability to extend credit or to carry large and varied stocks. In these circumstances the incidence of indispensable overheads is likely to be heavy.

There is a distinct preference on the part of African consumers for certain brands of merchandise, often for very good reasons. New entrants find it more difficult to establish consumer contacts if they cannot obtain supplies of the popular brands. Some of these brands are the property of established merchants and therefore are not available to competing newcomers. Others are subject to agreements between the suppliers and certain of the established merchants. In these circumstances the newcomer has to resort to the introduction and promotion of new brands, and it may be an expensive, risky and lengthy process.

These disadvantages press most heavily on new entrants who start direct importing or exporting without experience in these or other branches of West African trade. They press less heavily on firms or traders previously engaged in wholesaling or semi-wholesaling or small-scale produce buying, who have thus made some trading contacts, have some premises, are known to sources of capital or supplies, and have a nucleus of experienced staff. To some extent the former employees of existing firms are for similar reasons less handicapped in the establishment of new firms. Thus capital requirements in direct participation in external trade are reduced if entry into this activity is made easier for employees of the existing firms, or for traders previously engaged in local wholesaling or retailing. Conversely, capital requirements are likely to be increased and entry restricted by measures which ban the entry of newcomers into these small-scale activities, or which ban former employees from engaging in trade; such measures block the cheapest and most effective route to direct participation in external trade.

In short, newcomers in West African trade have to surmount a high threshold which acts as a partial bar to entry. This naturally strengthens the position of those already established, and enables them to increase the difficulties of entry for new firms. As a result, natural (inevitable) scarcities and contrived (institutional) obstacles interact to raise the threshold and to restrict entry.

5. THE ECONOMIES OF LARGE-SCALE OPERATION IN TRADE AND THEIR LIMITATIONS

In certain branches of tropical trade the advantages derived from the possession of large capital (especially the ability to survive vicissitudes) are reinforced by certain economies of large-scale operation. There are familiar economies from the bulk storage, handling and transport, especially of standardized products, such as flour, salt, cement and petroleum products. Similar economies to suppliers arising from large-scale transactions in these commodities enable them to grant quantity discounts to large-scale buyers which may represent genuine economies (especially in transportation) rather than extorted concessions. Somewhat analogous economies accrue to the substantial importer of textile prints, since printers often quote lower prices to buyers who place orders permitting long production runs on particular designs and specifications; they frequently refuse orders below certain large minimum quantities.

Because these commodities are highly standardized (with the exception of prints) a close study of market requirements or contact with consumers is less important and difficult, and it is comparatively simple to administer and control even a very large trade. Where these economies are significant, the costs of newcomers or recently established firms may often be high compared to those of their larger and more firmly established rivals.

But beyond a stage, which varies greatly between different activities, the economies to scale become exhausted or are counterbalanced by dis-economies. Beyond a certain point the expansion of scale often involves duplication of available facilities rather than the better use of facilities or the introduction of better methods. Even where improved methods are introduced the economies are eventually likely to be counterbalanced by higher costs of administration and control. The limit of the economies of size is likely to be reached most rapidly in trading in unstandardized commodities or services, and/or in markets in which supply and demand conditions change frequently and rapidly. These limitations are accentuated when it becomes necessary to rely on senior executives whose financial interests are not closely bound up with the success of the enterprise, with the outcome of the decisions they themselves make, or with the fruits of their own efforts. Moreover, the interests of paid executives may not always be the same as those of the firm as a whole. It is also likely that some executives may not display the same zeal and enterprise as would proprietors and their relatives in family-owned and controlled businesses. The division of functions and of control between overseas head offices and the local establishments strengthen these considerations. Divided control and delayed decisions raise costs and impede rapid response to profitable opportunities.[1]

In practice the disadvantages of large size and complexity in terms of economic efficiency are often masked by the strategic advantages enjoyed by firms by virtue of their size and early start. Important disabilities are often imposed on small, medium-sized and new firms by various types of administrative action and policy, in such spheres as the framing and administration of immigration regulations and trade controls.

[1] The limits of authority of even senior local executives are often surprisingly narrow. In a large enterprise operating in several territories with an annual turnover of many millions, no executive in West Africa, not even the head office representative, can grant an individual credit of over £300 without reference first to the overseas head office.

6. THE ECONOMICS OF INTEGRATION IN WEST AFRICAN TRADE

Some of the large importing firms have vertically integrated organizations. Although they are often not distinguished, the advantages and disadvantages of size and of integration are distinct and require separate analysis. Especially in West African conditions, only large firms can be integrated; but they could be large without this. Earlier sections dealt with the advantages of size and with their limitations; this section is concerned with integration.

The large merchant firms have their own wholesale, semi-wholesale and retail stores in West Africa as well as elaborate organization, including many small-scale buying points, for the purchase of export produce. The firms also obtain much of their merchandise through their own buying offices. The largest firm has its own offices in the principal supply centres of the world.

The merits of a system of integrated trading operations require careful analysis in view of the widely held opinion in West Africa that self-sufficiency and size are hallmarks of efficiency. There is no *a priori* reason why this should be so; indeed, the presumption would be the opposite. Integration is in a sense the opposite of specialization and of the division of labour; a non-integrated firm is one which specializes in certain activities or stages of trading activities, while an integrated firm performs a variety of functions and activities. As specialization is a key to efficiency and higher productivity, there is certainly no presumption that integration is necessarily conducive to efficiency.

In trading activities there is only one advantage (in terms of operational costs) of integration *per se*: by virtue of the existence of the organization each part of the integrated firm enjoys the continuous, compulsory and unsolicited patronage of the other parts. The non-integrated firm has no assurance that its customers will always place their orders with it; and this uncertainty increases the trading risks confronting it and may increase certain of its costs. In effect, for example, the merchandise orders of each of the many wholesale and retail branches of the United Africa Company are continuously and compulsorily centralized in the merchandise departments and buying offices of the company.

This advantage of secure sources of supply and clientèle (relatively to the position of independent non-integrated firms specializing in particular functions or stages of trading activity) involves the firm in certain costs of organization and certain other disadvantages (again relative to the position of independent non-integrated firms). The integrated firm maintains an apparatus of communication between its operational parts, and of control and communication between central management and all other parts. Most of the costs of this apparatus continue irrespective of the volume of trade. The independent non-integrated and therefore more specialized firm escapes these costs, but instead incurs the costs of soliciting custom and of seeking sources of supply, and also those costs occasioned by discontinuous and irregular variations of supplies and sales arising from the absence of tied sources and outlets. Most of these items tend to vary with the volume of trade which is transacted.

It is often thought that the small firm is necessarily at a disadvantage as it does not maintain overseas buying offices and does not itself arrange direct imports from overseas. This ignores the possibility that independent specialist firms in external trade can provide buying and importing services to others who are unable or unwilling to provide these services for themselves. This arrangement has the advantage that the firm is able to select from a wider range of alternatives than is open to its counterpart in an integrated concern. This flexibility may be a source of strength rather than an admission of weakness, even though the advantages of the compulsory and continuous contact between the parts of the integrated concern are absent. The economies of centralization and pooling are present even where the requirements of several firms are served by independent specialist firms; indeed, the economies may be greater than in the integrated firm, where some of its constituent parts may be handicapped by the limitation which is imposed on the scale of their output by the limited requirements of the firm. The import houses pool the large number of separate orders of independent wholesale and retail traders and maintain reserve stocks for them. The export merchant is in a position to place pooled orders with the suppliers and secures the economies of large-scale buying. These tasks are performed by wholesalers of all kinds, including import and export houses. In West Africa the importing sections of the integrated merchant houses, as well as the independent importers, perform these functions for local non-integrated wholesale traders, i.e. firms without an importing organization and specializing in wholesale trading.

As well as the direct costs of co-ordinating the parts of an integrated firm, there are certain disadvantages of integration (relative to the position of the non-integrated firm). The integrated organization is necessarily somewhat inflexible. The freedom of action of each constituent part is limited. The intermediate members cannot take advantage of favourable market opportunities; they have to buy from and sell to other members of their organization and thus do not operate in the market; as they are not directly subject to market forces, they tend to become passive channels of communication rather than active trading units, and this may tend to affect the morale and tone of executives and personnel, which frequently compare unfavourably with the greater alertness, energy and economy of the independent specialist.[1]

The burdens on the central management of large integrated firms are likely to be heavy partly because of the mere size of the concern and partly because of the diversity of its activities. Control is likely to be less effective because it is difficult or impossible to measure the success or efficiency of the constituent parts of an integrated firm, where the parts are interrelated and separated, partly or wholly, from the market. The economic efficiency of each constituent part of the organization cannot be accurately measured for several reasons. Responsibility for certain costs cannot be located with precision. It is impossible to assess the opportunities that are missed, and it is impossible to distinguish between, say, a failure to effect an advantageous purchase because of mistaken judgement, and a failure to do so because of enforced reliance upon other members of the firm. Again, the success of one part of the organization may be retarded by the failure of other parts, whose lack of success it meanwhile helps to obscure.[2] Moreover, the effectiveness of the control is reduced since the central management is unlikely to possess the special knowledge required for assessing performance in each of a number of diverse activities. This is an important aspect of the necessary absence of specialization in the integrated firm.

The efficiency of integration in terms of economy of resources depends on a balance of advantages and economies on the one hand and disadvantages and costs on the other. There is a general presumption that, other things being equal, there is less likely to be a true economy of resources the larger the numbers and variety of different activities embraced by the integrated firm; this presumption is a corollary of the advantages of specialization and of the costs of organization. The presence of large, complex and profitable integrated firms does not of course by itself affect the validity of this presumption or prove the superior economy of resources in integrated firms. The profitability

---

[1] This difficulty is sometimes met by permitting constituent parts of the firm to buy or sell outside the organization when they find it is to their advantage. To the extent that this is done the main advantage of integration—continuous and compulsory trading relationships—is forfeited. Moreover, it creates conflicts within the firm and severely adds to the complexity of administration. Such a course also diminishes the strategic advantages of integration, the obstruction of the growth of independent firms which might provide custom for rival suppliers.

[2] Integrated firms may attempt to measure the success of their individual constituent parts by using market prices in records of internal transfers. However, this fails to record the extent of missed opportunities. For instance, it may show that some purchases were made at unfavourable prices, but it cannot show what the volume of purchases would have been if the constituent parts had had free access to the market.

may have arisen from causes unconnected with integration, such as accidents of history or the services of highly efficient managers. Moreover, integration itself may confer strategic advantages upon the firm which increase its profits without representing a true economy of resources. In practice there is the usual difficulty of disentangling the component forces operating in a particular case.

The vertical integration of the large merchant firms in West Africa provides an example of the operation of several causes. The operation of integrated semi-wholesale and retail establishments is to a considerable extent the result of the absence of a local capitalist class capable of handling stocks of merchandise in wholesale quantities at the ports of entry or at the chief commercial centres. Moreover, considerations of market strategy, as well as these economic and historical forces, have influenced some importing firms in establishing or maintaining their own wholesale and retail outlets.[1]

7. INTEGRATION AND TRADE CONTROLS

The favourable aspect of integration may appear to be reinforced in certain conditions, notably in an international economy subject to different national controls and to sudden changes in these controls. An example may be taken from the experience of the United Africa Company.[2]

In the Company's Manchester office a decision may be made to buy, for example, some millions of yards of unprocessed ('grey') cloth for processing for the African market. This grey cloth might be bought in Lancashire and processed there. But Lancashire might be unable to supply either the cloth or the processing capacity; or the price might be too high. Consequently the grey cloth might be bought in Japan and shipped to the Continent, where it would be printed, using the Company's copper rollers despatched from the United Kingdom for the purpose. The finished cloth, as it became available, would then be allocated to the various West African territories in accordance with the import permits already obtained in liaison between the Company's Manchester office and the Coast organisation.

Under conditions of uncontrolled trade non-integrated firms in more or less continuous contact with one another would take advantage of mutually profitable opportunities on terms and conditions unlikely to

---

[1] Several West African merchant firms have expanded into non-trading activities. Some of these ventures have proved to be very profitable. The fact that predominantly trading firms have been able to finance and to administer these undertakings is not evidence either of the economies of large-scale operation in trade or of the benefits of integration. It more nearly reflects the advantages derived from access to capital, from the perception of economic opportunity and from an early start and a strong local position.

[2] United Africa Company, *Statistical and Economic Review*, September 1950, p. 5.

be more onerous than the costs of the integrated operation. But with diverse and changing controls each independent specialist at each of the several stages may not simultaneously have knowledge of available supplies and of unsatisfied requirements (coupled with permission to satisfy them). In general, each would only know a fraction of the required information; and the establishment of information services or of contacts is made difficult and costly by frequent and unpredictable changes in regulations and conditions. In these conditions transactions within a chain of specialist firms may be erratic, unreliable, discontinuous and costly, and there may be a real economy in the organized flow of information in an integrated undertaking. The particular economy depends on the somewhat accidental built-in readiness to match up the opportunities left open in different and unstable controls.[1]

This potential advantage should not be exaggerated. The independen merchants, who retain the large profits from the perception and exploitation of profitable opportunities, are likely to seek them out and to find the complementary parties who are the sources of supply or the effective outlets. Their counterparts, the employees of integrated firms, do not directly benefit from these opportunities and are thus much less likely to pursue them with the same energy and speed; moreover, their authority to act is likely to be circumscribed. Examples are given in the next section of the advantages secured by independent firms relying on specialist non-integrated contacts in unsettled and rapidly changing circumstances in which there is a premium on flexibility and speed of action.

8. EXAMPLES OF THE LIMITS OF THE ADVANTAGES OF SIZE AND OF INTEGRATION

The recent history of the external trade of West Africa has provided instructive examples of the advantages accruing to the smaller and more specialized firms against the large integrated organization.

The ability and readiness to act rapidly and thus to take advantage of market opportunities is often an important advantage of small or medium-sized firms managed by their owners; and it was a particularly important factor in the quickly changing but generally stringent supply conditions during the war. These factors have played an important part in the remarkable growth of the firm of A. G. Leventis and Company since its establishment in 1938. Offers of merchandise from unusual or unfamiliar sources of supply often reached West Africa subject to acceptance at very short notice. By working long hours and by attending to business at week-ends, the members of this firm were

---

[1] This type of economy is on the whole not open to an integrated firm operating substantially within a single framework of regional controls.

often able to deal with such offers a day or so before their rivals. Moreover, opportunities were frequently lost by competitors whose representatives had to refer to head offices while offers could be promptly accepted by Leventis, who did not have to refer to overseas principals.[1]

Again, this firm on many occasions secured supplies by relying upon well-chosen and alert buying agents in various overseas markets, remunerated on a commission basis, while their rivals relied on buying offices staffed by salaried personnel.[2]

The Sachs Report lists numerous documented instances of the failure of the executives of the larger firms to act promptly, or indeed to act at all, on written information about profitable trading opportunities; and the account in that report of the trading rivalry in the 1940's presents an instructive review of the advantages enjoyed in certain circumstances by medium-sized enterprises.[3]

There are other recent examples of the successful growth of new firms from small beginnings. As in the case of Leventis, the proprietors are former executives of established firms. There are a few medium-sized firms in Nigeria which have been established comparatively recently and which are directly managed and controlled by their proprietors. Two of these have made substantial headway. They were established in 1936 and 1946 respectively. One of these two, which I visited several times, specializes in the textile trade and maintains four establishments. The proprietor is French. He works far longer hours than is customary in the larger European firms. He has close personal contacts with his Lebanese and African customers, and has an intimate and up-to-date knowledge of their business requirements, as well as of their personal qualities. He invariably shows sketches of proposed designs of textile

---

[1] I have independent knowledge of two recent instances in which the firm was in the market for real estate against leading competitors and secured the substantial properties because it could act more quickly. The local representatives of the competing firms acted within a narrower range of instructions and referred to their European head offices for new instructions. In both cases the delays cost them the opportunities. In one instance a competitor offered the firm 20% more than the purchase price for the property within a few days of losing the right to buy it.

[2] It was this firm acting in conjunction with a small merchant in South Africa which pioneered and developed a substantial wartime trade between South Africa and the Gold Coast, discussed in the Sachs Report, para. 88; cf. Chapter 6, § 4, above.

[3] These examples again do not imply any assessment, either favourable or unfavourable, of the prospects of this firm, which by about 1950 had become one of the largest of the West African trading firms. The instances are presented here simply to indicate the limitations on efficiency experienced by very large organizations, and the advantages in certain conditions of small and medium-sized firms directly managed by their proprietors.

prints to his customers to gauge their preferences, and places orders only after these have been ascertained. The bulk of his substantial business is on credit terms, and since his establishment in 1946 he has not yet had one bad debt, despite the fact that in 1949 the textile market in Nigeria was heavily overstocked and many textile dealers were in difficulties. The business is conservatively administered, and the proprietor refrains from expanding too rapidly or from handling merchandise which in his opinion is unsuitable to the small firm. He instanced the trade in bulky standardized commodities, such as cement and salt, which require substantial capital and storage space, and in which the flexibility and close contacts of the smaller firms yields few significant advantages. He was emphatic that small or medium-sized enterprises in importing and wholesaling were viable, as long as they refrained from embarking on too rapid development or from entering unsuitable types of trade. He regarded the official policy and attitude towards new and small enterprises as the greatest obstacles to their establishment and progress. He himself has had great difficulty in securing permission to engage a European assistant.

An interesting difference between these two firms and their large competitors was the comparative absence in the former of signs of paper work. In the offices of the small enterprises a debtor's ledger and correspondence files were practically the only records to be noticed, while samples, sketches and some merchandise were conspicuous even on the desks. In the offices of the large firms the executives were fairly fully engaged perusing and preparing papers and returns. This type of visual evidence can of course be very misleading, but executives of the larger firms complained of their preoccupation with paper work and their consequent loss of contact with events in the market and the requirements of their customers. On the other hand, it was difficult to contact the European proprietors or managers of the smaller firms at their offices without appointments, since they spent a large part of their time in the market or on the premises of their customers. The proprietors emphasized the importance of this activity, and contrasted their methods with the inevitably heavy paper work and administrative routine they had to cope with when they were senior employees of the large firms.

The absence of heavy administrative overhead costs, coupled with a high degree of specialization, must have played a considerable part in the rapid rise of Mr S. Raccah in the groundnut buying trade, in which his turnover in 1938–9 was not far below that of the largest firm.[1] He claims with pardonable exaggeration that in those years all

---

[1] Mr Raccah's activities received considerable publicity in Sir Keith Hancock's chapter on West African trade in a *Survey of Commonwealth Affairs*, Part II, Vol. II, Chapter 2.

his records were contained in three books, his cheque book, his bank passbook and his cable book. Of course, Mr Raccah's methods are well known to be highly personal, and his enterprise has had its ups and downs; moreover, his former methods are not suitable to more complex trade nor to conditions in which statutory organizations and government departments insist on returns. Nevertheless, his progress in the late 1930's provides another example of the advantages of the informally operated enterprise closely controlled and managed by its proprietor.

9. RELATIVE DECLINE OF DIRECT AFRICAN PARTICIPATION IN EXTERNAL TRADE

The discussion of the earlier sections of this chapter on the advantages of financial strength and on the economies of scale bear on certain criticisms by Africans of the activities of European and Levantine merchants. Critics observe that in the nineteenth century there were many substantial African traders in both the export and import trades; and they argue that their position was undermined by the aggressive tactics of European firms and by the preferential treatment accorded by them to other non-African enterprises. There were indeed many Africans engaged in external trade in West Africa in the second half of the nineteenth century and the early years of this century, but in the aggregate their activities were on a very small scale compared with trade today. In Nigeria fifty years ago, for example, there were no exports, or only negligible exports, of groundnuts, cocoa, cotton, hides and skins or timber, and exports of palm produce were less than one-eighth by volume of what they are today. Exports of cocoa from the Gold Coast had barely begun. The import trade was similarly on a very small scale. Thus by present-day standards the operations of these African traders were very circumscribed, and were certainly a very small fraction of the trade handled by Africans today, largely as wholesalers and retailers or as produce buyers. The African share in direct foreign trade declined primarily as a combined result of the increased capital requirements of a rapidly growing trade and of a money economy,[1] and of the losses sustained in trade fluctuations. Moreover, the growing complexity and diversification of external trade called for a variety of technical, administrative and financial abilities which the majority of African traders were unable to command. In these circum-

---

[1] Many of the prominent African participants in external trade were chiefs who were able to command unpaid services. This became increasingly more difficult and less efficient with the advance of an economy in which money payments became more general. Similar developments occurred in the purchase of export produce, where the use of money both in payments and in the granting of advances increased capital requirements and also resulted in a rapid growth of trade.

stances there has been a pronounced tendency for weakly financed firms to disappear in times of adverse fluctuations. A number of African traders who had survived previous vissicitudes succumbed to the abrupt depression of 1920–1, especially as a result of losses suffered on unsold stocks of palm products.

The growth of the complexity as well as of the volume of the external trade after the turn of the century is not always fully appreciated, especially by those who see in the disappearance of the African trader evidence only of the malevolence of the European firms. The comparative simplicity of early West African trade is shown vividly in *The Diary of John Holt*, recently circulated privately by the well-known Liverpool firm of John Holt and Company. Had the nature of the trade remained substantially unchanged during the last century, the weakness in capital and in technical skill of African traders would have been of much less consequence.[1]

[1] In the nineteenth century it was often thought that the share of the African merchants in direct external trade might increase. A century ago the Governor of Sierra Leone wrote in his annual report: 'Whether (the commerce of the colony) will remain in the hands of the European merchants...is, I think, very problematical. Many of the wealthier liberated Africans resident in Freetown have already become large importers, and it will not be long ere they turn exporters on their own account. ...One thing certain is, that the number of liberated Africans engaged in commerce is annually on the increase, and where one of that class imported a single bale of goods fifteen or twenty years ago, numbers of them at the present day import whole cargoes; and as their trade expenses and their mode of living is considerably under those of the European merchants, they will necessarily, being a thrifty race, and in a comparatively short time, amass wealth and eventually and at no very distant period, become the real merchants of the colony' *Blue Book of the Colony of Sierra Leone for the year 1851*. I am indebted to Miss M. E. Hill for this reference.

CHAPTER 9

CONCENTRATION, MARKETING ARRANGEMENTS AND COMPETITION (I)

1. THE DEGREE OF CONCENTRATION AND THE BARRIERS TO ENTRY

The argument of the previous chapter suggests that new entry into West African trade may be difficult because capital requirements are often heavy and because there appear to be certain definite though limited economies of size. These forces, together with the advantages accruing from an early start, tend to bring about a measure of concentration. This in turn tends to perpetuate the strength of the large firms by conferring on them certain advantages which impede and inhibit the entry of new firms and the growth of smaller firms.

In earlier chapters it has been shown that by the middle of the 1930's one firm together with its subsidiaries and affiliates handled about one-third of the external trade of West Africa, while some five or six firms were responsible for about three-fifths of the total. In standardized staple imports and in the principal export products the concentration was appreciably larger. Moreover, groups of the largest firms frequently acted in concert. There were comprehensive market-sharing agreements in the purchase of the principal export crops and in the sale of imported merchandise.

A degree of concentration of this magnitude in such an extensive trade may raise the ordinary barriers to new entry and the expansion of small firms in four principal ways. First, firms may hesitate to start operations or expand in a trade in which they may have to face accentuated competition directed against them by powerful established firms, possibly acting in concert for the purpose. Newcomers have not only to reckon with the usual hazards of a risky competitive market, but also with the specific risk of incurring the commercial animosity of large firms or groups of firms who see in the newcomer a potential threat to their position. Secondly, there may be strategic advantages residing in the control or partial control by integrated firms of several successive stages of distribution. Thirdly, large entrenched firms or groups of firms may find it easier to receive supplies or to secure preferential treatment from important overseas suppliers, and this places less favoured firms at a distinct disadvantage. Fourthly, the presence of large firms or groups of firms may influence official policy and result in measures strengthening their position. These factors might enable the large established firms to earn exceptional returns and profits without attracting new entry.

The following chapters discuss these influences on the trading situation in West Africa. Certain deterrents to new entry stemming directly from the high degree of concentration and from certain results of integration are considered in this chapter. The implications and effects of special arrangements between overseas suppliers and merchants are reviewed next (Chapter 10). Thereafter the influence of official policies on the trading situation is examined (Chapters 11–13).

2. THE FEAR OF DESTRUCTIVE PRICE-CUTTING AS A POSSIBLE RESTRAINT ON ENTRY

A high degree of concentration, especially when coupled with concerted action, may deter prospective entrants if the latter fear destructive price-cutting aimed at their existence, or if they believe that pressure will be put upon important suppliers to withhold supplies from them.

Price reduction is the method par excellence of competition, and is generally of benefit to consumers and to the economy as a whole. Most of the protests against price-cutting are advanced to justify organized restriction of competition. But, as is apparent from a study of the history of the origins and maintenance of some modern monopolies, destructive price-cutting can be used by the dominant firm or group as a weapon to undermine otherwise viable competitors. The aim may be to destroy the competitor, or to limit his expansion by coercing him into an agreement. Although the manoeuvre appears to employ competitive price reductions, its objective is the elimination of competition and the preservation of monopoly. The price reductions are not forced on the large firms by conditions of supply and demand but are deliberately introduced, possibly at considerable temporary sacrifice, in order to inflict losses on competitors who are not expected to be in a position to bear them. Wherever practicable the price cuts are confined to localities in which the selected competitor operates.

Only firms with a dominant share of the market can successfully employ this type of aggressive price-cutting to strengthen their position by checking or destroying their competitors. Price-cutting by competing firms with small individual shares of the market cannot be destructive in this sense. It would not be profitable for one small competitor among many to attempt to enlarge his share of the market or his degree of market control by this method; he would not be able to eliminate a sufficient number of his many competitors, nor would he be able subsequently to raise his prices so as to recover his losses and to yield extra profits.

The issue of destructive and aggressive price-cutting looms large in discussions of the trading situation in West Africa. Critics of the large firms, especially of the United Africa Company, frequently maintain that the use of their financial resources to crush the smaller firms by temporary or local price reductions is a major influence obstructing the growth of competition. This is argued not only by Africans but also by Europeans, including some overseas suppliers.

The issue has been clouded by the belief of many Africans that all adverse market changes are engineered by European firms to put them out of business. Thus a few years ago many African importers placed orders on a large scale for commodities whose importation was temporarily very profitable. When prices had fallen by the time their supplies arrived, the African importers were apt to ascribe this to a deliberate policy on the part of the large trading firms to destroy them. Similarly, when the large firms reduce their prices to clear their stocks in anticipation of the arrival of large supplies, this again is often regarded as a deliberate attempt to destroy competitors. These allegations mistake the operation of market forces for aggressive price-cutting.

It is often difficult to distinguish between destructive price-cutting and a reduction in price to meet competition or dictated by ordinary market forces. The difficulty arises essentially because destructive price-cutting can be practised only by firms or groups of firms whose share in the market is in any case so substantial that they cannot help making the price and thus leading the market rather than following it; and in West Africa the share of the largest firm (and *a fortiori* of a group of firms sometimes acting in concert) in the trade is so large that its actions necessarily make the market.

While many of the complaints advanced by Africans are irrelevant or rest on a misapprehension, there may well have been cases of destructive price-cutting in West Africa. Conclusive evidence is very difficult to come by, largely because of the difficulty of attributing particular price changes, especially price reductions, to specific causes or motives. There is a *prima facie* case of destructive price-cutting in connexion with the manufacture and marketing of soap in Nigeria in 1940.[1] For some years the West African Soap Company, a subsidiary of Lever Brothers, had been manufacturing soap in Nigeria. In 1938 a merchant established in Kano a small soap company, the Niger Soap Factory which by 1940 had progressed sufficiently to make appreciable inroads into the market of the West African Soap Company. Its owner alleges that he was then presented with an ultimatum by the general manager of the West African Soap Company to close down within a fortnight. He refused to do this, and within a few days the West

---

[1] Documents relating to the incident are filed in the Provincial Office in Kano.

African Soap Company informed its distributors in the Kano area that its existing brand of soap would be withdrawn, and a new brand of identical weight and substantially similar quality would be put on the market at only just over one-half the previous price. This brand with its specially low price was distributed in the Kano area only. The sequel is not quite clear. It appears that the Niger Soap Factory closed down temporarily,[1] but subsequently resumed operations.

Some of the allegations, notably that of delivery of an ultimatum to the Niger Soap Factory, are denied by the West African Soap Company. But the introduction of a fighting brand at a special price is confirmed, and this is the aspect principally relevant to the discussion.

Similar transactions are said to have taken place in 1937 in the marketing of stockfish in the Port Harcourt area, where some African importers had entered the import trade in stockfish. A written statement submitted at the time to the authorities by an African importer alleges that an official of a large European firm called on him and threatened to destroy his business unless he desisted from importing stockfish. Although this is purely an *ex parte* statement, certain aspects of the sequence of events lend it some plausibility. The substance of the allegation closely resembles the alleged ultimatum for the closure of the Niger Soap Factory three years later. Records in the Nigerian Secretariat suggest that after the entry of the African importers into the stockfish trade the price fell substantially, in some instances below the invoiced value shown on the Norwegian bills of lading of the consignments shipped to the African traders. This may have been the result of localized, temporary price-cutting. But a decline in price to a level below that of the purchase price to the Africans is not conclusive evidence of destructive price-cutting, since it may have resulted from a glut of supplies, or from a lower purchase price to the larger importers.[2]

Allegations of destructive price-cutting generally refer to staple commodities, such as stockfish, matches and corned beef, in which the large

---

[1] It appears that for a while the company bought up some of its rival's soap in the Kano area and reshipped it elsewhere for re-sale at the higher price it could command.

[2] A somewhat similar instance seems to have occurred in the marketing of matches in the Lagos area in 1947 when several substantial African traders imported matches on a fairly large scale. When their shipments were cleared they found that the local price had dropped close on 40% in a few weeks and was about 15–20% below the invoiced value, which included only cash cost, freight and insurance. One or two of the importers were in a position to carry stocks until the price had reverted to its former level, but several had to sell at the lower prices as they were unable to hold out. Although one of these instances was substantially verified in an examination of the records of an African firm, the episode is not conclusive evidence of destructive price-cutting in view of the rapidly changing supply conditions at the time.

firms have a preponderant share of the trade and which they regard as their special preserve. Besides the examples already quoted, most of these allegations relate to the period of between fifteen and twenty years ago when the large firms attempted to consolidate their position in the West African market. They refer usually to the years 1934–9, the years of the establishment and operation of the Staple Lines Agreement and of the Merchandise Agreement. At least one of the firms which entered these agreements was reluctant to do so, but it feared a price war specifically directed against it unless it was prepared to join. The degree of concentration in the trade was by then sufficient to give plausibility to this danger.

A senior employee of one of the large firms said in private conversation that he had been advised by his superiors to send out petty traders and runners to sit outside the store of a Lebanese importer of corned beef and to sell the product at a lower price to discourage the importer from continuing in that trade. This is said to have occurred around 1935.

For the reasons stated it is exceedingly difficult to prove or disprove conclusively some of the alleged instances of destructive price-cutting. Most of the recent complaints of African importers are certainly unsubstantial. On the other hand, as we have seen in at least one instance relating to 1940, the substance of the allegation (the introduction of a fighting brand at a special price) is admitted by the dominant firm itself.

But it is the possibility of destructive price-cutting, the potential threat rather than actual exercise, which affects the market situation, as this would influence competitors in deciding to enter a trade or to expand their claim of operation. The threat of destructive price-cutting in the staple lines of the import trade may have had some deterrent effects on entry or expansion before or in the early years of the Second World War. For several reasons destructive price-cutting does not appear to have been significant in recent years. In a buoyant market for merchandise this danger is less likely to be an effective deterrent than in a buyers' market. The progress of several competitors of the larger firms has shown the comparative ineffectiveness of devices of commercial market strategy to obstruct competitors in the West African trade. Again, destructive price-cutting is a politically dangerous method of competition which the larger firms would be particularly reluctant to use in a politically highly charged atmosphere. Lastly, in recent years import licensing affected a number of those staple imports which might be the most suitable instruments of destructive price-cutting. For these various reasons neither destructive price-cutting nor its possible use has been a significant influence in West African trade in recent years.

3. VERTICAL INTEGRATION AND MARKET STRATEGY

Vertically integrated organization of successive stages of distribution in single firms may be found both in competitive and in monopolistic market situations; the fact of integration need not be a causal influence affecting the degree of competition. However, in certain circumstances integration may be used to strengthen existing elements of concentration or of monopoly and to strengthen the economic power of a firm or group of firms. Thus, to take an extreme example, if all retail outlets belong to one manufacturer or importer, no other manufacturers, importers or wholesalers could exist except on sufferance. Similarly, control or ownership of distributive outlets at any stage by an integrated firm limits the entry and potentialities of growth of independent firms at all earlier stages. In such circumstances independent firms at earlier stages may have to set up their own outlets if they wish to establish themselves or to safeguard and expand their position in the market at earlier stages. Heavy costs, especially capital costs, may have to be incurred; and this may prevent the establishment of new firms and impede the growth of others.

Integrated firms forfeit certain advantages of specialized operation, and are likely to incur higher costs of supervision than do firms more specialized in certain stages of the trade; and this may well outweigh any economies flowing from the more assured custom which results from the control of outlets. Nevertheless, even where integrated operations result in lower immediate profits than might otherwise be possible, there may be sound strategic reasons for preferring integration and the restriction of sales to units at subsequent stages of the firm's own organization. Independent wholesalers and retailers are likely to grow more readily if they have access, even on onerous terms, to the supplies of the dominant manufacturer or importer. Their growth enlarges the market which is available to independent specialist manufacturers or importers, and this in turn makes it more attractive for additional merchant firms to establish themselves. In this way the latter may gradually undermine the previously dominant position of the firm in question, unless continued superior efficiency enables it to check the inroads of competitors. In such circumstances the strategic advantages which the dominant firm may derive from an integrated structure have to be set against the disadvantages of the loss of specialization and the costs of administration which may result from integration in a large firm.[1]

---

[1] The argument of this paragraph raises a technical point. It is conceivable on certain extreme assumptions that a manufacturer or an importer in a quasi-monopoly position may charge such prices to his independent customers as to make each trans-

4. INTEGRATION IN WEST AFRICAN TRADE

In West Africa the large merchant firms do not confine their business to sales in large wholesale quantities at the ports or in other large wholesale trading centres; they operate large numbers of trading points throughout the territory both for the purchase of produce and for the sale of merchandise sometimes in small quantities.

This vertical integration is no recent development in West Africa. It accompanied the rapid growth of the external trade towards the end of the nineteenth century and the early decades of the present century. For reasons already indicated the growth of trade went hand in hand with a great increase in capital requirements; and there has never been in West Africa a strong local capitalist class capable of handling and financing the movement of merchandise from the principal supply centres into final consumption. Consequently the importing firms were drawn into (or perhaps forced into) the later stages of distribution by the absence of sufficient substantial local traders to whom they could sell imported commodities in wholesale quantities at a rapid rate of turnover. Some of the importers might well have preferred to use their capital exclusively in dealings in large quantities with a more rapid rate of turnover; the exigencies of the market may have forced them to extend their activities into smaller scale and far-flung merchanting activities which implies a slower rate of turnover.

The local conditions which probably compelled the importers to expand their operations vertically may, at the same time, have served their purposes by enabling them to strengthen their position. The conditions created difficulties; but once established, the firms may have found that the difficulties, and the measures they have taken to surmount these, provided a welcome shield against new competition. Where large firms adopt integration as a policy, it becomes difficult to judge the strength and relevance of considerations of market strategy. The result, however, is generally clear; forward integration of operations, together with a high degree of concentration, tend to act as a strong restrictive force obstructing entry.

action just worth their while. In this way he extracts the maximum from his situation and at the same time is in a position to regulate the trade of his independent customers and thus to secure all the strategic advantages of integration discussed in the text without actual integration and its costs. The assumptions involved are that the quasi-monopolist has complete knowledge of the situation of each of his customers, including their access to other supplies, and also that he is in a position to charge blatantly discriminating prices. In practice both assumptions are unreal, particularly in the conduct of large firms. It is likely that a monopoly position can be more effectively exploited in the relative certainty of an integrated operation than in the uncertainty of selling to intermediaries whose position cannot be known so exactly.

As has already been indicated briefly, in the last fifteen years some of the large trading firms in West Africa, notably the United Africa Company, have been divesting themselves of many of their so-called retail selling outlets as part of an avowed policy of withdrawing from the retail trade.[1] In the case of the United Africa Company this has been fairly rapid; according to statistics published by the firm, the number of its merchandise-selling stores in Nigeria and the Gold Coast was reduced from 1184 in 1939 to 667 in 1947.[2]

The policy is said to be based on both commercial and on wider political considerations. The cost of administering numerous, often small, retail stores was considered uneconomic, especially in view of the steady rise in the cost of European supervision; and, secondly, it was felt that African traders should be encouraged to expand in the so-called retail and semi-wholesale trades, for both commercial and political reasons. When the firms are engaged in direct importing and whole-saling as well as in semi-wholesaling and retailing, they to some extent compete with their own re-seller customers, which leads to friction and to arguments over the prices charged to these customers. Moreover, as African merchants are a vocal and an influential section of public opinion, the firms regard it particularly advantageous to reduce as far as possible the area of competition between themselves and these traders. Again, the strain on the capital resources of the larger firms would be reduced if the later stages of distribution were financed by African traders.

The process of contraction in retailing was accelerated during the war. At present (1951) some of the firms wish to carry the process still further, but they find it increasingly difficult to do so in view of the small number of local traders who have the necessary capital. In recent years there have been instances both in Nigeria and in the Gold Coast of administrators and members of the local population appealing to the firms not to close down some of their smaller establishments as this would inflict hardship on the people.

At first sight this withdrawal from the retail trade may suggest that

[1] The merger which resulted in the formation of the United Africa Company in 1929 was followed by a wholesale reduction in the number of smaller trading stations and stores belonging to the previously independent constituent firms. This process of reducing the number of outlets for reasons of redundancy was, however, largely completed by the mid-1930's, and the reduction of trading posts after 1936 (when the United Africa Company announced its policy of gradual withdrawal from the retail trade) was no longer an elimination of overlapping facilities. The fact that a large number of retail outlets were considered no longer necessary after the merger suggests that the retailing activities of the previously separate firms were to a material extent governed by considerations of market strategy and counter-strategy.

[2] United Africa Company, *Statistical and Economic Review*, March 1948, p. 33.

the motive of strategy in vertical integration is no longer important in West Africa. This, however, is not so; it merely suggests that other considerations, financial and political, have become more important in recent years. Moreover, the importers may still retain a fair measure of control over the trading activities of their successors in their discarded trading branches. Frequently the premises remain the property of the importing firm which lets them at low or nominal rents to the African trader, who is often a former employee. In many cases the importer merely treats the former employee as a credit customer; the goods dispatched to the store cease to be the property of the seller, even though he may continue to finance much of the stock-in-trade. Thus at a saving in costs (principally of supervision), and at some political advantage, many of the strategic advantages of integration are retained. Also, the withdrawal has not affected the earlier stages in the chain of distribution, that is the stages between importing and so-called retailing. Here the degree of integration has not been changed decisively.

In short, there has been a partial surrender of retail or petty whole-sale activity by the large firms, but this has not significantly affected the pre-existing degree of market control. Moreover, the surrender of retail outlets by the large importers has not been as risky as it would have been in earlier years, since over this period very few non-African firms have been permitted by government to enter West African trade except at the large-scale importing level. There has thus been less danger that the sacrificed control of retail trade would enable new non-African firms to become established and to expand to a size at which they could import direct or sustain efficient rival importers. Again, the apparent sacrifice of control over retail outlets took place over a period during which the large firms had seemed to safeguard their interests as importers by means of agreements among themselves, as well as with some principal sources of supply. Ground could be given up in the least profitable sector because the whole position had apparently become more secure.

Analogous reasoning may serve partly to explain the width and diversity of the range of merchandise handled by the merchant firms. Originally this presumably stemmed from the narrowness of local markets and the consequent limit on the extent of specialization by types of merchandise. But subsequently strategic considerations of pre-empting the market by forestalling competitors may have come to play a part. If the large firms do not carry a full range of merchandise small-scale and new independent competitors will find it easier to establish themselves in special lines. In this way these competitors may accumulate funds, gain knowledge of the market and establish contacts with customers. This may enable some of their number to develop into formidable competitors, to enlarge the range of merchandise carried and to extend the range of their activities. Thus the lower costs of more specialized operations may be outweighed by the greater risks of the emergence of serious competitors. The strategic advantages of increasing the difficulties of new competitors exist only in situations in which there is a large measure of concentration and in which there are difficulties of entry. In these conditions there is a close analogy between the strategic advantages of horizontal and vertical integration in trade.

Some of the largest firms are currently considering the desirability of curtailing the range of their merchandise in order to increase the rate of stock turnover and in order to achieve various economies in operational costs. Again, in present conditions the possible adverse strategic effects of this projected reversal of policy are presumably deemed less important than in the past.

It should not be inferred that the firms in West Africa necessarily and consciously adopted and pursued their policies in order to gain the strategic advantages outlined in the foregoing analysis. It is unlikely that in framing business policy these considerations of market strategy have been separately appreciated and weighed. However, here the concern is with the effects of courses of action and not with their motivation. In the general circumstances of West Africa the substantial measure of integration in the distributive trade, superimposed upon a marked degree of concentration, has been an influence restricting the entry and growth of competitive firms.

CHAPTER 10

CONCENTRATION, MARKETING ARRANGEMENTS AND COMPETITION (II)

I. SOLE AGENCIES AND OTHER EXCLUSIVE DISTRIBUTING ARRANGEMENTS

The manufacturers of many types of product distribute their products in some markets through merchants or agents to whom sole distributing rights are granted. This method is one of several open to a manufacturer who wishes to enter a particular market, and by it the distributor relieves the manufacturer of the necessity for local marketing activities, such as the carrying of adequate stocks, the promotion of sales (whether by advertising or by canvassing the trade), the handling and execution of orders and, where necessary, the provision of after-sale services. The satisfactory performance of these activities in some cases requires a substantial organization, as well as considerable knowledge of local trading conditions. An established distributor may be able to provide the necessary services for a new product or brand more cheaply and effectively than could the manufacturer if the latter were to set up a new organization specially for the purpose. The distributor may, however, incur appreciable costs for the introduction and promotion of the new product. These costs are in the nature of capital outlays, and the distributor is not likely to incur them unless he is reasonably certain to secure the profits for himself, at least for some years. Sole distributing rights ensure that the benefits of his efforts will accrue to his advantage and not to that of his competitors; the granting of such rights may be regarded as the necessary payment by the manufacturer for the investment and the service which he requires.[1] Sometimes the sole distributor in return for his exclusive rights undertakes not to handle competing brands; thus the exclusiveness may be reciprocal.

Although they are referred to as sole agents, the firms holding sole distributing rights often act as principals and not as agents. They own the stocks they carry, assume the credit and other trading risks, and may bear a substantial proportion of the cost of promoting the brand. Moreover, the sole distributor is usually free to determine the price at

---

[1] Frequently the reward for the special services takes the form of an overriding commission payable on all sales in the territory to the distributor or agent who first introduced the product or brand in recognition of his services in handling and popularizing a particular article or brand. The recipient of such an overriding commission is also frequently referred to as a sole agent.

which he will sell the brand, though there are exceptions to this. The character and the level of his remuneration are in the nature of a trader's profit margin rather than of an agent's commission.

Many branded commodities sold in West Africa are subject to sole agencies. They include the leading motor-cars, lorries, bicycles, tractors, tyres and also matches. A variant of the sole agency agreement is the practice of granting overriding commissions to a firm on all sales in a particular territory, whether effected by that firm or by another firm. This applies to many products, including certain petroleum products, cigarettes and some alcoholic drinks, including certain brands of beer and gin.

The decision to grant or to refuse sole distributing rights often depends on the general policy of the suppliers as well as on the situation in a particular market. Where the manufacturer or his brand is well known he may not consider it to his advantage to grant sole distributing rights. He may prefer to sell his products to all distributors who are prepared to pay his price. In this way he may secure a wider as well as a closer cover of the market he is about to enter. Moreover, the competition among distributors may reduce the price to retailers and consumers and may thus result in larger sales. These considerations are particularly likely to influence the policy of manufacturers of non-durable goods in the distribution of which after-sale service is not important, and where therefore the substantial capital involved or the special technical skill necessary for many types of after-sale service are not required.

An interesting example of the policy of refusing to grant sole agencies is the practice of the Unilever group, which does not generally grant such rights to those distributing its products; and accordingly the United Africa Company, although a member of that group, does not enjoy sole distributing rights of its products.

2. PREFERENTIAL ARRANGEMENTS BETWEEN SUPPLIERS AND MERCHANTS

Sole agency arrangements confine to one firm the right to handle a particular commodity or brand. Suppliers may also confine certain brands or types of commodities to a particular group of firms. This latter type of arrangement seems to have played a more important part in West African trade than elsewhere.

Arrangements restricting the supply of a particular commodity or type of commodity or brand to a group of firms has, for some time, been a feature of West African merchandise trade. In the 1930's certain popular types of brands of salt, sugar, dried fish (stockfish), corned beef, potable spirits, trade perfume and dyestuffs were largely or wholly confined to those permanent members of the Association of West African Merchants who participated in the Merchandise Agreement.

Some of these arrangements still operate. The principal suppliers of the leading brands of Scotch whisky, British salt and dyestuffs confine their products largely or wholly to this group. Some members of this group also occupy a special position in the distribution of cigarettes and of petroleum products. Some of these arrangements are both important and instructive.

British salt produced by the largest supplier (who controls the great bulk of the output) is almost wholly confined on a quota basis to a group of firms who dealt with this supplier in the early 1930's.[1] The same company is also the dominant supplier of British dyestuffs; the supply of these products also is confined to the participants in the former Merchandise Agreement. It seems that in return the group of merchants undertake normally not to import supplies from other sources —a reciprocal tying agreement. The company also exports paints and a whole range of other chemicals, in the supply of which it, however, does not have such a dominant position. No such exclusive marketing arrangements are made for these other products, and they are made available to the trade generally. Because of the easy availability of competing supplies from other sources, an assurance from one group of distributors not to buy elsewhere would not keep competing supplies off the West African market.

For some years past there was an agreement[2] between the same group of importers and the National Association of Norwegian Stockfish Exporters (to whose members the right to export is confined by statute) which covered the marketing of Norwegian stockfish, a commodity which is an important staple line in the Nigerian import trade. The agreement stipulated that a specified proportion of total shipments of Norwegian stockfish consigned to West Africa should be sold to the scheduled firms at a specified price. In recent years the proportion ranged from about 77 to about 90 %. The scheduled firms undertook to accept the available stockfish at that agreed price. The balance of stockfish available for the West African market could be sold by members of the exporters' association to any importer, subject to two conditions: the price was not to be less than that agreed between the association and the scheduled firms, and not more than $2\frac{1}{2}$ % of the total could be sold to any firm which had not imported stockfish before

[1] The favoured firms include a few merchants other than the participants to the former Merchandise Agreement. The share in total supplies of these outside merchants is small.

[2] This agreement was abandoned in the summer of 1951. Some aspects of its operation are discussed in Appendix 6.

the war. The Norwegian exporters undertook to bind purchasers in other markets not to resell stockfish directly or indirectly to West Africa. The restriction on the shares of new importers may have been designed to clip the wings of one or two substantial firms which have entered the Nigerian import trade since the outbreak of war.

Other arrangements between suppliers and distributors stipulate preferential treatment and discounts to the favoured distributor or group of distributors. Such discounts are distinct from quantity or cash discounts which are available to any buyer placing an order of the required size, or settling his account within a specified period. The granting of preferential discounts to favoured distributors does not formally exclude the less favoured firms from handling goods in question, but their activities are hampered and, in certain cases, crippled. Some merchants refuse to handle a line when they know that competitors receive better terms from suppliers.

In West Africa preferential terms and discounts have been frequently granted by suppliers of important lines of merchandise to individual firms or groups of firms, chiefly to the participants in the former Merchandise Agreement. In the course of the last fifteen years the commodities covered included flour, salt, whisky and sewing thread. In the handling of the latter, a substantial preferential discount (at about one-seventh of the selling price) was received by some of the larger firms until about 1950.

Provisions and stipulations for the maintenance of re-sale or retail prices are an important and familiar type of arrangement between supplier and distributor in many parts of the world. The practice of price maintenance may be adopted by suppliers for various reasons.[1] They may act under pressure from important distributors or groups of distributors who wish to have their margins guaranteed. Without this guarantee they may not be prepared to exert themselves in the sale of the suppliers' products, or they may threaten implicity or explicitly to discover and develop alternative sources of supply from which better terms or guarantees may be secured. On the other hand, suppliers may introduce re-sale price maintenance in order to make it more difficult for competing suppliers to enter the market; the guaranteed margin acts as an inducement to distributors to refrain from dealing with actual or potential rival sources of supply.

Re-sale price maintenance is not widespread in West Africa, but it covers certain important products. Cigarettes and sewing thread are sold subject to re-sale price agreements. These seem to be clear instances where a supplier in a quasi-monopolistic position uses re-sale price

---

[1] A comprehensive analysis of the cause and results of the practice is not presented here. Only those aspects which bear on West African trade are considered.

màintenance to make it more difficult or costly for possible rivals to enter the market by making it attractive for distributors to handle his own products; but the possibility of pressure by some powerful distributors cannot be excluded.[1]

3. THE DISTRIBUTION OF CIGARETTES AND PETROLEUM PRODUCTS

The arrangements in the distribution of cigarettes and petroleum products warrant further treatment because of the high degree of concentration, the considerable quantitative importance of these products and the certainty of further rapid expansion in the demand for them.

The British-American Tobacco Company, and its subsidiary the Nigerian Tobacco Company, which supply well over 90 % of all cigarettes in West Africa, largely confine their releases to the leading merchant firms. Sales are made subject to re-sale price maintenance, nominally down to the stage of petty retail but in fact effective only at the stage of first sale. In recent years demand has frequently exceeded supply at the officially or informally controlled prices. In such circumstances the suppliers naturally ration the trading firms, usually more or ess in proportion to past purchases over a recent period. But it appears that even when there is no excess demand supplies are released in the first instance almost entirely to certain of the largest firms only. In the Gold Coast, but not in Nigeria, the largest distributor is also in receipt of a commission on all sales of cigarettes of the only important supplier, chiefly in recognition for services in the operation of depots and in extending certain credit facilities to customers. These arrangements seem to be of the nature of reciprocal tying agreements by which the supplier largely confines the product to the favoured distributor, who undertakes not to handle products of rival suppliers; probably they are favoured for strategic reasons by both the supplier and the principal distributor.

Petroleum products are released by the four oil companies through

---

[1] In the distribution of petroleum products main distributors act as agents for the oil companies and are obliged to sell at their prices. With negligible exceptions the same prices are prescribed for bulk products by the four oil companies in much the same way as in other markets for petroleum products outside the United States. Some effects of these arrangements and practices resemble those of re-sale price maintenance. But in substance the situation is the familiar one of identical prices for a highly standardized product in the supply of which there is a high degree of concentration well-known examples include banking services, shipping services and a supply of bulk petroleum products. The identical prices may or may not be the result of price agreements; they are frequently brought about by the realization by the participants of the implications of the market structure without any definite agreement. This appears to be the position in the distribution of petroleum products in West Africa.

the principal merchant firms who act as their main distributors. The firms have to sell at prices prescribed by the oil companies and they receive a fixed commission on all sales. In some instances the oil companies recognize subsidiary distributors with whom the main distributor has to share the fixed commission. In addition to the distributor's commission on sales affected by them, the main distributors also receive an agency commission for such services as maintaining depots for the oil companies and bearing certain credit risks. One firm acts as main distributor for two oil companies.

These arrangements in the distribution of cigarettes and of petroleum products seem greatly to favour the larger firms, especially the participants in the former Merchandise Agreement. In the handling of these products there are certain economies of scale (especially in the early stages of the distribution of oil products) and also of widespread organization. But it seems probable that the overwhelming preponderance of the largest firms cannot be accounted for solely by these economies, but results partly from the special arrangements for the distribution of these products. This preponderance is far larger than the share of these firms in the import trade as a whole, or even in most of the staple lines.

As a result of the increase in demand for cigarettes and petroleum products in recent years, they have come to occupy an important position in the merchandise trade. Both in Nigeria and in the Gold Coast expenditure at market prices on these products together was in 1950 about one-tenth of the total expenditure on imported merchandise.[1]

In the trade of some of the largest firms the sales of these products loom very large indeed. Information very kindly supplied by the United Africa Company suggests that in 1950 sales of cigarettes and petroleum products together are represented by about one-quarter of the Company's total sales in Nigeria and about one-seventh in the Gold Coast, with cigarettes representing about three-fifths to two-thirds of the combined sales of these products.[2]

In West Africa the demand for cigarettes and petroleum products is certain to increase greatly, and almost certain to rise more rapidly than the demand for the aggregate of all imported merchandise. This is particularly likely in Nigeria, where cigarette consumption per head is still very low and motor transport comparatively inadequate, although growing rapidly in importance. Thus the advantages to the favoured distributors are likely to increase in importance. Not only do the special

---

[1] The figures include expenditure on locally manufactured cigarettes in Nigeria and also allow for the duty on these products.

[2] Some interesting information on the part of these products in the merchandise turnover of the Company is published in its *Statistical and Economic Review*, March 1950 and September 1950.

arrangements in the distribution of these commodities serve to provide the beneficiaries with a useful source of steady income, but the ability to supply these essential or desirable types of merchandise serves to attract custom for other goods.

4. DIFFICULTIES OF ASSESSING THE EFFECTS OF SOLE AGENCIES AND OTHER SPECIAL ARRANGEMENTS

In analysing the implications and results of marketing arrangements it is necessary to focus attention on substance rather than on terminology, since in some respects the explicit terminology is apt to mislead.

Thus, in spite of their monopolistic connotation, sole distributing rights do not necessarily restrict competition either among suppliers or among distributors. Reliance on sole distributors may be the most easily available efficient method of launching a new brand or product. In these circumstances competition is promoted by this method. Similarly, if sole distributing rights are fairly widely spread amongst distributors, competition amongst them need not be reduced to any material extent. The possibility of obtaining sole distributing rights and developing the markets for the products may help to maintain and strengthen the position of many smaller distributors. Since not all competing manufacturers can use the relatively few large merchants as sole distributors for their brands, they may be forced to use smaller firms, thus strengthening the position both of their brand and of the smaller merchants.[1]

In certain other circumstances, however, sole agencies and other exclusive dealing arrangements may restrict competition among distributors and manufacturers. A pre-existing high degree of concentration in the import trade tends to emphasize the restrictive potentialities of exclusive dealing arrangements. Manufacturers seeking entry into the market would naturally gravitate towards one or other of the few large import houses, because the majority of the smaller firms are much less useful for their purposes. Moreover, it is difficult for the overseas suppliers to assess the abilities and the potentialities of the smaller and relatively unknown importers. An accumulation or concentration of a large number of sole distributing rights in the possession of a particular distributor or small number of distributors tends to

---

[1] Thus a few years ago a new brand of beer was introduced in the Gold Coast by a medium-sized Lebanese importing firm. An intensive sales promotion campaign helped to create a demand for the brand which proved suitable to the local market. The sales effort proved successful, and the brand is now firmly established in competition with other beers. The success of the product has also substantially strengthened the position of the merchant who introduced it. The receipt of sole distributing rights was a major factor in inducing the trader to undertake the campaign.

restrict competition in distribution generally by hampering the entry and growth of new distributing firms. New or small firms are unable to offer their customers or potential customers a full range of desirable merchandise, and may find that their operations are seriously constricted or rendered altogether unprofitable. The process of concentration of distributing rights may thus be cumulative, and suppliers may offer sole distributing rights to the largest distributors without pressure from the latter. This process may greatly affect the degree of concentration and the extent of competition among distributors. It need not affect competition among overseas suppliers in their efforts to reach the market, though success may in these circumstances depend primarily on the decisions of a small group of distributors rather than on the choice of consumers among alternatives.

Where the exclusiveness is largely or wholly reciprocal, even strong overseas suppliers with well-known and well-established products may favour exclusive arrangements with the dominant distributors. Such tying arrangements make it more difficult for competing products or brands to enter the particular market, because the most favourable channels of distribution are denied to them. A tying arrangement may serve as a pre-emptive device by which the overseas supplier reserves the market for himself and for his distributors. In these circumstances the supplier does not adopt the practice of exclusive dealing to enter a new market; nor does he act under implied or expressed pressure of distributors. He introduces or accepts agreements to forestall potential competition, and does so by a method which restricts competition both in the supply of the products to the market and in their distribution.

Where there is a large measure of concentration in distribution, the inclination of manufacturers to deal with the largest firms rather than with the lesser-known smaller firms can be reinforced by actual or potential pressure or threats. There are some suppliers who would prefer to market their brands without sole-agency agreements; and there are others who would prefer to use small rising firms as their sole agents for various reasons, notably because their terms may be more favourable, or because they think that a smaller merchant would be more active in promoting the sales of the product. Nevertheless, the suppliers may be forced to grant sole distributing rights to one or more of the dominant firms, because of the fear that without this they might refuse to handle the products, or the fear that they might attempt to destroy the market for the brand if its sole agency is granted to an outsider. Fear of boycott or of retaliation may be as effective as actual suggestions or threats. Once there is heavy concentration in the import trade, the manufacturers are likely to take into account the possibilities inherent in that situation.

It is, moreover, not unlikely that the dominant importing firms may consciously or unconsciously give currency to the view that they in fact are the only reliable and available import houses, and that all other firms are of little substance or of doubtful integrity. In these circumstances exclusive dealing rights tend to be granted to the established distributors, strengthening the already strong position of the dominant firms.

In general it is not relevant whether a supplier has granted exclusive dealing rights (or adopted any particular marketing practice) on his own initiative or under pressure. The effects are clearly the same. In a sense all marketing agreements are voluntary, as the supplier need not accept them. However unwilling a supplier may be to enter a particular type of agreement, he may nevertheless accept it if on his assessment a different course might result in total or partial exclusion from the market. Where there is a dominant distributor, and even more so where a number of important firms act in concert, there is a strong implicit pressure for exclusive privileges, which is more potent when it is known or believed that pressure has on occasions been exerted.

The foregoing analysis applies closely to the granting of preferential terms by suppliers to favoured distributors, and in some respects also to the introduction of re-sale price maintenance arrangements by suppliers. Indeed, the granting of sole distributing rights is no more than the limiting case of preferential terms to the selected distributors; and to that extent the preferential treatment of some distributors is a possibly milder alternative to the issue of sole distributing rights.

The different marketing arrangements and agreements tend in practice to merge into one another, particularly in their results. Preferential terms shade into exclusive dealing agreements, and agreements covering a particular brand of commodity shade into arrangements covering an entire class of commodities. Preferential treatment and exclusive marketing arrangements may also succeed each other in time if preferential terms are granted to some distributors for a period and if supplies are subsequently confined to them. Again, the two types of arrangement may co-exist: some distributors are guaranteed both a minimum proportion of total supplies and preferential terms.

5. PRESUMPTION OF RESTRICTIVE EFFECTS OF SUCH ARRANGE-MENTS UNDER CERTAIN SPECIFIED CONDITIONS

In certain fairly clearly defined circumstances the presumption is strong that exclusive dealing arrangements tend to promote restriction rather than competition, both in the supply and in the distribution of the merchandise affected. This is so where the arrangements cover a commodity or commodity group rather than a particular brand of a commodity; where the agreement is with a group of distributors rather than with an individual distributor; and/or where the supplier is in a monopolistic or dominant position. Where one or more of these features is present it is probable that the agreement is in the nature of an induced boycott and/or an attempted pre-emption of existing channels of distribution. The favoured distributor(s) may have induced the supplier(s) to refrain from supplying other distributors; and/or the supplier(s) may have induced the favoured distributor(s) to refrain from purchasing from other suppliers.

In such circumstances the arrangements are particularly liable to be concluded with the large established distributors, whose position they serve to strengthen; and the practice may serve to induce these distributors to confine their dealings to the particular supplier(s). In these conditions the arrangements are likely to have restrictive effects in the sense of reducing the number of alternatives open to the public compared to the range of alternatives which would be available in their absence.

The high degree of concentration in the West African import trade, with a group of firms clustered round a dominant firm, sets up a presumption that marketing arrangements to which the group or its individual members are parties are likely to have a restrictive influence even where this is not specifically intended.

This presumption applies even to the granting of sole distributing rights to individual firms for individual brands, since in the circumstances of West African trade they are likely to be concentrated and their effects cumulative. This tendency cannot be expressed quantitatively, since the degree of concentration in the possession of sole distributing rights cannot be measured. The products are heterogeneous, and there are wide differences in their strategic values, in the profitability of the individual arrangements, in the condition on which they have been granted, and in the expenditure necessary to introduce and establish the product. But the impossibility of measuring the degree of concentration in this sphere does not affect the conclusion that the larger well-established firms almost certainly have a disproportionately large share of sole distributing rights,[1] particularly of branded goods of British origin.

What is known of preferential terms granted by overseas suppliers to the distributors in West Africa suggests that, even apart from quantity discounts, these were, and in some cases still are, to the advantage of the largest firms. This also applies to agreements between suppliers and groups of firms; all these seem to be between suppliers and members of the Merchandise Agreement group.

[1] I.e. much greater than their share in total merchandise imports.

6. COMPARATIVE UNIMPORTANCE OF SPECIAL DISTRIBUTING
   ARRANGEMENTS AS A FACTOR IN THE SHORTAGE
   OF MERCHANDISE

Since the early years of the war distributive arrangements between
importers and suppliers have frequently been blamed for specific shortages of commodities in West Africa. Moreover, aggrieved suppliers
were apt to consider these marketing arrangements as the principal
barrier to their participation in the highly lucrative import trade of the
war period and of the early post-war years.[1] These traders were inclined
to blame the large firms, especially the United Africa Company, for
their inability to obtain supplies. They failed to realize the implications
of the shortages, and of some of the complex reasons for the supply
difficulties. It was not generally appreciated that profits were high and
easy because not everybody could secure supplies, and that as soon as
market requirements could be met easily trading would be less profitable.
The difficulties of obtaining supplies were of various kinds: trade and
exchange controls, shortage of shipping, informal rationing by overseas
suppliers to regular customers, unwillingness of suppliers to accept new
customers in a strong sellers' market, and the existence of agreements
confining supplies of certain commodities or brands to particular importers or at least assuring them of strongly preferential treatment. The
agreements just mentioned aroused much criticism and their importance
was certainly exaggerated. In particular, results were ascribed to the
agreements which certainly cannot be attributed to them alone.

It is difficult to analyse and locate the causes of any particular
shortage in the trading conditions of the war and post-war years. Thus
if a brand of a commodity is in short supply[2] this limitation may be
principally the result of rationing by the overseas supplier. This may
be reinforced by the operation of import controls curtailing alternative
supplies, which, though less preferred, may nevertheless satisfy some of

---

[1] Figures have been made available to the writer by the Inland Revenue Department of Nigeria of aggregate profits of all limited liability companies in Nigeria from
1939-40 to 1948-9. The total taxable profits of trading companies, excluding mining,
banking and shipping, rose from £871,000 in 1939-40 to £7,100,000 in 1948-9. These
figures include profits on all trading activities; in so far as it is appropriate to apportion
total profits on diverse but connected activities, it is safe to say that the major share
both of the total and of the increase is attributable to the import trade. This is
particularly clear for the increase, since over most of these years the firms were acting
as agents only in the bulk of the export trade.

[2] This is a situation in which if the product is sold at a price equal to the landed
cost plus the customary rate of profit, the quantity demanded exceeds available
supplies; or in other words, those securing available supplies can dispose of them at
abnormally profitable prices.

the demands. If this brand is the subject of exclusive distributing agreements, the sole importer secures the whole of the available abnormal profits. Moreover, the sole importer may conceivably keep the market shorter than is absolutely necessary, and may thus secure true monopoly profits (arising from his control of supplies) as well as the abnormal scarcity profits (arising from the shortage of supplies). This need not be intentional, for the sole importer may merely fail to exercise the fullest pressure and foresight to obtain larger supplies. Again, the sole importer (or group acting in concert) may deliberately or unintentionally so distribute available supplies as to secure special advantages by keeping certain areas shorter than others.[1]

The effects of exclusive or preferential agreements are thus often interwoven with other supply difficulties which they tend to reinforce and emphasize. Moreover, trade controls and informal rationing by suppliers are likely to maintain and strengthen the preferential position of the beneficiaries of the agreements. But the effects of the arrangements and agreements between suppliers and distributors can be analytically distinguished from those of the trade controls. Further, these effects were already operative before the emergence of wartime shortages and can be expected to continue even in the absence of other supply difficulties.

7. THE THREAT OF INDUCED BOYCOTT AS A POSSIBLE BARRIER TO ENTRY

The trading situation as a whole, and particularly the prospects of new entrants, may be influenced by possible pressure on suppliers by established large distributors to withhold previously available supplies from specific firms, particularly more recently established firms. Especially in its results, this is to some extent related to exclusive or preferential dealing arrangements between suppliers and merchants. Nevertheless, there is a distinction. A firm may decide to establish itself even though it realizes that certain lines will be denied to it for a considerable time by the arrangements between suppliers and other merchant firms; it may be prepared to handle other lines unaffected by these agreements. But it may still have to face the risk that some of these might be

---

[1] The special advantages may take different forms. First, receipts on the sale of the brand may be increased by selling relatively more in markets where the demand is comparatively elastic and relatively less where the demand is comparatively inelastic. Secondly, regional releases may be adjusted so as to strengthen the firm's general trading position where competition is particularly strong. Thirdly, regional releases may be adjusted so as to attract a larger volume of profitable export produce. Fourthly, releases may be made direct to the employees of the sole importer or to regions in which a large proportion of the population is employed by the importing firm or its associates.

discontinued at the instance of its competitors if it threatens to develop an appreciable turnover.

Allegations that this type of pressure has been exercised by the dominant firms in West Africa, although often advanced, are less frequent than allegations of destructive price-cutting, or of the restrictive effects of the various agreements between suppliers and certain merchants. The validity and accuracy of these allegations are particularly difficult to assess, especially in conditions of intermittent shortages of supplies. Several specific complaints have been made to me by reliable firms of pressure on suppliers by the largest firms (in some cases acting together) to discontinue sales to competitors. These related to Scotch whiskies, a well-known brand of beer, processed cheese and the products of a well-known textile printer. The details relating to the last incident, which is said to have occurred shortly before the recent war, came independently from two sources and seemed trustworthy. It seems to have been an attempted induced boycott; his largest customers threatened to withdraw their business unless the printer refused to deal with a specified competitor. He rejected the ultimatum but the outbreak of war prevented the issue from being put to the test. In whisky the dominant supplier at first refused to confine supplies to a group of firms, but was apparently coerced into such an arrangement when the group in concert promoted the sales of a minor independent brand.[1]

The possibility of pressure on suppliers or of destructive price-cutting by itself may deter new entrants, particularly if they believe that these weapons have been used in West Africa. The frequency of their use is no measure of their inhibiting effects. Knowledge of the high degree of concentration, which is often exaggerated, and of the power to influence the market which is implicit in it, may strengthen the belief in their effectiveness. The necessarily inconclusive evidence on the use of these powers or practices is of secondary importance.

Nevertheless, for reasons very similar to those mentioned in connexion with the actual use, or the threat, of destructive price-cutting,[2] the threat of induced boycott does not appear to have been significant in the trading situation in West Africa in recent years.

---

[1] The incidents described in detail here took place before the war; those relating to beer and cheese are said to have occurred more recently. Although these were related by traders of standing they were essentially *ex parte*. I have not been able to secure evidence either to confirm or to refute them.

[2] Above, Chapter 9, § 2.

8. THE INFLUENCE OF THE MARKET SITUATION ON THE IMPLICATIONS OF MARKETING ARRANGEMENTS AND PRACTICES

The analysis of the preceding and present chapters points to an important general conclusion. A particular arrangement or practice may promote competition in some circumstances and strengthen restriction and concentration in others. The same practice may serve either to provide opportunities for newcomers and for small traders, or to consolidate the entrenched position of the dominant firms and suppliers by exclusion of competitors. Its effect depends essentially upon the situation and conditions in which the particular practice operates, as well as upon its width and scope. The practice is largely neutral; it is the situation which gives it colour; and this conclusion is reinforced by the fact that it is often the possibilities and potentialities inherent in a situation or a practice, as much as a practice itself, which are influential.[1]

This carries an important corollary for the devising and assessment of measures designed to curb concentration of economic power and restrictive practices generally. The proscription of certain defined practices and agreements, which may be clearly restrictive in some cases, may prevent their employment in other possibly important cases where their effects tend to promote competition. Conversely, the tolerance of generally harmless practices may in certain circumstances permit their use to strengthen and to promote concentration and restriction. Practices which may promote competition when adopted by some firms may be restrictive when employed by others; certain types of price-cutting are an example.

Although this study is not concerned with policy recommendations, it seems worth while to mention certain policy implications of the foregoing discussion. It suggests a serious difficulty of general anti-monopoly legislation. The comprehensive prohibition of a defined practice may be unwise; while the selective prohibition of its use in specified cases will always appear to be arbitrary (which on occasions it may largely be) and vindictive. The effectiveness of anti-monopoly action will be greatly increased, and its arbitrary elements will be minimized, if attention is focused primarily on situations and settings rather than on practices, agreements and arrangements. The latter may be important constituents of a situation, but they are rarely the causal or decisive elements in it.[2]

---

[1] There is, however, a strong presumption that certain classes of agreement are restrictive; cf. § 2 of this chapter.

[2] In many cases, though not in all, the strength of a marketing arrangement is not materially increased by a formal agreement, even if it is legally valid and enforceable

It is probable that the most effective[1] results will be achieved if remedial measures are framed after considering together the practices and the underlying situation, and if these measures are directed towards widening the range of alternatives open to the customers of the firms and towards improving the access of the population to these alternatives.

If a monopoly situation has been identified, it may or may not be sufficient to proscribe the particular marketing practice adopted. In some cases the proscription alone may be effective, for no alternative permitted marketing practice might be nearly as effective in maintaining or strengthening the monopoly as the one proscribed. In other cases the prohibition of a specific practice may be insufficient to achieve the desired results. Thus, where there is a dominant supplier and a dominant distributor the mere prohibition of re-sale price maintenance, or of exclusive dealing agreements, need not materially affect the ease of access of other suppliers to the market and of other distributors to the product.

9. SUMMARY OF THE EFFECTS OF CONCENTRATION AND COMMERCIAL ARRANGEMENTS ON THE ENTRY AND GROWTH OF COMPETITORS

The discussion of the last three chapters has disclosed the presence of a number of powerful influences, restraining the establishment and inhibiting the growth of new firms in the distributive trades. Nevertheless, in order to preserve a proper perspective it is necessary to emphasize again that despite all these difficulties, several new firms of substance have been able to enter the trade in recent years, and at least one has become a major competitor of the previously established firms. But for the formidable obstacles resulting from official policies and administrative action, the number and influence of effective competitors would have been much greater.[2]

---

in practice. The formal agreement may be a reflexion and a more or less temporary crystallization of existing relationships and forces. For example, if there is one dominant distributor it may well be necessary or profitable for a supplier to grant it special terms even in the absence of a formal agreement. Exclusive dealing and preferential treatment may be introduced apparently unilaterally by a supplier in recognition of the market situation and without formal contracts. Formalization in an agreement or understanding may, however, extend the arrangements for a longer period than would be warranted in its absence by changes in the situation.

[1] 'Most effective' need not be identical with the best. Conditions may well be envisaged under which the maintenance of a monopoly or quasi-monopoly situation, and the conditions of continuity and security of tenure for certain firms, may be deemed desirable. Examination of this possibility is outside the scope of this book.

[2] This was stated emphatically by the French proprietor of a medium-sized business in Nigeria mentioned in Chapter 8, § 8.

CHAPTER 11

OFFICIAL POLICIES AND ATTITUDES
AND ECONOMIC CONCENTRATION

1. EFFECTS OF OFFICIAL ATTITUDES ON THE TRADING SITUATION

In conditions in which official action impinges upon economic life closely at many points, administrative outlook and beliefs affect the trading situation substantially. In West Africa they condition the readiness with which administrators are prepared to accede to or to resist specific demands or suggestions made by trading interests or by African opinion. They can to a certain extent be regarded as independent causal influences in that they tend, consciously or unconsciously, to encourage or to discourage particular demands; vague and general discontent becomes crystallized in the course of interpretation by administrators into specific, and possibly quite different, ideas. Conversely, isolated personal grievances or complaints may be transformed in the course of administrative interpretation into generalized beliefs, and so produce generalized attitudes towards proposals for action and reform.

This chapter discusses, with some illustrations, the more pervasive attitudes and opinions that colour administrative action; some of the examples are drawn from the administration of wartime controls. Chapter 12 analyses the effects of immigration policy, the most important single influence of official policy on the trading situation. Some repercussions of other official measures are considered in Chapter 13.

2. ADMINISTRATIVE PREFERENCE FOR LARGE FIRMS, FOR ESTABLISHED FIRMS, AND FOR COLLECTIVE NEGOTIATION

The trading firms in West Africa often have to deal with the government in such matters as the allocation of trading licences and building plots, the administration of immigration regulations, the allocation of transport facilities, the operation of trade controls and proposals for development or for taxation policy.

In West Africa, as in other countries, administrators prefer to deal with a few large firms rather than with a number of small enterprises.[1] Administrators are less likely to know the latter, either because they are

[1] This refers in general to expatriate firms. There is no suggestion of any preference for expatriate over African enterprise. Indeed, as has already been stated and shown, there is at present intentional and explicit strong discrimination in favour of African firms in the administration of import licensing.

numerous and small, or because they are often comparatively recently established. Representatives of the large enterprises receive a different hearing, even though they may be executives or employees only, while smaller firms may be represented by their principals. There are many examples where the authorities have delayed for four to six months before answering letters from small or medium-sized enterprises of repute and standing; larger firms do not seem to experience similar difficulties. One of the medium-sized, prosperous and well-established trading enterprises in Nigeria is owned by a Frenchman who had been area manager of one of the larger firms. He said that he was often amused by the contrast between the reception accorded to him at government offices at present, and that extended to him in the past when he was merely manager of one of the large firms. He said that though his position at present was much more responsible, he formerly received greater attention.

Because there is widespread government intervention in economic life in its broadest sense, the general preference for dealing with the large firms is likely to strengthen their position against non-African competitors. This preference is sometimes rationalized on the ground of the alleged greater efficiency of the large firms, or the better conditions granted by them to labour and staff. Previous discussion has shown that the relative competitive strength of large and small enterprises in trade is a complex problem, and that no valid generalization can be established on this subject. In any event, even if there were some advantages attaching to large-scale operation, it would not follow that every large firm was more efficient than every small firm. And even if the large firms were more efficient generally (for which, as already stated, there is no conclusive evidence), this would not provide any justification for preferential treatment of the large firms by the authorities. Similarly, differences in labour conditions would not warrant preferential treatment for those firms which are believed to treat their staff best. If it were desired to help the better employers, the policy would need to be announced, and the nature of the favourable treatment indicated, as well as the terms on which it could be secured by firms of any size.[1]

The administrative preference in favour of large firms is coupled with

[1] Moreover, even if there were a consistent policy of favouring better employers of labour, its economic wisdom would not be obvious. The existence of better labour conditions in certain organizations prompts one to ask at whose expense these have been granted. They may in some cases be the result of quasi-monopolistic action by the firms concerned or by organized labour. In such cases the better working conditions are secured partly at the expense of higher prices to customers. But the main brunt is borne by workers or traders who are excluded as a result of this quasi-monopolistic action, and who have to accept less desirable occupations or remain unemployed.

a noticeable (and understandable) desire to deal with established firms rather than with newcomers or with firms set up comparatively recently. The administrative and personal convenience is obvious. The comparative unfamiliarity of newcomers with administrative procedures, regulations and channels of communication, inspires the belief that these firms are generally inefficient, as well as inconvenient to deal with. It is easy but fallacious to conclude that because their activities are likely to inconvenience administrators, they are also likely to harm the economy.[1] For obvious reasons these beliefs are encouraged by some of the established firms, who tend to be consulted by the administrators on many matters affecting the fate and fortunes of newcomers, including not infrequently their very admission.

The larger and longer established firms are also advantaged by greater ability to present their case in a well-prepared and acceptable form. Firms, even economically efficient and successful firms, differ greatly in their ability to present a case clearly, convincingly and in a manner acceptable to the authorities. While African deficiencies in this respect are likely to be excused in West Africa, similar disabilities of the smaller expatriate firms increase their disadvantages in official dealings. In the past the advantage of the large firms was at times increased by their direct contacts with the Colonial Office in London, which they owed to the fact that they have established offices in the United Kingdom. This is of little importance at present.

For reasons of political and administrative convenience, government departments and administrators the world over favour negotiations and dealings with groups of firms rather than with firms individually, even where the latter method is possible. In West African trade this has been evident in the operation of wartime controls in the administration of which the authorities relied for advice almost wholly on the Association of West African Merchants. At present, marketing boards and their executives negotiate with committees of buying agents rather than with individual firms. The remuneration of the buying agents and their reimbursement for expenses incurred are always collective. This practice tends to result in closer co-operation between the firms, which may in turn have the long-term effects which habitually flow from collaboration and meetings between firms and groups of firms, such as the encourage-

---

[1] This, of course, is not to call into question the value and importance of continuity in economic life, or to suggest that casual or *ad hoc* ventures and transactions are of the same value and usefulness as more permanent enterprises and business relations. The remarks in the text refer to the unfavourable attitude sometimes adopted towards viable enterprises with prospects of continuity, which happen to be recently established, or which are complete newcomers. It is sometimes overlooked that all established firms started as new entrants.

ment of price-fixing and market-sharing agreements and the growth of trade associations, joint organizations and amalgamations.[1]

In an assessment of the effects of these administrative attitudes it is necessary to recall certain influential views on economic activity and public policy. These include the belief that trade is unproductive; that arbitrage transactions (the profitable movement of commodities between places or seasons) are both unnecessary and undesirable; and that the amount of economic activity in general and of trade in particular is largely fixed, so that the activities of some groups, notably newcomers, are harmful to the interests of the majority, and indeed are likely to be largely at their expense. The familiar tidiness complex so influential in contemporary society reinforces these attitudes. A multiplicity of traders, especially of small or medium-sized firms, presents a chaotic and untidy appearance which is readily identified with inefficiency and administrative inconvenience. Substantially restrictive effects are likely to flow from the policies resulting from the combination of the attitudes and preferences discussed in this chapter and these more widely held beliefs.

3. DISTRUST OF THE LEVANTINE COMMUNITIES

Commercial life in West Africa has been much affected and is still affected by dislike and distrust of the Levantine communities, which is marked in official circles. Members of the Levantine communities are freely accused of black-market activities, that is, of selling commodities above their controlled prices. It is rarely asked whether members of other communities are doing likewise; whether the Levantine sellers themselves have been subjected to conditional sales in the purchase of controlled commodities; and whether it is either practicable or desirable to sell at controlled prices in the absence of effective official rationing.[2]

The denigration of the Levantine communities was a principal feature of the Martindale Report.[3] That report and its sequel revealed both the extent and depth of feeling against these communities held by the

---

[1] These effects should be familiar to readers of the *Wealth of Nations*: 'People of the same trade seldom meet together even for merriment and diversion but the conversation ends in a conspiracy against the public or in some contrivance to raise prices. It is impossible indeed to prevent such meetings by any law which either could be executed or would be consistent with liberty and justice.' Adam Smith also pointed the moral: 'But though the law cannot hinder people of the same trade from sometimes assembling together it ought to do nothing to facilitate such assemblies; much less to render them necessary' (Book 1, chapter 10).

[2] Levantines are also often accused of grain speculation and hoarding and are held responsible for occasional scarcity and high prices of grain. It should be apparent that without their activities the ultimate scarcity would be greater and prices higher.

[3] Discussed in Chapter 6 above.

administration and the European firms, and also the serious consequences to which this misguided prejudice can lead.

The distrust of Levantines, together with an administrative preference for uniformity, results in policies and measures tending to strengthen the position of the larger established firms against their expatriate rivals. The most important of these are the immigration regulations which are reviewed in the next chapter. In general the measures tend to make the racial composition of the traders less varied, to reduce the degree and the effectiveness of competition, and to protect the established firms. There is a general presumption that a racially more diverse group of traders is more likely to behave competitively and less likely to conclude and to observe effective market-sharing agreements than a more homogeneous group. This presumption is confirmed by the analysis of the trading situation and of its effects on producer prices in the purchase of groundnuts in Nigeria.[1]

The unfavourable attitude of many officials towards the Levantine communities contrasts notably with the financial support which European banks, manufacturers, export houses and merchants have given to many members of the Levantine communities in West Africa. Many of the Levantine enterprises enjoy the respect, confidence and financial backing of British banks and firms. In some instances the supporters are highly regarded old-established British firms whose names are household words the world over. It would seem that personal and commercial contacts between members of the Levantine community and their supporters have not confirmed the suspicions and fears entertained in official circles.

The administration is largely divorced from this important section of the commercial community.[2] This absence of contact renders the Levantines unfamiliar with the ways of the officials, and it enhances their difficulties of presenting their case or stating their grievances in an acceptable form. The dislike of the Levantines results in unfavourable treatment to them in the many matters which are controlled by the authorities, and in which officers possess a measure of discretionary power.

---

[1] Chapter 18 below.

[2] My visits to West Africa provided a trivial but relevant example. Levantines were not invited to the meetings with business men arranged for me under official auspices. I had to make my own arrangements to meet them. Inquiries addressed to officials tended to elicit the reply that they did not know many Levantines; moreover, they were not anxious to get to know them, partly because contacts with members of these communities might arouse suspicions of corruption.

4. SOME POLITICAL REPERCUSSIONS OF THESE
PREFERENCES AND ATTITUDES

The attitudes and predilections mentioned in the previous section are frequently rooted in supposed administrative advantages, including the supposed benefits of apparently tidy and neatly organized economies. But, in fact, most of these advantages are likely to be short-lived and are often only illusory. Apart from the adverse economic consequences which may flow from these preferences, there may also be unfortunate political repercussions. This is in evidence in West Africa, where the predominance of a few large firms, and the outstanding position of the United Africa group, create delicate situations. This concern occupies such a preponderant position and handles so large a share of trade, that it cannot fail to serve as a target for political discontent and criticism. It is expatriate; it operates on a very large scale; over a large field its share in the trade renders it inevitable that it should influence the market; and particularly in some areas its customers and servants often feel a sense of dependence owing to the comparatively restricted number of alternatives. Such a large firm is likely to attract more criticism and discontent than would be aroused by several smaller firms together handling an equivalent volume of trade. Moreover, active manifestations of discontent or disagreement with such a large organization have more disruptive effects. A strike against the United Africa Company seriously affects the economic life of large areas. The burden of administration, especially of political administration, is thus increased in many ways by the comparatively high degree of concentration, which is strengthened and fostered in many direct and indirect ways by official policy and action.

Administrative preference for dealing with organizations and associations of firms may at times also provoke political tension. African opinion, especially in the Gold Coast, is suspicious of the presence and activities of trade associations which they regard as monopolistic compacts of European firms directed against African interests. Africans in any case resent the presence and power of European firms; these sentiments are sharpened by the knowledge or belief that some of these firms act in concert, or are treated with as a group by government. Here again the administrative expediency of negotiating with organizations may be short-sighted.

It is recognized that with considerable government intervention in economic life it may be indispensable for the administration to consult those who possess expert and intimate knowledge of the trade, and whose interests are likely to be affected; and this may be possible only through their associations. But unless this reliance on trade associations and on representative committees is managed carefully and is confined to fields where it is not likely to be used to protect certain firms against competition from others, it may promote economic restrictionism, strengthen concentration in trade and increase political tension.

5. GENERAL ADMINISTRATION OF WARTIME TRADE CONTROLS

The history of the wartime administration of the principal controls of external trade in West Africa provides exceptionally clear examples both of the official attitudes and preferences mentioned in this chapter, and of their economic and political results; and it provides lessons of more than historical interest. It should be understood, however, that these controls are no longer in force. Import controls still operate, of course, but the principles on which they are administered differ greatly from those discussed in this chapter.

In effect, and in some cases even formally, the framing and administration of the most important controls were handed over by the British and West African governments to the Association of West African Merchants, a trade association with headquarters in the United Kingdom whose full members were a small group of large merchants. It represented only one section, albeit an important one, of West African trade; it comprised the large merchants who were parties to the Merchandise Agreement and to the various produce-buying syndicates of pre-war years. In the operation of the wartime controls only the full members played any significant part within the Association; in the import trade these were, for all practical purposes, the members of the Merchandise Agreement group. Neither Levantine firms, nor firms with headquarters outside Europe, were full members of the Association of West African Merchants.

At the outbreak of war it was obviously convenient, perhaps even necessary, for the government to take advantage of the existence of a trade organization with headquarters in the United Kingdom. The Association had much expert knowledge of West African trade, maintained widespread trade contacts, and was fully representative of the major share of both West African import and export trade. This possibly necessary step would not have had serious and lasting effects if it had not been coupled with important omissions. Only sporadic and incomplete attempts were made to replace reliance on the Association of West African Merchants by the formulation of a coherent policy against which to judge the need for and results of particular measures of control. This was the position even after the establishment in 1942 of the West African Produce Control Board and of the West African Supply Centre.

A coherent policy enunciated independently of trade interests, though framed after consulting them, would have been necessary even if the Association of West African Merchants had included all merchants of substance. This, however, was not the case. Little cognizance was taken of the presence of one or two important independent merchants, and of the serious rivalry between these firms and the full members of the Association. Moreover, the political dangers of prolonged and exclusive official recognition of the Association were neglected. This was unexpected in view of the widespread and explicit distrust of the Association by African opinion, and in view of the realization by several senior local administrators of the political dangers of the high degree of concentration in trade, the dominant position of the largest firm, and the sense of dependence of the population on the largest firms. For some years before the war suspicion and resentment were felt against the full members of the Association, who frequently acted in concert, and against the market-sharing arrangements which were the most important form of this concerted action. Yet it was this group which was singled out for official recognition, and the market-sharing practices were given official support and sanction with only a slight change in terminology.

6. THE ADMINISTRATION OF WARTIME IMPORT TRADE CONTROLS

The operation of the wartime export controls is of special interest as it affords a clear example of the introduction of a highly important set of regulations not required by the exigencies of war; the export quotas provide perhaps the least ambiguous example of certain results of these controls. This system is reviewed in Chapter 19, where it is shown that it was essentially an officially supported continuation and extension of the pre-war produce-buying syndicates. The present section is concerned with the operation of import control. Though they cannot be shown so clearly, the results of this control in some ways resembled those of the export quotas.

The official objectives of the wartime control of the import trade were somewhat vague and undefined. The primary objective was the maintenance of the level of supplies. But in the endeavour to secure supplies, especially supplies on offer, it was never explicit whether the controllers should have regard to West African interests only, or whether they should also consider the needs of the Commonwealth, or of the Allies as a whole.

In addition there was a secondary objective, namely, to maintain the *status quo* among merchants whenever restrictions were imposed. This secondary objective frequently clashed with the primary objective, and was, moreover, highly ambiguous in itself, for there are inevitably several sources of ambiguity in the interpretation of the term. In attempting to preserve the *status quo* decisions have to be made on a variety of matters, and these decisions materially affect the relative position of different firms. A base period has to be selected; it has to be decided whether the maintenance of the *status quo* is to apply separately to each source of supply or to a commodity in the aggregate,[1] whether the principle is to be applied to newly developed sources of supply, whether otherwise unrestricted supplies from a particular source should be brought under import control solely in order to maintain the relative position of different firms (this last issue was of particular quantitative importance in the administration of import control in West Africa), and whether account is to be taken of export controls imposed in supplying countries, and if so, how these are to be allowed for. It has also to be decided to which of the following alternatives the *status quo* should apply: the trade in individual commodities, the trade in all controlled commodities, the trade in all commodities, or possibly even the import and export trade together. Again, in the assessment of the maintenance of the *status quo* allowance may or may not be made for important incidental advantages accruing to the firms participating in the official machinery of control.

Thus an attempt to maintain one kind of *status quo* necessarily upsets some or all others. In changing circumstances, judgement must play a large part in the operation of controls, especially import controls. This makes clear the error of relying in the operation of controls solely on the advice of a particular group. Even public-spirited advisers are likely to be influenced by subconscious consideration of the interest of the firms they represent, which are all too plausibly equated with the general interest, particularly where the guiding objectives are sometimes contradictory and generally vague.

Without intending deliberately to take advantage of their position, the advisers will be in a position to suggest that if a certain firm makes special efforts to develop a new and unrestricted source of supply this trade should not be counted in the computation of the *status quo*, as this would sacrifice supplies otherwise available; on the other hand, they could argue that this trade would upset the *status quo*, and should there-

---

[1] This particular ambiguity is important when the available volume of supplies and their sources of origin vary and where the shares of different importers in the trade from different sources are unequal. In circumstances when some sources of supply disappear and others are developed, an attempt to maintain the *status quo* in the sense of unaltered shares in the total trade from all sources necessarily destroys the *status quo* in the trade from particular sources. It necessarily upsets the previously existing proportions between importers from a particular source, and might ruin a trader whose previous business was largely with a specific source of supply and whose share in the total trade was small.

fore be placed under control to preserve fair shares. Again, the adverse effects of a particular measure might be considered as inevitable hardships of the war; but, on the other hand, they might be thought to entitle those affected to receive compensating advantages in other directions. These would be only two instances among many where contradictory opinions and advice could be equally reasonably advanced, because of underlying ambiguities and incompatibility of objectives.

With the best of intentions controls must operate to the disadvantage of some interests. Where the control is advised or is operated by one group of interests, it is only too probable that it will tend relatively to benefit that group, the more so because any regulation affecting them adversely would either be vigorously opposed or used as a bargaining counter for other concessions. These results were noticeable in West Africa, where the administration of controls during the Second World War and the early post-war years was much influenced by the advice of one group of firms.

7. SOME REPERCUSSIONS OF WARTIME AND POST-WAR TRADE CONTROLS

In retrospect the economic consequences of the wartime controls are clear. The position of the Association of West African Merchants was strengthened. Their collaboration grew closer and more comprehensive. Controls also served to curb the activities of outside competitors. This support came at an opportune moment, since shortly before the war the competitors of the Association of West African Merchants were making substantial progress in groundnut and cocoa buying, as well as in the import trade of the Gold Coast. The wartime controls and their actual implementation not only barred the further progress of these competitors but in some cases actually reversed the trends.

The adverse political results of the administration of trade controls were much magnified by certain partly adventitious circumstances. In 1946 and 1947 the shortage of consumer goods was still acute, prices were very high and the import trade was extremely profitable. This created a tense situation, especially in the Gold Coast, where the authorities and the Association of West African Merchants were often blamed for the shortages and the prevailing high prices. It is almost certain that there was little the importers could do to relieve the shortages; but the high degree of concentration in the import trade made it particularly difficult to refute such charges as those of rigging the market, profiteering and monopolistic creation of scarcity. The official recognition of the Association of West African Merchants drew the criticism that the controls were unfairly administered and that they harmed the interests of consumers. It meant that any criticism of the

Association of West African Merchants was also directed at the government.

The tension set up by these forces was aggravated by the proceedings of the Martindale and Sachs Commissions which were much publicized locally. The reactions produced by these various influences and events contributed to the Accra riots of 1948.

The policies which led to these unfortunate results sprang to a considerable extent from the official attitudes discussed earlier in this chapter. Considerations of administrative convenience, preference for dealing with large firms and associations, the desire for an appearance of tidiness in administration, and the distrust of Levantine firms all played their part. Immediate advantages of administrative convenience were perhaps the most important; there can be few examples where these were bought at so high an eventual cost.

CHAPTER 12

EFFECTS OF THE IMMIGRATION POLICY ON
MONOPOLY AND COMPETITION

In West Africa (as in many other countries) governmental policies have
often had restrictive effects and have served to strengthen concentration
in trade. Those who have framed and administered these measures have
rarely deliberately intended to produce those results. Nevertheless, the
consequences have not been less serious or far-reaching for having been
largely unintended and unforeseen. The control of immigration is
among the most important of official policies to which this conclusion
applies. The immigration policy of the West African administrations is
a principal factor shielding the existing firms from effective competition.
Further, the immigration policy has important economic effects on the
formation of capital, on the provision of employment opportunities, and
on the general development of West Africa.

I. PURPOSE AND SCOPE OF THE DISCUSSION

The purpose of the discussion should not be misunderstood. Although
it is largely critical of the immigration policy of the last few decades, its
concern is with description and analysis of this policy and not with
recommendations for its revision, an issue which lies, of course, outside
the scope of this study. In so far as a discussion has any definite
implication for policy, it is the desirability of bringing into the open
certain dilemmas (illustrated in this chapter) underlying the objectives
of the current policy; and of bringing home to the local population
certain results of a policy followed largely in accordance with the
demands of a vocal minority.

Nor is it intended to suggest that either the problems of the control of
immigration, or the policies actually pursued differ fundamentally from
those often encountered in other countries, whether self-governing or
dependent. Certain important features of the situation in West Africa
are indeed unusual. The number of expatriates is extremely small, and
the contribution to economic development by comparatively small
numbers of additional immigrants might be considerable. The degree
of concentration in trade is exceptionally high, and the competition
offered to the existing firms by additional independent expatriate
merchants might have important effects in the market situation. But
the political and social resistance in West Africa to the admission of
immigrants, and the possible complications created by their presence,

are in many ways similar to these phenomena elsewhere; this should not be overlooked in reading the description and analysis of the West African policy presented here.

2. THE NUMBER OF EXPATRIATES IN NIGERIA AND THE GOLD COAST

A brief summary of the numbers of expatriates in West Africa is necessary as a background to the discussion of the immigration policy. As is well known, there is no substantial non-African population. Nevertheless, the comparative insignificance of the actual numbers, especially of Levantines and Indians, is not often realized. According to the 1931 census (the last population census in Nigeria) there were at that time 5442 non-Africans in Nigeria in a population of well over 20 millions. Syrians numbered 419 and Indians 97; Lebanese were not shown separately and were presumably included with Syrians. These figures almost certainly understate the true numbers, but they indicate the general order of magnitude. In February 1949 an official reply in the Legislative Council in Lagos gave the number of Syrian and Lebanese adults at just over 1000. In the Gold Coast, according to the 1948 census, there were at the time 6770 non-Africans (two-thirds of whom were British) in a total population of about 4¼ millions. Lebanese and Syrians together totalled 1370 and Indians 197.[1] Moreover, many of the expatriates are temporary residents.[2]

These low numbers are primarily the result of a consistent immigration policy. In view of the climatic conditions it is probable that even without this policy there might not have been any mass immigration into West Africa; but the stringency of the regulations and the large number of applications that are being refused make it clear that the policy is largely effective.

3. THE OBJECTIVES AND ASSUMPTIONS OF IMMIGRATION POLICY IN WEST AFRICA

Over the last ten or twenty years the essentials of immigration policy as they affect the structure of trade have been similar in Nigeria and the Gold Coast. This is still so today. The texts of the immigration

[1] It is certain that the figures are of the order indicated, and are far below the popular estimates which are sometimes shared by government officials, and which put the figures at tens of thousands. Thus a senior Gold Coast government officer in a responsible position suggested to me in September 1950 that the Indians and Syrians (the latter including Lebanese) in the Gold Coast each numbered about 15,000.

[2] It would seem that even a substantial increase in these small numbers is not likely to bring about the problems often (though by no means always) associated with a multi-racial society (cf. § 11 below).

ordinances (as well as of the regulations issued under these) in force in Nigeria and the Gold Coast are identical in all provisions of substance,[1] and administrative practice is alike in aim and emphasis. The policies can therefore be treated together.

There has also been over this period a somewhat greater continuity of policy than is sometimes believed. The control has become more severe, especially in its application to Levantines, but its general principles have been largely unchanged for a considerable period. When the Gold Coast government published a *Statement on Immigration Procedure* in a special number of the official *Gold Coast Gazette* in February 1949, defining the policy of the administration, there were protests in Great Britain, some of which were lodged by the merchant firms. This statement was more explicit and uncompromising than previous official pronouncements, especially in declaring that restrictions applied to British and non-British subjects alike. But the statement itself indicates that it was a summary of long-established policy rather than the announcement of a new policy.[2]

In an assessment of the operation and results of immigration policy, administrative procedure and practice are more important than the legislation and the regulations serving as a broad framework. This makes precise documentation impossible; but the principles of both official policy and administrative action are quite clear, and have been outlined to me by senior officials in Nigeria and the Gold Coast. They have also been confirmed by reference to statistics of immigration and by numerous discussions with firms which have been affected by the policy and its administration.

The principal declared objectives of immigration policy have been, first, the avoidance of possible complications arising from the presence of substantial non-African populations, and secondly, the promotion of the economic development and progress of the African population.[3]

[1] In Nigeria the immigration ordinance is Chapter 89 of 1947. In the Gold Coast it is Ordinance No. 7 of 1947. Administrative regulations have been gazetted under each of these.

[2] The statement of February 1949 was in effect a summary of instructions by the Executive Council to the Principal Immigration Officer. It was published on the front page of a *Gazette Extraordinary* containing little else, and in that form it could not fail to arouse much interest. As a result of protests in this country it was reviewed and replaced in June 1949. The revised statement was inconspicuously placed in the middle of an ordinary issue of the *Gazette*. The substance of the statement was the same as in the original, but the change in tenor and the method of publication ensured that it did not arouse comment.

[3] In the words of the Gold Coast official statement of February 1949: 'It has long been the policy of the Gold Coast Government to prevent non-African settlement in the Gold Coast. The purpose of this is to ensure that the indigenous population should be allowed to progress without the eventual complications of pressure from powerful

The translation of this general policy into practical administration has been largely influenced by two important assumptions. First, it is assumed that the amount of trade available is broadly fixed, so that an increase in the number of non-Africans in trade diminishes the opportunities available to Africans. A possible exception is admitted in direct importing on a large scale, or in the trade in technical goods and equipment, for which it is recognized that Africans to a certain extent lack the necessary skill and capital. Secondly, it is sometimes assumed that an increase in the number of expatriate trading enterprises would strengthen their monopoly in external trade. The analysis of immigration policy in this chapter considers the compatibility of the two main objectives and the validity of these assumptions.

4. GENERAL PRINCIPLES OF THE ADMINISTRATION OF THE IMMIGRATION POLICY

Expatriates are admitted into West Africa only if the immigration authorities are satisfied that their entry will not be detrimental to the economic development of the local population. The authorities have powers, which they use extensively, to limit severely the numbers admitted. The general aim is not to increase, and if possible to reduce, the number of non-Africans in the territories. The authorities are also allowed a large measure of discretion in deciding whether the activities of a would-be immigrant are likely to benefit or obstruct the progress and interests of the local population.

In the course of administration certain directing principles or criteria have emerged. First, the bar is much stricter against trading activities than against manufacturing; a prospective industrialist is admitted more readily than a trader. Secondly, the establishment of new expatriate semi-wholesale and retail trading enterprises is wholly barred. This is generally and confusingly referred to as barring expatriates from retailing or local trade.

Retail trade in this context differs greatly from the ordinary meaning attached to the term, and does not refer solely to selling to the ultimate consumer. The official interpretation of the term retailing usually refers to transactions which are several stages removed from sale to the ultimate consumer. Here again a substantial latitude is allowed to the authorities in determining whether a particular activity is wholesale or retail trading. In general, any breaking of bulk of imports appears to be regarded as retailing, even though the size of the transaction makes it clear that it is far removed from sale to the ultimate consumer. Thus

and strongly entrenched non-African interests, not only in the political sphere but also in the commercial and economic spheres.'

a senior officer of the Department of Commerce and Industries in Nigeria said that recently the immigration authorities had refused to permit a Lebanese firm of importers to continue trading if it opened bales of textiles, made assortments of the contents, and repacked them for sale in bale lots of assorted textiles. This activity was said to be semi-wholesaling, and the firm had a licence to operate only as a wholesaler.

Thirdly, the general administration of immigration policy is directed with special severity against Levantines and Indians, and especially against the former, who are probably most numerous among the applicants for immigration. Their trading activities are regarded as particularly unproductive, and they are the objects of a special degree of mistrust and apprehension in the eyes of the immigration authorities.

Similar principles are applied in the admission of employees. Trading firms receive immigration permits for a limited number of expatriate employees. The numbers are restricted in accordance with a quota, based either on the maximum number of employees in a past period, or on the numbers engaged at present. The numbers can be maintained at this level by means of holiday reliefs or replacements for retiring personnel; except in special circumstances increases are not allowed. Newly established firms are granted permission to employ expatriate staff in accordance with the requirements of their trade as approved by the immigration authorities. These restrictions apply usually to administrative and executive staff only; technically qualified personnel are often excluded from the quota. In the application of these principles the police have substantial discretionary authority.

5. GENERAL EFFECTS OF THE IMMIGRATION POLICY

The immigration regulations greatly strengthen the position of the established firms, which they shield from the competition of newcomers in many different ways. This conclusion is not substantially affected by the fact that the entry of new firms into direct importing is not completely barred. The permission of the immigration authorities has to be obtained even here. This may be refused, and is likely to be refused where the applicant is a Levantine, or where he cannot show that he has the capital which the authorities consider necessary.

The official immigration restrictions bearing on the so-called semi-wholesale and retail trades in imported merchandise (which, however, are very largely wholesale activities) have certain obvious and direct effects on these trades, as well as other less obvious but equally important, or more important, effects on the general trading situation, especially on the extent of competition and concentration in direct importing. Immigration restrictions operate on the so-called semi-wholesale and retail trades in three ways: the entry of new expatriate firms is practically prohibited; the expansion of existing firms is hampered by control over the immigration of non-African staff; and the spread of the activities of purely importing firms into other stages of distribution is curtailed by both types of control.

The direct result of this policy is to reduce the degree of competition in these trades and increase the profits and strengthen the position of the firms already established in these non-importing activities; the established firms include, of course, the large vertically integrated merchant houses.

It is often argued that competition in semi-wholesaling and retailing will be preserved by the entry of African intermediaries to take the place of the excluded or restricted expatriates. Indeed, this has always been a principal assumption of the immigration policy. It is assumed that African traders can adequately perform the necessary functions of distribution after first importation. Whatever may be the merits of the policy on wider grounds, this particular argument is invalid, for if African traders in the required numbers were as efficient as expatriate traders there would have been no need for official exclusion or restraint of the latter. This is not to imply that Africans are not capable of performing these functions at all, but that excluded expatriate competitors can do so on better terms and at lower cost than those African merchants who owe their trade directly to the shelter provided by the regulations. This conclusion can be deduced from the fact that the regulations have to be used to exclude would-be entrants and to curb the activities of existing firms. It is confirmed by the difficulties experienced by the United Africa Company in finding suitable local traders to take over its smaller-scale activities.[1]

The restrictions on entry and expansion in the stages of trade after importation substantially affect the degree of competition and of concentration in direct importing. There is likely to be a smaller total volume of trade, a corollary of the restrictions on the activities of more efficient traders with lower costs. Moreover, as a result of the restrictions non-African firms are less likely to grow to a stature and size at which they would be able to enter direct importing in competition with the established firms of importers. Further, the market for the services and merchandise of new or growing non-integrated importers is narrowed, thus weakening this possible source of increased competition in the import trade. The presence and possible growth of African firms in the non-importing stages of distribution are unlikely either to provide new

[1] Further confirmation is furnished by the difficulties experienced by some of the large importers, particularly the United Africa Company, in diverting their trade from Levantine to African traders except on unfavourable terms. For political reasons the policy is nevertheless followed to a considerable extent.

entrants into the import trade, or to provide so satisfactory a market for rising non-integrated importing firms. This is suggested by the higher costs and more modest qualifications of those African traders who owe their position to the operation of the restrictions. Their weakness in capital resources, combined with other disabilities, suggest that many of these traders are more likely to be tied to particular sources of supply, which again tends to increase the difficulties facing new or small import firms.

The distribution of commodities imported by other merchants is probably the best apprenticeship for subsequent entry into the import trade itself; it may also provide a source of capital to the hard-working and efficient trader. Experience of the local market, knowledge of customers and the possession of capital are necessary in the West African import trade where credit has to be granted extensively and where lack of experience or of capital tells heavily against the new-comer. The restriction or control of entry into non-importing trading activities therefore closes a particularly suitable avenue of entry into the import trade itself.

The diary of the founder of the firm of John Holt and Company not only provides a vivid account of the growth of this well-known West African enterprise, but is also an illuminating case study of entry into the import trade and into industrial activities from humble beginnings in small-scale wholesaling and retailing.

The first John Holt went out to West Africa as a clerk, storekeeper and foreman in the employ of the British consul at Fernando Po, who was a trader and had two shops and a farm. After the death of the owner Holt managed the small trading enterprise for some time for his widow, and later bought it from her out of his own savings, beginning to trade on his own account. Most of his trade was of a type which today would be regarded as retail trade. Eventually he became the founder of a highly respected enterprise, which today is one of the foremost firms of direct importers in West Africa. Its activities include the operation of a shipping line and a river fleet, and it controls or is associated with several industrial enterprises.

John Holt went to West Africa as a commercial employee without capital; the enterprise in which he was employed and which he subse-quently took over was a retail business or at best only a petty whole-saling establishment; and the activities of the business included trade in local foodstuffs. Having started trading on his own account he eventually established a direct importing business. All these activities are at present either barred, or controlled by statute, or prohibited by administrative practice. All his earlier activities would today be barred or hedged about with crippling restrictions. Indeed, they would fall foul of the basic principles of the present immigration policy.

6. SPECIAL ASPECTS AND RESULTS OF THE IMMIGRATION POLICY

Certain further specific aspects of the immigration policy and of its administration reinforce its effects in shielding the large firms against effective competition from newcomers and from the growth of smaller firms.

The size of the expatriate staffs which the trading firms are permitted to employ is to some extent regulated on an informal quota basis. Applications for permission to employ non-technical expatriate staff tend to be considered favourably if the total number of such staff employed by the firm does not exceed the number employed at some earlier date, usually a pre-war year. In the course of the 1930's and in the early war years the larger established firms, especially the constituent parts of the United Africa group, greatly reduced the number of European personnel in their employ by closing down outlying stations, by effecting various other economies, and by substituting, wherever possible, African personnel for expatriate staff. To a certain extent they have been able subsequently to base their applications for immigrant staff on the larger numbers formerly employed, and to that extent the restrictions do not bear so harshly on them. Similarly, most of the larger firms have technical departments or associate companies specializing in the supply and maintenance of equipment. Technicians are not normally subjected to the ordinary immigration quota restrictions. They can thus be employed to free other personnel for administrative duties; moreover, they add to the reserves available as reliefs for personnel away on leave or to help to deal with exceptional pressure of business. The smaller firms generally employ few expatriate staff and have little or no reserve of personnel; and they are apt to find it difficult to obtain permission quickly to secure even replacements in an emergency.

Immigration permits are usually granted on condition that the recipient engages in a specific activity or in a particular employment. Changes in occupation or employment are therefore very difficult or impossible. These conditions bar an immigrant employee from starting a trading concern of his own which might perhaps gradually develop (as it has often done in the past) into a substantial competitor of the existing firms. As has been shown, in West African conditions these restraints seriously affect new entry, the degree of concentration and the extent of competition in direct importing.

In the administration of the immigration regulations the police authorities have much discretion. In particular, they have to decide whether an enterprise is in their opinion likely to promote or to retard the interests of the African population; and their judgement is likely to be influenced by the belief that the activities of expatriates tend to diminish the opportunities for Africans. They are likely to have before them at any given time a large number of applications, and almost on principle they are unlikely to grant them all. In such circumstances the discretion is likely to be exercised in favour of the large and well-established firms whose executives are almost certainly better known to the authorities than newcomers or the principals of small and comparatively recently established firms.[1]

The practical results of immigration control are affected by the marked official dislike of Levantine traders. Levantine firms are usually medium-sized or small enterprises on which the immigration regulations bear harshly. As many of them are not direct importers they fall under the general head of retail trade. They were established when restrictions were not so severe as they are at present, but they feel the pressure of present policy in their attempts to obtain expatriate personnel. Specific examples were readily provided to me in the course of two visits to West Africa. In the Gold Coast the future of a small furniture workshop employing some thirty Africans was in jeopardy in 1950 owing to the refusal of the immigration authorities to sanction the employment of one Lebanese in a wholesale textile business from which the capital for this enterprise was derived. Levantine enterprises, even when largely or even exclusively engaged in importing, find it difficult to secure permission for additional staff.

The Levantines in West Africa represent types of immigrant who have an important part to perform in the economic development of many under-developed countries. Although they are rarely highly educated, they are resourceful, industrious, enterprising, and exceptionally gifted in the perception of economic opportunity. They are independent of existing commercial interests, and in many branches of trading activity are important and effective competitors of the large European firms. As they are prepared to accept a lower remuneration than western European personnel, the services they render are performed at a correspondingly lower cost. In West Africa, as in many other parts of the world, the immigrants who could contribute most to economic development are regarded with the greatest suspicion by influential sections of the administration, their admission particularly resisted, and their activities restricted under pressure from local sectional interests and from already established expatriate commercial interests.

The implications of these considerations are reinforced in West

---

[1] This attitude and its corollaries reflect merely a preference for the large and well-established firm among expatriate enterprises, and not a preference in favour of expatriate against African enterprise.

Africa by the high cost of maintaining British personnel. In 1949 the then managing director of the United Africa Company in a public address estimated the cost to his company of employing and maintaining the most junior European employee in West Africa at over £1400 a year. The cost of employing and maintaining a Levantine is much lower, and is almost certainly less than half this figure. New enterprises, which are in some circumstances well advised to start on a small scale, cannot afford to carry such costly British personnel in the early stages of their growth; their commercial prospects would be improved if they were able to employ less expensive Levantine.

7. IMMIGRATION RESTRICTIONS AND COMPETITION IN TRADE

The assumption that restrictions on the activites of expatriate traders reduces the monopoly elements in West African trade conceals an important ambiguity in the use of the term monopoly.[1] The restrictions on expatriate traders, and particularly on the entry of newcomers, clearly promote monopoly and/or oligopoly, in that they maintain the existing degree of concentration. They thus limit the range and efficacy of independent alternatives available to those who use the services of traders. Indeed, these restrictions are an important buttress to the high degree of concentration in West African trade. On the other hand, restrictions on the activities of expatriates tends to give African traders a larger share of a smaller volume of trade in certain stages of distribution. But this does not mean a reduction in the degree of monopoly or of concentration from the point of view of the customers of the traders.

As a result of the restrictive control of immigration, the protected firms, both expatriate and African, operate in a less competitive environment in which profit margins tend to be higher and more secure, and in which the possibilities of formal or informal price-fixing and market-sharing arrangements are increased. The rest of the African community (producers, consumers and other traders) tends to receive their services on less favourable terms. The fact that some of the beneficiaries are African traders does not alleviate the impact of reduced competition and of higher profit margins. Moreover, those African traders who owe their existence as traders to the immigration restrictions are not as effective or efficient competitors as the excluded expatriates; therefore the real dependence of the population on the large and established expatriate firms is increased.

There is a contradiction in certain current African demands. The Africans protest against the power of the existing firms and particularly

[1] Which has already been discussed (cf. note to Chapter 7).

against the power of the United Africa Company and of the other members of the Merchandise Agreement group. But they also protest against the admission of new expatriate firms, or the growth of other expatriate firms, which could offer effective competition to these large firms.

8. THE EFFECTS OF THE IMMIGRATION POLICY ON THE GROWTH OF CAPITAL AND ON THE CREATION OF EMPLOYMENT OPPORTUNITIES

The immigration policy has important effects on the growth of the West African economies. An earlier chapter has discussed the productivity of trade in securing the most economic distribution of existing resources and in promoting the growth of resources.[1] The role of traders in the accumulation of capital and in its productive use has been stressed as being of special significance.

The restrictions on the activities of certain traders and the exclusion of others necessarily retard the growth of capital. Unemployment caused by lack of co-operant productive resources, including capital and skill, is among the most serious economic and political problems in West Africa.[2] Much of the missing administrative and technical skill is furnished by immigrant expatriates, and the trading activities of European and Levantine enterprises are an important source of capital formation. This is so even where the owners or employees enter West Africa without capital. They create capital in the course of their activities by consuming less than their earnings, and the capital thus created is as useful in raising production and providing employment as if it had been brought in by the management in the first instance.

In the course of their mercantile activities the trading firms gain a knowledge of local conditions which enables them to discover useful opportunities and to take advantage of the most profitable employment for their capital, possibly in spheres other than trading. In West Africa most of the comparatively small number of successful industrial enterprises have been founded without official assistance by the trading firms. Examples include saw-milling, tanning, beer brewing, the manufacture of plywood, soap, furniture, groundnut oil and stationery. The capital and skill employed in these activities provide substantial employment for African labour.

The operation of the immigration regulations also tends to discourage the extension of trade into more remote areas where the presence of traders would stimulate production, both by making consumer goods available and by providing a market for agricultural products even where production is small. The curtailment of the activities of Levantines,

---

[1] Chapter 2 above.   [2] Chapter 1 above.

whether as employees or as traders on their own account, bears particularly harshly on the development of trade and thus on the growth of production in more remote rural areas. Levantine traders or firms employing Levantines can operate on a slower rate of turnover and on a smaller volume of trade than is necessary to sustain British or western European personnel; and they can thus trade in areas where production is not so intensive or where the population is more scattered.

A listing of the specific functions performed by trade and traders is apt to distract attention from the essential and pervasive influence of expatriate enterprise in the opening up and economic development of the West African territories. Professor Hancock has justly discussed the economic development of West Africa in terms of the extension of the traders' frontier.[1] The part played by traders in the promotion of economic growth is today less immediately obvious but hardly less valuable than in the past.

9. CRITIQUE OF THE ASSUMPTIONS OF THE PRESENT IMMIGRATION POLICY

The assumptions underlying West African immigration policy[2] are incorrect in the form in which they are usually stated. The volume of trade is not fixed: restrictions on the activity of expatriate firms do not increase but diminish the economic activity of Africans, retard the growth of the volume of trade, and tend to strengthen the elements of monopoly in West African trade and to reduce the alternatives open to the customers of the traders.

If there were no restrictions on expatriates, some African traders would be displaced. But against these losses to some Africans there would be much larger gains to the Africans as consumers and as producers using the services of intermediaries. Moreover, the expansion of trade would benefit African traders in those branches of the trade which would remain in African hands.[3] On all but the most extreme assumptions the absolute volume of trade handled by African traders would increase, even though some African traders were displaced in certain branches of trade. This high probability, based on the increase in trade resulting from the more effective use of existing resources, becomes a certainty when the results of the activities of expatriates on the growth of resources are also considered. In short, on strictly economic grounds there is certain to be a net gain to the African population as a whole from the expansion of the activities of expatriate traders and from the

[1] *Survey of British Commonwealth Affairs*, Part II, vol. II, ch. II, passim.
[2] Cf. § 3 of this chapter.
[3] Quantitatively the most important of these are the concluding stages in the distribution of merchandise and the initial stages in the assembly of export produce.

reduction in the costs of trading services; and there is a high probability that this would increase the demand for the services of African traders in the aggregate.[1]

10. POLITICAL ECONOMY OF THE IMMIGRATION REGULATIONS

In an assessment of the motives of the immigration restrictions, of their method of operation and of their results, it is necessary to remember that those who benefit from the activities of the expatriate traders rarely appreciate this fact clearly, while those who suffer or may suffer from their competition are highly sensitive to this danger to their interests; further, it is also necessary to take note of considerations beyond those which fall within the purview of technical economic analysis. This section deals briefly with certain quasi-political issues related to these matters.

The displacement of some African traders as the result of the less restricted entry of expatriate firms would be obvious both to themselves and to the public generally, whereas the benefits would be widely diffused, and some of these (the benefits resulting from the growth of the economy rather than from the more efficient use of existing resources) would permeate the economy only gradually.[2] The displacement of African traders would tend to take place among distributors who operate on a fairly substantial scale, while the benefits (largely unperceived) would accrue largely to the small-scale traders and to the final consumers. This localization of the losses to particular African trading interests would give rise to the impression that the subservience of Africans to the expatriate traders had increased. It would also strengthen the impression that the African population is cut off from the outside world by an impenetrable layer of alien trade.

For these reasons it would be difficult for the administration to reverse its immigration policy, or even to modify it materially. The vocal section of the public is recruited largely from among those African traders who benefit, or at least appear to benefit, from present restrictions. The much larger numbers of Africans who would benefit from a relaxation of restrictions are unlikely to appreciate that they would; moreover, they are largely inarticulate and uninfluential.

---

[1] It is sometimes suggested that the given level of development of which a territory is capable would in any case be reached sooner or later and that development is therefore not permanently restricted by the effects of the immigration policy. This argument is considered in Chapter 3 above.

[2] This is an instance of the general tendency for the competitive relationship between certain groups and participants in economic life to be perceived more readily than the complementary (or mutually beneficial) relationship. This asymmetry in the perception of gains and losses is discussed in some detail in Chapter 3 above and in the note appended to it.

The West African administrations clearly dread the political consequences of attempting to influence African opinion in a direction contrary to what appears to be a strong current trend, and are apprehensive of adding even slightly to the number of non-Africans. Yet it seems doubtful whether the official policy is the result only of political considerations and pressure. In general, the authorities seem to show little inclination to influence African opinion in assessing the full results of the restrictive immigration policy. Indeed, they seem to share the belief that an increase in the activities of expatriate traders (with the possible exception of those exclusively engaged in direct importing) diminishes the opportunities and damages the interests of the African population. They do not seem to be clearly aware of the role of trade and of expatriate traders in promoting the growth of capital in suitable hands, and thus in providing additional employment to Africans. There is also a failure to realize that the economic interests of different groups of Africans are not the same, and that the special interests of sectional groups do not coincide with the interests of the general population as purchasers of merchandise, sellers of produce, or as actual or prospective employees and wage-earners.

Even some of the Africans who may benefit in the short run probably lose part or all of the supposed benefits if long-run effects on the growth of the economy are included in the calculation. Meanwhile some of the immediate gains accruing from restriction will go to established expatriate interests, since these also benefit from the reduced competition.

It may be argued that the economic disadvantages of a policy of restriction are temporary, and that they have to be set against the possibly larger advantages resulting from the acquisition by the sheltered African traders of experience and skill in the initiation and management of larger scale mercantile enterprises. Although some benefits of this kind may be expected, they are likely to be small in relation to the costs of the policy. Mercantile skill may be generally acquired at much lower cost by Africans who obtain responsible employment in expatriate firms.

Moreover, the acquisition of experience and skill with the help of protection afforded by substantial restrictions on the activities of expatriate merchants may in some respects mislead the beneficiaries of the policy. It is likely to lead these traders to underestimate the difficulties and requirements of successful participation in external trade, a consideration of some practical importance in a comparatively early stage of economic development. In conjunction with the operation of specific licensing,[1] the immigration restrictions are likely

---

[1] Specific licensing presents all recipients of licences with windfall gains. African traders benefit further from the discrimination in their favour in the administration of licensing.

to strengthen the belief that external trade in the aggregate is fixed in amount; and further, that it normally yields easy profits not commensurate with the service rendered. This would naturally tend to attract numerous entrants into this activity who could make a more valuable contribution to the economy in another occupation. Moreover, the substantial benefits accruing to the favoured groups from these measures tend to divert the interest and efforts of some of the most alert members of the population away from normal commercial activity into politics and especially towards a quest for political influence.

The previous considerations summarize the principal conclusions that may be derived from economic analysis. On a somewhat different plane certain other considerations may be and indeed have been advanced in favour of present immigration policy. Thus it is argued that much African discontent derives from knowledge and rumour of the opulence of expatriate traders; and that the important part played by these communities in the economic life of the colonies is a grievance in itself. The feelings of dissatisfaction are not assuaged even where it is realized, as it very rarely is, that the activities of the expatriate traders are productive and that their wealth is not secured at the expense of the African community whose incomes are increased. The implied corollary is that the total satisfaction enjoyed by Africans may be increased by policies which curtail expatriate activities even though African command over material resources is reduced.

While these considerations are relevant, they appear to be much more in evidence among politicians, journalists and larger-scale African traders than among the producers and smaller traders, who seem to be much more concerned with improving their economic position. The inarticulate members of these groups do not necessarily like the expatriate traders; but they are interested in improving the terms on which they deal, and in widening the range of alternatives available to them. In so far as they object to the activities of the expatriate trader, their objections and their resentment often spring at least partly from a sense of dependence on the comparatively few expatriate firms; a dependence which tends to be increased by the restrictive results of the immigration policy.

11. INCOMPATIBILITY OF THE TWO PRINCIPAL OBJECTIVES OF IMMIGRATION POLICY

There is an incompatibility between the twin objectives of immigration policy, the maintenance of a homogeneous population and the promotion of the economic development of these territories. Some of the complications of a mixed racial society may be relieved by a restrictive immigration policy, but only at the cost of retarding economic development and growth. Moreover, concessions to demands for exclusion and restriction of expatriate activities tend to have cumulative effects. In West Africa they encourage similar demands for restrictions on the internal movement of Africans and their freedom to engage in trading activities. The racial and tribal composition of the populations of Nigeria and the Gold Coast furnishes ready pretexts for restrictive measures on inter-regional (even inter-district) trade and migration[1] with further unfavourable effects on economic progress.

It would not be appropriate here to attempt an assessment of the dangers and merits of a multi-racial society or to suggest which of the two objectives of immigration policy should take priority.[2] But failure to appreciate the incompatibility of the two objectives can only cloud the issues involved; and it may well bring about policies of restriction even on internal movement with a resulting fragmentation of these economies.

[1] These tendencies have been discussed in Chapter 3 above.

[2] It might perhaps be possible to devise a system under which a somewhat larger number of immigrants would be admitted than at present, with freedom to change occupations and with some assurance of permission to reside for a given number of years, but without expectation of political rights or assurance of an extension of the stated period of residence. If found politically acceptable, such a system might promote development while avoiding some of the more difficult problems of plural societies. It would be inappropriate to attempt to discuss such wide issues here.

CHAPTER 13

FURTHER INFLUENCES OF OFFICIAL POLICY ON THE TRADING SITUATION

1. COMPARATIVE IRRELEVANCE OF PRESENT IMPORT AND EXPORT CONTROLS TO THE RELATIVE POSITION OF THE NON-AFRICAN (EXPATRIATE) MERCHANT FIRMS

The operation of import licensing and exchange control in West Africa does not at present significantly affect the competitive position of the various trading firms in West Africa; it cannot be said to offer substantial advantages to the large firms.[1] With the exception of certain specified commodities, imports from the sterling area are admitted under open general licence, that is, they can be imported without restrictions on source, quantity or importer. The principal exceptions are sugar, flour, oils and fats, tinned meats and petroleum products. In most cases the reason for these exceptions is that the sterling area is on balance a net importer from dollar sources; in one or two instances the shortage in the United Kingdom is a principal or a contributory factor. Much the same controls apply to imports from soft currency sources outside the sterling area; with the exceptions just listed, they are admitted practically freely.[2]

Imports of all commodities from hard currency sources, as well as the import of certain commodities from other sources, are subject to specific controls (specific licences). At present, therefore, import controls or exchange controls substantially affect only American and Japanese goods, as well as flour, sugar, petroleum products, tinned meats and oils and fats from all sources. In 1949–50 these restrictions affected sources and commodities which in a reasonably prosperous pre-war year represented about 20–25 % of West African imports; as a result of relaxations in 1950 the corresponding proportion in the second half of that year was about 15–20 %. This applies to the pre-war pattern of the import trade; with free importation the proportion of imports from these sources in recent years might have been higher.

---

[1] This chapter describes the operation of import and price controls in force in 1950. The range of import controls was extended in 1952 as a result of the deterioration of the foreign exchange position of the sterling area in the previous year. But these changes did not influence those aspects of the controls relevant to the discussion of this chapter. The relative competitive position of the different expatriate firms, and the discrimination in favour of Africans in the administration of licensing remained substantially unaffected.

[2] For technical reasons the terminology of the import licensing procedure differs from that applied to sterling area sources.

With few exceptions, import licensing does not at present greatly affect the relative position of the different non-African (expatriate) firms. The total volume of controlled imports is, of course, determined by the amount of licences granted. At present the limited licences are not allocated on the basis of past imports by applicants, but principally on the basis of their ability to secure supplies, and to handle and distribute imports. Individual applications are scaled down when in the aggregate they exceed the import limit. The administration is now wholly in the hands of government departments.

In accordance with government policy, African traders are preferentially treated in the administration of specific licensing.[1] It has been shown in Chapter 5 above, that in the importation of staples subject to licensing, notably sugar and flour, African traders handle a substantially larger share than they would in the absence of licensing.

As has already been stated, the importation of standardized staple commodities is not particularly suitable for small traders.[2] It is rarely realized by African traders that they in fact receive preferential treatment. They note that the trade in controlled commodities is particularly profitable, and they resent any limitation on the volume of their imports of these commodities.[3] They do not perceive that the profits are high and easy only because imports are restricted.

By reducing the range of alternatives open to competing merchants import control often strengthens the position of holders of sole agencies and of the beneficiaries of preferential agreements with overseas suppliers. In recent years this factor was of some importance in certain chemicals, certain types of hardware, sewing thread and one or two other commodities. With the relaxation of import controls in 1950 these protective features have become much less marked.

---

[1] This is quite compatible with the frequent drastic reduction in African applications for licences, where these are grossly inflated in relation to the applicant's resources and organization.

[2] In the Gold Coast in the autumn of 1950 some African traders approached the general manager of a large European firm, suggesting that it should handle their licensed imports of flour on a commission basis, as they found it difficult to import and handle economically this standardized staple line.

[3] There are of course frequent instances of individual hardship of the kind familiar in the administration of specific controls. Such instances appear to have occurred especially in connexion with the licensing of flour imports, the administration of which is partly affected by the operation of the International Wheat Agreement. Import licences for flour are valid for comparatively short periods only, and bona fide traders have found that their licences expired before they could exercise them. Some traders have incurred appreciable expense and have suffered losses as a result of short delays in shipment beyond the comparatively brief period of validity of the licences. Moreover, such adverse experience prejudices the applicant's prospects in future application for licences.

The present pattern of control over the export trade is simple. The great bulk of exports is in the hands of the marketing boards which are statutory export monopolies. Their operations do not directly affect the relative position of the trading firms. Their establishment has resulted in a reduction in the status of the former export merchants to that of buying agents on behalf of the marketing boards. This reduction in status (which does not necessarily involve a reduction in profits) may discourage entry into produce buying and into the export trade. Indirectly this also affects the import trade, since successful firms tend to extend their activities from one branch of external trade to another branch. This aspect of the establishment of the marketing boards is thus likely to be welcomed by the merchant firms.

2. THE OPERATION OF PRICE CONTROL

Until comparatively recently, there was extensive price control in Nigeria. By 1950, however, statutory price control was limited to flour, stockfish, whisky and kerosene; the prices of a few other commodities, including sugar, salt, Raleigh bicycles and cigarettes, are now controlled by informal agreements between the government and the importers. In the Gold Coast, price control is very extensive and detailed. It covers the bulk of the standard staple lines of trade in great detail; for example, the official price list for textiles extends to fifteen foolscap pages in the official *Gazette* and contains close on two-and-a-half thousand separate entries covering each line imported by each firm. Forty different brands of whisky are listed separately.[1]

The object of maximum price control is presumably to protect the consumer in times of exceptional scarcity. This aim is not fulfilled by the publication of a list of maximum prices in the *Gazette*. Even where it is observed in the first stage or stages of merchandise distribution, the effectiveness of price control is dubious in the absence of consumer rationing. Formal rationing is impossible as the great majority of West African petty traders and consumers are illiterate. Therefore price control is not effective in the final stages of distribution; the bulk of merchandise subject to price control moves into consumption at open market prices and not at controlled prices. This in turn renders it difficult to maintain the controlled prices at the earlier stages, because to sell at the controlled price amounts to giving the buying intermediary an effortless profit indistinguishable from a free gift of money. Where the importer

---

[1] In the Gold Coast much of the price control is inoperative, since over a large field prevailing prices are often below the controlled maxima. In such circumstances price control has no bearing on the situation, and is ineffective not in the sense of being unenforceable but as being redundant and irrelevant. The analysis in the text refers to situations where the controlled price is lower than the uncontrolled price.

attempts to adhere strictly to controlled prices he has to ration the scarce supplies among the large number of applicants. In some instances he will endeavour to confine supplies to established customers; in other instances to allocate supplies piece by piece on a first-come first-served basis; and in yet other cases to evade the letter or the spirit of price control by conditional sales. In practice these methods tend to be combined. In all these instances, however, the bulk of the sales is to resellers who are likely to sell to further resellers or to consumers at open market prices. The consumers benefit little.[1]

It has been argued that the operation of price control does at least secure for the local population a part, or most, of the windfall which in its absence would accrue to the importers. There is an element of truth in this contention, though the extent of the possible gain is difficult to assess, particularly in view of the prevalence of conditional sales. Where price control is observed at the importing or wholesaling stage, it leads to allocation and informal rationing by the European firms with resulting discontent and accusations of favouritism and of discrimination between communities and individuals. When it is thought necessary to skim off the easy profits of scarcity conditions, the disadvantages just mentioned could be avoided by a system of higher and more flexible import or excise duties, or by special taxation of importers' profits.[2]

One feature of the price-control regulations in the Gold Coast tends to prejudice the interests of the non-integrated intermediaries. The gazetted maximum prices for a wide range of commodities, including all textiles, do not distinguish between wholesale and retail prices. Where importers sell to resellers (which applies to the bulk of textile sales) at the controlled price, the resellers are unable to make any profit without a technical breach of the law. In practice these maxima were charged to resellers in 1948 and 1949 and to some extent in 1950 on those classes of merchandise for which the controlled prices were not above market prices. Under this type of price control the reseller can exist only on sufferance of the importer and/or by an official disregard

---

[1] I repeatedly asked responsible officials for their opinion of the effectiveness of price control, in particular for their estimate of the proportion of controlled commodities moving into consumption at controlled prices. This matter does not seem to have been much considered at the official level. A senior executive of one of the large European firms replied without hesitation that with few exceptions the consumer beneficiaries belong to three classes: the police force, civil servants and employees of importing firms. He was emphatic that the African consumers at large are unaffected. The prominent position of whisky among controlled commodities lends support to this opinion.

[2] There is a disadvantage in removing such profits where the volume of supplies partly depends on the exertions of importers. In such circumstances the removal of profits may discourage importers in seeking out supplies.

of limited breaches of the formal provisions of price control. As it is manifestly impossible for resellers to continue in business unless they can sell at higher prices than are charged to them by importers, the authorities in the Gold Coast in general do not prosecute where the reseller's price is no more than 5 % above the price at which he bought from the importer. However, this is hardly a satisfactory procedure. First, 5 % is not a sufficient gross margin on many lines of textiles to which this rule is principally applied. Secondly, no public announcement appears to have been made of this concession, and resellers are legally still liable to penalties if they sell over the officially gazetted maximum prices, and proceedings can be instituted at the discretion of the authorities. Nor does there appear to be any provision for the second or third link in the distributive chain. Last but not least, official tolerance of, or connivance at, breaches of formal statutory provisions is likely to bring the law into disrespect.

3. BOTTLENECKS, ALLOCATION AND CAPITAL REQUIREMENTS

As a result of the rapid but uneven rate of development in West Africa there have been bottlenecks and frequent instances of serious congestion in the transport system and the ports.[1] The experience of West Africa exemplifies markedly certain difficulties which are apt to appear at a high and unaccustomed level of economic activity. These difficulties have been aggravated by inability to obtain prompt delivery of essential equipment.

A principal effect of consequential delays in the movements of merchandise has been to raise significantly the heavy capital requirements of large-scale trading operations in West Africa. The effect of this on the difficulties of new firms in West African trade has already been analysed. However, this is not the only effect of bottlenecks in transport on the trading situation.

The emergence of bottlenecks immediately tends to stimulate apparent demand at the prevailing price. Users of the commodity or service

---

[1] The contemporary use of the term bottleneck refers to a situation in which the quantity of a commodity or service demanded at the prevailing price exceeds the quantity available, and in which the quantity available cannot be increased sufficiently rapidly to close the gap. It thus refers to a situation where demand exceeds supply at a price which for various reasons has not been raised to the level at which supply and demand are equated. It is an overworked but useful expression which is frequently used in this study in this particular sense. It is assumed here that the prevailing price is above the long-period supply price (i.e. the price at which the demanded supplies will eventually be forthcoming); if the prevailing price were below this price the supplies would not be forthcoming without subsidy.

inflate their demands, partly in order to lay in stocks to meet emergencies, and partly to secure the largest possible share under prospective systems of allocation. Firms and individuals who are not normally in this particular market are tempted to enter, as the fact of the bottleneck indicates that the commercial or market value of the commodity or service is greater than the prevailing price at which supplies, if available, can be bought. Thus the fact that the prevailing price is below the price at which supply and demand would balance (the equilibrium price) tends to bring about an excess demand for two reasons: demand is extended because of the relatively low price; and the realization of supply difficulties (including expectations of the prospective introduction of some form of rationing or allocation), and the possibility of windfall gains through riskless dealings, lead to a further increase in expressed demand.[1]

For various reasons the price charged for the commodity or service may not be raised to the level of the equilibrium price which would ensure the disappearance of the excess demand and thus of the bottleneck. The reluctance to raise the price is often understandably great where the supply of the commodity or service is in official hands, as with West African railways and port facilities which are the most important examples in the present context. Thus rationing and allocation inevitably emerge where the bottleneck appears. This tends to favour the established users as against new entrants or comparative newcomers. Moreover, the larger firms which are regarded as more valuable customers, and which are better able to present their case, tend to be favoured. This result of bottlenecks tends to reinforce the advantage which accrues to large and well-established firms from the increased capital requirements also flowing from the same cause. The authorities discriminate in favour of African enterprise where formal allocation operates, but this does not substantially affect the general tendency.

It is possible that the extent and impact of these difficulties might have been lessened in some measure by modifications of official policy. The frequency and severity of scarcities might well have been reduced if official action had been directed more towards overcoming, or at least easing, specific shortages rather than towards more spectacular ventures of general development. The insistent and indiscriminate demands for rapid and general development seem to have been accepted somewhat too readily, and at times seem even to have been encouraged by the authorities. The difficulties, the costs, and the political dangers of disappointed expectations were not realized. Again, the authorities in pressing for larger supplies of essential equipment or

---

[1] In technical language there is both an extension in demand and a speculative shift in the demand curve.

for allocations of foreign exchange from the British authorities might well have emphasized with some insistence the heavy contributions to the economy of the United Kingdom made by the West African colonies in recent years. Lastly, the authorities might have been bolder in the use of the price mechanism, and especially of fiscal devices (notably import and excise duties), in dealing with bottlenecks and thus in eliminating the need for allocation.[1] Besides the economic results already mentioned, in West African conditions bottlenecks and the consequent necessity for allocation, inevitably result in charges of favouritism and corruption, and they conduce to political tension and discontent.

4. ALLOCATION OF TRADING SITES

There is one particular type of shortage or bottleneck which is likely to become more rather than less serious with the passage of time. This is the shortage of suitable trading and building sites in many commercial centres. Leases and titles of rights to occupancy for these plots are issued largely at the discretion of the authorities. In some localities the authorities are loath to allocate new sites, partly for political reasons and partly because they fail to see the need for it, or again because they wish to reserve the available sites for other uses. In other localities the suitable sites may already have been completely allocated. But, generally speaking, wherever the authorities dispose of new or vacant building sites, whether available sites are many or few, the method of allocation at a predetermined rent is usually preferred to disposal by auction. The authorities largely decide whether sites are available, on what terms they are available, to whom they are available and to what uses they may be put. In general, the policy is to favour African firms and, less explicitly, to discriminate against Levantines.

5. REPERCUSSIONS OF HIGH RATES OF DIRECT TAXATION

The present system and level of direct taxation in West Africa also serve to strengthen the position of the established firms, especially the larger firms. Direct taxation is levied on all companies, all expatriates, and on Africans in certain commercial centres in Nigeria. Both in Nigeria and in the Gold Coast company profits are taxed at 9s. in the £. Income taxation on the lower or middle ranges of non-company incomes is at a lower rate, but on very high incomes of £10,000 or more the marginal rate is 10s. in the £ both in Nigeria and in the Gold Coast. These very high rates of direct taxation are in accordance with contemporary ideas on company and individual taxation.

---

[1] In West African conditions such a policy has little adverse effect on the final consumers for in any case they would pay the market (equilibrium) price.

It is doubtful whether those who advance these ideas have fully realized how greatly such a system assists established or entrenched firms to maintain their position against new entrants or young firms. This heavy taxation acts as an obvious deterrent to prospective entrants, and it also tends to discourage the expansion of their activities by established enterprises. This deterrent is likely to be particularly prominent in comparatively risky activities, such as external trade in tropical countries. Against these difficulties placed by severe taxation in the way of newcomers and recently established enterprises, firms which have been established for some decades have been in a position to accumulate reserves and to build up their organizations out of profits taxed at much lower rates than are current at present. Their competitors today cannot accumulate such reserves, since their profits attract much heavier taxes and they are thus unable to build up their businesses, even if they are equally efficient and conduct their finances equally conservatively.

Large corporations the world over are paying very heavy taxes on their profits and complain about this; they are apt to overlook that if taxation were not so heavy their profits might not be so large, for they would tend to be exposed to more severe competition. These general considerations apply with particular force in West Africa, where, owing to the comparatively recent development of these territories, there has been little time for substantial local capital to accumulate.[1]

---

[1] A further aspect of the heavy company taxation in West Africa deserves mention as having some bearing on the trading situation. At the lower or middle ranges of income, individual taxation compares favourably with company taxation, and this acts as a deterrent to the establishment and growth of solidly financed commercial enterprises, especially African companies.

CHAPTER 14

THE SUPPLY OF ANCILLARY SERVICES

I. POSSIBLE RESULTS OF CONCENTRATION IN BANKING AND SHIPPING

There is a high degree of concentration in West Africa in banking and shipping, two ancillary services essential to trade. In this situation competition among suppliers is apt to be weak or absent, and the prices of the services likely to be high. The high degree of concentration may also affect the degree of competition among users of the services.[1] This possible influence is of greater interest than the effects of concentration on the price of the services. African traders frequently allege that their trade in competition with expatriate traders is greatly prejudiced, because the latter are in close contact with the banks and to a lesser extent with the shipping companies. In substance the allegation is either that Africans are denied access to these ancillary services, or that they are available on terms which compare unfavourably with those on which they are available to expatriate firms.

2. HIGH DEGREE OF CONCENTRATION IN BANKING IN WEST AFRICA

There are only two important banks in British West Africa: the Bank of British West Africa and Barclays Bank (D.C. and O.). Very recently a third European bank, the British and French Bank for Commerce and Industry, has opened an office in Nigeria. This bank, which as yet operates there only on a very small scale, is associated with an important French bank extensively represented in French West Africa. In Nigeria there are several African banks, one of which, the National Bank of Nigeria, has been working successfully for seventeen years. Its scale of operations is very small compared with that of the two British banks. In the Gold Coast only the two British banks operate;[2] until recently there was a statutory bar on the establishment of other banks.

There are written agreements between the two large banks governing the level of the principal bank charges.[3] Agreements on bank charges

---

[1] This well-known effect has already been illustrated in the account of the import trade in West Africa. It has been shown that a high degree of concentration among overseas suppliers promotes a high degree of concentration in the import trade.

[2] Since this was written the National Bank of the Gold Coast has been established.

[3] The National Bank of Nigeria and the British and French Bank also charge these rates.

are common throughout the world and are generally effectively maintained.

For familiar reasons entry into commercial banking on a substantial scale in competition with established banks is generally very difficult. In West Africa there are additional difficulties in the way of the establishment of any new expatriate enterprise which have already been discussed in previous chapters. In banking the difficulties are accentuated because there is a heavy concentration of the demand for banking services; the bulk of the business comes from the government, the marketing boards and a handful of large trading enterprises. Large customers of banks are loath to change their allegiance, particularly as new or small banks are unlikely to inspire the same confidence or to provide the same range of services when they start business.

The largest of these customers, the governments and other official organizations, naturally and properly tend to be conservative in their banking habits. In West Africa the Bank of British West Africa acts as the agents of the West African Currency Board and also handles most government accounts. Other large government accounts, including that of the Nigerian Railway, are kept with Barclays Bank. The marketing boards divide their business between the two banks. Very recently the Nigeria Cocoa Marketing Board has placed a small deposit with the National Bank of Nigeria.

3. THE LEVEL OF BANK CHARGES

Bank charges in West Africa are heavy. It is believed that they are heavier than the charges of British banks in any other colony. Bankers attribute this to the highly seasonal demand for currency, the absence of suitable outlets for funds in the off season, the cost of moving currency within these territories, the heavy charge of the West African Currency Board for transfers to and from London, and the low rate of interest which can at present be earned in the London money market. While the operation of most of these factors is undeniable, it does not follow that the charges are not higher than they would be if there were more actual or potential competition, in the sense of easier entry, or the presence of a larger number of banks, or a less rigid observance of the agreements between the existing banks. Given the difficulties of entry, the high degree of concentration, and the effectiveness of the agreements, it is impossible to assess whether the charges are excessive. It cannot be determined whether the banks receive a higher rate of return on capital than is necessary to secure the enterprise and capital, or whether costs are higher than they would be if competition were more effective.

Some of the charges certainly appear high. For example, the banks still make substantial charges for the transfer of funds between trading centres in individual colonies, even though the West African Currency Board now makes notes and coins available at the same rate in all principal trading centres. In the past the Currency Board used to charge for internal remittances, and the banks still make substantial charges for this service.[1]

On remittances between the United Kingdom and West Africa the banks invariably debit their customers with the full Currency Board charge, although the banks have recourse to the Currency Board only when they are short of funds at the destination. This latter cannot be the normal situation; and funds obtained by the banks from the Currency Board can be used to finance several times their own volume of commercial or private transfers. The banks argue that the standard charge, though it may be highly profitable at times, is nevertheless necessary to cover the cost of maintaining large idle balances in West Africa in the off season.

This argument, which is undoubtedly relevant, would have more force if the banks adopted devices to minimize actual transfers of currency between the United Kingdom and West Africa. Thus if the discount rate for bills on London were raised in winter and reduced in summer it is possible, and indeed likely, that there would be some reduction in the peak demand for West Africa currency in the produce season and a somewhat better use of the banks' funds in the off season. The present system of standard charges throughout the year does not encourage this economy.

The charge for discounting in Lagos a sight bill on London is $\frac{7}{8}\%$, of which $\frac{1}{2}\%$ is the Currency Board's standard charge for remitting funds[2] and $\frac{3}{8}\%$ is the bank's charge for discounting the bill. This latter includes a negligible element of interest, since bills are sent to London by air mail and presented immediately. Thus the $\frac{3}{8}\%$ is a service charge; for bills other than sight bills there are additional interest charges. There is also an additional charge, usually of $\frac{1}{2}\%$, for opening a letter of credit. The bills are normally drawn under a confirmed credit opened in London covering hypothecated produce, usually with guaranteed minimum prices, so that there is no credit risk.

---

[1] The merchants are often obliged to use the banks for these internal transfers, as the Currency Board is accessible to the public only for large dealings. The banks of course incur the costs of breaking bulk, but this hardly explains substantial *ad valorem* charges, generally of the order of $\frac{1}{2}-\frac{3}{4}\%$, for transfers between important trading centres.

[2] This $\frac{1}{2}\%$ Currency Board charge is always debited, though as has already been explained it is not incurred by the banks unless exchange is actually required from the Board. The charge of $\frac{7}{8}\%$ refers to Lagos; there are differential additions of up to another $\frac{3}{4}\%$ for up-country trading centres, even though there may be no charges for moving funds from Lagos to these centres.

Traders endeavouring to turn over their capital reasonably rapidly find these charges heavy, and they attempt to minimize them by private compensation transactions. The banks object to this indirect competition, and traders known to indulge in it are less favourably treated by the banks in other matters.

Until the end of 1949 the Currency Board dealt only with the banks, and firms which required remittances had to use the banks. Since then the Currency Board has been accessible to traders at its standard charge of $\frac{1}{2}$ % for remittances above a certain minimum. At the same time the banks reduced their remittance charges from $\frac{3}{4}$ to $\frac{1}{2}$ %. This suggests the power of competition.

These examples are not conclusive evidence that the bank charges, though high, are necessarily excessive. This cannot be proved or disproved in the present conditions of West African banking.

4. MISCONCEIVED AFRICAN GRIEVANCES AGAINST THE BANKS

The high cost of banking services applies to all customers in a non-discriminatory way.[1] It inevitably tends to press more heavily on the small-scale Levantine and African enterprises which do not have access to capital in Western Europe. Moreover, the large firms are better able to minimize remittance charges, either because they have funds available both in Africa and in the United Kingdom as a result of their two-way trade, or because they are better placed to arrange remittances without using the banks.

These advantages conferred on the larger enterprises are of only minor importance. The main African criticism is directed at the alleged discrimination of the banks in their credit operations. According to the standard African view the credit facilities of the banks are open to European and Levantine firms only, and Africans cannot secure bank loans even if they offer impeccable security which would amply cover advances several times over. As a result African enterprise is said to be placed at a severe competitive disadvantage.

African business men in possession of good security are apt to consider the banks as a source of permanent capital. They see that they have good security to offer, they wish to use the funds for establishing or for expanding a lucrative and sound enterprise, and cannot understand why the bank refuses to accommodate them. Yet a similar refusal may be given in Britain to a would-be borrower, since it is a familiar principle of British deposit banking not to grant loans for permanent capital. Many British businessmen have complained about

---

[1] As elsewhere some large permanent customers may receive preferential terms which are essentially quantity discounts.

the attitude of the banks on much the same grounds as the Africans, without of course the accusation of racial discrimination.

This issue is much confused by the fact that British bankers follow a tradition which has a solid basis, but the logic of which they rarely explain to their customers. The essence of the matter derives from the dual function of British and American deposit banking. The banks act as transmitters of the savings of the community to those who want to use them; but they also provide the principal supply of money in these communities, since their obligations (deposits) are the most widely used medium of payment. A bank advance is therefore not only a loan but also an increase in the supply of money which becomes immediately available for the purchase of goods and services. If bank advances were used for the financing of fixed capital on any substantial scale, the resulting increase in purchasing power would become immediately available for expenditure, and there is no assurance that the public intends to increase its savings correspondingly and would refrain from exercising its purchasing power over the long period during which the advance is outstanding. If the public chose not to leave the increased supply of money on deposit, such bank loans for fixed capital purposes might result in inflationary tendencies or precipitate a banking crisis. The banks normally cannot know what portion of deposits represents the permanent savings of the depositors and what part is liable to be withdrawn at short notice for various types of expenditure. Thus under the British and American system of banking, long-term finance for enterprise is not normally available from the banks, though it may be obtained from their investment subsidiaries whose own obligations do not circulate as general purchasing power.

Though they often find it difficult to explain it to their customers, British bankers pursue this policy consistently. It would be useful if it could be made clear to would-be African borrowers that they cannot expect to use banks as a source of permanent finance, even if their integrity is unquestioned and their security impeccable. There are obvious difficulties in driving this point home in Africa, and they are aggravated by the absence of a developed money market and institutions which could provide more permanent finance by mobilizing available savings.

Not only is the supply of savings in West Africa low, but in addition the small supply often runs to waste or remains unproductive, because it is hoarded in the form of currency, or is accumulated in the form of low-grade gold trinkets or of textiles. While these have proved a useful hedge against inflation, the savings might have been used more productively if there had been in existence suitable channels for the transmission of savings into sound enterprises, possibly on an equity basis.

There are other reasons for the apparent reluctance of the banks to lend to Africans even on good security. British bankers are more lenient in their dealings with those customers who pass all their transactions through their bank accounts than they are with those who disclose only some of their business. The banker has good reason for this preference, since unless he knows the business of his customer more or less in its entirety he cannot gauge his financial position. Moreover, bankers generally also insist on detailed knowledge of the purpose for which the loan is required. Many sound and prosperous African businessmen do not pass all their transactions through their bank accounts. They fear that the bank clerks might disclose their financial position either to their competitors or to their families. Even though the transaction may be perfectly straightforward, they are often reluctant to inform their banker of the precise purpose for which the loan is required. For these reasons they find it more difficult to secure an advance than would a European or Levantine customer of equal financial standing.

In some cases security which appears to the African to be ample might nevertheless be unsatisfactory to the banker. The complexities of African family relationships and the insecurities of land tenure often make bankers reluctant to advance money to an apparently sound borrower. Even in the absence of these complications African fixed property may be an unsatisfactory type of security. It might be politically embarrassing for the bank to force the sale of the assets of the African debtor even if the purchaser were to be another African. Auctions are also frequently 'rigged' so as to depress the realized value of the property.

Most of these complications do not arise with European or Levantine borrowers. The banks can easily lend to European or Levantine firms. These customers generally borrow from the banks for working capital and loans to them are self-liquidating and are rarely outstanding for long periods. Moreover they normally pass all their transactions through their bank accounts.[1] Contrary to frequent allegations, the banks find that their Levantine customers are as satisfactory as their other customers.

There is of course no complete bar on African borrowing from the banks and African customers are frequently accommodated. Moreover, African traders have access to trade credit often on a large scale. Those dealing with the large European firms, whether as customers for merchandise imports or as middlemen purchasing export produce for the

---

[1] The important exception is provided by compensation transactions between firms to minimize remittance costs. There is also another less important exception. In West Africa, as elsewhere, transactions implying an infringement of price control regulations are sometimes settled by means of banknotes which are not deposited.

firms, have easy access to European capital, since the firms frequently deal with them on a credit basis. In many instances the firms do not run any real credit risk since they possess security of various kinds;[1] but in other instances there is a net credit risk. Over a wide range of trade the European firms have in fact assumed functions fulfilled in Europe by bankers, in particular the short-term financing of trade for periods varying from a fortnight to two months. Certain branches of the United Africa Company also accept cash deposits from old customers for investment in London. This facility, more extensive in the past, is now confined to the continuance of past arrangements.

Before the war certain European suppliers who consigned goods to Africans were prepared to grant short-term credits by drawing sixty- or ninety-day bills on the importers instead of insisting on payment against documents. This practice is now extinct, partly as the result of the temporary eclipse of German exporters, partly owing to the sellers' market in Great Britain, but largely as a result of experience of the failure of many African importers to pay their bills. The absence of bankruptcy legislation, and the various imperfections of the legal machinery, make it extremely difficult to bring defaulting importers to book, with the result that reliable importers are also denied such credit facilities.

5. THE ELEMENT OF SUBSTANCE IN THE COMPLAINTS

Even when full allowance is made for the various good reasons for the reluctance of the banks to lend to African customers, there nevertheless appears to be some substance in the African complaint that the banking and credit machinery is not adequate to their needs and potentialities. For example, the conservatism of at least one of the banks may possibly be excessive. This seems to be suggested by the two examples that follow.

In Freetown I called on the English general manager of a well-known British enterprise, established for forty years, which is closely connected with another firm which has operated in Sierra Leone since 1874. Both enterprises are of high standing. The general manager told me that his request for an increase in his overdraft had recently been refused by one bank. The security offered would have covered the overdraft at least ten times and the reasons for the request were sound. After the bank had refused to grant the credit, the general manager approached the

---

[1] Sometimes the African customers leave substantial cash deposits (frequently accumulated discounts and commissions) with the firms and yet receive advances which are regarded as credit transactions. This is regarded as mutually convenient. In such circumstances there is of course no credit risk. The terminology is misleading because it is the European firm and not the African who is the debtor.

other bank, which immediately granted his request. The firm thereupon transferred all its business to this bank.

A well-known African trader, highly regarded in official circles, who owns extensive unencumbered property in the centre of Lagos and successfully operates a small factory as well as a very large trading enterprise, recently received a consignment from abroad worth about £4000, and asked his bank[1] for an overdraft of a few hundred pounds for a period of two weeks. The bank insisted on repayment within six days and refused to grant an extension. The trader showed me the counterfoils of his cheque book from which it appeared that his turnover with the bank had exceeded £18,000 in the previous three months.

As the banks are in West Africa in order to earn profits it seems at first sight improbable that they should fail to take advantage of profitable business offered. There are various factors which may explain their conservatism, and particularly that of one of the banks.

Until recently there were only two European banks in West Africa and the third bank has only recently begun operations. Over large areas only one of the two banks is established. Thus even in such an important trading centre as Onitsha there is only one bank. In fact, the Bank of British West Africa is the only one operating in the extensive and commercially important area between Lagos and Port Harcourt. Moreover, it is the official banker to the West African governments, as well as the official agent of the West African Currency Board. It obtains a substantial part of its income from government business, much of which is of a routine character. As it is free from competition over very large areas, its representatives understandably wish to confine themselves to safe and trouble-free operations. The quasi-monopolistic position of the banks may thus possibly be partly responsible for their exceptional conservatism, as well as for the high level of bank charges.

This inclination is strengthened by the fact that the head offices of the banks grant very limited freedom of action to their local managers. Several senior bank managers told me that they felt that this control was unduly close and irksome, and that if they were given a slightly freer hand from London they could expand their business in a manner consistent with sound banking principles. The managers concerned may not always have fully realized the extent of the total claims on the resources of their banks; generally only the head office is in a position to appreciate the overall position of a bank which operates in different territories. But even allowing for this, there was almost certainly some substance in the contention that they had to work within extremely narrow limits of authority, and on the basis of leading criteria not fully applicable to

---

[1] This was the same bank that refused the overdraft request in the previous example.

local conditions. At most local centres there is only one European in charge of the branch, and, particularly if he is a young man, he is likely to be reluctant to lend to an African customer on his own initiative. Lastly, there are as yet very few personal contacts between bank managers and members of the African community, with the result that the bankers often find it difficult to discriminate and distinguish between individual Africans.

Thus there are circumstances in which African borrowers find it difficult or even impossible to obtain short-term bank accommodation even if their financial position is sound and they are prepared to disclose their business to the bank managers. This is not the result of undue influence of European competitors anxious to retard the growth of African business. It seems to arise because the banks are assured of a reasonably secure income at little risk; and also because they tend to employ European lending criteria. This in turn retards the growth of the banking habit, and by restricting the use of funds outside the produce-buying season, raises costs and thus bank charges.

It is necessary, in conclusion, to recognize that West Africa has derived substantial benefits from the presence of two strong and well-established banks, the solvency of which has been beyond question for many years past in good times as well as bad. The growing money economy of these territories has thus been spared the shock of banking crises or bank failures. This is rarely recognized by African critics, who take the banks' presence for granted, and who are apt to overstate the possible element of substance in their complaints.

6. THE LENDING CRITERIA OF OFFICIALLY SPONSORED ORGANIZATIONS

The difficulties of obtaining bank credit affect African *traders* more than other members of the African community for two reasons. First, where it is available, bank credit is proportionately more important for traders than for other entrepreneurs. Secondly, traders receive less favourable treatment from various other credit sources than do other Africans of comparable ability and financial standing. The various government-sponsored and government-financed boards and organizations practically confine their assistance to agricultural and industrial applicants. The same appears to be true of Barclays Overseas Development Corporation. Moreover, present government policy is unlikely to encourage these institutions or concerns to lend to traders. The motives for this discrimination are not quite clear. They seem to derive partly from the view that trade is unproductive; partly from a desire to encourage types of enterprise producing a tangible output since the results of the assistance are then obvious; and partly from a desire to avoid the administrative and political complications of having to choose from among many applicants, some of whom are likely to be business competitors.

The difficulties of African traders are increased by the absorption of the bulk of African savings by the marketing boards.[1] The activities of the boards reduce African expenditure and thus the turnover of African traders; they also absorb and centralize the incomes they have withheld in a form in which the savings do not become available for borrowing by traders. The ability of traders to borrow from individuals, especially from members of their families, has been materially impaired by the retention centrally of surplus incomes which in part would have been loanable. In Nigeria part of the reserves is allocated to Regional Production Development Boards to be used eventually for various development purposes. Traders would not qualify for assistance from these sources.

7. INTEGRATION IN TRADE AND CONCENTRATION IN SHIPPING

There is a close conference of shipping lines serving West African trade; it includes four full members and a few less important associate members. Practically the entire trade between British West Africa and the United Kingdom and the great bulk of the trade between British West Africa and northern Europe is handled by three British lines, two of which, owned by large merchant houses trading in West Africa, carry over one-half of the homeward tonnage and over two-fifths of the outward tonnage between the United Kingdom and West Africa. There is very close co-operation between the three lines in the arrangement of sailing schedules, the distribution of cargo, arrangements for berthing and the chartering of additional vessels. During the last few years the capacity of their ships has been chronically insufficient to meet the demand for freight, and the lines have chartered vessels to augment their services. Owing to the bulkiness of West African exports the pressure has been particularly severe on homeward capacity, and for years past the conference lines have frequently had to resort to a system of allocation for timber exports. Thus, while there is no pooling of profits, the co-operation is so close as to resemble joint management in some important respects.

There are a few smaller shipping lines outside the conference while one or two other lines recently had plans for entering the West African trade, which have not all been abandoned. Approaches have been made

[1] Of course the marketing boards retain out of the proceeds of sales much more than would be saved by the African producers.

by them to the West African marketing boards for freight, but the results have been discouraging.

Before the war a fair volume of tonnage was carried by tramp steamers. Successful charters at very favourable rates were an important factor in the success of Mr Raccah in the groundnut export trade. These charters served to keep down freight rates generally. At present (1950–51) the situation is reversed. The lines are chartering additional vessels at rates above their own freight rates; and although the latter are gradually being raised, they have not yet reached the levels which would correspond to prevailing charter rates. There may be various reasons for the readiness of the lines to continue chartering on unfavourable terms and at times at direct money losses to themselves. It may reflect a desire of the firms or their executives to maintain a regular and adequate service without very abrupt changes in freight rates. It may also reflect a desire to handle the great bulk of the trade themselves and to prevent other operators from establishing connexions in West Africa.

In recent years the effects of the high degree of concentration in shipping have at times been reinforced by the general world shipping shortage, and, more important, by the fact that the major share of the demand for homeward tonnage is centralized and concentrated in the marketing boards. The latter practically confine their homeward shipping to the conference lines. Concentration in the demand for a service tends to encourage concentration in its supply, and the present case is no exception. The three British conference lines are anxious to ensure that the marketing boards should not use the services of other lines on the homeward run. The prospects of new entrants securing tonnage from the boards are poor; the boards are in present conditions dependent upon the established lines, which go out of their way to render special services to them.

Freight rates in the West African trade do not appear to be high compared with rates on other runs. However, this comparison is inconclusive, because the incidence of the factors determining freight rates and shipping profits on different runs differs greatly.

8. SUBSIDARY ASPECTS OF THE RELATION BETWEEN CONCENTRATION IN SHIPPING AND CONCENTRATION IN TRADE

The high degree of concentration and the prominent position in the shipping trade of the largest merchant firm serve to emphasize the high degree of concentration in West African trade generally, and also to recall the economic power of the largest firm. This firm entered the shipping trade on a large scale after it had failed to secure special freight rates from the largest shipping company. When its request for special terms was refused it withdrew its custom and provided its own shipping. This was a major influence in the financial difficulties and subsequent capital reconstruction of the shipping line concerned.

During a shipping shortage ship-owning merchant firms may naturally and understandably secure an important advantage by pre-empting a large part of the available space for their own use. Being certain that shipping space will be available for themselves, the firms may be able to reduce their investments in stocks of merchandise with important reductions in costs and in capital requirements relative to those of their competitors. These advantages would be additional to the high shipping earnings in a period of shortage. Moreover, their participation in the allocation machinery for shipping may also secure these firms certain advantages in the form of preferential treatment and more reliable information about the trade of some competitors, especially in the export trade not controlled by the marketing boards. These influences are unlikely to be of major importance.

The same two firms have developed and alone operate river shipping services on the Niger and the Benue. In certain areas, notably the middle Niger, parts of the Niger delta and along the Benue, they handle almost the entire trade. The advantages derived from owning and operating these services are the same as those already indicated for ocean shipping, and they are greatly reinforced by the absence of independent alternatives. It should, however, be remembered that the development of these services was due entirely to the foresight and enterprise of these two companies (and in one instance of a predecessor), and that for various reasons their operation is difficult and complex.

PART 4

THE EXPORT TRADE

CHAPTER 15

OUTLINE OF THE GROWTH, COMPOSITION AND
RECENT HISTORY OF THE EXPORT TRADE

1. THE GROWTH AND PRESENT COMPOSITION OF EXPORTS
FROM NIGERIA AND THE GOLD COAST

The rapid growth in volume of the principal West African exports is shown in Table 11.

With the exception of palm produce these exports date from about 1900. Such staples of the present West African export trade as groundnuts and cocoa were either absent from the trade returns fifty years ago, or were of negligible importance. Palm produce, which was by far the most important Nigerian export at the turn of the century, had increased about eightfold by the mid-1930's; nevertheless, despite this remarkable rate of increase, palm produce is now only one of three principal agricultural exports. The phenomenal history of the Gold Coast cocoa industry is well known. The annual value of cocoa exports from West Africa at present is about £80 m. Cocoa in West Africa and rubber in south-east Asia are in a class by themselves, as they are by far the most important cash crops produced by local populations in the Colonial Empire. After several decades of rapid expansion the volume of the principal export crops has been rather erratic since the mid-1930's.

Table 11. *Exports of certain commodities from Nigeria and the Gold Coast, 1899–1951*

Nigeria

	1899–1901	1919–21	1929–31	1935–37	1951
Palm oil (000's tons)	14	80	129	150	150
Palm kernels (000's tons)	52	192	255	346	347
Groundnuts (000's tons)	—	45	151	242	141
Cocoa (000's tons)	—	20	53	91	122
Cotton (000's tons)	—	4	6	11	15
Hides and skins (000's tons)	—	4	6	7	14
Timber (000's tons)	27	29	34	44	394(a)

(a) Estimated from cubic feet

Gold Coast

	1899–1901	1909–11	1919–21	1929–31	1935–37	1951
Cocoa (000's tons)	1	28	145	218	272	230
Timber (£000's)	70	123	217	104	112	4977

Generally there was a decline until the late 1940's, with a recovery
in the last few years which for oil-palm produce and groundnuts has
carried exports back to, or even somewhat above, the level of the
mid-1930's.[1]

The comparative stagnation or stability in recent years was probably
the result of several causes. In some areas of southern Nigeria and of
the Gold Coast there was little scope for further expansion of production
for export. But this was certainly not the only factor, and almost
certainly not the principal factor in the situation. In the Gold Coast
production of cocoa was affected adversely by swollen shoot disease,
as well as by a ban on cocoa planting in force in Ashanti from 1938 to
1944 inclusive. The further growth of the money economy and of the
production of export crops in these territories over this period was also
retarded by such influences as the shortage of all kinds of merchandise
(including transport equipment) and of some foodstuffs; the severe
restriction on the immigration of expatriates; and the payment of low
prices to producers until about 1950. As a matter of some interest, it
will be noted that the volume of exports of the principal products not
subject to statutory marketing (hides and skins and timber) has increased
very rapidly in recent years.

The present composition of exports from Nigeria and the Gold Coast
is shown in Tables 12 and 13.

Non-mineral exports are produced by large numbers of peasant
producers, each operating on a comparatively small scale.[2] The vast
bulk of the exports is in the form of unprocessed produce. The exceptions are small or insignificant, the most important being sawn timber,
groundnut oil and tanned skins. The processing plants are in most cases
owned and operated by expatriate firms.

---

[1] In Table 11 the volume of exports of groundnuts in 1951 shows a substantial
decline compared to 1935-7. This, however, is exceptional; in 1950-1 the crop failed.
Exports of groundnuts from Nigeria in recent years have been about 300,000 tons
or more. Indeed, this is the only crop the exports of which in recent years were
generally above the level of the late 1930's. The higher volume of exports of Nigerian
cocoa for 1951 shown in the table is accidental and includes substantial shipments
from stocks; the crop in recent years has been around 100,000 tons.

[2] There are a few exceptions. There are some rubber and oil-palm estates in
Nigeria, and a lime plantation in the Gold Coast. In rubber production estate output
is about one-quarter of the total; the production of estate palm oil is a very small
proportion of the total. A more important exception is provided by the banana
plantations owned and operated by the Cameroons Development Corporation (a
government-controlled statutory body) and by Elders and Fyffes.

Table 12. *Principal exports from Nigeria, 1949–51*

Item	Average, 1949–51			1951		
	£000's	Percentage of total exports	Percentage of non-mineral exports	£000's	Percentage of total exports	Percentage of non-mineral exports
Cocoa	23,415	23·9	25·8	35,565	28·0	30·4
Palm kernels	18,499	18·9	20·4	21,890	17·3	18·7
Groundnuts	14,766	15·0	16·3	10,144	8·0	8·7
Palm oil	12,708	13·0	14·0	14,142	11·2	12·1
Tin	6,836	7·0	—	8,974	7·1	—
Rubber	3,860	3·9	4·2	8,154	6·4	7·0
Raw cotton	3,246	3·3	3·6	5,316	4·2	4·5
Unmanufactured timber	3,061	3·1	3·4	5,556	4·4	4·7
Untanned goat skins	2,888	2·9	3·2	3,110	2·5	2·7
Hides (cattle, untanned)	2,350	2·4	2·6	3,806	3·0	3·2
Bananas	1,961	2·0	2·2	2,202	1·7	1·9
Benniseed	794	0·8	0·9	708	0·6	0·6
Other skins (sheep and reptiles)	658	0·7	0·7	800	0·6	0·7
Total of above	95,042	96·9	—	120,367	94·9	—
All others	3,089	3·1	—	6,458	5·1	—
All others, non-mineral	2,630	2·7	2·9	5,619	4·4	4·8
Total non-mineral exports	90,836	92·6	100·0	117,112	92·3	100·0
Total exports	98,131	100·0	—	126,825	100·0	—

H

Table 13. *Principal exports from the Gold Coast, 1949–51*

Item	Average, 1949–51			1951		
	£ooo's	Percentage of total exports	Percentage of non-mineral exports	£ooo's	Percentage of total exports	Percentage of non-mineral exports
Cocoa	49,644	69·8	91·2	60,310	67·6	89·6
Gold	7,898	11·1	—	8,562	9·6	—
Manganese	5,410	7·6	—	7,217	8·1	—
Unmanufactured timber	3,676	5·2	6·8	4,977	5·6	7·4
Diamonds	3,066	4·3	—	5,971	6·7	—
Bauxite	241	0·3	0·3	226	0·3	—
Palm kernels and oil	145	0·2	0·1	143	0·2	0·2
Copra	72	0·1	0·1	129	0·1	0·2
Rubber	36	0·1	0·1	49	0·1	0·1
Total of above	70,188	98·8	—	87,584	98·1	—
All others	885	1·2	1·6	1,666	1·9	2·5
Total non-mineral exports	54,458	76·6	100·0	67,274	75·4	100·0
Total exports	71,073	100·0	—	89,250	100·0	—

2. OUTLINE OF THE ORGANIZATION OF THE EXPORT TRADE AND OF THE PRINCIPAL WARTIME AND POST-WAR CHANGES

Before the recent war, produce was exported by merchant firms which generally acted as import merchants also. The principal exceptions were one or two substantial shippers of cocoa and groundnuts who did not deal in imported merchandise. The exporters were practically all expatriates.[1]

During the war the marketing of the principal West African exports was gradually taken over by statutory organizations, and the former export merchants became shipping or purchasing agents acting for these organizations.

The marketing of cocoa was the first to come under statutory control. On the outbreak of war a collapse of cocoa prices in West Africa was widely feared. This was, indeed, very possible in view of the closure of part of the European market and the probability of shipping difficulties. This prospect of a sharp fall in the local price would have made the crop unsaleable; and, especially in the Gold Coast, this might have had serious social and political results. To avert this the British government undertook to purchase, through a statutory export monopoly, at annually fixed prices, all cocoa offered for sale. The organization responsible was the Cocoa Control of the Ministry of Food. In 1940 the responsibility was transferred to the Colonial Office, operating through the Cocoa Control Board, a body specially created for this purpose. In 1942 the functions of the Cocoa Control Board were extended to cover the purchase of all vegetable oils and oilseeds, and its title was changed to the West African Produce Control Board.

Minimum buying prices for cocoa were announced for a number of buying stations throughout the producing area. The merchants acted first in a somewhat ambiguous capacity somewhere between buying agents for the authorities and shippers acting under their direction. Their status, however, soon became specifically that of agents buying on a commission basis.

The early wartime arrangements in the purchase of palm produce and goundnuts differed somewhat from those adopted for cocoa. These products were directed to the Ministry of Food by a system of export licensing. The former merchants continued to act as shippers selling as principals to the Ministry. The Ministry issued contracts to the shippers through the Association of West African Merchants on the basis of pre-war shares in the trade as calculated by the Association. The price was agreed between the Ministry and the Association. Until 1942 the

---

[1] There were a number of African exporters a few decades ago when the export trade was on a much smaller scale and its capital requirements much less.

merchants were not paid on commission; they earned the difference
between the Ministry's price and the buying price in West Africa. The
prices at which the produce was bought from the producers were agreed
with the authorities. The Association submitted a schedule of expenses
to the Ministry, and these expenses, together with an agreed margin of
profit, determined the producer price in West Africa.

When expansion of oilseed supplies became very important after the
loss of the Far East in 1942, the marketing of these crops was entrusted
to the West African Produce Control Board. This organization had
a statutory export monopoly. Henceforth the marketing arrangements
for oilseeds and cocoa were identical.[1] Minimum producer prices were
fixed seasonally for all products under the control of the West African
Produce Control Board. The former merchants acted as buying agents
for all products handled by the Board, and were remunerated by commissions calculated to cover expenses and an agreed margin of profit.

Thus while cocoa was taken over by a statutory export monopoly
because the market had contracted, the system was extended to oilseeds
because of a sudden expansion of demand. In fact, neither circum-
stance postulated an export monopoly. A collapse of local cocoa prices
could always be averted without a monopoly if the government was
prepared to act as residual buyer, and to give an unequivocal assurance
to offer a minimum price for the crop. Again, an export monopoly was
not necessary to secure increased supplies of oilseeds; in practice it had
the opposite effect.[2]

The less important export products (except for some minor oilseeds)
were not handled by the West African Produce Control Board. In
general they were bought and shipped by the merchants and were
largely directed to the purchasing departments in the United Kingdom.

The major export products have not returned to private purchase and
export, although hides and skins and timber have done so. The operations of the West African Produce Control Board were continued by the
West African marketing boards which succeeded it. The boards have
statutory monopoly of export and purchase for export. They prescribe
seasonally fixed producer prices, which are technically minimum prices,
but as the merchant firms acting as licensed buying agents are reimbursed on the basis of these gazetted minima, any excess (or over-pay-
ment) represents the surrender by the licensed buying agents or their

---

[1] Palm oil came under the control of the West African Produce Control Board in
1943 only.

[2] Indeed, the establishment and operation of the export monopoly rather tended
to curtail supplies primarily because it secured from the Ministry of Food, and paid
to producers, very low prices; and also because it facilitated the administration of
a quota system in the purchasing of products; cf. Chapters 19 and 20 below.

intermediaries of part of their reimbursement for expenses or part of their profits. Over-payments do at times emerge in the purchase of some of these products; they are considered at some length in Chapter 18 below; their level is of necessity generally small compared with the producer price or with the surplus margins of the marketing boards. Unless otherwise stated, reference to producer prices under statutory marketing[1] is to these prescribed minimum prices.

NOTE TO CHAPTER 15

The production and internal consumption of palm oil in Nigeria

The statistics of the exports of palm kernels and of palm oil can be used to show that contrary to often-expressed fears the production of palm oil in Nigeria has not been stationary or declining, and that an increasing volume of production has been largely absorbed by internal consumption instead of being offered for export. This conclusion is based on the following reasoning and calculations.

The annual exports of palm kernels and palm oil[2] are known exactly. The ratio of the production of palm oil to palm kernels is known within reasonable limits, and with negligible exceptions no palm kernels are consumed in Nigeria; thus the quantity of palm oil retained for internal consumption can be estimated fairly closely.

Palm kernels are about 14% by weight of the palm fruit. The oil secured by local methods of extraction[3] ranges from 8 to 15% of the total weight of the fruit. There are fairly wide variations in the extraction rate in different areas and different seasons, but it rarely falls outside these limits. In recent years there has been a tendency for the extraction rate to increase as part of a general improvement of native methods. It can be assumed to average about 10–12% of the total weight of the fruit, it may be higher with a tendency to increase. From this it can be inferred that the production of oil would be about six-sevenths of the production of kernels, perhaps more, as kernels are sometimes thrown away, and they also suffer a loss in weight between collection and export. The total volume of palm oil production may thus be equal to the total export of kernels and may even be more. If the volume of palm oil exports is deducted from that of palm kernels, the difference provides an approximate estimate of the local consumption of palm oil. This difference was of the order of 40,000 tons around 1900, about 120,000 tons around 1925, and it has been rather over 200,000 tons since the mid-1930's. This suggests that the palm oil industry of Nigeria has not been stagnant or decadent.

[1] Throughout this study the term 'statutory marketing' refers to the marketing of export produce by statutory export monopolies.

[2] Palm oil is produced from the fleshy outer layer of the fruit; this outer layer or pericarp encloses the nut which contains the kernel. Thus palm oil is produced before the kernel becomes available.

[3] Extraction from the outer layer (pericarp); this has nothing to do with the crushing of the kernel.

CHAPTER 16

THE BUYING ORGANIZATIONS AND METHODS
OF THE MERCHANTS AND OF OTHER INTER-
MEDIARIES IN THE EXPORT TRADE

I. PRE-WAR ORGANIZATION OF THE EXPORT TRADE

Before the war the merchants acted as principals in the purchase and
shipment of export produce. The firms bought produce at their buying
stations, which were generally situated up-country in, or close to, the
areas of production.

The actual buying for the firms was undertaken by their clerks or by
various categories of middlemen who depended, in differing degrees,
upon the firms' funds, premises, labour, equipment and so on. The
clerks bought direct from producers, from middlemen who had collected small parcels from producers, or from other smaller intermediaries. Many of the more substantial middlemen had their own
organization of employees and sub-middlemen, often running parallel
with those of the merchant firms. Thus a middleman selling to an
intermediary acting for a particular trading firm often competed with
other intermediaries also buying for that firm, and/or with that firm's
salaried employees engaged in produce buying.[1]

The middlemen were paid commission by the merchant firms; moreover, they kept any differences between the prices they paid for produce
and those they received from the firms. Some of the smaller middlemen
received agreed payments (as salaries), as well as commission on purchases. Clerks also sometimes received small commission payments, as
well as their salaries.[2]

---

[1] The analogy will be readily perceived with the organization of the import trade,
where customers of the import merchants often sell merchandize in competition with
the semi-wholesale and retail establishments of the firms from which they buy their
own supplies.

[2] This short summary sets out the essentials of the pre-war buying organizations of
the merchant firms. In practice the features were often blurred by local terminology,
by having distinctive names for different types of middlemen. A useful detailed
description of the organization of cocoa buying before the war is presented in the
Report of the Commission on the Marketing of West African Cocoa, Cmd. 5845, 1938 (the
Nowell Report), chapters IV and VIII. A description of the post-war buying organization of the United Africa Company is presented in the *Statistical and Economic Review*
of the United Africa Company, September 1948 (cocoa), March 1949 (oil-palm
produce), September 1949 (groundnuts) and September 1951 (cotton). In general,
the organization of the other firms is on similar lines though on a smaller scale.

Although the actual shippers were expatriate firms, there was in every case large-scale African participation in the purchase and movement of export produce. Except in the groundnut trade all the middlemen and clerks were Africans; in that trade an appreciable proportion of the crop was bought by Levantine middlemen for the merchant shippers. But here too these middlemen obtained the bulk of their supplies from smaller-scale African intermediaries. There was a clear analogy with the racial participation in the trade in imported merchandise. In both branches of external trade the overseas suppliers or buyers dealt directly with West African expatriate firms, while at the other end African producers and consumers were in commercial contact with African intermediaries. Between the first and last stages of the distributive process, African intermediaries occupied the bulk of the trade with a share that declined the nearer direct importing and exporting was approached.

In the purchase of export produce the merchant firms frequently granted to their intermediaries advances which were used by the latter to buy from sub-intermediaries (to whom they in turn frequently also made advances). These advances were repaid by the intermediaries from the proceeds of the produce they delivered. On repayment they were granted new advances which they settled in the same way, and this was repeated throughout the season.

The granting of advances was, and still is, one result of the low level of local capital; it represents the function of European capital in the financing of the collection and transport of export produce. The readiness with which advances are granted tends also to be influenced by the degree of competition among the firms. It is a form of competition which enables local executives to attract intermediaries by valuable concessions without exceeding the buying price prescribed by their superiors and/or agreed with other firms. For many years, for instance, advances, usually on slender security, have been granted freely for the purchase of hides and skins, where competition is severe. These advances are particularly risky, both because of the lack of security, and because the purchases take place over very large areas of northern Nigeria and the adjacent French colonies.

There was little government intervention and control in the West African export trade before the war. There was, however, compulsory inspection of the principal classes of export produce both in Nigeria and in the Gold Coast. Certain minimum standards of exportable quality were laid down, and produce falling below these could not be exported. For cocoa there was also compulsory grading in addition to the stipulation of minimum standards. There was some official control over the marketing of Nigerian cotton in which the sale of cotton destined for export was officially restricted to certain designated (scheduled) markets, and there were certain restrictions on the activities of middlemen.

2. EXAMINATION OF THE CRITICISMS OF THE PRE-WAR ARRANGEMENTS IN THE NOWELL REPORT AND ELSEWHERE

The pre-war organization and system of export marketing was subjected to frequent criticism. The multiplicity of intermediaries and the large number of stages in the distributive chain were often thought to be unnecessarily wasteful and to serve to exploit the producers. These criticisms generally failed to take into account those special features of the West African economy which are the subject of Part 1 of this study, notably the low level of capital and the availability of a large and otherwise unoccupied or partially occupied labour force, and the obvious possibilities open to the population of by-passing redundant traders. They also failed to recognize that the activities of the many traders widened the market for the produce of remote areas and stimulated the intensive and extensive expansion of production.

Other criticisms referred to alleged abuses, such as false declarations by middlemen and clerks to their principals (over-stating stocks on a falling market and under-stating them on a rising one), and to the use of incorrect weights. No doubt these practices were prevalent, but the results were not necessarily detrimental to the producers. The severe competition among middlemen and clerks generally ensured that any gains from these practices were not retained; the level of earnings and margins secured by these intermediaries were limited (then as now) by the intensity of competition and the ease of entry into the trade.[1]

In general, these criticisms were directed against the organization, practices and methods of the West African export trade rather than against the high degree of concentration among the merchants. Yet it was this oligopolistic market situation which brought about the frequent market-sharing agreements in the purchase of export crops; these were very unpopular with the local population, and one of them led to the cocoa hold-up in the Gold Coast in 1937–8.

Much the most important and influential criticisms of the pre-war system of marketing were those of the Nowell Commission which reported on the cocoa hold-up.[2] The Commission considered that the cocoa trade presented certain general undesirable features as well as more specific abuses. The parts of its report dealing with these features and abuses was reproduced in the second White Paper on the *Future*

---

[1] This subject is discussed at greater length in Chapter 18 below.
[2] *Report of the Commission on the Marketing of West African Cocoa*, Cmd. 5845, 1938.

Marketing of West African Cocoa[1] in support of the proposals for establishing statutory export monopolies; and they were important influences in the establishment and extension of statutory marketing organizations. Moreover, the views of the Nowell Commission are the most detailed and specific expression of the criticisms of pre-war marketing methods. They are still often quoted against the pre-war organization of the export trade and the marketing methods in the remaining private sector of West African trade; and they are still advanced in support of statutory marketing. An extended examination of these views is therefore justified.

The following is the text of the passages of the Nowell Report reproduced in the second Cocoa White Paper:

Having carefully examined the representations of Africans, including producers, Chiefs, middlemen and others in the Gold Coast and Nigeria, and of the buying firms in Africa and in London and having obtained the views of the local Governments, we reached conclusions regarding conditions of cocoa marketing on the West Coast which may be summarized as follows:

(i) that the trade has not in general been remunerative to the buying firms in recent years;

(ii) that this was due largely to intense competition between the firms on the Coast which led

to their offering prices frequently out of parity with current world prices;

to various forms of increases of the remuneration paid to middlemen;

to an increase in the advances made to middlemen and the extension of the period for which they were allowed to remain outstanding (especially in the Gold Coast);

and

to the free and even unscrupulous interpretation, largely tolerated by the firms, of certain conventions under which middlemen were entitled to declare purchases whenever a price change was made;

(iii) that as a result of these circumstances the cost of buying cocoa on the Coast and of shipping it to world markets frequently, and even usually, exceeded the price that would be realised on an immediate sale, so that a conservative marketing policy became impossible;

and

(iv) that a number of practices and conditions existing in the trade must be regarded as undesirable, notably:

the sale of badly prepared cocoa by producers, especially in Nigeria;

the fact that producers are not generally paid at different rates for cocoa of different qualities;

the purchase of cocoa in advance of the season by African moneylenders and middlemen at fixed prices allowing a large margin of profit;

[1] Cmd. 6950, 1946.

the pledging of farms as security and of crops as interest for loans;

the use of false weights and measures by African buyers;

the issue of large advances to middlemen in part before the season by the European firms;

speculation by the larger middlemen with cash advanced by the firms, in the form of over-declarations of purchases on a fall in price and under-declarations on a rise; and similar speculation by sub-buyers with the advances passed on to them;

the use of expedients such as a temporary and artificial lowering of prices by the firms in order to induce declarations of middlemen's purchases before a genuine rise occurred;

the conditions of strain created for firms' agents and middlemen, caused by the rivalry for tonnage, the fear of defaults on advances, and generally the intense competition;
and

the danger that the remaining small firms might be unable to stand the pace set by competition and be forced to leave a still larger share of the trade in the hands of two or three firms.

The White Paper of 1946 drew the inference that the Nowell Report

showed in particular how the producer, through the practices of the trade and particularly the activities of middlemen in West Africa, failed to obtain a fair price for his crop while at the same time the trade in general became unremunerative to buying firms and a conservative marketing policy was made impossible.

These passages support views which have been widely current over the last fifteen or twenty years. Examination of these arguments, as well as of the assumptions underlying them, casts doubts on some of the conclusions. For example, it is not clear why the firms continued the export trade in cocoa, if it was so unremunerative; nor is it clear why these alleged losses should have been a matter of public concern which could serve as a partial justification of drastic changes in marketing arrangements.

The Nowell Commission did not consider the firms' trading activities as a whole; yet it is obvious that the profitability of an enterprise must be judged from its total activities and not from one section of its trade alone. There was nothing to prevent the firms from discontinuing their cocoa-buying activities if they were so disposed; the fact that they remained very active in this trade is proof that they considered it necessary or desirable to do so, either for the direct or indirect advantages they derived. The principal indirect advantage of produce buying was said to be its beneficial effect on the firms' trade in imported merchandise; many firms claimed that produce buying was essential to promote and support their merchandise trade. But if this contention were valid, part of the profits on merchandise trade should have been credited against the expenses of cocoa buying, if strict accounting of the single activity were thought necessary. Without this adjustment it was misleading to attempt to assess the profitability of cocoa buying purely on the basis of direct costs and receipts.

There was good evidence that cocoa buying was regarded by some firms as profitable in itself and not only as an adjunct to the import trade. Both in the Gold Coast and in Nigeria several important cocoa-buying firms were engaged solely in the export trade. Before the war these purchased about one-third of all cocoa in the Gold Coast and about one-sixth in Nigeria. There is no evidence that these firms, which obviously could not derive any indirect benefits from their produce-buying activities, were disposed to curtail their activities despite the alleged unprofitability of the trade. In fact, during and shortly after the deliberations of the Nowell Commission several new firms entered or wished to enter cocoa buying, and one large prospective entrant had no interest in the import trade.[1] Moreover, the evidence of the alleged lossess was misleading. The schedule of buying expenses, which the firms used to determine the local parity of world market prices, was generously calculated. Not only did they fail to credit the buying expenses with any of the profits on merchandise trade, but they also debited them with a substantial part of the total overheads of the firms; and many cost items were rather liberally allowed for. Payments of prices in excess of the calculated local parity prices were therefore not surprising.[2]

Firms occasionally suffered heavy capital losses as a result of the maintenance of speculative open positions on falling markets. In some cases these were maintained because the principals of the firms deliberately chose to take up an uncovered speculative position. In other cases it was partly enforced, because the largest firm represented such a large proportion of total purchases that it was unable to maintain an effectively covered position by selling forward regularly at the prices at which it bought. The quantitative importance of this particular cause of loss is difficult to assess; but if it was significant it was caused

[1] The indirect advantages of participation in produce buying should not be exaggerated; it was certainly not indispensable for the maintenance of the merchandise business of individual firms. There were many importers, including a substantial and prosperous European firm in the Gold Coast, not interested in the export trade. In the aggregate the share of these non-exporters in the import trade was between one-third and two-fifths of commercial merchandise imports both in the Gold Coast and in Nigeria.

[2] They were analogous with the payments by the licensed buying agents in excess of the statutory minima prescribed by the marketing boards; cf. Chapter 18 below.

largely by the preponderant share of the trade handled by one group.[1] It could have been eliminated if this firm had reduced its commitments to avoid this risk; and it showed no inclination to do this. Moreover, even if cocoa buying had been unprofitable, this would not have been evidence of abuses or ground for public concern. It is quite normal for businesses to make losses at times without this being regarded either as damaging to their customers or as a matter for official concern or action.[2]

The producers clearly could not have been harmed by competitive 'over-payments'. These allegedly excessive payments must have been received by farmers or middlemen, all of whom (in cocoa buying) were Africans. It is a paradoxical feature of the Nowell Report and of the second Cocoa White Paper that they allege that the buying firms paid 'excessive' prices while the farmer failed to secure a 'proper' price for his crop. The argument would seem to be that both the buying firms and the producers were exploited by the middlemen. This, however, was plainly impossible in view of the severe competition among middlemen and the ease of entry into their ranks. Any advantage they could have secured from sharp practices was certain to be competed away in favour of the parties they served, that is, the producers and the buying firms. Had their charges for their services (including their allegedly improperly secured advantages), been excessive, they would have been by-passed by their customers even if these margins had not been competed away. The references in the Nowell Report to the allegedly excessive remuneration or earnings of intermediaries were attempts to resolve the paradox of allegedly excessive payments by the buying firms and allegedly unduly low prices received by the producers. They also represented an expression of a vague and unanalysed hostility to middlemen, and, in the White Paper, an attempted justification of the establishment of statutory export monopolies.

Nor were the allegations of other specific abuses more substantial. Buying the crop by paying advances was simply a method of financing

[1] This was recognized by the Nowell Commission: 'It was not, however, impossible for a firm, provided that it was handling moderate quantities of cocoa, to pursue such a policy of having a covered position if it was thought to be essential. That is to say, a buyer of moderate tonnage could, though perhaps only at a loss, either dispose of his actual cocoa day by day or, if that was impracticable, could secure temporary protection against a decline by effecting sales on one or other of the terminal markets without depressing the price level. This would not be true of a firm handling a large tonnage.' *Report*, para. 411. In this context large refers obviously to the share in exports.

[2] Concerted monopoly action by the buyers and its repercussions may well have been matters for public concern—witness the cocoa-buying agreement of 1937. But this is quite different from suggesting that the alleged unprofitability of cocoa buying was of concern to the government.

the harvesting and movement of a seasonal and expensive crop with European capital. Far from being an abuse, it was (and still is) a valuable contribution of expatriate capital to the functioning of economies very short of local capital. Similarly, the multiplicity of middlemen was an inevitable and by no means undesirable feature of economies in which the export crops were produced by tens of thousands of small-scale and dispersed cultivators.

The system of false declarations was largely an inevitable result of that absence of a local capitalist class of small merchants which made it necessary to buy through agents, for the agents tried to make a profit by understating their purchases when the prices had risen between the time they received instructions to buy and the date of delivery, and by overstating them on a fall in price.

But as there was strong competition among these intermediaries and agents any improper gains were passed on ultimately to the farmers or back to the principals. Much the same would apply to the alleged malpractice of giving false weights. The profits of the middlemen derived from such cheating can be secured only if tonnage is obtained. Under competitive conditions the resulting desire for tonnage forces the competitors to give up all or the bulk of the extra gains either to their principals or to the producers.[1]

The various other alleged abuses are irrelevant to the method of marketing. The pledging of land or of the crop to moneylenders is an aspect partly of the lack of local capital, and partly of the peculiarities of the systems of land tenure and the social habits of the population. It is certainly not clear why mortgaging property should necessarily be undesirable, much less that it is an abuse of cocoa *marketing*. Again, the failure of buyers to pay different rates for cocoa of different qualities can hardly be termed an abuse in conditions of buying competition, especially since the world market does not pay significant price differentials for different qualities of West African cocoa. Lastly, there was little justification for the fear that the continuation of the intense competition would have resulted in an even larger measure of concentration than existed already. A substantial competitor had appeared during the 1937–8 season, and other prospective new entrants were about to make their appearance. Moreover, even if competition had resulted in an increased measure of concentration this could have done no harm as long as new entry remained possible.

So it would appear that most of the general and specific allegations of abuses were advanced by the buying firms as a justification for the establishment of a buyers' monopoly, which had itself provoked the producers' strike of 1937–8; and these were accepted somewhat un-

---

[1] These propositions are examined in some detail in § 3 below.

critically by the Nowell Commission. No action was taken on the Nowell Report before the outbreak of war. The ideas it advanced came to the surface again some years later.

3. THE ORGANIZATION OF PRODUCE BUYING ON BEHALF OF THE MARKETING BOARDS AND THE REMUNERATION OF LICENSED BUYING AGENTS

Both in Nigeria and the Gold Coast the organization and physical structure of the export trade between the farmer and the port of shipment have remained largely unaffected by the establishment of the marketing boards. The former produce buyers and shippers now act as licensed buying agents for the boards; and though they operate under the general directions of the boards' executives, their organization is much the same as before the war. The important difference is that they now act as agents and not as independent traders.

The reimbursement and remuneration of the licensed buying agents are among the minor problems of the export trade. The block allowance, or payment per ton, which is intended to reimburse the licensed buyers for their expenses and remunerate them for their services, is small compared with the surplus margins of the boards; the extent to which the block allowance could be compressed is even smaller, particularly as the margins secured by licensed buying agents in practice are often lower than those provided for under the scheme. Competition among the buying agents often results in the payment of producer prices somewhat higher than the statutory minima, while the buyers are reimbursed on the basis of the statutory minima only.

The rates of commission (profit) payable to licensed buying agents of the marketing boards range at present (1950–51) from $1\frac{1}{2}\%$ of the producer price for Nigerian cocoa to $2\frac{1}{2}\%$ for palm oil. For the other products, including Gold Coast cocoa, the commission is 2% of the producer price. This remuneration is based on turnover and not on capital employed by the licensed buying agents. It is possible to turn over capital between three and four times a season.

In Nigeria some of the smaller licensed buying agents who are not engaged in the purchase of oil-palm produce have in personal discussion raised an interesting complaint about the computation of the block allowance. They argued that the large firms whose representatives negotiate the block allowances with the boards have so allocated overhead expenses as to throw a large proportion on to oil-palm products and proportionately less on to groundnuts. They were said to have done this partly because the largest firms have a greater interest in the purchase of oil-palm produce than in the purchase of groundnuts, and partly because competition is less severe in the purchase of palm oil than in the purchase of groundnuts; generous agreed margins can be retained in the former trade, while competition in groundnut buying would force the buying agents to compete away part or the whole of any excessive agreed remuneration. It is noteworthy that the remuneration (profit) element in the block allowance is fixed at 2 % for groundnuts and 2½ % for palm oil, though the purchase of groundnuts entails greater risks than the purchase of palm oil, as the latter is rarely bought with advances, while in the buying of groundnuts (a highly seasonal product) advances are general.[1]

It is difficult to assess the validity of this complaint; to the extent that it is valid, an adjusted apportionment of overheads between the trades would reduce the retained earnings of the palm-oil buyers in favour of the marketing board or of the producers directly. On the other hand, competition among groundnut buyers would cause them to surrender a part or the whole of any additional agreed allowances in favour of producers. The groundnut buyers would benefit only if competition did not compel them to surrender the whole of the extra allowance.

The block allowances are negotiated between the boards or their executives and the representatives of the licensed buying agents. Such collective negotiations are likely to foster closer collaboration among the merchants, and collaboration may lead to its familiar results, such as the strengthening of market-sharing agreements and more effective united pressure for the exclusion of newcomers.

4. THE REMUNERATION OF THE SMALLER INTERMEDIARIES

Produce continues to be bought on behalf of the former export merchants (acting as licensed buying agents) either by intermediaries (brokers, commission buyers or factors) or by salaried employees such as clerks or storekeepers. There may be one or more sub-middlemen or other intermediaries between the middlemen or clerks and the actual producers. The remuneration of the commission buyers operating on behalf of the licensed buying agents is provided for either by the inclusion of this item in the block allowance, or by the prescription of different statutory minimum prices payable for produce purchased unsifted and ungraded (i.e. purchased from producers or petty middlemen), and for produce cleaned and graded (i.e. purchased from commission buyers).

In general, the commission rates to middlemen, as provided in the

---

[1] The collection and transport of palm oil is more intricate than that of groundnuts, but this is provided for by the depreciation item and various other cost elements in the block allowance.

block allowance or in the price structure, envisage commission at a rate approximately between $\frac{1}{2}$ and 2 % of the producer price.[1] The actual margins secured by the intermediaries depend not so much on the formal provisions of the block allowance as on the prevailing degree of competition. Intermediaries may legitimately make further profits where they can secure transport at lower rates than the officially calculated transport cost. Conversely, competition may force them to surrender such profits in the form of prices to producers higher than the gazetted minima.

Owing to the diversity of conditions, and the absence of consistent price quotations and clear-cut distinctions between the different stages of produce buying, it is difficult to assess closely the structure of profit margins. Detailed discussion and analysis would be unrewarding, chiefly because the results would be of very limited meaning.[2] It seems, however, worth while to summarize some of the information on this subject, since it differs considerably from widely held opinions about the width of the margins secured by the smaller intermediaries. Estimates prepared in the produce departments of the United Africa Company in Lagos, Port Harcourt, Kano and Accra by senior members of the staff of the company suggest that the margins are far narrower than is generally believed. In western Nigeria in 1950 the port price of cocoa was £100 per ton and the port price of palm kernels £26 per ton. The Lagos general manager of the United Africa Company estimated that the great majority of producers or members of their families received £90 per ton or more for cocoa and £20 to £22 per ton for palm kernels. Information gathered in the course of visits to seven or eight markets in

---

[1] The arrangements in the purchase of Gold Coast cocoa furnish a convenient example. In 1949–50 the producer price was £84 per ton; this was a net price payable at the railway station exclusive of brokerage. The block allowance included 28s. a ton for brokerage and commission. The arrangements between the individual buying agents and their intermediaries vary substantially, chiefly because of the practice of paying salary as well as commission on large tonnage. The salary may range from £6 to £12 per month, and the rate of commission from 18s. to 30s. per ton. There are also varying arrangements about advances and the loan or sale of equipment. The gross margins of the intermediaries buying cocoa on behalf of the licensed buying agents at gazetted stations represent from about $\frac{3}{4}$ to $1\frac{1}{2}$% of the producer price. In many instances the intermediaries have to share this with various sub-intermediaries, since the remuneration of all intermediaries between the gazetted station and the licensed buying agent must be met from the salary and brokerage paid by the licensed buying agent. The recipient of the money at the buying station is the farmer, or a relative, or a neighbour or a petty village trader, but practically always a member of the rural community. The rate of remuneration provided for other products of lower value tends to be a somewhat higher percentage of the producer price, but the difference is not significant.

[2] In much the same way as details of the structure of margins in the import trade are of little significance (cf. Chapter 5, § 8 above).

the Ibadan area in the summer of 1950 confirmed these estimates, though it was not always easy to distinguish between small-scale intermediaries and actual producers.[1] These price differences are narrow when it is remembered that they have to defray the cost of transport from up-country stations to the ports (the cost of which ranged from about £1 to £3 per ton of produce), as well as the expenses and remuneration of one or more intermediaries.

The general managers of the United Africa Company in eastern Nigeria and in the Gold Coast supplied independently compiled information on this topic, presented in somewhat different form but yielding very similar results. This suggests that the prices received by producers or petty village traders were generally between 4 and 12% below the statutory prices at the nearest gazetted station. This differential has to provide for the remuneration of the services of the intermediaries who buy from the dispersed producers or the smallest-scale village traders (who in almost every case are members of the rural community), and for the cost of transport to the gazetted stations.

5. RECENT INFLUENCES RESTRICTING ENTRY INTO PRODUCE TRADING

Even allowing for the approximate nature of the opinions presented in the preceding section, it seems that the margins of these intermediaries are not excessive, either in the sense of providing generous returns on the capital and labour employed, or in the sense that their compression could significantly improve producers' returns.

These comparatively narrow margins are the result principally of competition in buying and, in particular, the ease of entry into small-scale produce buying. The readiness of the African producer (especially in the south) to spend much time and effort in seeking out the best buyers for his produce also serves to restrain the margins of intermediaries. A comparatively small measure of competition can make its influence felt over a fairly wide area through a chain reaction. If the competition in a particular market results in payments above the statutory minima, these higher prices have to be paid in the next village, as otherwise producers take their crop to the other market. These higher prices have the same effect at the next stage and so on for perhaps half a dozen markets.

It is possible that the present degree of competition among intermediaries may not continue, since influences are at work to restrict

---

[1] These intermediaries were always members of the rural community and the distinction is not of great practical significance. The price may have been received by a relative or a creditor of the producer. The relevance of this is considered in a note at the end of this chapter.

the freedom of entry into produce buying. The Gold Coast Cocoa Marketing Board has begun to license the intermediaries acting on behalf of its own licensed buying agents, and the Nigeria Cocoa and Groundnut Marketing Boards have similar licensing powers, which have not yet been exercised. The assumption of these powers probably reflects in part the desire to control these industries as closely as possible, and in part the mistaken belief that an enforced reduction in the number of intermediaries would serve to reduce the margin and to improve the price received by the producer. They may also stem from a desire to see these trades present a tidier appearance. The limitation of the number of intermediaries can only result in giving those left in the trade a measure of monopoly power at the expense of the producer.

In western Nigeria produce buyers are endeavouring to restrict new entry into their trade and to diminish competition in the purchase of cocoa and palm kernels. In Ibadan and Ife there are influential produce buyers' unions of which the Ibadan Produce Traders' Union is the most important. This well-financed and efficiently organized body is represented in almost every produce market in the Ibadan area. It seems to exercise substantial local pressure, and to be able to influence the various native authorities who in turn can limit the number of buyers in various local markets.

Some members of the Produce Traders' Union complain that they are being exposed to severe competition from buyers outside the Union and from buyers from other areas who send lorries to collect produce far afield. Some of the complainants emphasize that the presence of one produce buyer from outside the neighbourhood (and thus less susceptible to pressure from the Union or from the native authorities, or from public opinion) can influence prices in a number of villages. The Produce Traders' Union have already made representations for the official licensing of all produce buyers to reduce the intense buying competition which is cutting into their margins.

NOTE TO CHAPTER 16

The extent and the effects of indebtedness

Rural indebtedness is often instanced in West Africa as a factor affecting adversely producers' returns and ensuring inflated returns to the intermediaries, or at least margins much higher than might appear from the structure of market prices. Some information on this topic is presented in this note.

Although not much is known of the extent of peasant indebtedness in West Africa, nor of the membership and status of the creditor class, nevertheless it is unlikely that indebtedness seriously affects the price received by the rural sections of the economy for the crops produced. If the creditor is a member of the agricultural class the rural sector is unaffected by the actual terms agreed between creditor and debtor, so long as the standard of cultivation is maintained. It appears that much of the indebtedness in areas where it exists is between debtors and creditors within the same village (and often between close relatives). In the cocoa- and kola-producing areas of south-western Nigeria the indebtedness may be between wife and husband. In eastern Nigeria there appears to be very little rural indebtedness. In the groundnut area the relatively restricted indebtedness appears to be mainly instances of short-term seasonal debts between the farmer debtors and other members of the agricultural community.[1]

Where the creditor is a produce buyer from outside the debtor's village, a distinction should be made between his two functions, viz. the functions of money-lending and those of produce buying. If the buyer did not also act as a money-lender the debtor would presumably borrow from some other source, and there is no *prima facie* reason why he should be in a better position.

On the practical level much more research will have to be undertaken before the effects of rural indebtedness can be assessed. Even if they appear in the nature of consumption loans, some of these advances may be productive and may help the farmer to produce more. In an industrialized society the entrepreneur class as a whole, including farmers, is generally in debt to the banks, but this does not cause alarm. In less advanced communities farmers may also operate with borrowed capital, without this necessarily being a sign of distress.

Many advances appear to be made without interest; the creditor receives a lien on the crop, either at a fixed price or at the purchase price ruling at the time of the harvest. In other instances an interest element is stipulated, but the total amount repayable might remain the same, even if the duration of the loan is extended. It is also often informally understood that if the crop fails the advance will not be repaid. Where the producer receives less than the market value on the sale of his crop to the creditor, the reduction in price may well be a substitute for interest payments. The two separate transactions —sale and loan—may in practice be merged; it is then incorrect to confine the examination to the apparent terms of one transaction alone.

Much of the indebtedness is undoubtedly between members of the same village community. The balance represents the provision of finance from outside the village, the bulk of which is ultimately obtained from the ex-patriate merchant firms. Moreover, as many loans do not stipulate the payment of interest and as some advances are never repaid, it is not

[1] Information presented by various chiefs, dignitaries and local authorities to the chairman of the Nigeria Groundnut Marketing Board in the course of a tour by the latter in northern Nigeria in December 1949 also suggests that indebtedness is not a major problem of groundnut producers. As the producers of groundnuts are among the poorest producers of export crops and their production is highly seasonal they would be more likely to be in debt than other farmers. Some references to this may be found in *Minimum Prices for Gazetted Buying Stations in the Kano Area*, published by the Nigeria Groundnut Marketing Board in 1950.

improbable that on balance the outside capital is available at relatively low real rates of interest.

The general presumption that the level of agricultural indebtedness to urban creditors is not as high as is sometimes suggested seems to be confirmed by a simple but useful piece of empirical evidence. Throughout the producing areas most of the sellers of groundnuts and of cocoa, the two most important seasonal crops, spend the proceeds of their sales of merchandise either at the time of the sale or shortly afterwards. This suggests that they are largely free to dispose of the proceeds, and that the obligation to repay debts is not wide-spread or serious. It is also generally agreed that the producers of oil-palm products (which are largely non-seasonal and which are not cultivated products) in eastern Nigeria are rarely in debt, except possibly to close relatives.

CHAPTER 17

THE SHARES OF FIRMS IN THE TRADE IN EXPORT PRODUCE

1. INFORMATION ON THE SHARES OF FIRMS IN THE TRADE IN EXPORT PRODUCE

There is much information available on the shares of individual firms in the export trade of West Africa. It is derived partly from returns furnished by the buying agents to the executives of the marketing boards and circulated by the boards, and partly from analysis of customs entries. Considerable information has also been made available by private sources.

The export of agricultural products from Nigeria and the Gold Coast is in the hands of marketing boards which are statutory export monopolies. In the actual export of these products, the concentration is of course 100 %. The merchant firms act as buying agents for the boards, and for these commodities the statistics of concentration shown here refer to their operations as buying agents and not as actual exporters. For hides and skins and timber the information refers to the shares of firms in actual exports.

With the exception of the buying of cocoa, confidential market-sharing syndicates are operated by most of the licensed buying agents in the purchase of produce for export on behalf of the marketing boards.[1] In a review of statistics of this degree of concentration it is necessary to take cognisance of such syndicates for two reasons. First, their presence implies that in effect the members share their purchases. The shares of individual firms in total purchases do not give a full picture of the degree of concentration; in addition, the share of all the syndicate members taken together must be considered because they act largely in concert and in their purchasing activities voluntarily limit their independence of action. Secondly, the share of an individual firm in total purchases in any year may give a misleading indication of its quantitative importance if it is a member of a syndicate. A firm may intentionally reduce its purchases in one year in accordance with the provisions of the market-sharing arrangements. This tends to increase the tonnage bought by others, whether members of the syndicate or not. Conversely, a syndicate member which was buying less than its agreed

[1] The syndicates in the purchase of oil-palm produce seem recently to have been suspended (cf. note to Table 14 below).

share might make a special effort to recover its position; and this tends to reduce the tonnage bought by others.[1]

These difficulties have been met by providing some supplementary information. Where appropriate, the combined share of syndicate members in total purchase is shown, as well as the *adjusted* shares of the largest firm and of the three largest firms together. The adjusted share for this purpose is the firm's participation share in the syndicate multiplied by the syndicate's share in total purchases.[2]

2. THE PARTICIPATION OF FIRMS IN THE TRADE IN EXPORT PRODUCE

The available information about the participation of firms in the export trade is summarized in Table 14. Details of the shares in purchases for export[3] or in actual exports[4] are shown for each firm for the most important non-mineral exports. In addition, the shares of the firms in the total trade in Nigerian non-mineral exports have been calculated. No similar calculation for the Gold Coast is presented; in view of the preponderance there of cocoa in non-mineral exports the shares of firms in cocoa buying are sufficient indication of their participation in produce buying generally. The products listed represent over 90 % of all non-mineral exports from Nigeria; in the Gold Coast cocoa alone accounts for about 90 % of non-mineral exports.

Details are shown for each firm with a share of 0·4 % or more in purchases of Nigerian non-mineral exports or of 1½ % or more in purchases of Gold Coast cocoa. The percentage figures are shown to one decimal place for the major products and to the nearest whole number for the others.

Table 14 shows clearly the measure of concentration present in produce buying for export. A high degree of concentration, somewhat higher than in the import trade, is shown by the fact that in each case the three largest firms purchase more than one-half of the quantity exported. The low value, bulk, and standardized nature of the export products provide less scope for the activities of the smaller trader than does the more varied import trade, especially outside the bulky staple products.

[1] The principal provisions and the methods of operation of the syndicates are discussed briefly in § 4 below.

[2] For instance, if in a particular year the quota of firm X in the syndicate is 50 % and the syndicate in the aggregate has handled 90 % of all purchases, the adjusted share of firm X is taken as 45 %, even though its actual purchases may have been larger or smaller than this percentage.

[3] That is, their purchases as licensed buying agents on behalf of the marketing boards.

[4] That is, their exports as shippers on their own account.

Institutional arrangements have served to reinforce these influences. In recent years the most important have been the wartime controls, especially the export quotas, which have increased the degree of concentration and the scope and effectiveness of the various market-sharing agreements.

The establishment of statutory marketing has also had some restricting effects on new entry and has thus tended to strengthen concentration. This has been so even though buying agents are licensed with reasonable freedom by the Nigerian marketing boards, and the entry of new buying agents is definitely encouraged by the Gold Coast Cocoa Marketing Board. Licensed buying agents operate largely on a fixed commission basis; they cannot ship or sell abroad, and merchants are thus unable to take advantage of special opportunities for advantageous marketing. There is not the same incentive to attract enterprise as there would be if the scope and possibilities were less restricted. This dampening effect is quite compatible with rates of return higher under the present system than under the system it has replaced.

In addition, in Nigeria the established licensed buying agents can influence entry of newcomers, since they are represented on the various representative committees which have to be consulted by the boards on the admission of new buying agents. The established firms are unlikely to be successful if they were to oppose the entry of African buying agents, but they are likely to be more influential in restraining or hampering the entry of new expatriate firms. Finally, though the executives of the boards may not wish to limit entry deliberately, considerations of administrative convenience and the application of tests and criteria unconnected with economic efficiency may themselves be restrictive in effect even if not in intention. These considerations are likely to become more important if the number of buying agents or of applicants should increase.[1]

In spite of the high degree of concentration there has been fairly lively competition in recent years in several branches of the produce trade. Thus, in the buying of groundnuts and of palm kernels the statutory minimum prices have been frequently appreciably exceeded, although these are activities which, statistically, appear to be dominated by a few large firms, and in which buying syndicates handle a large part of purchases.

---

[1] In Sierra Leone the licensing system is being used frankly for political purposes to discriminate against Lebanese traders. It is not improbable that the same will eventually occur elsewhere in West Africa. The influences listed in the foregoing paragraphs are, of course, distinct from (and additional to) the more general influences restricting the establishment of new expatriate enterprises discussed in Part 3 of this study.

Table 14. Shares of merchant firms in purchases for export or in exports in Nigeria and the Gold Coast, 1949 or 1950 (percentages)

Firms	Nigeria (1) Nigerian non-mineral exports	(2) Cocoa 1949–50	(3) Palm kernels 1950	(4) Palm oil 1950	(5) Ground-nuts 1949–50	(6) Cotton 1949–50	(7) Timber in logs 1949	(8) Sawn timber 1949	(9) Skins 1949	(10) Hides 1949	(11) Rubber 1949	Gold Coast (12) Cocoa 1949–50
A	43·3	33·2	48·9	68·2	37·1	48·8	37	69	28	50	17	38·8
C	9·1	10·9	11·3	5·7	7·8	14·6	—	—	8	14	3	2·7
B	6·5	5·4	7·3	5·4	6·9	8·6	—	—	12	15	—	6·4
E	6·0	8·2	7·1	6·2	4·6	8·3	—	—	2	1	—	1·9
J	3·6	11·7	2·8	—	—	—	—	—	—	—	—	13·6
D	2·8	1·4	4·6	5·0	1·3	2·8	—	—	7	—	—	2·4
K	2·6	—	—	—	13·2	—	—	—	—	—	—	—
L	2·3	8·8	—	—	6·0	15·4	—	—	8	6	—	11·7
M	2·2	2·0	1·7	—	—	—	—	—	—	—	—	4·5
H	1·6	—	—	—	—	—	—	—	24	11	—	—
N	1·4	1·1	3·0	2·4	—	—	—	—	—	—	—	5·0
O	1·3	3·1	2·3	—	—	—	—	—	—	—	—	—
P	1·3	3·2	1·3	—	—	—	—	—	—	—	—	3·4
F	1·1	—	—	—	—	—	—	—	—	—	—	—
Q	0·9	—	—	—	4·5	—	—	—	—	—	—	—
R	0·9	—	—	—	4·3	—	—	—	—	—	—	—
S	0·8	1·5	—	1·1	—	—	—	—	—	—	6	—
T	0·8	—	1·0	—	—	—	—	—	—	—	—	—
U	0·7	—	—	—	—	—	—	—	6	—	19	—
V	0·6	—	—	—	—	—	—	—	—	—	14	—
W	0·4	—	—	—	—	—	4	—	—	—	19	—
X	0·0	—	—	—	—	—	—	—	—	—	10	3·7
Y	0·0	—	—	—	—	—	—	—	—	—	—	3·3
All others	9·8	9·5	8·7	6·0	10·9	1·5	59	31	5	3	12	2·6
Total	100	100	100	100	100	100	100	100	100	100	100	100

Share of three largest firms	59	56	68	80	79	54	80	64	79	55	59
Share of five largest firms	69	78	82	93	96	71	83	87	97	79	75
Aggregate share of syndicate members	—	—	85	93	100	—	—	—	—	—	—
Adjusted share of largest syndicate member	—	—	55	71	48	—	—	—	—	—	—
Aggregate adjusted share of three largest syndicate members	—	—	71	83	72	—	—	—	—	—	—

Notes

(1) The firms are listed in order of their participation in purchases for export of Nigerian non-mineral exports. As the code letters are the same as those in Chapter 5, which deals with the import trade, and the order of importance of firms in the export trade is not the same as in the import trade (among other reasons, because there are some firms acting only as import merchants and others only as export merchants), the order in this table is not the same as in the tables in Chapter 5. The figures are percentages of values where they refer to shares in total Nigerian exports and to exports of timber and hides and skins. For other commodities (that is, cocoa, groundnuts, palm kernels, palm oil, cotton and rubber) they are percentages of volume. As these crops are standardized products the difference between percentage shares in value and volume is not significant.

(2) The figures in column (1) are averages of those in columns (2) to (12), weighted by the relative values of the individual commodities in aggregate exports in 1950. The weighting is thus by export values and not by aggregate producer payments. The relative shares would not have been significantly affected if the latter basis had been adopted. This, however, would have introduced a capricious element into the calculations, as these would have been influenced by differences in the price policies of individual marketing boards in a particular year.

(3) The shares of the three and five largest firms exclude the shares of firm M, which refers to the African co-operatives.

(4) Associated firms and subsidiaries have been grouped together as single firms. In groundnut buying one firm financially linked with another large buyer has, however, been treated separately, as their association is more loose and does not include elements of ownership such as participation in profits. To this extent the degree of concentration is understated.

(5) The figures referring to the buying syndicates in palm products are subject to a small margin of error. The shares of the individual firms in the syndicate refer to 1949 and the share of the syndicates in total purchases refer to 1950. Moreover, it is understood that the palm-kernels syndicate, which in 1949 still handled 95% of all purchases, was dissolved in the autumn of 1950 in the face of rapid progress by outside firms. More recently (about 1952) the palm oil syndicate was also suspended.

(6) The system of production and export of rubber differ considerably not only from that of the products controlled by the marketing boards but also from that of other non-controlled export products. Whereas the other crops are produced by small peasant farmers, there are several rubber estates, of which those controlled by the Cameroons Development Corporation are the most important. These estates export their own production, which is a significant proportion of total exports. It is for this reason that the pattern of concentration in the export of this crop differs from that in other branches of the export trade.

(7) Special aspects of the structure of the timber trade are discussed in a note appended to this chapter.

3. REGIONAL TRADING REPRESENTATION

To assess the alternatives open to producers and smaller middlemen in the selling of export produce it is necessary to investigate, if only briefly, the representation of buying agents in different regions or districts. For various reasons detailed inquiry on this subject would be of limited value. In the trade in the most important products the merchant firms no longer act as principals, but only as agents of the marketing boards; ultimately sellers of produce have no alternative buyers, since all produce is bought by the boards. As the boards prescribe minimum prices and reimburse their buying agents on the basis of these minimum prices, the influence which differences in the number of firms can exercise on the prices paid for produce is necessarily restricted. Moreover, inquiry into regional trading representation can yield approximate results only, since the conclusions regarding the number of buying firms to whom producers have access would depend on a number of factors which cannot be expressed easily in a quantitative form. However, it seems worth while to present certain information on the regional trading representation.

In the Gold Coast the Cocoa Marketing Board divides the territory in which it operates into forty-four districts and collects information on the number of buying agents operating in each. In 1949–50 there were only five districts in which less than five buying agents operated and less than 4 % of the crop was purchased there. Such detailed information is not available for Nigeria, but from the data in the possession of the produce inspectorate it appears that at least three-fifths of the tonnage graded in the cocoa season of 1949–50 was bought at stations at which seven or more buyers operated; for Nigeria as a whole the average number of buyers per station, weighted by tonnage, was over twelve.

Fairly detailed information is available on the regional representation of licensed buying agents in the purchasing of groundnuts. It would seem that in the northern or Kano area, where between 92 and 95 % of the exportable crop is bought, the great majority of producers have access to six or more buyers. Twenty-one buying agents operate in Kano Province, which, with the immediately adjoining part of Bauchi Province, produces between one-half and three-fifths of the exportable crop; some ten are represented in Katsina Province, which produces another fifth, and in Bornu Province, which produces another tenth.

Information is presented in greater detail in the next chapter of the position at thirty-two road stations at which some two-fifths of total purchases of the crop and about three-fifths of the purchases at road stations are effected. At these stations in 1949–50 the average number of firms per station, weighted by tonnage, was 7·4. With the exception of a few remote outlying areas, the great majority of the groundnut producers in the northern area seem to have access to half a dozen or more buyers.

In the Middle Belt or Rivers area, where between 5 and 8 % of the crop is bought, the position is different. At present only two firms operate there, and informal zoning arrangements are generally in force between them. The degree of concentration in the purchase of palm produce is appreciably larger than in produce buying generally. This general picture is reflected in local trading representation.

In the eastern region, which supplies about six-sevenths of the exports of palm oil and just over one-half of the exports of palm kernels, there are extensive areas where only one or two firms are established. This is partly the result of the long distances and poor communications between the outlying areas of the palm belt and the principal trading centres. The economies of bulk storage and transport of palm oil also tend to promote concentration. Historical factors have also played a part, as this area was the centre of the operations of the Niger Company. The records of the produce inspection service suggest that in 1949 about one-half of the tonnage of oil-palm produce bought in the eastern palm belt was purchased by stations at which there were three firms or less. Since then, however, several buyers have established themselves in this area (including even Opobo, a traditional stronghold of the United Africa Company). Therefore, new entry into this area can also be expected.

In the western area, in which communications are much more highly developed, and which is easily accessible to Lagos and Ibadan, the position is different. Only about one-eighth or one-tenth of the tonnage of oil-palm produce is purchased at stations where there are three buyers or less, and about one-half of the tonnage is bought at stations where there are seven or more firms. Moreover, as communications in the western area are much better than in the eastern palm belt, the effective number of alternative buyers accessible to producers (or other small-scale sellers) is larger than would appear from figures of trading representation at particular stations.

This brief description suggests that with the exception of certain fairly clearly defined areas, notably the Middle Belt (the so-called Rivers area) and parts of the Niger delta and Cross River area in the eastern palm belt, the degree of local concentration is not significantly smaller than is indicated by the data presented in earlier sections for the territories as a whole. With the gradual improvement of internal transport the significance of local trading representation is certain to diminish, as sellers will have easier access to the various firms operating in a particular territory.[1]

---

[1] Unless obstructed by restrictions on the movement of traders or commodities.

4. MARKET-SHARING ARRANGEMENTS IN THE PURCHASE
OF EXPORT PRODUCE

Confidential market-sharing agreements had been in operation in the purchase of the principal West African export crops for several decades before the outbreak of the Second World War. Their methods of operation received wide publicity as a result of the cocoa-buying agreement in 1937 in the Gold Coast, which gave rise to the cocoa hold-up of 1937–8. That agreement was essentially similar to the confidential arrangements in force from time to time in the purchase of oil-palm produce and groundnuts. In the purchase of certain products similar arrangements are practised today. Since the war these have included oil-palm produce, groundnuts, cotton and ginger.

The methods of operation of these agreements (sometimes known as syndicates or pools) are simple. The participants agree on the proportions (quotas) that their individual purchases shall bear to one another. The prices to be paid for the crops are generally also agreed formally or informally. Purchases are made separately by each participant, and information about them is periodically collated. Participants who have bought more than their agreed shares are required to make penalty payments in favour of those who have bought less than their agreed shares. The penalty payments are calculated so as to deprive the payer of all contributions to overheads and profits on the excess purchases.[1] The incentive to buy more than the quota is thus reduced or removed altogether. In the calculation of the penalty payments recourse is had to agreed schedules of expenses known as buying schedules. These schedules include estimates of the overheads incurred in buying operations, which can be used to assess the level of penalty payments to be exacted from participants who have exceeded their quotas. In the past these schedules were also sometimes used to arrive at the maximum prices to be paid to producers.

Most of the arrangements appear to have followed a characteristic cycle. Agreements would be concluded regulating the purchase of a product and they would continue for some years. There would be internal dissensions more or less from the very beginning. The ambitions of local executives and the desire to strengthen the merchandise trade would cause some participants to expand their purchases despite the penalty arrangements. External competition would tend to reinforce

---

[1] An earlier arrangement required those who had bought excessive purchases to deliver the excess to the underbought firms in return for the cash outlay of purchase. The market-sharing arrangements in the purchase of cotton and ginger differ in some respects from those in the other products. In particular, the participants agree not to establish new buying points without the consent of the other members.

internal dissensions; the prospect of a possible dissolution of the syndicate would induce some participants to increase their purchases, as well as in the hope of securing more favourable quotas should a new agreement come to be negotiated at a later date. Entry of newcomers or the expansion of outside firms would eventually disrupt the arrangements, generally after internal tension had come close to breaking point. This would be followed by years of intense competition which might then be succeeded by a renewal of the agreement, including certain firms which had previously been outside the syndicate. This would be the beginning of the next cycle.

The most stable of the syndicates tended to be those covering palm produce. Here the degree of concentration was exceptionally high and the dominant firm was in a strong position. But even in these products the agreements broke down occasionally; a temporary collapse occurred a few years before the war.

In the purchase of groundnuts the progress of the largest of the outside merchants was so rapid after 1937 that in 1939 the syndicate had become largely ineffective and was abandoned in the summer of 1939. This was but one instance of the re-assertion of the forces of competition. At about the same time substantial new entrants appeared or were about to appear in cocoa buying.

During the war and early post-war years the operation of the buying syndicates was officially sanctioned, strengthened and extended by the quota system in the purchase for export and by the ban on new entry. These arrangements were finally withdrawn in 1947. Since then private syndicates have operated in the purchase of all major export products except cocoa, hides and skins and timber;[1] their scope in 1950 is indicated in Table 14. It is only in the purchase of cotton for export that all buyers are members of the syndicate. The particularly comprehensive scope of the cotton syndicate may be partly the result of the system of scheduled markets (the restriction of purchase to certain specified markets), which promotes concentration and increases the effectiveness of market-sharing arrangements.

Neither the presence of fairly comprehensive syndicates nor a high degree of concentration has served to remove all competition in produce buying for export; competition is still in evidence, particularly in the purchase of groundnuts and palm kernels.[2]

[1] The absence of syndicates in cocoa buying may be due to political reasons, particularly the memory of the hold-up of 1937–8, and/or to the comparative importance of one or two buyers (including the co-operative societies) who did not readily participate in these agreements. The absence of syndicates in hides and skins and timber is partly the result of the comparatively unstandardized nature of these products; cf. § 5 below.

[2] See Chapter 18.

5. THE CONNEXION BETWEEN THE DEGREE OF STANDARDIZA-
TION AND THE DEGREE OF CONCENTRATION

The structure, organization and recent history of the export trade offer instructive examples of the connexions between the degree of standardization of the principal export products and the degree of concentration and the presence of monopolistic arrangements in their purchase, similar to those already established for the import trade.[1]

The more standardized the commodity, the more probable is a high degree of concentration, and, with a given degree of concentration, the more effective are market-sharing agreements. The degree of concentration is particularly high in the purchase of standardized staple exports. Moreover, the establishment and operation of produce-buying syndicates or pools have always been confined to the more standardized exports, such as cocoa, groundnuts, cotton, oil-palm produce; they never operated in hides and skins or timber. Similarly, the wartime export quotas applied largely to the former class of commodity and only intermittently and imperfectly to the latter. The tendency has continued to the present, since the former commodities are subject to statutory export monopolies while the latter are not.

NOTE TO CHAPTER 17

Special features of the timber export trade

The participation of firms in the export of timber[2] differs from that in the other branches of the export trade. This pattern of participation, as well as some other related aspects of the timber trade, deserve brief consideration, particularly in view of the rapid growth of timber exports in recent years both from Nigeria and from the Gold Coast.

The statistics of the Nigerian export trade in sawn timber are a useful reminder of the need for some care in interpreting this type of information. In 1949 over two-thirds of these exports were handled by one firm. This simply reflects the operation by that firm of some large sawmills, as well as a large plywood factory, which are the most important enterprises processing Nigerian export produce. The logs are, however, purchased in competition with the smaller processors, exporters of logs, and local users, while sawn timber is sold overseas in competition with timber from many other sources. Thus the high proportion of exports of sawn timber handled by one firm does not indicate a high degree of concentration (much less does it indicate monopoly power) either in the purchase of logs, or in the sales of sawn timber.

---

[1] Chapter 5 above.
[2] The export of timber is not controlled by a marketing board and the firms act as actual exporters.

Although exports of sawn timber have been rising very rapidly in recent years, around 1949–50 logs were still quantitatively more important. In 1949, in both Nigeria and the Gold Coast, logs were about two-thirds of the value of timber exports and sawn timber about one-third.[1] It is almost certain that the proportion of sawn timber and of veneers will increase in the next few years.

Much of the export trade in logs has for years past been in the hands of African shippers; this is the only section of the West African export trade in which Africans have played an important part as shippers in recent years. From information made available by the Forestry Department in the Gold Coast, it appears that in 1949 African shippers handled about two-thirds of the export trade in logs, while all sawn-timber exports were shipped by some eleven sawmills owned by European firms. In the same year in Nigeria some 28–30 % of the export trade in logs was in African hands, against some 10 % of the combined exports of sawn timber and plywood.

The preponderance of expatriate enterprise in the export trade in sawn timber reflects the relatively greater capital and technical skill required in its production and export. An increase in the relative importance of sawn timber is almost certain to increase the relative share of all timber exports handled by non-African firms; it is, indeed, even possible that the absolute volume of the export trade remaining in African hands might be reduced.[2] But these developments would not result in a decrease in the volume of timber handled by African traders in their capacity as intermediaries. The total volume of timber business transacted by Africans is likely to increase, since the sawmills are likely to use the services of African dealers and contractors. In assessing the African interest in the timber trade it would therefore be misleading to focus attention on the shipping stage of the export trade; other African interests are likely to benefit greatly from an expansion in the volume of exports, even if African direct exporters should lose some ground to non-Africans, relatively or even absolutely.

[1] Including veneers and plywood in Nigeria.
[2] It will tend to diminish, though this may be counteracted by official action, or obscured by various devices such as joint commercial enterprises with African participation.

CHAPTER 18

ASPECTS OF COMPETITION IN
PRODUCE BUYING

There has been repeated reference in previous chapters to the presence
of competition in branches of external trade which appear to be dominated by a few firms and in which market-sharing agreements operate.
This chapter and the appended note present information on the operation of competition under apparently unpropitious, and certainly unexpected, conditions. The bulk of the material is derived from the
groundnut trade. Certain well-documented episodes in the history of
that trade are of much interest for this study.

1. THE ROLE OF TRADERS IN THE GROWTH OF THE NIGERIAN GROUNDNUT INDUSTRY

In discussions of the rapid growth of the Nigerian groundnut industry
the two influences most frequently mentioned are the extension of the
railway to Kano and the establishment of law and order over the
previously turbulent regions of northern Nigeria. There were, however,
two further indispensable factors. One of these was the initiative and
enterprise of the Hausa peasant who rapidly extended the cultivation
of this crop over large areas. The other factor was the activity of European and Levantine shippers and of Levantine and African merchants,
who brought consumer goods, which served as an inducement for the
cultivation of a cash crop, within the reach of the peasants of these large
and often remote regions. The merchants also brought into being
organizations which were able to arrange for the collection and removal
of very large volumes of produce, originating in areas from eight
hundred to eleven hundred miles from the coast.

The large European firms which had operated in southern Nigeria
before the rise of the groundnut industry soon established themselves in
the north, both for the sale of merchandise and for the purchase of
groundnuts. Besides the large European firms there were also a number
of Levantine traders acting both as shippers and as intermediaries,
especially in groundnut buying.

There were informal market-sharing arrangements between the large
European firms by the early 1920's, and a formal groundnut-buying
syndicate was established in 1926. The membership of this syndicate
was repeatedly extended. By the mid-1930's it comprised several of the

largest European firms, which together handled about 70 % of total exports. But while these arrangements reduced buying competition, they were appreciably less effective than similar arrangements in the purchase of oil-palm produce. This was due to many reasons, the most important of which was the presence of a number of traders, chiefly Levantine, who were outside the syndicate. Although until about 1936 the share of Levantines in total purchases was comparatively small, it was never negligible. Members of the syndicate could not pay much lower prices than the independent firms, since this would have immediately increased the share of the latter.

The most important of these Levantine traders was Mr S. Raccah, a Tripolitanian merchant to whose activities wide publicity was given in Professor Hancock's chapters on West African trade in *A Survey of Commonwealth Affairs*. By 1938–9 his purchases and shipments were not far behind those of the largest European shippers, and were more than treble those of any other shipper. His success was due principally to widespread contacts in northern Nigeria and the adjacent French territories, to the low level of his overhead costs, and to a keen competitive spirit. At times he was also able to effect substantial economies on freight by chartering vessels instead of relying on conference lines, saving as much as 15s. to 18s. a ton in this way.[1]

Mr Raccah claims that when competition between himself and the syndicate was at its height, the margins at which he worked were so narrow that at one stage the principal element in his profit margin was the gain in weight of groundnuts bought during the dry season and shipped rapidly. Groundnuts bought during the desiccating *hamattan* gain about $\frac{1}{4}$–$\frac{1}{2}$ % in weight between purchase in Kano and delivery in the United Kingdom or in north-west Europe. It is certain that profit margins were extremely narrow in the season before the outbreak of war. Mr Raccah's rapid progress resulted in a suspension of the syndicate at the end of the 1938–9 groundnut season. It was re-established at the beginning of the war as a result of the purchasing arrangements of the Ministry of Food.

2. AN EXAMPLE OF UNEXPECTED EMERGENCE OF COMPETITION

A small episode in the purchase of groundnuts during the war affords an interesting example of the unexpected emergence of competition under unpromising conditions, and of the influences which are apt to come into play to suppress it.

[1] These charters were probably a major influence in bringing about a reduction of the conference freight on groundnuts from 32s. a ton to about 21s. a ton around 1938; this benefited all shippers and producers.

I

The operations of the groundnut-buying syndicates have always been confined to the so-called Kano or northern area, which normally produces more than nine-tenths of the exportable groundnut crop. The balance is produced and bought for export in the so-called Rivers area, along the middle Niger and Benue in the Middle Belt of Nigeria. Before the war only two firms operated in that area and informal zoning arrangements were generally in force between them. Accordingly it was not necessary to include this area in syndicate operations; and for the same reason the wartime quota system was not extended to this area. After the establishment of the West African Produce Control Board in 1942 the two firms operating in this area were gazetted as buying agents, and minimum prices were fixed at a number of stations, chiefly along the rivers. The prices were generally higher down-stream nearer to the ultimate port of shipment; the difference between these prices and the lower prices up-river were estimated to cover the cost of river freight.

Among the various obscure tribes living in the vicinity of the Benue are the Kakanda, a comparatively backward tribe inhabiting a remote part of the eastern half of the Middle Belt. The Kakanda frequently travel long distances by canoe, and during the war they often engaged in taking various types of merchandise from Onitsha to Yola some five hundred miles or more up the river. As they had to make the return journey down-stream again, they were prepared to carry groundnuts at a very low charge. The tribesmen were thus in a position to buy them up-country at higher than the gazetted price and sell them to the licensed buying agents down-stream where the gazetted price was higher. They also sold small quantities of groundnuts for local consumption in Onitsha. But principally they resold the supplies they bought to licensed buying agents on the lower reaches of the Benue or the Niger. Towards the end of 1942 these Kakanda canoe men began to outbid the two large and powerful firms established on the upper Benue.

The firms concerned protested against the intrusion of these tribesmen into their markets. The Resident of Adamawa Province, to whom the complaint was first addressed, refused to intervene, as in his opinion no harm could result from these operations, since the producers received the guaranteed price or even higher prices, while the canoe transport served to relieve the strain on the shipping space and storage accommodation of the firms. However, the firms did not accept this, and carried their protests to the Nigerian Supply Board, on which they themselves were represented. They requested a suppression of this buying competition by prohibiting the Kakanda to buy groundnuts for shipment down the river. They argued that the action of the tribesmen increased the cost of groundnut purchases, as they offered them for sale at a place where higher prices were gazetted. This was plainly an unsubstantial argument, since the price differential was calculated to represent the cost of transport. However, the Nigerian Supply Board overrode the Resident, and an order was issued prohibiting the movement of groundnuts on the Benue except with official sanction, which was withheld from the canoe men. A blockade was also established to intercept the groundnuts carried by them. Some of the Kakanda tried to run the blockade, almost certainly with groundnuts purchased before the publication of the order, but they were unsuccessful. Their stock of groundnuts was confiscated and criminal summonses were also issued against them, but they managed to escape.

3. THE INFLUENCE OF THE NUMBER OF INTERMEDIARIES ON TRADING MARGINS

An examination of the influence of the number of merchants operating in an area on the prices offered for produce and charged for merchandise (i.e. on the merchants' gross margins) is a topic of wide general interest. It bears on important aspects of economic policy and administrative practice, as well as on certain controversial issues in economic theory on the effects of the number of traders on the terms on which trading services are available to the population. But this topic is also of special interest for the present study, one principal object of which is an attempt to assess the effects of concentration on the trading situation in West Africa, as well as to consider the number of independent alternative trading channels accessible to the local population.

For various reasons such an inquiry meets with very great difficulties, some of which are particularly telling in West African conditions. Ideally, complete and reliable price statistics would be required for two or more areas alike in all relevant respects except in the numbers of trading firms operating in each. For a number of obvious reasons it is difficult to find such comparable areas; two areas can never be completely alike, and it becomes necessary to ascertain whether the differences confuse the comparison.

Most of the difficulties of such on inquiry have their origin in the familiar problem of finding situations in which all other factors are constant except the one under investigation. They arise principally from four sources. First, the number of traders operating in a particular area does not necessarily indicate the number of alternatives open to the population, since the inhabitants may have access to stores in neighbouring areas or may be served by itinerant traders. Secondly, reliable and useful price statistics are rarely available; this is true *a fortiori* of statistics of gross margins. Thirdly, it is exceedingly difficult to find different areas which are alike in all relevant respects except in the number of trading alternatives open to the population. In particular, costs may differ owing to differences in money incomes, wage rates, density of population, the nature of the trade and many other factors. Fourthly, there is the difficulty common to many types of statistical inquiry, in that two series of statistics may either be causally connected, or may be independent results of a common cause, or may be unconnected though exhibiting some degree of statistical association.[1]

Most of these difficulties are, however, more acute in the analysis of the distribution of consumer goods to the users than in the purchase of standardized and bulky staple farm produce such as the principal export crops of West Africa. Fairly reliable data are available of prices paid in specific markets for export produce, and they generally relate to highly standardized commodities, often at a clearly defined stage in the chain of collection.

Where the population has access to traders in other areas or to their agents or to itinerant traders, the number of trading firms effectively operating in a particular area cannot be reliably ascertained. But this crucial difficulty is absent where the comparison is between market situations affecting bulky commodities (the transport costs of which are comparatively heavy) in large isolated areas. Fortunately for the purposes of this inquiry, the physical conditions and the trading situation in the groundnut-producing areas of Nigeria make such a comparison possible. Moreover, sufficient information is available for the purpose.

A comparison of this nature on a small scale has been presented by Professor Hancock in his celebrated chapters on West African trade in his *Survey of British Commonwealth Affairs*. Professor Hancock compared groundnut prices ruling in the towns of Kano and Baro in Nigeria over a number of pre-war years; from the findings he suggested that the larger number of traders in Kano secured higher prices for producers than in Baro where only two firms operated. Professor Hancock's pioneer effort related to a comparatively small sample and to somewhat fragmentary price statistics. He therefore advanced his conclusions tentatively. The comprehensive comparison set out in the following sections overwhelmingly confirms his findings.

4. BUYING ARRANGEMENTS FOR NIGERIAN GROUNDNUTS

Groundnuts are produced in Nigeria in two geographically distinct regions. Approximately 92–95 % of the total bought for export is produced in the so-called Northern or Kano area, while the balance is

---

[1] For example, the presence of only a small number of firms and high gross margins need not be causally connected but may both be symptoms of the inability of a sparsely populated or remote area to support more than one or two stores, the costs of which are likely to be high in such conditions.

produced in the Rivers area (or Upper Niger–Benue area). The two areas are divided by large and thinly populated stretches of country. In the periods covered by the investigation, groundnuts were not moved either by producers or traders from one area to the other. The produce of both areas is exported by the Nigeria Groundnut Marketing Board, and is bought on its behalf by trading firms which act as its licensed buying agents. In the season 1948–9 there were seventeen licensed buyers operating in the Northern area, and in 1949–50 there were twenty-one. In the Rivers area there were only two firms buying for the Board; both of these firms also operated in the Northern area.

The licensed buying agents purchase either through middlemen acting for them on a commission basis, or through their own clerks who are employees, and who are generally remunerated partly by salary and partly by commission. The middlemen have their own network of sub-middlemen. In the Rivers area the two buying agents purchase through clerks only and do not employ middlemen.

Each season the Groundnut Marketing Board prescribes statutory minimum prices to be paid for purchases at a large number of designated markets (gazetted stations) spread throughout the groundnut-producing areas. In the Kano area the structure of minimum prices pivots on the uniform prices prescribed for all railway stations.[1] In 1949–50 the railway line price was £21. 4s. 0d. per ton. In the Rivers area the structure pivots on two basic prices payable along the rivers; the difference in the two river prices (£1 per ton in the period under review) is to allow for the approximate differences in the cost of shipment to the ports. In 1949–50 the two basic river prices were £20 and £19 per ton.

At buying stations away from the railway line or the rivers (i.e. at road stations) lower minimum prices are prescribed to allow for the cost of transport to the railway or river stations; the difference is known as the transport differential. At a number of road stations in the Kano area the gazetted minimum prices are fixed at higher levels in relation to the basic price at railway stations than would be warranted by the officially calculated transport differentials. This is designed to encourage production in outlying areas. At these stations (subsidy stations) licensed buying agents receive transport subsidies from the Board for their purchases, to compensate them for the officially calculated loss which they are assumed to incur by paying the prescribed subsidized prices.

The buying agents receive from the Board no more than the relevant minimum prices (and transport subsidies where applicable) for the tonnages bought. They are reimbursed for their expenses and

---

[1] The Nigerian railway charges a flat rate for the movement of groundnuts throughout the Kano area.

remunerated for their services by the tonnage payments known as block allowances. In 1949–50 this block allowance was £4. 10s. 6d. per ton for the Kano area and £4. 17s. 9d. for the Rivers area. The principal items include the cost of bags, interest, insurance and other finance charges, an allowance for overhead expenses, middlemen's commission and the agents' remuneration. In 1949–50 middlemen's commission was allowed for at 14s. a ton on all purchases in the Kano area. There was naturally no similar item in the Rivers area; but the overhead allowance was raised by over 13s. in recognition of the fact that all purchases were made through the salaried clerks of the trading firms. The licensed agents' remuneration was 8s. 6d. and 7s. 8d. per ton in the Kano and Rivers areas respectively. This was 2% of the basic price. There is no item for transport costs in the block allowance, since the transport differentials and subsidies are deemed to cover the transport expenses of the firms from the stations to the railway line or the rivers.

The block allowances in the two groundnut areas are settled by negotiation between the Marketing Board and the licensed buying agents. There is no reason to believe that they are less generous in the Rivers area than in the Kano area. The absolute level is higher in the Rivers area, in acceptance of the claims of the buying agents that their costs are higher. Within the total allowance the overhead items are both absolutely and relatively larger in the Rivers area.

5. THE NUMBER OF BUYING AGENTS IN THE TWO PRODUCING REGIONS

Although a fair number of buying agents operate in the Kano area, the organization of the trade might suggest that little buying competition would take place there. First, in 1948–9 sixteen of the seventeen agents were members of a confidential market-sharing syndicate operating along familiar lines; in 1949–50 sixteen out of twenty-one were members of the syndicate. In both 1948–9 and 1949–50 the combined share of members of the syndicate in total purchases was over 90%. Secondly, there is a marked degree of concentration in groundnut buying; three of the licensed buying agents, handling between one-half and three-fifths of total purchases, are financially linked, though their operations locally are largely independent. Thirdly, with quantitatively negligible exceptions, all licensed buying agents are European and Levantine (i.e. non-African) firms or traders who operate with substantial capital and who possess a large measure of commercial skill; their middlemen are in many cases non-African. They buy from customers (producers and small African traders) who in the great majority of instances are illiterate, have little capital and are geographically dispersed.

From these considerations it might well be inferred that in spite of the apparently large number of licensed buyers price competition, or indeed any form of buying competition, would be negligible. In short, it might be expected that the intensity of buying competition in the Kano area would not differ materially from that in the Rivers area, where there are only two buyers.

The main reasons for the small number of traders in the Rivers area are fairly clear. The area is comparatively poor, undeveloped, sparsely populated and backward, and is therefore not an easy market for traders to enter. However, the comparative backwardness is not a complete explanation; it is known that trading in this area has been distinctly profitable to the firms established there. These two firms own and operate the cheapest form of transport, river shipping, which they developed over a number of years, and this may have acted as a deterrent to new entry. It would be costly, and possibly impracticable, for a new trading firm to develop its own river-shipping services, while reliance upon the services of the ships owned and operated by the established trading firms would increase the risks and inconvenience of trading. Nevertheless, some firms have recently investigated the possibility of establishing themselves in this region and are likely to start operations in the near future.[1]

6. PAYMENTS IN EXCESS OF STATUTORY MINIMUM PRICES IN THE KANO AREA

There has been a substantial measure of buying competition in the Kano area for many years past in spite of confidential buying syndicates and other influences tending to discourage it. Buying competition in the Kano area continued even during the war, despite an officially established and administered system of buying quotas with fines for overpurchases, and a ban on new entry. The statutory minimum producer prices, which from 1942 to 1946 ranged from £6 to £16 per ton at rail stations, were frequently and increasingly exceeded. At first, overpayments were of the order of a few shillings per ton, but by 1946 overpayments of 40s. and 50s. per ton were frequent at outlying road stations where the minimum prices were appreciably lower than those fixed for rail stations. These overpayments were particularly large in

---

[1] Information on the volume of groundnut purchases at individual markets in the Rivers area seems to suggest that the number of firms operating in them is not limited solely by the extent of the market. In many markets in the Rivers area the volume of groundnut purchases per firm is much greater than the corresponding averages at many markets in the Kano area (including many stations in outlying districts where nevertheless several buyers operate). Moreover, cotton, benniseed, ginger and shea-nuts are also brought to markets in the Rivers area.

areas where there were wide transport differentials or where transport subsidies were paid.

Overpayments have been widespread since 1947; and more specific and more comprehensive information has become available on this subject, chiefly because for administrative reasons more detailed data have been collected. Sufficiently detailed and consistently compiled information is available for thirty-two road stations, at which about two-fifths of the tonnage was bought in 1948–9 and 1949–50.[1]

In 1948–9 there was a good harvest, but in the following year it was

Table 15. *Groundnut purchases and overpayments at thirty-two road stations in northern Nigeria, 1948–9 and 1949–50*

	1948–9	1949–50
Total groundnut purchases in Kano area (tons)	315,000	178,000
Groundnut purchases at the 32 road stations (tons)	119,000	76,000
Average number of licensed buying agents [a] · represented at the 32 road stations (weighted by tonnage of purchases at each station)	6	7
Statutory minimum price at railway line (per ton)	£19. 4s. 0d.	£21. 4s. 0d.
Average prescribed minimum price at the 32 road stations (per ton)	£16. 19s. 9d.	£19. 3s. 0d.
Average price paid at the 32 road stations (per ton) [b]	£18. 0s. 1d.	£20. 8s. 8d.
Average overpayment at the 32 road stations (per ton)	£1. 0s. 4d.	£1. 5s. 8d.
Range of overpayments at the 32 road stations (per ton)	From 1s. to £3. 10s. 0d.	From 1s. to £4. 5s. 0d.

[a] The numbers of middlemen and clerks operating in different localities tend to be proportional to the number of licensed buying agents. The degree of competition among the clerks and middlemen is largely influenced by the number of licensed buying agents and the market positions of the latter (cf. also § 10 below).

[b] For 1948–9 the prices paid are the averages for the whole season; for 1949–50 they refer to the first half of the season, by which time rather more than one-half of the crop had been bought. For various reasons overpayments tend to be larger in the second half of the season, chiefly because greater competition among the owners of transport leaves the buyers with a more generous real allowance on transport differentials. Thus the 1949–50 figures may tend to understate the extent of overpayments for the season as a whole.

[1] The prices were collected partly by the authorities and partly by the licensed buying agents. Each price represents a simple arithmetic mean of a more or less continuous series of recorded prices containing a large number of successive items. Though the figures are imprecise, and in a sense incomplete, they are close approximations. A personal test check in December 1949 at two stations confirmed that the ruling prices accorded closely with the recorded data.

bad. Wherever the information is available the investigation covers both years to allow for the possible influence of the size of the crop on the intensity of competition. In fact this influence appears to have been small.

The principal statistics relevant to the present investigation are presented in Table 15.

In both years the gazetted minimum prices were exceeded at every station. The highest overpayments were recorded at road stations where the gazetted minimum prices were lowest and where, therefore, the transport differentials, usually augmented by subsidies, were greatest; in 1948–9 overpayments of £3. 10s. 0d. were frequent at stations where the minimum prices were slightly over £13 per ton.

7. ABSENCE OF OVERPAYMENTS IN THE RIVERS AREA

The presence and the extent of these overpayments in the Kano area are themselves significant; and they gain in significance when contrasted with the position in the Rivers area, where there were only two licensed buying agents. With one interesting but quantitatively negligible exception,[1] there has been no record or suggestion of overpayments for groundnuts by licensed buying agents or their representatives in the Rivers area during or since the war. The statutory minima have been observed but have nowhere been exceeded. This is undoubtedly due to the absence of competition, and not to the lack of available margins, which, given competition, would have been competed away in favour of sellers. In the Rivers area four-fifths of the tonnage was bought in 1949–50 at buying stations at which only one or other of the two firms were operating. For this large portion of the area informal market-sharing by means of zoning was in effect in force.

8. THE RELATION BETWEEN THE NUMBER OF TRADERS AND THE LEVEL OF OVERPAYMENTS

It would have been interesting to investigate the correlation between the extent of overpayments and the numbers at each road station in the group analysed in the preceding section. Unfortunately, the available data cannot be used for this special purpose. The amount of the overpayment depends not only on the extent of competition, but also on the margin available to be competed away in this way. This margin is not the same at each road station, principally because it is greatly influenced by the difference between the officially recognized transport differential (and subsidy where this applies) and the actual

---

[1] Reviewed in § 2 of this chapter.

transport costs incurred.[1] Sufficiently detailed information about the latter in the two seasons under review is not available.

However, there is some information, more limited in scope but of considerable interest, of prices paid in 1949–50 at nine buying stations on the railway line.[2] The figures are tentatively advanced, but it is most unlikely that any errors they may contain would significantly alter the conclusions they suggest.

In 1949–50, 24,000 tons were bought at these stations—about 15 % of total purchases in the Kano area and 45 % of total purchases at rail stations. The gazetted minimum price was £21. 4s. 0d. per ton. As there were no transport differentials or subsidies, the prime costs of buying groundnuts were about the same at each station; hence the margin which could be competed away was also fairly constant. The major influence vitiating the comparability of overpayments at different road stations is absent.

Information on buying operations at the nine railway stations is shown in Table 16.

There were overpayments at six of the nine markets along the railway

Table 16. *Groundnut purchases and overpayments at nine markets at railway stations in northern Nigeria, 1949–50*

Station	Number of licensed buying agents	Average overpayment in shillings per ton	Tonnage bought	Average tonnage per buying agent
A	1	0	1196	1196
B	2	0	666	333
C	2	0	1412	706
D	2	10	1968	984
E	3	11	3107	1036
F	4	6	1975	494
G	6	16	2885	481
H	7	6	2756	394
I	10	20	8967	897

[1] Generally speaking, the margin available to be competed away was greatest at the outlying stations, especially at the subsidy stations where the transport differential and the subsidy together in some cases exceeded £9 per ton. On the other hand, at road stations near the railway line the differential was only a few shillings. Thus, even though there might have been a large number of buyers operating under keenly competitive conditions at road stations near the railway line, the overpayments would perforce have been less than at the more remote stations with fewer buyers but larger transport differentials.

[2] This information was kindly collected for this inquiry by the produce department of the United Africa Company in Kano.

line. Moreover, the data suggest strongly that the extent of overpayments is much influenced by the number of traders present.[1] There were only one or two buying agents represented at the three stations at which no overpayments were recorded. At the other end there were three stations at which six or more buying agents were represented, and two of these had the heaviest overpayments.

But numbers of traders alone do not give a full picture of the degree of buying competition at the different stations. It may be expected that, apart from numbers, the intensity of competition would depend upon various other factors, some of which cannot be expressed quantitatively. These would include the presence of newcomers trying to force their way into the trade generally or into the particular trading centre, and the presence of firms outside the buying syndicate. A further factor may be the presence of firms without extensive organization in the particular area who might therefore have to a greater extent to rely on price inducements to secure supplies. A racially heterogeneous group of traders comprising Europeans, Levantines and Africans is likely to behave more competitively (even despite agreements) than a homogeneous group of the same size, as the contacts between members are likely to be less continuous and smooth, In addition, Levantine firms tend to be more individualistic in outlook and behaviour.

The influence of competition on prices becomes even clearer when the figures in Table 16, which by themselves are instructive, are subjected to qualitative analysis. Thus station D, which at first sight appears to be an exception, falls into place; for there a newcomer, who was not in the syndicate, had entered the market for the first time in that season and had, moreover, to contend with the difficulties of a late start in the season. Qualitative analysis also clarifies the position at E. One new firm, again not a member of the syndicate, entered the market here. This firm is a comparatively recently established Levantine firm with no extensive organization. The comparatively modest overpayments at F and H coincide with the absence of firms outside the syndicate. At F, with one exception, only large established European firms operated; the exception was a Levantine trader financially linked with one of the large European firms. Six of the seven firms which operated at H are the largest members of the syndicate, and three of them are linked financially. The situation at I, where substantial overpayments occurred, is one of some interest in that all ten firms which operated there were members of the buying syndicate, but four of them were comparatively small firms, including three Levantine enterprises.

A study of the entries in the final column of the table (average

[1] The correlation coefficient between the second and the third column in the table is $+0.76$.

tonnages per buyer) suggests that differences in overpayments were independent of the scale of operations as measured by average volumes handled. There is evidently no correlation between the average tonnage purchased per firm and the size of overpayment.

The statistics of this section, although on a small scale, suggest several conclusions. They confirm that the emergence of competition under apparently unpropitious circumstances has resulted in substantial overpayment, and they suggest that these overpayments are largely a function of the intensity of competition. It appears that the number of firms is an important element in the competitive situation, and that even small numbers may result in a substantial measure of price competition. But numbers alone do not provide a full explanation; qualitative assessment is also necessary. Here the role of new entry and of the composition of the group of competitors appear to have been particularly important.

9. THE SOURCE AND INCIDENCE OF OVERPAYMENTS

It is easier to discover the beneficiaries of overpayments than it is to determine who bears their cost. The statistics of actual prices in the preceding sections refer to prices paid by middlemen and clerks of licensed buying agents to producers or to those petty middlemen, not affiliated to any licensed buying agent, who bring produce to the buying stations. As the unaffiliated petty middlemen are members of the rural community, and in many cases are themselves producers, overpayments represent additions to the income of the agricultural community.

The heaviest overpayments since 1942–3 (when they were first recorded) have occurred in the comparatively distant Bornu Province. In 1949–50 overpayments at the principal buying stations in that province were of the order of £3 to £4 per ton on a basic minimum road station price of about £16. In this area the transport differentials and subsidies are high and are in effect the main source from which competition has produced overpayments, since the actual transport rates tend to be much lower. In 1949–50 the officially calculated transport costs from the principal buying stations in Bornu to Kano were of the order of £10 per ton, while the actual costs were about £4 per ton, mainly because of the cheap rate quoted by owners of lorries returning lightly laden from the Lake Chad area. This example suggests that some of these overpayments represent and reflect the fruits of the actual creation of new wealth through improvements in the methods of transport and marketing.[1]

---

[1] This traffic was not peculiar to 1949–50. In recent years groundnuts appear to have been carried from Bornu to Kano or Jos for about 2½d. per ton-mile, which is remarkably low for an area with a poor road system about a thousand miles from the ports.

The groundnut producers of Bornu are not only generally illiterate but are among the most backward sections of the peasantry of northern Nigeria. According to the views held in some influential circles the 'bargaining position' of these producers *vis-a-vis* a handful of generally well-financed and organized alien traders, frequently acting in concert, would have been extremely weak. Yet so far from being exploited by the so-called rapacious alien and other middlemen, competition amongst buyers has secured for them prices far in excess of the minima laid down for their protection.

Overpayments represent the surrender by those participating in the trade of part of the incomes and reimbursements provided for in the official structure of prices and block allowances.[1] They are made in order to secure additional supplies, and are enforced by competition upon licensed buyers and middlemen.

It is not possible to determine precisely how the burden of any particular overpayment has been shared by the buying agents, clerks and middlemen, who are all members of the urban community. However, the magnitude of overpayments at rail stations, where the basic minimum price is payable (i.e. where there are no transport differentials and subsidies) makes it clear that in many cases a share of the burden is carried by the licensed buying agents themselves; some of the overpayments exceed the gross commission payable to middlemen.

10. VALUABLE INDIRECT CONCESSIONS BY BUYING AGENTS AND OTHER INTERMEDIARIES

Although this analysis is concerned with the influence of the number of traders on the prices received by producers, it would be misleading to neglect other advantages derived by producers and rural middlemen from buying competition among licensed buyers and their employees and middlemen; the benefits of competition are not confined to overpayments.

Local executives of the merchant firms acting as buying agents frequently wish to secure additional tonnage without making overpayments, which may meet with displeasure from senior executives. Additional purchases may be secured without actual overpayments by selling equipment and merchandise to favoured middlemen at prices lower than the prevailing market prices. An important special case of

---

[1] It is conceivable that overpayments and out-of-pocket expenses together might in some cases exceed the gross receipts allowed for by the prescribed price structure. This would represent an instance of a notional loss on one branch of the activities of what is in effect a multi-product firm, for the benefit of the business as a whole. There is some evidence that middlemen occasionally 'lost' on groundnut buying but continued operating because of market opportunities in the related grain trade.

this practice is the favourable allocation of price-controlled (so-called short supply) equipment and merchandise to these customers. Other concessions take the form of the use of premises at nominal rents or the granting of advances or trade credits for long periods.

Wherever possible clerks prefer to secure additional tonnage by means of valuable concessions rather than by undisguised overpayments. Such concessions are not at the expense of their own commission or salary, and can be made at the expense of their firm without requiring specific approval from their superiors.

There may be further reasons for preferring indirect (but valuable) concessions to direct overpayments as a means for securing additional tonnage. Some of these concessions can, at least for a short period, be restricted to a limited number of selected customers, whereas overpayments must generally be granted to all comers, as knowledge of them tends to spread more quickly. Moreover, even where the granting of the concession cannot be concealed, the differential treatment is less likely to cause resentment than differential overpayments, since certain concessions (such as the use of premises on favourable terms) by their very nature cannot be made to all customers.

The presence of a number of firms is in itself of value to the producer by reducing his dependence on individual firms or their intermediaries or employees, and especially by providing more buying stations closer to individual producers. This is generally beneficial to producers, and is of special importance in such very large regions as the groundnut producing area of northern Nigeria.

II. PRACTICAL IMPLICATIONS OF THE ANALYSIS OF THIS CHAPTER

The results of competition in produce buying shown here bear on a wide range of topics in economic theory, in administrative practice and in discussions of the reform of marketing. The evidence suggests that an increase in the number of traders improves the terms on which trading services are made available to the rest of the community. In other words, it tends to increase the volume and range of goods and services obtained by the producers for a given amount of effort. This evidence has important implications for official policy in such diverse fields as the control of immigration and internal migration, the various measures of control over the numbers and activities of traders, and certain proposals for the reform of marketing methods in produce buying and in internal trade.[1]

---

[1] Some of these proposals are considered in Part 6 below.

NOTE TO CHAPTER 18

Supplementary information on the influence of competition among traders on the price of trading services

The analysis of this chapter refers to groundnut buying, for which reliable data are available, and for which conditions in the producing areas make detailed comparisons possible. But the influence of competition on the margins secured by intermediaries, from the licensed buying agents to the smallest petty trader, is evident throughout Nigeria and the Gold Coast.

Certain results of competition among intermediaries were discernible in the purchase of palm kernels in western Nigeria in 1950. In the summer of that year several visits were made to five or six markets in the Ibadan area; substantial overpayments over the gazetted minimum prices were noted in each of these markets. Overpayments were frequently in excess of the total commission of the middlemen, and must have been derived either from the profits of transport (i.e. by securing transport at a lower rate than that provided for in the calculation of the structure of minimum prices at stations away from the railway line), or from overpayments sanctioned by licensed buying agents.

The arrangements in the marketing of palm kernels exemplify another source of profit for middlemen, and thus ultimately a source of overpayment, and this deserves more detailed analysis as it suggests lessons of some general interest. Palm kernels generally lose weight in storage and transport. This is recognized in the present marketing arrangements in Nigeria, which allow a franchise of 4 lb. per bag of 185 lb. between purchase up-country and check-weighing at the port of shipment. The licensed buying agents, or the commission buyers operating on their behalf, must pack palm kernels to a standard pack of 185 lb. per bag. As long as they comply with these instructions and subsequent check-weighing at port of shipment shows an average weight of not less than 181 lb. per bag, the buying agent is not held accountable for the difference. The franchise is supposed to represent a fair average of the loss on a bag weighing 185 lb. at the time of purchase. However, in western Nigeria the average loss of weight is appreciably less than 4 lb., and this presents a possible source of profit. If as a result of collusion between the buying clerk or the commission buyer on the one hand and the up-country produce inspector[1] on the other, the latter passes bags of palm kernels weighing only 183 lb. or even 182 lb. instead of 185 lb., it is possible to secure a profit of over 1 % as long as the consignment passes the check weighing test at port of shipment. This gain is occasionally increased by further collusion with the checkweigher, who can so choose a sample that only the heaviest bags are weighed.

These arrangements open up possibilities of illicit gains for the commission buyers and the clerks of the licensed buying agents. But as these buyers

---

[1] The produce inspector has to pass and seal at the time of purchase the produce bought by the commission buyer or the buying clerk.

operate in an area where there is much competition, the bulk of the illicit gains is passed on to the producers in the form of overpayments in excess of the statutory minimum prices. Ultimately the improper practice simply results in a transfer to the producer of what would otherwise be a very small addition to the surplus margin of the Oil Palm Produce Marketing Board. This process illustrates the general proposition that abuses in produce buying are of little significance when competitive conditions force the transmission of the illicit gains to the producer as a result of the efforts of middlemen to obtain tonnage; the prices received by producers or the margins of intermediaries are influenced more by the degree of competition than by the prevalence of sharp practices.

Thus in the purchase of palm kernels, as in groundnut buying, competition among the intermediaries has produced substantial overpayments above the gazetted minimum prices with favourable effects on the terms of trade of the population, closely similar to those reviewed in this chapter.[1] And whatever was the source of the gain, it was only competition which forced the intermediaries to pass it on to the producers.

It will be recalled that the difficulties of assessing the effects of the numbers of traders in a particular area (the trading representation) on trading margins are appreciably greater in merchandise trade than in produce buying, principally because of the varied nature of merchandise, the non-uniformity of consumer tastes, the ease of moving merchandise between adjacent areas, and the absence of reliable price records. But sporadic evidence in West Africa confirms that, other things being equal, an increase in the number of firms tends to result in lower prices of imported merchandise as well as in other valuable concessions to buyers.

Local agreements among sellers of merchandise are rarely concluded in areas in which many firms operate; and (even when concluded) they tend to be ineffective where there are more than three firms. There are various local agreements among the different firms, but it is generally agreed that they are inoperative except in areas where there are not more than three firms and/or which are outside the reach of transport from the larger trading centres. Again, the larger the number of firms operating in an area, the more likely it is that one or another of these should at any given time find itself pressed for capital and so be induced to liquidate stocks with a resulting fall in prices.

One or two more specific pieces of evidence tend to confirm these general impressions. I was shown the margin secured on bafts and shirtings by a large importing house in a particular year in different districts in Nigeria. They referred to standardized lines and the necessary adjustment for transport costs from the coast had been made. These margins were in every case appreciably higher in those districts where the firm had no competitor, or

---

[1] The effect of buying competition on producer prices was reflected in recent years in two minor export products of northern Nigeria, gum arabic and reptile skins. In the purchase of these commodities one or two medium-sized Levantine firms entered the market in competition with one or two of the largest European firms, and their intervention resulted in a remarkable reduction in both the absolute and the percentage margins between world prices and local prices.

had only one, than in those areas where there were a number of competitors. This evidence is not conclusive, since the high margins and the small number of firms may both be the result of comparative inaccessibility of certain regions and of high costs of operations, and the higher margins may not represent higher returns on capital. Nevertheless, it is suggestive of the influence of numbers of competitors on the level of selling prices.

The impression conveyed by these figures was again confirmed in discussions with executives of some of the largest firms in Nigeria. The opinion was unanimous that trading in the Middle Belt of Nigeria, especially along the middle Niger and the Benue, was far easier and more profitable, though much smaller in total, than in the Kano area, where competition was much livelier.

Again, over large areas in northern Nigeria there are price agreements between the principal firms for minimum prices of salt and certain standardized textiles. They seem to be effective only in the more outlying parts of Sokoto and Bornu, or along the middle Niger and the Benue.

Administrators, as well as the more articulate members of the local population, with whom I discussed the question of the influence of trading representation on prices, were generally of the opinion that an increase in the number of stores tends to keep down the prices of imported goods. In some areas this feeling is so pronounced that it has led to a reversal of the previous trend of African opinion, which had been pressing for a withdrawal of the non-African firms from the petty wholesale or retail trade. More recently there have been instances of requests by the local population for the opening of more stores by the firms to assist in keeping down the prices of imported goods.

Competition in the merchandise trade often also takes the form of covert price concessions and the provision of additional services. The reasons for these practices, which are additional to ordinary price competition, are in general much the same as for the similar practices in groundnut buying discussed in § 10 above. Important examples of such concessions are the granting of liberal credit terms, the allocation of short supply merchandise, the provision of transport and containers, and efforts to meet customers' special quality requirements. And as in the produce trade, the presence of a larger number of traders in merchandise benefits the population by providing more stores nearer to their homes.

CHAPTER 19

WARTIME ARRANGEMENTS IN THE WEST AFRICAN EXPORT TRADE AND THEIR RESULTS

1. SIGNIFICANCE OF THE WARTIME CONTROLS IN THE EXPORT TRADE

There were three principal objectives of the wartime control over West African exports. The first was to deny supplies to the enemy and to secure them for the Allies, particularly the United Kingdom. The second objective was the prevention of a collapse of the local price of cocoa. The third principal objective was to increase exports of groundnuts and of oil palm produce after 1942. There were also three principal elements in the machinery of export control. The first was licensing of exports to direct these to specific destinations. The second was statutory monopoly in the handling of the principal exports. The third element was a system of quotas in the purchase of export produce. Licensing of exports to direct these to specific destinations was an obvious necessity. Neither this aim of policy nor its administration differed substantially from similar arrangements elsewhere, including the United Kingdom. Moreover, this aspect of the controls did not affect permanently the structure of the trade. Accordingly it will not be considered further in this study. On the other hand, the establishment of statutory monopoly in the export of agricultural produce, and the operation of a quota system in their purchase, differed greatly from the controls over similar commodities elsewhere in the British colonies. These arrangements, which do not appear to have been necessary for any of the declared objectives of the controls, have had far-reaching and lasting effects on the marketing of West African produce. For these reasons this chapter examines in some detail their wartime establishment and operation.

2. WARTIME ESTABLISHMENT OF STATUTORY EXPORT MONOPOLIES AND SOME OF ITS RESULTS

The wartime establishment of statutory export monopolies in West Africa has come to be taken so much for granted that the grounds for their establishment do not appear to have been examined. Yet it is clear that their introduction was not necessary.

Monopoly of export was obviously not required for the support of the local price of cocoa; an official guarantee to act as residual buyer at a seasonally fixed price was all that was necessary.[1] A statutory export monopoly was equally unnecessary for the increase of the supplies of groundnuts and of oil-palm produce after the fall of the Far East in 1942.

Indeed, the marketing arrangements and price policies of the West African Produce Control Board were not calculated to increase supplies of groundnuts or oil-palm produce. These products were sold exclusively to the Ministry of Food. The Ministry took them over from the West African Produce Control Board at cost prices, that is, at prices paid by this organization to the producers plus charges to cost and freight United Kingdom. Both the prices paid by the Ministry of Food and the local producer prices were exceedingly low.[2]

Some results of the establishment of statutory marketing are suggested by Table 17, which shows the relation between the prices paid by the Ministry of Food for bulk supplies of Nigerian and Indian groundnuts before and after the export of the Nigerian product was taken over by the West African Produce Control Board.[3] Throughout the entire period covered by the table the Ministry was the sole buyer of Nigerian groundnuts. The data are derived from the official trade returns.

The much higher prices paid for Indian groundnuts from 1942 were those paid for bulk supplies and not for marginal quantities. Indeed, up to 1946 imports from India were much larger than from Nigeria. It was only in 1947–8 that imports from India were reduced to small quantities.[4] The figures do not suggest that the establishment of statutory marketing could have served to increase supplies, since the low prices secured and paid by the statutory monopoly were hardly calculated to

[1] Price supports in the form of guaranteed minimum prices have been introduced many times in different parts of the world without establishing purchasing monopolies.

[2] In Parts 4 and 5 of this study, especially in Chapters 19 and 22 and in Appendix 1, there are repeated references to the differences between the prices secured by the statutory marketing organizations from the Ministry of Food and those received by other bulk suppliers. In any assessment of these policies the circumstances of the war years must be remembered. The information on the differences in prices paid for West African and other produce is presented here not as a review or as a criticism of the wartime arrangements, but because of its bearing on the policies of the marketing boards and on some of the claims advanced on behalf of this type of marketing organization. In assessing the price policies of the marketing boards, especially in their effects on producers and on the long-term competitive position of these territories, the length of the period over which producer prices have been kept below market prices and below the price received by other suppliers is a relevant factor. Secondly, the danger of weak selling by merchants is frequently adduced as an argument for statutory monopolies, and the marketing of West African produce during the war has been invoked in support of this argument.

[3] Broadly comparable information for oil-palm produce is presented in Appendix 1.

[4] From 1949 onwards they were negligible. The reduction in supplies from India from 1947 was the result principally of the revival of outside markets and partly of a reduction in total exports.

increase exports. They also dispose of the argument occasionally advanced in support of the establishment of statutory marketing in West Africa that it has served to eliminate weak selling by merchants.

From February 1947 the selling arrangements were modified, and the prices paid by the Ministry of Food were no longer fixed by reference to the costs of the West African Produce Control Board. Although the prices paid were still well below market levels, they were nevertheless appreciably raised. Much of this increase was, however, retained by the West African Produce Control Board. The Board was able to do this, since by virtue of its statutory export monopoly it was in a position to prescribe the prices paid to producers, and to divorce these both from world prices and from selling prices. As a result of the policy of accumulating surpluses the prices received by the producers remained far below commercial values. But while before 1947 the difference accrued wholly to the Ministry of Food, thereafter much of it was retained and accumulated by the West African Produce Control Board.

In cocoa marketing the selling arrangements were more successful, since the prices received by the West African Cocoa Control Board and the West African Produce Control Board were much closer to market levels than those secured for the other products. But almost from their inception the Boards began to accumulate surpluses by withholding from producers part of the net sale proceeds.

Not only was the establishment of statutory export monopolies unnecessary for the purposes which were stated to be the reason for their

Table 17. *Imports of groundnuts into the United Kingdom, 1939–48*

	From Nigeria		From India		B as a percentage of D	
	Quantity 000's tons	Price £ per ton	Quantity 000's tons	Price £ per ton		
	A	B	C	D		
1939	41	10·4	209	11·0	95	Nigerian exports by merchants
1940	123	14·7	247	15·8	93	
1941	214	17·3	377	18·1	96	
1942 (a)	201	17·3	253	20·4	85	
1943	96	19·8	292	35·9	55	Nigerian exports by W.A.P.C.B.
1944	169	22·6	312	35·6	63	
1945	154	24·6	238	33·0	75	
1946	271	24·9	120	34·2	73	
1947	229	28·4	12	61·1	46	
1948	264	42·4	41	62·2	68	

(a) Marketing of groundnuts taken over by West African Produce Control Board in August 1942.

Source. Annual Statement of Trade of the United Kingdom.

introduction, but the policies pursued by these organizations were irrelevant or disadvantageous to the attainment of the officially stated aims of policy. On cocoa transactions the Cocoa Control Board and the West African Produce Control Board began to accumulate surpluses almost from their inception by paying producers less than the sale proceeds received. This was clearly quite irrelevant to the maintenance of the local price of cocoa, which was stated to be the reason for the establishment of statutory marketing; and this policy was continued throughout the existence of these bodies. Again, as soon as the Ministry of Food raised the very low prices paid for oilseeds (calculated on the basis of the cost of these products to the West African Produce Control Board), the Board began to accumulate surpluses on these products as well. This could only serve to discourage supplies in contrast to the official aim of expanding supplies.

Thus during these years the prices received by West African producers were below those received by other suppliers of the same or similar commodities for two reasons. First, because the marketing authority received lower prices from the Ministry of Food than were paid to other bulk suppliers. Secondly, because of the retention of part of the sale proceeds from the producers. These arrangements brought about a marked reduction in the real incomes of the producers of West African exports through a sharp deterioration in their real terms of trade.[1]

3. ESTABLISHMENT AND METHOD OF OPERATION OF THE EXPORT QUOTAS

During the war the export, or purchase for export, of all major West African agricultural products was subject to official quotas; in the purchase of oil-seeds the system operated from 1939 to 1945 and in the purchase of cocoa until 1947. There were unimportant differences in its administration in the various colonies.

When it was announced in November 1939 that the British Government would purchase through an official monopoly[2] at a fixed price all cocoa offered for sale in the Gold Coast and Nigeria, it was also stated that the merchant firms would act as agents in the purchase of the crop and as shippers under the direction of the authorities, and that they would share the trade on a quota basis.

---

[1] The course of the terms of trade of the producers is examined in Chapter 23 and in Appendix 2 below. These show very steep deterioration in the terms of trade during the war. They also show that when the West African Produce Control Board ceased to handle the products under its control (in 1947 for cocoa and in 1949 for the other products), the terms of trade of the producers were still less favourable than they had been in the mid-1930's.

[2] First the Cocoa Control of the Ministry of Food, and subsequently the West African Cocoa Control Board and the West African Produce Control Board.

The firms were allotted percentage quotas[1] based on past performance, and they were supposed to keep their purchases and shipments as near to these as possible; new entry into the trade was banned. Those who exceeded their quotas were debited by the authorities for the benefit of those who were under-bought. These settlements were easily effected, since the authorities had to make periodic payments to the firms reimbursing them for their expenses (including the cost of the purchase of the products) and remunerating them for their services. The rate of penalty payments per ton (for over-purchases) and of premia per ton (for under-purchases) was equivalent to the sum of the commission and the overhead items in the schedule of expenses. This method of calculating penalties was exactly the same as that provided for in the cocoa-buying agreement of 1937 and in the other produce-buying agreements or syndicates before the war. After 1942 the West African Produce Control Board became the actual shipper, and the former exporters became its licensed buying agents. The quota system continued without substantial modifications, but the former shipping quotas now became buying quotas.

The quotas, which were calculated by the Cocoa Committee of the Association of West African Merchants, were based on the firms' exports for the three seasons from 1936 to 1939 with certain minor modifications for firms which had not operated throughout this period.[2] The results of the calculations were gazetted by the authorities; the rate of penalty payments was also made public.

Somewhat different arrangements applied to the export of oilseeds, in which the merchants continued to act as principals until 1942. Exports were directed to the United Kingdom where the Ministry of Food was the sole buyer. This department arranged the shipments with the Association of West African Merchants; and this body in turn allocated the contracts in accordance with quotas calculated by itself. As export licenses were granted for exports to the United Kingdom only, pre-war shippers who had not been members of the Association were now forced to join it, because membership was a condition for the receipt of export licences for these commodities.

---

[1] Some of the smaller traders (the so-called B shippers) received fixed specific tonnage quotas.

[2] The authorities appear to have had no part in the arrangement of the quotas beyond mere publication of the results of the decisions and calculations of the Cocoa Committee of the Association of West African Merchants. So complete was the recognition accorded to the Association of West African Merchants that for long periods the authorities in West Africa did not even know either the size of the individual quotas or the basis on which they were computed, and issued licences in accordance with instructions from the Colonial Office. The latter in turn simply transmitted the calculations of the Association.

When the West African Produce Control Board took over the export of West African oilseeds in 1942 (and of palm oil in 1943), the former shipping quotas became buying quotas for the licensed buying agents purchasing on behalf of the Board. Payments and receipts for over- and under-purchased positions were settled through the Board in accordance with published quotas and penalty rates.

Nigerian cotton was purchased by the merchant firms for the British Cotton Growing Association, which in turn acted on behalf of the British purchasing departments. There was no formal quota system, but it was informally agreed between the merchants and the authorities that the purchases of the merchants would be kept in line with the relative shares at the beginning of the war. Relative shares were to be maintained by altering buying representation at the different scheduled markets (where all cotton had to be bought) in accordance with over-bought or under-bought positions. This, again, was the method of the cotton-buying syndicate, but it did not function very smoothly during the war. The aim was roughly achieved, but only after much friction and argument.

Hides and skins were bought by the British purchasing departments broadly in accordance with the relative shares of the shippers in the pre-war export trade. There had been no syndicate in these products, largely because they are unstandardized; this also rendered difficult the administration of a quota system.

These arrangements continued in the case of cocoa until 1947. For other products the quotas were abolished in 1945, but the ban on new entry remained in force until 1947.[1]

4. THE PARADOX OF THE QUOTA SYSTEM

In the export trade, as distinct from the import trade, the quota system was unnecessary and harmful. Indeed, its introduction and operation were paradoxical.

Quotas are normally introduced to share out limited supplies or a limited market; neither of these limitations applied to the West African export trade. The quotas were imposed and maintained in the face of an unrestricted market. This was implicitly recognized in that no limit was placed on aggregate purchases or shipments of any of the products in the quota system; the quotas simply referred to shares in unspecified or unlimited totals. From this it was clear that the quotas were not required by the exigencies of war. However, these considerations appear to have been ignored; quotas based on past performance were such

---

[1] A ban on new entry is, of course, a corollary of a quota system based on past performance, but not vice versa; a ban on new entry is compatible with the absence of quotas.

a widespread feature of controls that they came to be regarded as natural adjuncts of government intervention.[1] Yet it is noteworthy that the same products when exported from other British colonies (for example, oil-palm products from Malaya) were not subject to quotas.

The absence of any limit or quota on the total quantity to be purchased or shipped was not the only obvious piece of evidence of the lack of restriction on the market. In the purchases of cocoa the paradox was evident from the inception of the quota system, the introduction of which was announced in the same official statement as the British guarantee to purchase the entire crop at seasonally fixed prices which ensured an unlimited market locally. In the purchase of groundnuts and of oil-palm produce the paradox of the quota system became particularly evident when an acute shortage of these products developed further after the loss of Malaya and the Netherlands East Indies in 1942. In West Africa intensive production drives were undertaken to stimulate the production of these crops. Extreme measures were also introduced to reduce local consumption, even if only by a few tons, and much hardship was inflicted on the local population and on individual traders to force every ton or donkey-load of groundnuts into export. Expensive publicity campaigns were undertaken; officers toured the districts and leaflets were dropped from aeroplanes to explain to women and children, cracking palm kernels in the remote African bush or growing groundnuts in the arid semi-desert south of the Sahara, that their produce was urgently required in the war for freedom. But the quota system was firmly retained, and buyers were fined if they exceeded their shares.[2] Though in the nature of things it is not possible to measure how far supplies were curtailed by this system, there can be little doubt that they were adversely affected by these restrictions on the activities of the merchants and on the competition between them.

5. GENERAL EFFECTS OF THE QUOTA SYSTEM ON THE DEGREE OF CONCENTRATION

Some of the results of compulsory quotas in trade are the same wherever quotas are practised.[3] They necessarily freeze the pattern of trade and prevent or hinder the growth of new firms. As quotas impede buying

[1] This was explicitly stated in the first Cocoa White Paper, *Report on Cocoa Control in West Africa*, Cmd. 6554, 1943, para. 24.

[2] There were some small buying agents who had fixed tonnage quotas and they were completely barred from exceeding these.

[3] The most important result of the quota system was probably its contribution to the establishment of statutory monopolies in the West African export trade (which in turn have served as patterns for similar organizations elsewhere in Africa). This aspect of the quota system is not discussed in this section, but is reviewed in § 7 of this chapter.

competition, they bring about somewhat lower prices to producers, which tends to reduce supplies. The incentive to buyers to increase their purchases is reduced, and this again adversely affects supplies. These effects are particularly marked in conditions in which the market is clearly unlimited and in which there are no market obstacles to competitive activity.

The wartime quotas in the West African export trade offer an exceptional opportunity for presenting quantitative information on the effects

Table 18. *Changes in participation in produce buying since the abolition of the quota system*

	(a) Purchases of firms which commenced buying since 1947 as percentages of total purchases in 1949–50 or 1950	Combined share of three largest wartime quota holders (percentages)		
		(b) Share in wartime quotas	(c) Share in actual purchases 1949–50	(d) Adjusted share in purchases, 1949–50, or 1950, allowing for syndicate arrangements
Cocoa, Gold Coast	1	63	59⎫	No
Cocoa, Nigeria	9	65	56⎭	syndicate
Palm kernels, Nigera	14	82	67	71
Palm oil, Nigeria	5	86	79	83
Groundnuts, Nigeria	11	70	57	58

Notes

(1) In the purchase of oilseeds the quotas were abolished in July 1945, but the prohibition on the entry of new firms continued until 1947. In cocoa buying the quota system and bar on entry were removed together in 1947.

(2) Both in the Gold Coast and in Nigeria certain classes of small cocoa buyers (so-called B shippers and agents) were in receipt of fixed specific tonnage quotas as distinct from percentage quotas. In the Gold Coast, after several revisions, these tonnage quotas came to total about 10 % of the crop exported. In Nigeria eventually only the co-operatives remained with tonnage quotas and all other buyers received percentage quotas. The tonnage quotas of the co-operative societies were about 10 % of the total crop exported. In the table allowance has been made for the tonnage quotas by reducing the percentage quotas of the three largest quota holders by the appropriate amount, i.e. by deflating the percentage quotas by one-tenth. Thus the percentages are comparable throughout the table.

(3) The figures in the column headed 'Adjusted share in purchases,' are in the nature of a refinement and are the result of certain adjustments which are useful to illustrate the position of firms where market-sharing syndicates are in operation (as they were for the purchase of products in the table, with the exception of cocoa). The nature and purpose of the adjustments are indicated in Chapter 17, § 4, above.

of such a system in freezing the pattern of trade and in preventing the growth of new firms. By comparing the quotas of the firms with their shares in purchases of export produce shown in Table 14, it is possible to measure the effects of the entry of new firms and the expansion of some established firms which have taken place since the quota system was abolished. In the circumstances of West African trade in the late 1930's it is reasonable to assume that these or similar developments, probably on a larger scale, would have taken place sooner if the quota system had not been imposed.[1]

The salient facts are summarized in Table 18. It suggests that the share of newcomers who entered the various branches of produce buying since 1947 is about equal to the reduction in the shares of the largest quota holders since the abolition of official quotas. There has been a general decline in the relative participation of the principal wartime quota holders, which is particularly marked in the purchase of Nigerian cocoa, palm kernels and groundnuts. This loss of ground is particularly noteworthy in view of the comparatively short period since the lifting of the ban on new entry, and in view of the various obstacles (of which the immigration restrictions are by far the most important) to the establishment and growth of the smaller non-African firms.[2]

6. SPECIAL RESULTS OF THE ESTABLISHMENT OF QUOTAS IN GROUNDNUT AND COCOA BUYING

The inhibiting effects of the quota system on the projects of certain firms were accentuated in West Africa, because a small group of merchants effectively administered the quota system and was primarily responsible for calculating individual quotas. In a few instances there were substantial and growing individual competitors whose interests were at variance with those of the particular group which controlled the bulk of the trade. In 1938 and 1939 rapid progress was made in the groundnut and cocoa export trade by competitors of the large firms and of the buying syndicates. The effects of the quotas in re-

---

[1] This is a reasonable assumption in view of the rapid progress in 1938–9 of certain non-syndicate members in the purchase of cocoa and groundnuts, and in view of the proposed establishment in 1939 of a cocoa-buying organization by a large American consumer, which was prevented by the introduction of export controls which confined the trade to quota holders with past performance in the trade. There were several other prospective newcomers, but this was the most important.

[2] With the exception of the purchase of cocoa in the Gold Coast, the loss of ground cannot be ascribed to official assistance given to African produce buyers, especially to the co-operative societies. In Nigeria the most important instances of relative gains have been registered by independent firms, chiefly expatriate enterprises not assisted by the Government.

stricting the progress of some firms were thus particularly significant in these two trades.

In the groundnut export trade Mr Raccah had become the second largest exporter of groundnuts and by far the most important exporter who was not a member of the groundnut-buying syndicate or of the Association of West African Merchants. In September 1939 the Director of the Department of Imported Oils and Fats in the Ministry of Food stated in an official letter to a well-known firm of produce merchants in London, who acted as Mr Raccah's agents, that the Department would not purchase groundnuts from Mr Raccah or from his agents, since it was the policy to purchase only from shippers established in the United Kingdom who were liable to United Kingdom tax. This ruling implied the exclusion of local merchants and sole reliance on the Association of West African Merchants, membership of which was confined to firms with head offices in the United Kingdom or in Europe. In this instance it also meant that the Ministry's purchases would be limited to members of the groundnut syndicate. This decision was taken at a time when this same department was buying large quantities of groundnuts and of oil-palm products from other colonies and other sterling area sources in which there were many suppliers and shippers not liable to income tax in the United Kingdom; nor was this question raised with these suppliers.[1]

After protests by Mr Raccah and his London agents, supported by the then Governor of Nigeria, the Ministry of Food, or rather the Director of Imported Oils and Fats, agreed to purchase groundnuts also from merchants who had not been members of the pre-war syndicate, on condition that they became temporary members of the Association. Membership of the Association entailed acceptance of a system of export quotas with penalties for over-purchase calculated strictly along the lines of the groundnut buying syndicate. In fact, membership of the syndicate was made compulsory.[2]

In the purchase of cocoa both the unnecessary nature of the quota system, as well as its political risks, were evident from its inception. The British guarantee to purchase the entire crop at seasonally fixed prices was announced simultaneously with the quota system. Thus the market was unlimited from the beginning and this was recognized by the quota system, since no limit was placed on aggregate purchases or

[1] In many instances some suppliers were liable to British income tax and others were not. This, however, was not considered in deciding on purchases from them nor was this question raised with them. Suppliers of Malayan oil-palm products were one example.

[2] To leave no doubt on this matter, the United Africa Company sent to Mr Raccah's London agents a copy of the secret syndicate agreement which he now had to accept as a condition for receiving a share in the Ministry of Food purchases.

shipments. There were obvious political dangers in a system which was quite clearly a resumption in a different guise of the 1937–8 cocoa-buying agreement; the important differences were that its provisions were now officially enforced and that membership was necessary for participation in cocoa buying.[1]

The quotas were calculated by the Association of West African Merchants and transmitted by the Colonial Office to the West African administrations. The firm of A. G. Leventis was by far the most dangerous competitor of the members of the Association in the Gold Coast, and as it happened the results of the quota system and of the method of calculation of the quotas bore especially harshly on this firm. This was explicitly recognized by the local administration and by the Colonial Office, and subsequently by the Sachs Commission.[2]

It must not be inferred from the foregoing that the profits of the firms of Raccah or Leventis (or of any other firm) were actually reduced by the operation of the quota scheme below what they would have been without it. By restraining competition among established firms and barring the entry of newcomers, the system protected profit margins per ton which were appreciably higher than they would have been without this restraint. This protection of the merchants' margins was significant because in the early years of the war the buying schedules for the reimbursement of expenses and the calculation of the remunera-

---

[1] As is well known, the support given by the Colonial Office to the pre-war cocoa-buying agreement was much criticized by African opinion, and also by certain members of the administration; this is set out in some detail in the Nowell Report. When the hold-up ended, export quotas were established and enforced until September 1938 to secure the orderly liquidation of accumulated stocks; and this again was much criticized. The cocoa-buying agreement was formally suspended on 28 April 1938. The participants agreed informally to keep their purchases in line with pre-existing shares. The agreement was finally abandoned on 30 November 1939 on the introduction of the official quota scheme which had been announced on 17 November. Thus it was finally withdrawn only when official quotas took its place.

[2] The average exports of the three cocoa seasons 1936–9 were chosen as the basis for calculating past performance. Special adjustments were provided for firms which had operated only for one or two years. The firm of Leventis began operations in March 1938, and owing to the imposition of quotas (again largely based on past performance) at the termination of the hold-up in April 1938, it was able to ship only a small quantity in that year. In the computation of the wartime quotas it was, however, assumed that the firm had operated for a full season in 1937–8. In February 1940 the Cocoa Control officially thanked the Association of West African Merchants for consenting to a slight increase in the quota of this firm, from 3·21 to 3·63 % of the quota of all A shippers; in the weeks before the imposition of the quota the firm had been buying 9 % of the total. When making that concession the Association of West African Merchants informed the Cocoa Control that this was a wholly exceptional concession, and they would not entertain any further representations. It is interesting to speculate on what would have happened if the authorities had stated in reply that they would discontinue the quota system altogether.

tion of merchants were generous. The remuneration (that is the agreed rate of profit) was generally of the order of 5–7 % of the f.o.b. price; and the schedules of expenses were generously calculated. The history of the West African produce trade, especially of the groundnut and cocoa trade, both before and since the war, suggests that profit margins much less generous than those provided for by the early wartime buying schedules tend to be compressed by buying competition.

Even under the quota system there was some competition in the purchase of export produce. It is obvious from the high level of penalty payments in force throughout the operation of the system that without it buying competition would have been much more vigorous, with substantial compression of margins through overpayment of the statutory minimum prices. Thus it is certain that aggregate profits in produce buying were larger than they would have been without the quota system, and it is not unlikely that the trading profits, even of those firms whose quotas were unfavourable, and whose competitive progress was retarded, were larger than they would have been without this system.

7. THE CONNEXION BETWEEN THE QUOTA SYSTEM AND THE ESTABLISHMENT OF STATUTORY MARKETING

Apart from the obvious aim of denying supplies to the enemy and securing them for the allies, the two principal declared objectives of wartime controls over West African exports were to avoid a collapse in cocoa prices locally and to stimulate the export of groundnuts and of oil-palm produce after 1942. Neither of these required either a statutory monopoly or the introduction of export quotas; nor does the one system require the other. But although both the principal measures were unnecessary for, and indeed rather harmful to, the achievement of these objectives, there appears to have been a causal connexion between the quota system and the establishment of statutory export monopoly.

The quota system was originated by the merchants in order to restrict competition among themselves and to bar new entry. Export quotas (including quotas in buying for export) are easier to establish, to enforce and to administer when there is only a single buyer, especially if that buyer is prepared to arrange a settlement between those who exceed their allotted shares and those who fall short of them. Thus contrary to the more usual attitude of export merchants, the West African merchants were inclined to favour statutory export monopolies, especially for commodities for which there was more than one buyer overseas. Thus the draft scheme for cocoa control submitted by the Association of West African Merchants to the Colonial Office in November 1939, and approved by the authorities, provided both for the purchase of the entire crop by a statutory export monopoly at seasonally fixed prices, and for a quota system based on past performance. The merchants may have proposed a statutory monopoly because they did not realize that effective price support was practicable without it. But more probably their proposals were influenced at least in part by a realization that a statutory monopoly would facilitate the operation of a quota system and increase its effectiveness, particularly in the purchase and export of cocoa in which there were a number of markets and an even greater number of buyers overseas.

There was also another connexion between the quota system and the establishment of statutory marketing. Some senior officers in West Africa realized, as they could not fail to realize, that the quota system was imposed and ultimately managed by the Association of West African Merchants. This greatly strengthened their determination to see a radical change in marketing methods, and in particular the establishment of statutory export control to restrain the power of the large firms. This attitude was not altogether logical, since it was only the statutory controls enforced by the authorities which gave the firms the great powers they possessed. The progress of the competitors of the largest firms before the introduction of the quota system was ample evidence of the limits of their commercial power. But this inconsistency was not fully perceived. Two successive Governors of Nigeria in particular saw in this display of power an important argument for a radical change in marketing methods, without examining too closely what exactly provided the basis of this power.

The quota system was a principal factor in the wartime establishment of statutory monopolies in the West African export trade. And once such a system is introduced its continuation depends on influences and considerations quite different from those which brought about its establishment. This form of marketing was continued and extended after the war; and the system has been introduced into other British colonies as well. The marketing of colonial exports through statutory monopolies has far-reaching political and economic results, some of which are already obvious, while others are emerging gradually. It seems that this has been much the most important legacy of the wartime trade controls in West Africa.

8. SOME SECONDARY RESULTS OF THE QUOTA SYSTEM

In West Africa there were obvious political dangers in a quota system operated along the lines of the produce-buying syndicates. The memories of the cocoa hold-up of 1937–8, which was prompted by the cocoa-buying agreement, were still vivid in the Gold Coast. The operation of the other produce-buying syndicates, though less widely publicized, were also the object of widespread suspicion. Accordingly, the association of the authorities with the quota system was widely criticized.

Although there were no violent or overt political reactions, the system was not without its repercussions in that field. The establishment and the calculation of the cocoa quotas were an early move in the struggle between the members of the Association of West African Merchants and the firm of Leventis, which has had far-reaching political results in the Gold Coast; and it was probably the first attempt, possibly a subconscious one, to use the machinery of control to influence the course of this commercial struggle.

The quota system also brought home the advantages and profitability of market-sharing agreements to traders previously outside the buying syndicates. It suggested to them the advantages of continuing these arrangements after the abolition of the quota system. When the quotas were withdrawn the confidential buying syndicates resumed their operations on a more comprehensive basis than before. In groundnut buying every buying agent, including even the smallest, joined the syndicate; the membership of the oil-palm produce syndicate was also extended. Some of these arrangements did not prove lasting; but the groundnut-buying syndicate remains more comprehensive than it was before the establishment of the official quota system.

PART 5

THE STATUTORY MARKETING BOARDS AND THEIR POLICIES

63

CHAPTER 20

THE GENESIS OF THE MARKETING BOARDS

I. THE SIGNIFICANCE OF THE MARKETING BOARDS AND THE SCOPE OF THIS PART OF THE STUDY

The most striking and important instance of monopoly in West Africa is to be found in the export trade. By their comprehensive nature and their statutory powers the organizations controlling West African exports present instances of monopoly power not approached in any other sector of West African trade; and their operations have far-reaching influence on the well-being of these territories.

The West African marketing boards are by far the largest statutory export monopolies in the British Colonial Empire and possibly in the Commonwealth; they are indeed among the most important in the world. Already their financial resources exceed those of the West African governments, and the disposal of their large reserves will be a major influence in the political and economic situation in these territories.

But quantitative information alone does not convey adequately the significance of these organizations Their decisions in fixing the prices paid to producers are a major factor in determining the level of incomes, the standard of living and the ability to save of the people, and through their influence on the flow of incomes these decisions largely affect the balance of payments of the colonies. By prescribing producer prices they exercise a potent influence on the production of different crops. The policies of the boards and the use of their accumulated reserves raise difficult and delicate issues of relationship between the United Kingdom and the colonies. The results (some unintended) and repercussions of these policies can be expected to extend well into the future, particularly since they also affect the future scale of output.

The description and analysis of the boards' activities necessarily differ from the treatment appropriate to an examination of the degree of concentration and of monopolistic tendencies in the private sector of West African trade. In the latter, the factors influencing entry and those underlying the extent of concentration, together with the resulting market situation, are the principal topics of inquiry. These matters are irrelevant to the activities of statutory monopolies, since entry is barred by statute and there is 100 % concentration in their field of operations. On the other hand, detailed analysis of the policies pursued in such conditions, and of the results of these policies, becomes the appropriate subject for inquiry.

Much of this part of the study is taken up by a critical examination of the official documents proposing the establishment of statutory marketing, of the policies pursued by the boards, of the results and implications of these policies, and of the arguments advanced in their support.

The scope and purpose of the discussion should be clearly understood. In accordance with the general purpose and plan of this book it is concerned solely with discussion, examination and analysis of ideas and proposals put forward and of policies pursued over the period under review, and with their results and implications. It is not concerned with policy recommendations. In particular, it must not be inferred from these chapters that certain types of stabilization measure, clearly defined and specified, would not have solid advantage in West Africa or in any other primary producing countries. It seems necessary to be explicit on this point to avoid misunderstanding.

The frequent and often wide fluctuations in the prices and incomes of producers in these territories may amount to daily revaluation of producers' services, and this can entail important social, political and economic disadvantages. Such fluctuations are likely to have unsettling effects in all communities, and the strains which are set up may be serious in communities on which the impact of a money economy is comparatively recent, and in which the population is apt to ascribe adverse price changes to the decisions and even to the malice of merchant firms. The same applies to the results of wide and often erratic fluctuations in prices and incomes between seasons. In West Africa, as in many other countries, the proceeds of exports are the most important component element of the flow of money incomes, and such wide discontinuous variations affect the entire economy. Again, sharp short-term variations in prices may set up expectations by producers which bring about changes in capacity not called for by long-term trends. Moreover, discontinuous fluctuations retard the growth of a sense of continuity in economic affairs which for various reasons is often very imperfectly developed in primary producing countries. Smoothing of the erratic and discontinuous fluctuations in prices and incomes might serve to promote a sense of continuity and thereby extend the economic horizon of the producers and increase their inclination to save; in these and other respects it may serve to promote development.

Thus the possibility of successful stabilization of prices and incomes deserves serious consideration. But worth while treatment of this topic requires extended discussion with a clear recognition of the conceptual and practical problems involved. Reliance on vague general ideas may result in the pursuit of very dangerous policies which may bring about a situation even less satisfactory than that which they are designed to remedy. As the primary concern of this study is description and analysis rather than the presentation of suggestions for policy, this subject is not pursued here.[1]

2. UNDERLYING INFLUENCES IN THE ESTABLISHMENT OF THE MARKETING BOARDS

The documents relating to the establishment of the marketing boards, the powers granted to these organizations and the pronouncements of their spokesmen, suggest that their introduction was the result of several different and distinct opinions and ideas, and that chance played an important part.

The first strand of ideas derived from the criticisms of the pre-war marketing system, especially those embodied in the Nowell Report. These criticisms have already been examined at some length in Chapter 16, where it was suggested that though reflecting widely held views, they were, nevertheless, largely misconceived, and had disregarded essential factors of the local economies and of the market situation. They were, however, widely accepted, without perception of the defects of the underlying arguments. The ready acceptance of the findings of the Nowell Commission can be partly explained by their appeal to ideas and attitudes which are influential in contemporary society. The Commission criticized the seemingly chaotic and unorganized system of marketing; and the collective marketing agencies which it proposed had the appearance of simplicity, efficiency and neatness.[2] Moreover, the establishment of such agencies would result in the creation of large-scale organizations and of important official positions. Although these criticisms of the pre-war system were undoubtedly a major influence in the establishment of statutory marketing, it is noteworthy that neither the West African Produce Control Board nor the marketing boards undertook, or were asked to undertake, a reorganization of the machinery of produce buying. In particular, the establishment of statutory export monopolies left largely unaffected the market structure between the producer and the merchants, that is, the sphere in which many of the alleged abuses were said to have occurred. The former export merchants have continued to buy the crops as agents

---

[1] The possibilities and difficulties of certain types of stabilization scheme are considered at some length in an article by Professor Paish and the present writer in the *Economic Journal* for December 1952.

[2] In the Nowell Report (p. 196) there are two diagrams which show the channels and stages of cocoa marketing in 1938, together with the results of certain changes envisaged by the Commission, who recommended in fact a compulsory reduction in the number of stages of intermediaries. The diagrams and the text imply that the elimination of certain stages in distribution, even by compulsion, is economic; and that the intermediaries were used without performing any service.

of the boards, and they have used the same organization of clerks and middlemen as before.[1]

The establishment of statutory marketing has resulted in seasonally prescribed statutory minimum prices; and it has been suggested that this has greatly reduced the likelihood of exploitation of producers by intermediaries, and the scope of the alleged abuses in produce buying. This suggestion is not convincing. As has already been shown, if there is competition among buyers the producers will be protected from exploitation, or from the adverse effects of sharp practices on the part of buyers. Under competitive conditions buyers can secure supplies only by offering to the producers prices which, even after allowing for 'abuses', leave the intermediary with only the competitive margin for the performance of his services. Nor is it certain either that the prescription of minimum prices will, in fact, protect producers effectively in the absence of competition (a matter considered further in Chapter 25 below), or that statutory monopolies are necessary for the establishment and enforcement of minimum prices. If it is thought that in certain areas the producers are in danger of exploitation (a term which would need to be more precisely defined) by intermediaries, it might still be possible to prescribe and enforce minimum prices without statutory monopoly, if it is held that this form of protection is likely to be most effective.

Nor is the system likely to have enabled farmers to borrow on more favourable terms from intermediaries than they would be able to do in its absence. It is not clear why frequent fluctuations in prices should materially increase the desire of producers to borrow, or to render the terms more onerous than they would be otherwise. Between seasons prices have continued to vary greatly, often by large discontinuous jumps, so that there is still ample opportunity for unsuccessful forward sales. What is certain is that the retention of large surpluses (and the realization of very low selling prices by the West African Produce Control Board) increased the peasant's need for money, especially in view of the steady rise in the cost of imported merchandise; and at the same time it served to reduce the flow of private saving. On both counts, statutory marketing is more likely to have weakened rather than strengthened the position of the peasant vis-a-vis the intermediaries.

The administrative experience of the West African Produce Control Board and its performance in the marketing of West African exports were repeatedly mentioned in important official publications in support of the decision to continue statutory marketing after the war. In particular, three kinds of inference have been drawn from the experience of

---

[1] During the war the arrangements of the West African Produce Control Board, so far from rectifying any defects of the pre-war system, gave official sanction to the buying syndicates through the official quota system.

the West African Produce Control Board. First, it has been inferred that it was very successful in the marketing of West African produce. Thus in West Africa the substantial surpluses accumulated by the West African Produce Control Board were hailed as evidence of its successful trading operations. In fact these surpluses simply indicated the proportion of sale proceeds it decided to withhold from producers, and they were no indication of its success in marketing the crops.[1] Secondly, it has been argued that its operations were evidence of the feasibility of organized marketing of peasant crops in backward areas. In fact it merely shows that where there is a statutory export monopoly all exports will necessarily take place through the monopoly. Thirdly, it has been inferred that this war-time experience showed the feasibility of price stabilization as well as its beneficial results. In fact what it did show was that a statutory export monopoly can prescribe producer prices more or less at any level (below the world level) it thinks desirable, and that it can fix prices at levels which would not be permitted by the government if attempted by private organizations. Whatever the merits of the West African Produce Control Board as an instrument of wartime control, its experience cannot be adduced in support of the establishment of permanent statutory export monopolies.

But the presence of the Board at the end of the war was a principal factor in the establishment of the marketing boards. Once an organization such as a statutory export monopoly has been in existence for some years, strong tendencies for self-perpetuation come into play, since it creates strong administrative, intellectual and material vested interests. It is generally easier to continue with a system once established than to discard it, which may involve weighing and comparing numerous arguments and considerations, and taking specific and possibly embarrassing decisions, including the abolition of important administrative posts. Moreover, the operations of such an organization enable individuals to maintain and to extend their influence and prestige, since credit for the organization's activities is frequently given to particular persons, which is rarely possible under conditions of unorganized economic growth. When these inclinations and interests reinforce the preference for tidiness, for large-scale operations and for administrative convenience (whether apparent or real), the tendency for the continuation of statutory export monopolies becomes practically irresistible.[2]

---

[1] The same opinion was expressed in the Nigerian Sessional Paper No. 18 of 1948, which announced the extension of the proposed marketing boards to products other than cocoa. As has been shown in Chapter 19, the selling transactions of the West African Produce Control Board were extremely unfavourable.

[2] The importance of the tendency for self-perpetuation was explicitly recognized in the important Nigerian Sessional Paper No. 18 of 1948 (cf. § 4 below).

Chance occurrences have also played their part in the introduction of statutory marketing. The most important of these was the causal connexion between the quota system and the wartime introduction of statutory export monopoly discussed in the preceding chapter.

All these factors were reinforced by a widespread but vague belief that the marketing boards would bring about stabilization of producer prices, an aim which was regarded as both practicable and desirable. These ideas are well reflected in the two important British Parliamentary White Papers which dealt with the post-war arrangements proposed for the marketing of West African cocoa.

3. THE PROPOSALS OF THE COCOA WHITE PAPERS

The Cocoa White Papers were published in 1944 and 1946 respectively.[1] Both emphasized the undesirable features of the pre-war marketing system of cocoa described in the Nowell Report, but they insisted particularly on the necessity of avoiding short-term price fluctuations. In the words of the first White Paper:

War experience has added weight to the view that a prime need of the cocoa industry, if it is to have attendant prosperity and efficiency, is a reasonably stable price basis, *by which is meant not necessarily prices fixed over periods of several years, but the avoidance of short term fluctuations.* To achieve this result it is necessary to break the direct link between the producer's price and world market prices.[2]

It will be noted that this passage implies very short-period price stabilization over perhaps a few months, or over one or two seasons at most. This was also implied in the second White Paper:

The experience of the war years has shown that Government can achieve a *stabilisation of seasonal prices to the West African cocoa producer,* despite heavy fluctuations in supply and demand. This stability of price has been generally welcomed, and it is reasonable to assume that its continuance would be considered to be far preferable to a return to the fluctuating day-to-day prices of the pre-war era.[2]

All these considerations point to one conclusion, namely that the remedy for many of the evils afflicting the West African cocoa industry lies in imposing a buffer between the producer and the international market *which will protect him from short term fluctuations of world prices* and allow him a greater stability of income.[2]

The second White Paper also revealed a distinct dislike of traders and intermediaries, to whom it referred generally as middlemen-specu-

---

[1] *Report on Cocoa Control in West Africa 1939-1943 and Statement on Future Policy,* Cmd. 6554, 1944. *Statement on Future Marketing of West African Cocoa,* Cmd. 6950, 1946.
[2] Author's italics.

lators. Their allegedly nefarious activities were instanced as a major reason for drastic changes in marketing arrangements.

The White Papers proposed in effect to attain their aim by continuing the wartime arrangements of statutory export monopolies. The functions of the proposed export boards were described in the second White Paper. This envisaged the establishment of export monopolies for cocoa in the Gold Coast and in Nigeria which would fix seasonally stable prices to producers and sell the produce to the best advantage. Their surplus funds would be used primarily for price stabilization and to a lesser extent for research, disease eradication and similar purposes.

The White Papers did not specify the period over which prices were to be stabilized. But it was implied that they were principally concerned with avoiding price fluctuations within a season or with stabilization over a few years of fluctuating world prices. This is suggested by the passages already quoted and also by this remark in the concluding section of Cmd. 6950:

> By fixing a steady buying price in advance of the sale of each season's crop the Boards will cut the link between the price of cocoa in West Africa and the *day-to-day price on the world market*.[1]

It was also implied that the long-period accumulation of surpluses was not contemplated.

> In some seasons when world prices are high, the price paid to the producer will be less than the average realisation on overseas sales. The Boards will, on such occasions, show a 'surplus.' There will, however, be other seasons in which the average world price is below the price paid to producers. On these occasions the Boards will make a 'loss', which will be financed from the 'surpluses' accrued in years of high world prices. The intention is that 'profits' will be utilized primarily to maintain the maximum possible stability in the price paid to the producer. Thus on the average of a period of years, it is to be expected that the average price paid in West Africa will be substantially equal to the average net price realised on world markets and that the Boards' buying and selling transactions will therefore approximately balance.

It is noteworthy that the words 'profits', 'surplus' and 'loss' were used in inverted commas, indicating that the authors realized the true nature of such balances and in particular the radical difference between these and commercial profits and losses.

Both in the Gold Coast and in Nigeria the Cocoa Marketing Boards envisaged in the second White Paper took over from the West African Produce Control Board in 1947. These newly constituted boards were henceforth to decide producer prices, and future policy generally, in

---

[1] Author's italics.

both the buying and selling of cocoa. The selling arrangements, and the administrative and executive personnel of the West African Produce Control Board in London, were left substantially unchanged, as were the buying arrangements in West Africa.

4. THE EXTENSION OF THESE PROPOSALS TO OTHER PRODUCTS

The proposals of the White Papers referred to cocoa marketing only. It was soon decided to extend these proposals to the marketing of the other West African staple exports. The official reasons for this extension were published in a little-known but easily accessible Nigerian Sessional Paper, *Statement of the Policy proposed for the Future Marketing of Nigerian Oils, Oilseeds and Cotton.*[1] This paper in effect repeated the general argument of the Cocoa White Papers and stressed their applicability to other products. But it added further reasons for the maintenance of statutory export monopolies.

First, it emphasized the desirability of maintaining the type of marketing organization which was said to have functioned so well during the war. The proposals for statutory export monopolies were claimed to

represent in fact the adaptation of marketing arrangements created and developed by the necessities of war to the purposes of peace.... Over a period of years an orderly structure, integrating the pre-war commercial system, has been built up. To take over that structure for maintenance, improvement and extension is, in the opinion of the Government, far wiser than to destroy it and so expose the whole economy and particularly the producers' economy, to the risks, uncertainties and price fluctuations which characterized the inter-war period.

The Sessional Paper also instanced the substantial surplus of the West African Produce Control Board as a reason for establishing statutory marketing boards for oils and oilseeds. In this connexion it emphasized and extended an argument advanced in one of the Cocoa White Papers. In the words of the Sessional Paper:

In the event of the abandonment of the present arrangements, the disposal of the considerable sums which have already accumulated would present a problem of no little difficulty. In one way or another, since the return of a contribution made to those funds by each individual farmer is plainly impracticable and, even if practicable, would be of negligible benefit to the individual, these sums would have to be expended for the benefit of the producing communities. That by itself implies the establishment of representative boards to direct the process.

[1] Sessional Paper No. 18 of 1948.

This argument implies that surpluses can never be returned to producers. But this applies with equal force to funds of the marketing boards, the establishment of which was proposed in the Sessional Paper. Indeed, it would apply much more to the marketing boards. The Sessional Paper was issued in 1948. The West African Produce Control Board had accumulated surpluses on oil-palm produce and groundnuts (the Sessional Paper did not deal with cocoa) only since March 1947. Thus a distribution of its funds at the time by subsidizing producer prices would have benefited very largely those producers at whose expense the funds had been accumulated. But the operations of the marketing boards would extend over years or decades, and the accumulated surpluses would at times be much larger than those accumulated by the West African Produce Control Board; and drafts on reserves after years of surpluses would benefit groups of persons very different from those from whom the funds had been collected.

Altogether, the reasoning of the Sessional Paper provides an explicit and interesting example of the almost irresistible self-perpetuating force of this type of organization.

Statutory export monopolies for oil-palm products, groundnuts and cotton were established in Nigeria in April 1949, and took over the marketing of these products from the West African Produce Control Board when this organization was dissolved. At about the same time the marketing of the minor agricultural exports of the Gold Coast was entrusted to the Agricultural Products Marketing Board established there for that purpose. Practically all non-mineral exports from Sierra Leone and from the Gambia were also taken over by similar organizations. The initial arrangements for the marketing of these products were the same as those described in the immediately preceding section dealing with the establishment of the Cocoa Boards.

5. AMBIGUITIES OF THE IDEA OF STABILIZATION

The aims and methods of stabilization as outlined in these official documents, notably the two Cocoa White Papers, appear very simple. The proposed marketing boards would withhold part of the proceeds from producers in times of high prices and pay out the accumulated funds in years of low prices, thus evening out peaks and troughs.

Unfortunately, the problem is far more difficult than was suggested. While it is widely regarded as desirable, there are fundamental ambiguities and difficulties in the idea of stabilization, especially as a guide to policy; there seems to be a general failure to appreciate these, and the Cocoa White Papers were no exception. It seems worth while to list some of these difficulties.

The concept of stabilization may refer to prices, money incomes and real incomes. Stabilization of any one of these may destabilize the others; and in certain likely circumstances, such as a rise in import prices or fluctuations in crops, it will necessarily do so.

The White Papers assumed as self-evident that fluctuations in prices cause or enhance fluctuations in producer incomes. In fact price fluctuations which are caused by variations in supply serve to stabilize producer incomes, and their removal would thus destabilize incomes. This is particularly obvious in a crop such as cocoa, where the British West African output is a large part (about one-half) of world supplies. Thus when the cocoa crop is short this tends to lead to a rise in prices, which partly compensates farmers for the lower crop; to stabilize prices in these conditions is to remove the compensating factor and to destabilize income. Moreover, in conditions of a general rise in prices and costs the stabilization of money incomes and *a fortiori* of money prices would result in a destabilization and depression of the real incomes of producers.

The concept is again meaningless without reference to a specific period over which the accumulated forced savings and their subsequent disbursement balance. As the future course of prices is uncertain, it can always be argued that the larger the surpluses, the greater is the ability of the organization to weather possible storms. When there is no stated or even contemplated finite period over which stable prices are to be achieved, the continuous accumulation of increasing reserves could provide its own perpetual superficial justification. In these circumstances even the most austere producer price policy could be justified by postulating an indefinitely large and prolonged fall in market prices in the undefined future.[1]

In addition, stabilization is meaningless without some reference to

[1] Certain implications of a long-period upward trend of prices serve both to illustrate these difficulties and to show the limitations of undefined stabilization as a guide to policy. The higher are prices, the larger are the absolute amounts required to maintain them at a given level over a stated period, and therefore a given sum is more likely to appear insufficient as stabilization reserve. Surpluses accumulated over a number of years of relatively low prices, and representing large percentages of producer prices at the time of their accumulation, may be held to constitute an insufficient reserve at a subsequent date (by which prices have risen greatly), even though the fear of a decline had been adduced as a reason for their accumulation. When prices are rising over a number of years it is therefore quite likely (in the absence of a clear definition of stabilization, or of the period of accumulation) that the producers who receive the low prices of the early part of the period are called upon to surrender a proportionately large part of their incomes for the creation of reserves which may either be accumulated indefinitely, or used to subsidize much higher producer prices in face of a possible decline. This decline may represent a much smaller proportion of the higher prices than the proportion which the producers have to surrender at a time of much lower prices. And of course the beneficiaries of this process are a group of persons quite different from those who have had to make the sacrifice.

the relation between the price envisaged under stabilization and the open-market level. The lower the absolute level received by the producer, the longer can it be maintained; a zero price would ensure maximum safety and stability.

There are fundamental difficulties of measurement and definition in the concept of stability; and it is not clear whether a large number of frequent and small changes represent a greater or lesser measure of stability than a smaller number of large and discontinuous jumps, such as are often found in the operation of the so-called stabilization schemes.[1]

There is a further ambiguity when producers are not individually registered. When the process of accumulation is continued beyond a comparatively short period, and is then followed by a disbursement of funds, the beneficiaries of these drafts on the reserves will be different from those at whose expense the surpluses were accumulated. This sub-sidization of some producers at the expense of others is inevitable in the absence of individual contact between the marketing authority and the producers.[2] When part of the proceeds is withheld over a number of years the difference between payers and recipients will be significant, even if the surpluses are eventually returned to producers by a sub-sidization of the producer prices. In such circumstances this process does not stabilize incomes; it reduces the incomes of some producers and augments the incomes of others.

Finally, there is a practical corollary of these ambiguities. Without clearly defined concepts of stabilization and of measures for attaining it, stabilization is apt to become interwoven with entirely different aims of policy, especially of public finance, such as compulsory saving or the raising of revenue.

Quite apart from these ambiguities, the desirability of stabilization (whether of prices or incomes or real incomes) is not obvious. First, the aim of the policy is presumably not the stabilization of incomes in the sense of keeping these at or near current levels, since it is to be hoped and to be expected that they will show a long-period upward trend, especially in under-developed countries. The implied aim seems to be the removal or reduction of random fluctuations about this long-period trend, and this is even more difficult than stabilization at a particular level.

There is a familiar risk in stabilization measures of a loss of contact with the trend of prices or of money incomes, and this is a risk which

---

[1] The latter type of price change looks neater on a diagram than the former, and is often presented with pride in official reports. But this is no indication of a real measurement of stability.

[2] As we have seen, it was suggested in the Nigerian Sessional Paper No. 18, as well as in the second Cocoa White Paper, that surpluses cannot be returned to individual producers at all.

implies serious dangers. As all long-term price changes begin as short-term movements, it is not possible to say until well after the event whether a particular price change was a short-term fluctuation or a phase of a long-term change. Thus, unless they are hedged about with special safeguards, stabilization measures may easily result in a loss of contact with the trend. This is particularly likely when there is a long-period change in the value of money or a shift in underlying conditions of supply and demand.

Again, when the rate of exchange with the outside world is fixed, an improvement in the terms of trade postulates a rise in local prices and wages relatively to import prices; if stabilization is rigidly interpreted, no improvement in the terms of trade resulting from a rise in export prices can be transmitted to the local population.

Moreover, in the absence of highly centralized and closely administered planned economy, prices and incomes serve to direct resources into and out of different lines of production, and stabilization of prices may remove desirable inducements for expansion or contraction.

In much contemporary discussion of stabilization, including the Cocoa White Papers, there is a tendency to overlook the role of prices, notably their function to direct resources into the production of various commodities in accordance with changes in supply and demand conditions. If a substantial proportion of the commercial value of the crop is withheld from producers, this cannot fail to influence the volume and direction of effort they put forward. This in turn will tend to affect adversely the maintenance and extension of capacity and the volume of output. It will tend to do so not only by affecting the producers already cultivating the crop, but also by making it less attractive to potential producers, compared to other crops or, indeed, to other forms of activity.[1]

Further, the area over which the cultivation of the crop is profitable necessarily decreases. The cultivation and collection of the crops in outlying areas requires a price sufficient to cover heavy transport costs and still yield a worth while return to the producer to enable and to induce him to establish capacity and to cultivate the particular crop. For these reasons prices below commercial values tend to diminish the area over which production for the market takes place.

---

[1] It has been argued that there will be no discouraging effect if returns in other forms of activity are reduced equally with those which can be secured in the cultivation of the particular product. This view is erroneous. First, both production and the extension of capacity in outlying areas would still be adversely affected. Again, for many producers subsistence production or leisure would become relatively more attractive than cultivation for the market. In practice there is, of course, no question of reduction in the attractiveness and profitability of other forms of activity, corresponding to the withholding of a substantial part of the sale proceeds under the various stabilization schemes.

If over a number of years the prices ruling in some producing territories are less attractive than they are in others, conditions will be relatively less conducive to the maintenance and extension of capacity, with a resulting danger to the long-period competitive position of these territories. Lastly, even if stabilization measures are adopted which face these ambiguities and risks explicitly, and are designed to reduce these as far as possible, it is still necessary to examine and argue the case for compulsory stabilization or smoothing instead of leaving these to the voluntary decisions of individuals by setting aside part of their incomes at times of prosperity.

There are thus real risks involved in stabilization policies, and in certain fairly clearly defined circumstances these risks and difficulties are much increased. This is probable when there is a change in the trend of prices or in the long run equilibrium price. The consequences of a loss of contact with the trend are much more serious when those policies are pursued unilaterally and contact is severed with market prices in one territory or group of territories, while it is retained elsewhere.[1]

It would seem that every one of these conceptual and practical problems is essential for serious and meaningful consideration of the aims and methods of stabilization. Yet not one is even mentioned in the official statements announcing the establishment of the marketing boards.

Thus the marketing boards were not warned of the fundamental difficulties[2] they were likely to encounter, and they were certainly not given a mandate sufficiently specific to serve as a guide to policy. While it is difficult to reconcile the policies actually pursued with any reasonable interpretation of the idea of price stabilization, it is nevertheless necessary to state, in fairness to the boards, that they were never provided with any useful directive; indeed, the documents announcing their establishment served only to obscure the difficulties of the problem.

Further, in fairness to the draftsmen of the White Papers and to those who have had to frame and administer policy on the basis of these ideas, it should also be stated that these vague notions were (and usually still are) widely and uncritically accepted. It may also be stated that although the widest publicity was given to the White Papers, which obviously bore on major issues of public policy and also raised issues of considerable analytical interest, they do not seem to have attracted any critical discussion by professional economists.

[1] These considerations suggest that indiscriminate quest for security may often amount to the substitution of less obvious but equally real or even greater hazards for those it is intended to eliminate; and that after a point the covert risks increase cumulatively without compensating increase in safety or any other advantage. This may be of wider relevance than policies of price and income stabilization.

[2] There was much discussion of less fundamental issues such as technical and administrative details, and of the problems of meeting the next American slump.

CHAPTER 21

THE SCOPE AND POWERS OF THE
MARKETING BOARDS

1. LIST OF THE WEST AFRICAN MARKETING BOARDS

Statutory marketing boards operate in all four British West African colonies. The following is a list of the boards.

Nigeria: Nigeria Cocoa Marketing Board (established 1947).
             Nigeria Groundnut Marketing Board (established 1949).
             Nigeria Oil Palm Produce Marketing Board (established 1949).
             Nigeria Cotton Marketing Board (established 1949).
Gold Coast: Gold Coast Cocoa Marketing Board (established 1947).
             Gold Coast Agricultural Products Marketing Board (established 1949).
Sierra Leone: Sierra Leone Agricultural Marketing Board (established 1949).
Gambia: Gambia Oil Seeds Marketing Board (established 1949).

In Nigeria in 1951 the four boards controlled 69 % by value of all exports and 78 % of all non-mineral exports. In the Gold Coast the corresponding percentages were 69 and 90 %. In Sierra Leone and the Gambia the percentages tend to be rather higher. In all four colonies the marketing boards control practically 100 % of agricultural exports produced by Africans, including quite minor and even insignificant production. Thus in Nigeria, the Groundnut Marketing Board now controls sunflower seed, which is not even listed in the trade returns.

2. POWERS AND FUNCTIONS OF THE BOARDS

The functions of the Gold Coast Cocoa Marketing Board are statutorily defined in these terms:[1]

> It shall be the duty of the Board to secure the most favourable arrangements for the purchase, grading, export and selling of Gold Coast cocoa, and to assist in the development by all possible means of the cocoa industry of the Gold Coast for the benefit and prosperity of the producers.

The statutes establishing the other boards contain similar clauses.

These provisions are no exception to the general tendency for such 'objects clauses' to be vague and indefinite. But it is noteworthy that

[1] Gold Coast Ordinance No. 16 of 1947.

although price stabilization was understood to be the principal purpose of establishing the marketing boards, there is no mention of this objective either in the Gold Coast or in the Nigeria Cocoa Marketing Ordinances; and it is mentioned only casually in a sub-clause in the other Nigerian ordinances, as one of the objects on which the funds of the boards may be spent. There is, of course, no reference to the period over which stabilization is to be achieved, or over which the boards' surpluses and deficits should balance.

In Nigeria each board consists of three official members and three nominated unofficial members; all six are appointed by the Governor and hold office at his pleasure. The three official members are the same for each of the boards, while the unofficial members are different for each board. The Department of Marketing and Exports serves as the executive of all the Nigerian boards, and its Director is one of the official members of each board.

In the Gold Coast until 1951 the Cocoa Marketing Board comprised twelve members, six Europeans and six Africans. Four of the Europeans were official members and one of these acted as chairman. The Board was reconstituted after two amending ordinances in 1951 and 1952 and it now consists of nine members, all appointed by the Minister of Commerce, Industries and Mines. The producer prices prescribed by the Board must be approved by the Minister, who also has powers to direct the Board in the use or management of its funds. It is obvious that the Board is simply an organ of government. It will be argued subsequently that these changes are not likely to result in radical changes in price policy.

The most important power of the boards is their sole right to export, and to buy for export, produce under their control, including all processed products derived from these crops. They can extend their control to other products with the approval of the Governor in Council. Under the Nigerian legislation the powers of the boards can be extended to the few products at present outside their scope without further legislation, or without the establishment of new boards. The authority of the Nigerian Groundnut Marketing Board covers not only groundnuts, benniseed and all derivatives thereof, but also sunflower seed, to which it was extended by an Order in Council in 1950.

As a corollary or derivative of their statutory monopoly, the powers of the boards include the fixing of prices payable to producers and the prescription of different grades of produce with different prices to be paid for these. They can define the exportable grades, and produce falling below these grades cannot be exported.

Both in Nigeria and in the Gold Coast the boards are obliged to purchase all produce offered to them which is 'suitable for export'. But they alone have the right to decide what is suitable, and they need pay no regard to the acceptability to overseas buyers in making their decisions. Similarly, they alone decide the prices and price differentials they offer for the produce under their control. Thus from the producers' point of view the obligation to purchase all produce offered is of very limited significance only, especially in view of the absence of any reference in that guarantee to the prices the boards have to offer. West African export produce has never been unsaleable. There was always a market for the exportable surplus, and the only question was that of the price at which the crops could be sold.

The boards purchase the crops through merchants whom they license as their buying agents. The licensing powers of the Cocoa Boards and of the Nigerian Groundnut Marketing Board extend beyond their own buying agents; they can license all persons dealing in these products.[1] The Nigerian boards have not yet exercised this particular power. In the Gold Coast, the Cocoa Board licenses the intermediaries from whom its buying agents obtain supplies. The formal provisions of the legislation would empower the Board to license even the pettiest village or bush trader.

Local processors are not allowed to export except by permission of the boards, and on such conditions as the boards may impose at their absolute discretion. Moreover, control is not confined to the export of processed products. The boards can lay down the terms and conditions on which the processors buy their raw material.

The boards can allocate or spend their funds for purposes which, in their opinion, are likely to benefit the producers. They have a large measure of discretion in determining what are the legitimate purposes. In the Gold Coast, expenditure for purposes other than the purchase of cocoa requires the approval of the Governor in Council; since 1951 the Minister of Commerce is empowered to issue directives to the Cocoa Marketing Board for the disposal of its funds.

In Nigeria expenditure can take the form of the allocation of funds to specially constituted Regional Development Boards. It has, however, been repeatedly emphasized in official statements that the bulk of the available funds would be used for price stablization, while development and research would have only a secondary claim on the boards' resources.

---

[1] This statement was challenged by a senior officer in Nigeria. It can easily be verified by reference to the legislation. The relevant clauses are Section 8 of the Gold Coast and Section 17 of the Nigeria Cocoa Marketing Ordinances, and Section 17 of the Nigeria Groundnut Marketing Ordinance. The relevant passages are reproduced in the note appended to this chapter.

3. IMPLICATIONS OF THE SCOPE AND POWERS
OF THE BOARDS

Many of the powers of the boards are unconnected with price stabilization in any sense of the term. This is not unexpected, since stabilization is not listed among the functions of the Cocoa Boards and is mentioned only incidentally among the functions of the other Nigerian boards.

Thus the extensive licensing powers over the activities of all intermediaries in cocoa and groundnut buying are obviously quite irrelevant to price stabilization. The same applies to some of the powers of the boards over the activities of processors.

Statutory marketing in the form in which it operates in West Africa postulates some control over the exporting activities of the processors, as without it they could purchase the raw product at the low internal price, sell the processed products at open-market levels, and thus secure windfall profits. But this can be prevented by simple control over their exports, notably by the imposition of levies to skim off these profits.[1] It does not require any other form of control, such as the power to prescribe prices and conditions on which the processors can purchase their raw material, or the right of a board to insist that the processors must purchase their supplies from the board. Under these conditions processors can operate only on the sufferance of the boards.[2]

It is clear from their powers and organization that the boards are organs of government, and not independent commercial organizations, as has been officially claimed on their behalf. In the Gold Coast the governmental character of the Cocoa Marketing Board has been placed beyond doubt by the amending ordinances of 1951 and 1952 referred to in the previous section. The official character of the Nigerian boards is

[1] It has been suggested that in the absence of strict control over processors they might make large profits on local sales. Even if this were so it would not be a concern of the marketing boards. It would in no way be the result of low producer prices enforced by the boards, since these are also reflected in the local price of the processed product. If the processors were to make large profits on local sales, this would reflect the superior efficiency of their processes over hand methods.

[2] It has at times been influentially suggested that the need to protect producers from exploitation by merchants and middlemen has been a principal reason both for the establishment of statutory marketing with prescription of minimum prices, and for the granting of such extensive powers to the marketing boards. This is more in the nature of an *ex post* rationalization for the introduction of certain measures than a satisfactory explanation for their establishment. As already argued, where there is competition in produce buying and free entry into the trade producers are unlikely to be exploited; and when they are in danger of exploitation the granting of extensive powers, especially licensing powers, to a statutory monopoly will not protect them. In fact, the licensing of dealers can only weaken the position of producers by reducing competition for their product.

evident from the numerous references in the ordinances to 'the Governor in Council' in connexion with such matters as the appointment of members of the boards, the drafting of regulations and standing orders, the extension of the boards' authority to other products, and so forth.

Apart from these formal considerations, organizations with the functions, scope, influence and powers, especially compulsory powers, such as those of the boards are essentially and necessarily governmental organs and not independent commercial organizations.

The extension of the authority of the boards to minor products also seems to be unrelated to stabilization. There may have been various reasons for this extension. It may have been thought that the production of some of these crops would increase if their producers received significantly higher prices than were paid to producers of the major crops; such a discrepancy might also create political and administrative embarrassment. Again, if the system was held to benefit the producers of major crops, it would seem proper to extend it to other products. The familiar desire for expansion and comprehensiveness may have also played a part.

These considerations, however, do not wholly explain either the extension of the authority of the boards, or the assumption of such wide powers unrelated to their ostensible functions. Both these aspects seem to reflect the intention, or at least the inclination, to use this machinery to enlarge and to strengthen official control over these industries and over peasant producers as much as possible.

NOTE TO CHAPTER 21

Extracts from the ordinances establishing the boards

The text of this chapter paraphrased the principal contents of the ordinances establishing the Nigerian and Gold Coast marketing boards.

This note presents the text of some of the provisions of these ordinances which illustrate the wide powers vested in these organisations.

Gold Coast Cocoa Marketing Ordinance (No. 16 of 1947)

Section 6: (1) It shall be the duty of the Board to secure the most favourable arrangements for the purchase, grading, export and selling of Gold Coast cocoa, and to assist in the development by all possible means of the cocoa industry of the Gold Coast for the benefit and prosperity[1] of the producers.

(2) In particular, and without prejudice to the generality of the foregoing, the Board shall have the power

(a) to control and fix the prices to be paid from time to time to Gold Coast producers for their cocoa and similarly to arrange in such manner as the Board shall think fit, to notify such prices;

[1] The definition and interpretation of these terms is left entirely to the discretion of the boards.

(b) to purchase cocoa and to do all things necessary for and in conection with the purchase from producers of Gold Coast cocoa;

(c) to appoint licensed buying agents for the purchase of cocoa on behalf of the Board;

(d) to grant, renew or withhold licenses for each crop year to such agents, to impose conditions upon the grant of such licences, and to cancel or suspend any such licences for breach of any such conditions or other good cause;

Section 8: From and after the commencement of this Ordinance

(1) No person shall purchase cocoa except

(a) The Board, or a person authorised to purchase cocoa for sale to the Board; or

(b) a licensed buying agent or a person authorised to purchase for sale to such an agent; or

(c) a person acting upon the written instructions of the Board.[1]

(2) No person shall export any cocoa except

(a) cocoa which is the property of the Board; or

(b) cocoa the export of which has been authorised.

Nigeria Cocoa Marketing Ordinance (No. 33 of 1947)

Section 16: It shall be the duty of the Board to secure the most favourable arrangements for the purchase, grading, export and marketing of Nigerian cocoa and to assist in the development by all possible means of the cocoa industry of Nigeria for the benefit and prosperity of the producers.

Section 17: In particular, and without prejudice to the generality of Section 16, the Board shall have the power

(a) to control and fix the prices to be paid from time to time for cocoa or for any grade thereof at any place or within any specified area, and similarly to notify such prices in such manner as the Board may deem requisite;

(b) to prescribe grades of cocoa;

(c) to purchase cocoa and to do all things necessary for and in connection with the purchase of cocoa;

(d) to appoint licensed buying agents for the purchase of cocoa on behalf of the Board;

(e) to control and fix the prices to be paid from time to time to licensed buying agents for cocoa;

(f) to control and regulate the activities and remuneration, by licence or otherwise, of all persons or classes of persons connected with the sale, purchase or other disposition of cocoa and if necessary to prohibit any person or class of persons from dealing in cocoa;[2]

---

[1] Thus the formal powers of licensing of the Board extend to all dealers in cocoa and not only to the licensed buying agents.

[2] Cf. the immediately preceding footnote.

(*g*) to grant, renew or withhold licences for each crop year in respect of licensed buying agents, to impose conditions upon the grant or renewal of such licences, whether in respect of the area in which cocoa is to be sold or otherwise disposed of, and to cancel or suspend any licence for breach of any such conditions or for other good cause;

Section 37: From and after the commencement of this ordinance no person shall export cocoa other than

(*a*) cocoa which is the property of the Board; or
(*b*) cocoa the export of which has been duly authorised in writing by the Board.

Section 38: From and after the commencement of this ordinance, cocoa purchased for processing within Nigeria shall be

(*a*) cocoa which is the property of the Board and the purchase of which has been authorised by the Board; or
(*b*) any other cocoa the purchase of which for such processing has been authorised by the Board in writing, subject to the conditions contained in such authority.

Provided that the provisions of this section shall not apply to cocoa purchased for processing within Nigeria where the product of such processing is consumed within Nigeria.

It would be repetitive to quote lengthy extracts from the other Nigerian ordinances. The provisions relating to the control over exports and the prescription of prices are essentially the same in all. The control over processors and dealers is, however, of special interest in oilseeds and cotton, and the relevant clauses of the Groundnut Marketing Ordinance (No. 11 of 1949) deserve quotation:

Section 17: [the Board shall have power]

(*f*) to control and regulate the activities and remuneration, by licence or otherwise, of all persons or classes of persons connected with the sale and purchase for export of produce subject to this Ordinance and, if necessary, to prohibit any person or class of person from dealing in such produce for export;

Section 60: (1) The Marketing Board may direct that any produce subject to this Ordinance which is purchased for mechanized processing in Nigeria shall be purchased from the Marketing Board.

(2) No oil or other product resulting from the local processing of produce subject to this Ordinance shall be exported except by the Marketing Board.

CHAPTER 22

THE PRICE POLICIES OF THE
MARKETING BOARDS (I)[1]

This chapter and Chapter 23 review the price policies of the marketing boards from their establishment in 1947 and 1949 to the end of 1951, as well as, more briefly, some results of the operations of the West African Produce Control Board. In assessing the policies of the present boards, it should be remembered that the years covered were to some extent the experimental, or formative, period of these organizations.[2] This does not affect the description of the policies, nor the analysis of their effects, nor the discussion of the arguments advanced in their support; indeed, it only serves to bring out more clearly some of the problems created by an experimental, *ad hoc* approach. But in a critical assessment of the decisions taken it is relevant that over this period the boards could be said to be feeling their way; and further that they have had to do so without a clearly defined mandate.

I. SUMMARY OF THE OPERATIONS OF THE BOARDS

The marketing boards began their operations with important advantages. The two Cocoa Boards inherited some £22 m. from the West African Produce Control Board. That organization did not begin to accumulate surpluses on other products until February 1947 (since up to that time it sold to the Ministry of Food on a cost basis), and in the space of about two years it accumulated £11 m. on oil-palm produce and £10 m. on groundnuts, which it handed over to the successor boards in April 1949. These last two figures were higher than the total paid to producers by the successor boards in their first year of operation. Moreover, the demand for cocoa was high, and oilseeds were still in acutely short supply; the Ministry of Food had guaranteed minimum prices for

---

[1] The detailed discussion of the price policies of the marketing boards is confined to the Nigerian boards and to the Gold Coast Cocoa Marketing Board, that is, all the boards operating in these two colonies with the exception of the Gold Coast Agricultural Products Marketing Board. Some of the detailed statistics are not shown for the Nigeria Cotton Marketing Board which is much less important than the other boards.

[2] There was here an asymmetry between the position of the boards and that of their constituents. The present boards came into being in 1947 and 1949; but the producers have been affected by statutory marketing continuously since the establishment of cocoa control in 1939 and the West African Produce Control Board in 1942.

Table 19. *Summary of the operations of the marketing boards, 1947–51*

	(1) Producer price per ton (£)	(2) F.o.b. cost per ton (£)	(3) Average f.o.b. price per ton (£)	(4) Surplus (including interest) per ton (£)	(5) Surplus per ton as percen- tage of producer price (i.e. 4 as percentage of 1)	(6) Total annual surplus (£m.)
Gold Coast cocoa:						
1947–48	75	85	201	117	183	24·1
1948–49	121	139	136	−0·5	−0·5	−0·1
1949–50	84	110	178	71	86	18·0
1950–51	130	196	269	77	59	20·1
Nigerian cocoa:						
1947–48	63	70	195	126	200	9·3
1948–49	120	135	138	8	7	0·8
1949–50	100	117	178	69	69	6·9
1950–51	120	173	268	102	85	11·2
Nigerian palm oil:						
1949	40	52	68	16	40	2·5
1950	40	52	65	13	32	2·1
1951	52	65	83	18	35	2·3
Nigerian palm kernels:						
1949	26	33	45	12	46	3·2
1950	26	34	41	8	31	2·9
1951	32	41	57	16	50	5·4
Nigerian groundnuts:						
1949–50	21	35	48	13	62	3
1950–51	21	41	63	24	114	3·3
Nigerian cotton:						
1949–50	37	43	82	39	105	1·2
1950–51	37	56	107	51	138	2·2

Note

The producer price for Nigerian cocoa shown here refers to grade 1 cocoa and thus slightly overstates the actual average producer price, as a small part of the output consists of lower grades. For palm oil the producer price shown is the average (weighed by tonnage purchased) of the price of grades 1, 2 and 3; the very small quantities of grades 4 and 5 have been excluded. For cotton the price is the seed-cotton price.

All producer prices refer to the basic prices payable at the ports or at railway-line stations. They are higher than those payable at road stations.

groundnuts and oil-palm produce for three years at levels well above those which were being paid to producers in 1949. From their establishment the boards pursued austere price policies in paying producers much less than the disposable proceeds.

Table 20. *Surpluses of the marketing boards to the end of crop year
1950–1 or calendar year 1951*

	Taken over from the West African Produce Control Board (£ m.)	Surplus on operations (£ m.)	Total surpluses (£ m.)
Gold Coast Cocoa Board	14	62	76
Nigeria Cocoa Board	8	28	36
Nigeria Oil Palm Produce Board	11	18	29
Nigeria Groundnut Board	10	6	16
Nigeria Cotton Board	0·2 [a]	3	3
	43	117	160

[a] Grant from Raw Cotton Commission

Note

These are official figures of the annually accruing surpluses. A minor part of these has been allocated (though usually not spent) for certain specific purposes, or to other organizations, and is therefore formally not part of the boards' reserves. For this reason the figures do not agree in every case with published figures of reserves.

Table 19 summarizes the operations of the boards. The figures disregard any differences between market prices and the sales proceeds of the boards, a matter discussed in § 2. The surpluses are struck after the payment of export duties, which are included in the f.o.b. cost and represent a substantial part of the difference between columns 1 and 2. In practice the level of these duties seems to be influenced largely by the size of the margins (surpluses) of the boards, since when these are large, export duties diminish only the margins per ton and do not directly affect producer prices. The presence of the large surpluses was probably the principal reason for the very sharp increases in recent years[1]

[1] In the Gold Coast the export duty on cocoa in 1950–1 was £51·1 per ton, which was 39 % of the basic producer price; in 1939–40 the figures had been £2·1 and 15 %. In Nigeria in 1950–1 the cocoa export duty was £40 per ton, which was 33 % of the basic producer price: in 1939–40 the figures had been £1·3 and 7·6 %. On non-mineral exports not controlled by marketing boards, e.g. rubber, timber, hides and skins, the duties were then (and have been since) 10 % or less of f.o.b. values, or about what they had been on all exports before statutory marketing. Since then the discrepancy has widened greatly with the big increases in the cocoa export duty, which in 1953–54 reached at times about £200 per ton both in Nigeria and in the Gold Coast, equal to about 40–45 % of f.o.b. values and about 150 % of producer prices. These large figures are of the duty only, excluding the surplus.

in the rates of export duties on these products to levels far higher than the rates of duty on those non-mineral exports (e.g., rubber and hides and skins) which the boards do not control. In its effects on the economy, and on the individual producer, an increase in export duty to transfer part of the surplus from a marketing board to the government is a paper transaction which substitutes one type of levy for another.

Column 5 of the table shows the percentage by which producer prices in any one year could have been raised without drafts on reserves. Only in one instance was there a draft on reserves, and that was very small. The aggregate surpluses are shown in Table 20; the overall total is not far short of the amounts paid to the producers from the establishment of the boards up to the autumn of 1951.

2. THE PRINCIPAL LEVIES ON THE PRODUCERS OF WEST AFRICAN EXPORTS

The accumulation of surpluses by the marketing boards is not the only levy on the West African farmers in their capacity as exporters.

There are heavy export duties, the rates of which tend to be connected with the supluses.[1]

Differences between market prices and the sale proceeds realized by the marketing organizations need also to be examined.[2] Where the

---

[1] The connexion between the surpluses and rates of duty was confirmed in 1951 in the *Report of the Commission on Revenue Allocation* (Lagos, 1951) by the then Chairman of the Nigerian boards: '...an important objection to this form of taxation in present Nigerian circumstances is the extreme facility with which it can be collected from the Marketing Boards. The dangers involved in this are obvious....At present the rates of duty are reasonable enough, though in the aggregate they probably produce rather an excessive proportion of Nigerian revenues...but to raise the present rates substantially...might be injurious' (para. 19). The duties on marketing board produce have since been raised greatly. These considerations are sufficient to meet the argument sometimes advanced (e.g. by Dr A. R. Prest, *Journal of the Royal Statistical Society*, 1954, Part I) that the export duties and surpluses should not be considered together, as the former are part of general revenue. It seems best to consider these together but show them separately, as is done here. They are both compulsory levies on producers in their capacity as exporters, and they thus bear on a discussion largely concerned with the relation between producer prices and commercial values. Moreover, duties at given percentages of f.o.b. values are a higher percentage of producer prices when surpluses are accumulated (i.e. when producers receive less than the commercial values of their products) than in the absence of statutory marketing, and thus represent a much heavier rate of taxation on producers than they would otherwise.

[2] The terms 'market prices', 'market values' and 'commercial values' are largely interchangeable in this study. They always refer to prices obtained or obtainable for bulk supplies. But in some cases they refer to market quotations, in others to prices paid (especially by the Ministry of Food) for bulk supplies without an open-market quotation; and they may also refer to the local equivalent of such quotations and prices,

former regularly exceed the latter and producers must sell to the statutory organizations, this difference must also be considered when assessing the effects of the marketing system on producers.

The necessity for this procedure is obvious from the history of statutory marketing over a number of years. Until 1947 the Ministry of Food bought the crops (except cocoa) from the West African Produce Control Board at cost price, and the board thus did not accumulate surpluses; prices were much less than those paid by the Ministry of Food for bulk supplies of these commodities from other sources, and also much less than open-market prices.

Examination of this matter is of interest for several reasons. First, in assessing the effects of statutory marketing it is necessary to consider the length of the period over which the prices received by producers have differed substantially from market prices or from those received by other suppliers. Both the length of the period and the extent of the difference are relevant. Secondly, the selling arrangements and results bear on the argument, frequently advanced on behalf of statutory export monopolies, that their position as strong sellers enables them to secure much more favourable prices than would be received by individual exporters. Further, in an assessment of the retention of a substantial proportion of the sales proceeds from producers over this period it is relevant that the proceeds (other than the proceeds of cocoa) were generally well below the market prices of the war and post-war years. It must however be noted that while computation of this item is of considerable interest, the interest is chiefly historical, since under selling arrangements which came into force at the end of 1951 the Ministry of Food pays open-market prices for its bulk purchases of West African produce, so that this item does not, and indeed cannot, arise at present.

These differences between sales proceeds and commercial values as shown by open-market prices or by the prices paid to other bulk suppliers are, of course, affected by the prices chosen for purposes of comparison. But it is clear that on sales of groundnuts and of oil-palm produce these differences were large over most of the period of statutory marketing, chiefly over the period covered by the West African Produce Control Board.

Thus when discussing the effect of statutory marketing on producers, three items, or types of levy, must be considered; the surpluses of th

---

after deduction of transport costs and of similar items. The term 'sale proceeds' refers to the f.o.b. or c.i.f. selling price realized. In some instances the term 'net sale proceeds' is used to indicate proceeds net of all marketing expenses other than export duty, that is, the amount available to be shared between the government, the marketing organizations and the producer. The meaning will either be clear from the context or indicated in a note.

marketing organizations; export duties; and the differences between commercial values and the sale proceeds realized. This last item is referred to in the discussion as under-realization. Although it cannot be computed and presented as precisely as can other items, it is possible to assess it closely for all major West African exports. But as this item is not in every respect *in pari materia* with the others, the three types of levy (the surplus of the marketing organizations, export duty and under-realization) are distinguished in all statistics presented in this study to enable separate assessment to be made.

The bases of the calculations are discussed in Appendix 1, but an outline is necessary here as without it the tables may not be fully intelligible.

(*a*) The market prices and values with which the sales proceeds of the marketing organizations are compared refer in every case to prices paid for bulk supplies, and not for marginal quantities. In the marketing of groundnuts and oil-palm produce over most of the period the prices are those paid by the Ministry of Food for bulk supplies of identical or closely similar commodities. From about 1948 some of these were no longer purchased by the Ministry of Food in significant quantities, but since that year consistent series of market prices are available relating to substantial transactions, and these serve as basis for comparison. As is well known, the principal vegetable oils and oilseeds are widely substitutable for each other in the production of edible fats and soap. Their prices are always inter-related, and usually move together closely. For this reason, changes in the market prices of any one oilseed are generally a reliable guide to changes in the market values of similar products, as long as substantial quantities of the principal oils and oil-seeds are traded in the markets under review. West African vegetable oils and oilseeds are a small proportion of the total of such supplies reaching the market over a period; thus if they are sold on the open market they will fetch a price closely related to market quotations.

(*b*) In a discussion of cocoa marketing such comparisons require special care because the selling agencies of the marketing boards control such a large proportion of total world supplies that they necessarily influence world prices. Their sales tend to depress the market; and conversely when they do not sell prices tend to rise. It is thus generally not significant to compare the market prices received by them with the average daily or monthly quotations which are often nominal. Nevertheless, from 1940 to 1948 a firm and meaningful comparison is possible between commercial values and the prices received by the marketing organizations. Over this period the price paid by the Ministry of Food for West African cocoa was based at first on the prices ruling in the United Kingdom when the distribution of cocoa was taken over by the

Ministry of Food; and from 1942 it was based on a formula (explained in the first Cocoa White Paper) which resulted in the Ministry obtaining its cocoa at a lower price than that ruling in the United States. The difference is significant between the c.i.f. New York price (converted at the official rate of exchange) and that paid by the Ministry of Food, since over most of this period the price of cocoa in the United States was controlled so that additional supplies could have been sold at the New York price.[1]

This price was controlled from 1941 to 1946; for the seasons over which it was not controlled one-third of the difference between the New York price and that paid by the Ministry of Food was taken in recognition of the fact that if more had been sold in New York the price there would have been lower. On a very modest estimate the differences in the aggregate exceeded £12 million on total imports of West African cocoa into the United Kingdom from 1940 to 1948 (private purchase of cocoa was restored in 1949). This is over £3 a ton on the total tonnage handled by the statutory marketing organizations from 1939–40 to 1950–51. A figure of £3 per ton has been adopted in the tables under the heading of under-realization for the period as a whole.[2] As approximately seven-eighths of the total dates from the operations of the West African Produce Control Board, no figures are shown under this heading for the period since 1947. In considering this item for cocoa it should be remembered that the British Government underwrote the purchase of the entire West African crop (though at an unspecified price) when in the early years of the war the market prospects appeared very bleak indeed.

(c) As a corollary of (a) and (b), the comparisons between commercial values and sales proceeds are not vitiated by the familiar objection that if larger amounts had been sold in higher-priced markets the prices there would have been lower. The considerations set out in (a) meet this objection for groundnuts and oil-palm produce, and those in (b) meet it for cocoa.

---

[1] In outside markets prices for substantial quantities were much higher than the New York price. And the fact that the New York price was controlled throughout practically the whole of this period meets any objection that it may have been influenced by the strong selling position of the West African Produce Control Board.

[2] These calculations are discussed in Appendix 1. Since 1949 the Cocoa Boards have realized lower prices on their sales to the United States than in soft currency markets. It seems that more was sold in hard currency markets than would have been dictated by commercial considerations, possibly largely in the interests of the sterling area dollar pool. This may have represented another levy on the producers, which is, however, neglected here. It has been suggested that the motive for these sales was to retain American goodwill for West African cocoa. This is an insubstantial argument in the marketing of a standardized primary product.

(d) The discrepancies between market prices and selling prices considered in the discussion do not refer to unsuccessful forward sales in the accepted sense of the term. The great bulk refers to differences in prices paid for supplies sold on identical or closely similar conditions of delivery (usually spot or near deliveries), but paid for at different prices. This was the position for the crops purchased by the Ministry of Food from the West African Produce Control Board and from other sources. In recent years the bulk sales of the Groundnut, Oil Palm Produce and Cotton Boards have also been unsuccessful. Most of these transactions seem to have stemmed principally from the desire to make certain of a price showing an appreciable surplus on the producer price, especially perhaps over this formative period of the boards' operations. This supposition is confirmed by the frequent references in the reports of the boards to surpluses as evidence of commercial success.

This conclusion probably does not apply with the same force to the bulk sales of the Groundnut Marketing Board and the Oil Palm Produce Marketing Board for 1951. The decision of these two boards to sell forward the entire exportable output under their control at prices which turned out to have been unsuccessful, may have been the result partly of an unfortunate judgement of market prospects, as well as of the desire to ensure sales at prices showing substantial margins on the producer prices.[1]

The inclusion of the 1951 figures in the calculation of the under-realization would not affect greatly the rates of this levy, either over the period as a whole or since 1947. They have, nevertheless, been excluded from the calculation of the averages of the under-realization (to ensure that these should not be influenced by what may have been simply unsuccessful forward sales), but included in the computation of the total levies over the period, shown in Table 23. As these figures are shown separately in Tables 21 and 22, as well as in Apendix 1, the under-realization can be easily subtracted from the total in Table 23 if so desired.

(e) The information on the three types of levy is shown in this chapter in the form of averages and totals over certain periods; in Appendix 1 the data are presented year by year. Table 23 summarizes the figures for the entire period of statutory marketing. In Tables 21 and 22 they are shown

---

[1] It was partly because of these unsuccessful sales that from the end of that year the selling arrangements were greatly altered. Since the end of 1951 the prices received by the boards from the Ministry of Food have been based on independently assessed and declared average market prices of the previous quarter. This interesting tribute to the validity of market prices as a guide to commercial values incidentally confirms the validity and relevance of the use of market prices in the computation of the discrepancies between commercial values and the sales proceeds realized by the marketing organizations.

Table 21. Levies on the producers of West African exports under statutory marketing (£ per ton)

Year	(1) Producer price	(2) Export duty	(3) Surplus of marketing organization	(4) Net sales proceeds, i.e. (1)+(2)+(3)[a]	(5) Under-realization	(6) Net commercial values, i.e. (4)+(5)[b]
Gold Coast cocoa						
1939-40 to 1950-51	46·7	7·2	27·5	81·4	3·0	84·4
1947-48 to 1950-51	102·5	18·5	64·1	185·1	n.a.	185·1
1950-51	130·7	51·1	72·7	254·5	(c)	254·5
Nigerian cocoa						
1939-40 to 1950-51	47·9	6·0	31·6	85·5	3·0	88·5
1947-48 to 1950-51	100·6	14·1	71·8	186·5	n.a.	186·5
1950-51	120·0	40·0	95·0	255·0	(c)	255·0
Nigerian groundnuts						
1942-43 to 1949-50	14·0	1·5	5·6	21·1	16·3	37·4
1947-48 to 1949-50	18·8	3·1	14·9	36·8	16·1	52·9
1949-50	21·2	3·3	13·0	37·5	18·0	55·5
1950-51	21·2	6·4	22·0	49·6	17·0	66·6
Nigerian palm kernels						
1942-50	14·5	1·2	3·9	19·6	12·6	32·2
1947-50	22·15	2·15	8·75	33·05	14·35	47·4
1949-50	26·0	2·55	9·75	38·3	10·75	49·05
1951	32·0	5·3	14·2	51·5	15·0	66·5
Nigerian palm oil						
1943-50	23·2	1·8	7·4	32·4	11·4	43·8
1947-50	34·0	2·9	14·8	51·7	12·9	64·6
1949-50	40·0	4·3	14·3	58·6	10·4	69·0
1951	52·0	7·8	17·8	77·6	46·0	123·6

(a) I.e. sales proceeds f.o.b., less marketing expenses to f.o.b. other than export duty, that is, amount available to be shared locally between the government, the marketing organization and the producer.

(b) I.e. amount which would have been available to be shared locally between the government, the marketing organization and the producer if market prices had been realized.

(c) Private purchase of cocoa restored in 1949.

n.a. Not available, or more precisely not computed (see text).

Table 22. *Levies on the producers of West African exports under statutory marketing (percentages)*

Year	(1) Export duty	(2) Surplus	(3) Under-realization	(4) Total levies, i.e. (1)+(2)+(3)	(5) Producer price	(6) Export duty	(7) Surplus	(8) Duty and surplus, i.e. (6)+(7)	(9) Producer price	(10) Export duty	(11) Surplus	(12) Under-realization	(13) Total levies i.e. (10)+(11)+(12)
	As percentage of producer price (i.e. percentage of (1) in Table 21)				As percentage of sales proceeds (i.e. percentage of (4) in Table 21)				As percentage of commercial values (i.e. percentage of (6) in Table 21)				
Gold Coast cocoa													
1939–40 to 1950–51	15	59	6	81	57	9	34	43	55	9	33	4	45
1947–48 to 1950–51	18	63	n.a.	81	55	10	35	45	55	10	35	n.a.	45
1950–51	39	56	(a)	95	51	20	29	49	51	20	29	(a)	49
Nigerian cocoa													
1939–40 to 1950–51	13	66	6	85	56	7	37	44	54	7	36	4	46
1947–48 to 1950–51	14	71	n.a.	85	54	8	38	46	54	8	38	n.a.	46
1950–51	33	79	(a)	112	47	16	37	53	47	16	37	(a)	53
Nigerian groundnuts													
1942–43 to 1949–50	11	40	116	167	66	7	27	34	37	4	15	44	63
1947–48 to 1949–50	16	79	86	181	51	8	40	49	36	6	28	30	64
1949–50	16	61	85	162	57	9	35	43	38	6	23	32	62
1950–51	30	104	80	214	43	13	44	57	32	10	33	26	68
Nigerian palm kernels													
1942–50	8	27	87	122	74	6	20	26	45	4	12	39	55
1947–50	10	40	65	114	67	7	26	33	47	5	18	30	53
1949–50	10	37	41	89	68	7	25	32	53	5	20	22	47
1951	17	44	47	108	62	10	28	38	48	8	21	23	52
Nigerian palm oil													
1943–50	8	32	49	89	72	6	23	28	53	4	17	26	47
1947–50	9	44	38	90	66	6	29	34	53	4	23	20	47
1949–50	11	36	26	73	68	7	24	32	58	6	21	15	42
1951	15	34	88	138	67	10	23	33	42	6	14	37	58

(a) Private purchase of cocoa restored in 1949.   n.a. Not available or, more precisely, not computed (see text).

Notes to Tables 21 and 22

The data are derived from detailed tables in Appendix 1 where the basis of the information is set out in detail in the notes.

The surpluses of the boards used in these calculations and shown in the tables are very slightly lower than those in Table 19. The latter, taken from the published reports of the boards, include interest. This small item, which has arisen only comparatively recently, is excluded, partly to ensure the comparability of the rates of the levies with the earlier years of statutory marketing, but chiefly for a less obvious reason.

Interest arises only because the boards have accumulated surpluses, that is, because part of the sales proceeds have been withheld. Thus, unless this item is excluded, the average rate of the levies (even if weighted) over a number of years cannot be used in strict logic to indicate the extent by which producer prices could have been raised in their absence.

both for the entire period of statutory marketing (beginning in 1939 for cocoa, 1942 for groundnuts and palm kernels and 1943 for palm oil), and also for certain sub-periods. These mark important changes in administrative and selling arrangements, such as the revision of the selling arrangements for groundnuts and oil-palm produce in 1947, or the change-over from the West African Produce Control Board to the present marketing boards. For cocoa the information is presented for the period as a whole, separately for the period since 1947 (the inception of the present boards), and separately for 1950–1. For groundnuts and oil-palm produce the information is presented in the tables for the period as a whole, separately for the periods 1947–51 (the period of the accumulation of surpluses) and 1949–51, and separately for 1950–1 or 1951 as appropriate. The various changes in organization and in selling arrangements were sufficiently important to justify presentation of the information separately for these sub-periods. But, as will be seen, there was remarkable consistency in producer price policy over the period as a whole.

(f) The figures are shown both in unweighted and in weighted form. This presentation has been adopted to meet a familiar difficulty. Unweighted averages are required to show the varying rates of levies through time; and weighted figures to show the total amounts involved. Here this difficulty is not important quantitatively because of the

Table 23. *Levies on the producers of West African exports under statutory marketing (£ m.)*

	(1) Producers' gross proceeds	(2) Export duty	(3) Surplus	(4) Under-realization	(5) Total levies	(6) Levies as percentage of proceeds
Gold Coast cocoa	138	22	77	8	107	71
Nigerian cocoa	58	7	37	3	47	81
Nigerian groundnuts	33	4	16	36	56	170
Nigerian palm kernels	55	6	17	42	65	118
Nigerian palm oil	33	3	12	18	33	100

Notes

Gross proceeds denote the basic producer price multiplied by the tonnage marketed. The figures necessarily appreciably exceed producers' total receipts, since most of the output is sold at stations where lower prices apply.

In the text the contribution to buyers in cocoa marketing is estimated at £12 m.; of this £8½ m. has been allotted to the Gold Coast, and £3½ m. to Nigeria in approximate proportion to the tonnage marketed (the figures have been rounded off to £8 m. and £3 m.).

L

consistent behaviour of producer price policy reflected in Tables 21 and 22. But as a special check and as a matter of interest both the weighted and unweighted figures are shown. In Tables 21 and 22 the levies are expressed as averages (simple arithmetic mean) of annual amounts per ton and of percentages respectively. In Table 23 they are shown as totals, that is, as the sums of annual amounts multiplied by tonnages, thus presenting the information in a weighted form. The results are closely similar to those obtained by the use of the simple arithmetic mean, which is remarkable in view of the large changes in the absolute amounts involved, especially in view of the much larger absolute figures of recent years.[1]

3. THE BURDEN OF THE LEVIES

The principal conclusions from Tables 21–23 emerge clearly. In round figures the surpluses of the boards and the export duties together totalled about £200 m. over the whole period of statutory marketing. Under-realization in the aggregate exceeded another £100 m. The total of the combined levies approximately equalled the total of gross proceeds.

In the most important single effect or aspect of statutory marketing, the relation of producer prices to market prices, there was over this period remarkable continuity of policy since the inception of this form of marketing. This is clear from the comparative consistency of the figures for individual products in column 9 of Table 22. For particular products these do not differ greatly for the period as a whole or for parts of the period. As selling prices improved a larger proportion was withheld from producers, leaving producer prices at about the same proportion of commercial values as before. This tendency was, for instance, evident in 1947, when, after the changes of the selling arrangements of the West African Produce Control Board with the Ministry of Food, the Board received substantially higher prices than before and immediately began to withhold a large part of the increases in prices.

Over the period as a whole, and over the various sub-periods, producer prices have been kept generally at between two-fifths to three-fifths of commercial values. The proportion received by groundnut producers has tended to be less, generally about one-third to two-fifths of commercial values.

This comparative consistency is of particular interest in the levies on cocoa and groundnut producers, since in these figures the element of

[1] In more specific terms the dilemma might be put as follows. In recent years the absolute level of prices has been much higher than in the early years of statutory marketing. Thus if weighted averages are used the recent years would swamp the earlier period. On the other hand, reliance on the simple arithmetic mean might give rise to the usual objections, in particular to the objection that the results present a misleading idea of the amounts involved.

estimate is very small indeed, and the risk of overestimate is negligible. Surpluses and export duties amounted to over 90 % of the aggregate of the levies on cocoa producers as here computed; and for these two items official figures are available throughout the period. In the calculation of the levies on groundnut producers the element of estimate is very small, for two reasons: first, in recent years the surplus of the board represented most of the levies; and secondly, under-realization can be assessed very closely indeed in view of the comparison between the prices paid (generally by the Ministry of Food) for Nigerian and Indian groundnuts.

In these tables the levies are related to the basic producer prices payable at ports or at railway-line stations; to gross proceeds in the sense of basic producer prices multiplied by the tonnages marketed; to proceeds available at the points where the basic producer prices are payable; and to commercial values at these points. Thus the relation of the levies to the receipts of producers pivots on the basic prices. These prices necessarily substantially overstate producers' proceeds per ton, and overstate producer incomes per ton to an even greater extent. First, basic prices are port prices or railway-line prices, and most producers necessarily sell at prices which are lower than these by the transport costs [1] and the costs of the services of intermediaries. Secondly, expenses of production must be deducted from the prices received by the producers before arriving at their incomes from the sale of a ton of produce. Thus all percentages in the table substantially understate the levies as proportions of producers' cash receipts, as proportions of incomes available in their absence (i.e. as percentages of pre-tax incomes), and as percentages of retained incomes.

But even in relation to gross proceeds as here defined, the levies on the producers of groundnuts and palm kernels, the most important exports from northern and eastern Nigeria, were over this period as a whole and over all sub-periods (with only one unimportant exception) at rates of over 50 %.

When the necessary adjustments are made to convert gross proceeds per ton at port or railway-line prices to producer incomes, the proportions become significantly higher. Expressed as percentages of producer incomes available in their absence, the levies on the producers of every one of these crops have averaged well over 50 %, both over the period as a whole and since 1947. In 1950–1 they were again of that order.

---

[1] With the exception of Gold Coast cocoa lower producer prices are gazetted for buying stations other than those to which the basic prices used here refer. Most of the output is bought by the boards' licensed buying agents at such stations. The initial sale by producers is often at non-gazetted markets, still farther from the ports or the railway line and at correspondingly lower prices.

The position of the groundnut producers deserves more detailed consideration. Disregarding the heavy under-realization, in the year 1950–1 export duty and the board's surplus (excluding interest) amounted to about 57 % of the disposable proceeds at railway stations.[1] Without these levies the average cash income of groundnut producers in 1950–1 from the sale of groundnuts would have been of the general order of £10–15 per year; after the levies it was about £4 or £5.[2]

The burden of these levies on the producers of the other major export crops was proportionately somewhat less,[3] though still necessarily at appreciably higher rates than suggested by the figures in the table. The incomes of the producers of oil-palm produce and of cocoa are higher than those of groundnut producers, those of the cocoa producers being much higher.[4]

The information presented in Tables 21–23 is reproduced in Charts 1 and 2. Chart 1 shows producer prices and all the three levies; Chart 2 omits the under-realization and is confined to the two levies—the surpluses and the export duties—which can be precisely ascertained

[1] The selling price was £70 c. and f. United Kingdom; total transport and marketing expenses, excluding export duty, were about £20, leaving £50 to be shared between the government, the board and the producer. The export duty and the board's surplus amounted to about £28·5, and the producer price at these stations was £21·2. If interest is included in the board's surplus the total of the two levies is raised to over £30, or more than 60 % of sales proceeds.

[2] The basis of these figures is easily explained. In 1949–50 and 1950–1 the basic railway-line price was £21·2 a ton; at road stations it ranged from £16·2 to £21. In money terms these were the highest prices for at least 25 years. Most producers cultivate altogether about three or four acres, and about one acre of this is under groundnuts; with their equipment and technique they could not cultivate much more. One acre of groundnuts yields about one-quarter of a ton. Thus if producers sell at gazetted stations and have no expenses, they are left with about £4–5 for a season's production of groundnuts if the entire output is sold. There are unavoidable expenses of production and of transport, and net cash incomes from groundnut production would be nearer to £3.

[3] The burden on the cotton producers has been very similar to that on the groundnut producers (cf. Table 19 and § 4 below).

[4] The discussion and calculations in the text assume that the incidence of levies is on the producers (sellers) and not on the consumers, i.e. that the payment of prices below commercial values did not affect market prices through curtailment of supplies. This is undoubtedly correct for groundnuts, oil-palm produce and cotton, since Nigerian exports are a very small proportion of all exports of vegetable oils, oilseeds, and cotton. West African exports of cocoa, on the other hand, are an appreciable part (about one-half) of world supplies, and sustained payment of prices below market values certainly affects the maintenance and extension of capacity, and thus the long-period supply from West Africa, with some resulting repercussion on world prices. But in the production of cocoa this factor operates much more on long-period supply, i.e. through repercussions on capacity rather than on production from given capacity. It is certain that the influence of this factor on market prices was negligible over this period, though eventually it is likely to be of some significance.

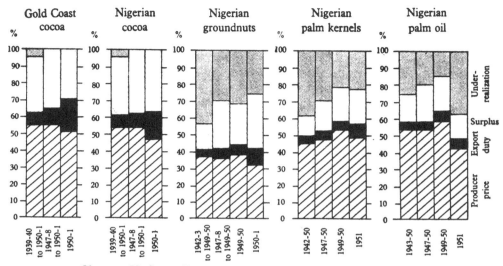

Chart 1. Under-realization, surplus, export duty and producer price
as percentages of commercial values.

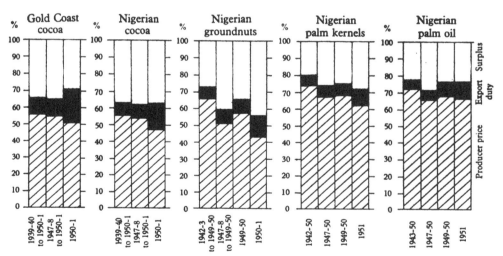

Chart 2. Surplus, export duty and producer price as percentages
of sales proceeds.

from published official sources. But the element of estimate is small
even for the information presented in Chart 1.

The diagrams illustrate conveniently the principal conclusions emerging from the tables. The high rates of the levies, the relation of producer
prices to sale proceeds and to commercial values, the continuity of

policy since the establishment of statutory marketing and the particularly heavy burden of groundnut producers can all be seen easily.

There are certain other levies on West African producers under statutory marketing. These are not of the same magnitude as the items already listed, and their incidence cannot be easily expressed quantitatively, but they deserve mention. Thus, the boards' surpluses are calculated after allowing for certain costs which would not be incurred under a commercial system. Thus the Nigeria Cotton Marketing Board finances a Cotton Development Team, the cost of which is charged in the accounts before computing the margin accruing to the Board. Similarly, the cost of various types of transport subsidy and certain other available elements of costs, particularly in the marketing of groundnuts, are also debited to expenses before computing the margin.[1]

4. STATUTORY MARKETING ARRANGEMENTS FOR MINOR EXPORT PRODUCTS

The four products so far reviewed are quantitatively by far the most important exports controlled by the marketing boards. It is not proposed to present detailed statistics for the less important products marketed by statutory export monopolies; but a general indication can be given of the price policies pursued by the organizations in charge of these products.

Nigerian cotton is the most important of these secondary export crops controlled by statutory marketing organizations. In the later war years and early post-war years the British purchasing authorities (the Board of Trade, the Ministry of Supply and eventually the Raw Cotton Commission) took over this crop at very low prices which, after 1946, were generally of the order of one-half of the prices paid for comparable growths in the world markets[2] or paid by these authorities when purchasing from other sources. From its inception the Cotton Marketing Board pursued an exceedingly conservative policy. In the first two seasons of its operations its accumulated surplus was rather more than total payments to producers; it thus withheld about one-half of the proceeds available for distribution. As cotton prices rose substantially

---

[1] The producers also pay various local taxes which are often substantial, as well as import and excise duties on the merchandise they buy. Total receipts from import and excise duties are about one-fifth of the total c.i.f. value of imports.

[2] Thus in 1947–8 the average f.o.b. price for first-quality Nigerian cotton lint was about 11d. per lb.; and it was on this basis that the c. and f. price paid by the purchasing departments was calculated. In the same season the average New York spot price for middling cotton (converted at the official rate of exchange) was 1s. 10d. per lb. Nigerian cotton is of higher quality than American middling and normally carries a premium of about 1d. per lb.

above the levels at which the Cotton Board had sold forward the entire exportable crop, the producer price turned out to be appreciably less than one-half of the local equivalent of the commercial value. In 1951 it was about one-third or two-fifths of this figure.

In Nigeria benniseed is marketed by the Groundnut Marketing Board. The marketing arrangements and the price policy are similar to those for groundnuts. The proportion of proceeds withheld by the Board is much the same as for groundnuts, but this represents a somewhat higher percentage of the price paid to producers. Benniseed is produced by very backward and poor tribes (especially the Tiv) who have barely emerged from the most primitive subsistence production. The operation of statutory marketing has necessarily retarded the emergence of a substantial cash and exchange economy among these people.

In the Gold Coast several minor agricultural exports, including copra, palm kernels and coffee, are marketed by another statutory monopoly, the Agricultural Products Marketing Board. Towards the end of 1950 and the beginning of 1951 producers received about one-third or one-quarter of the commercial value of their crops. As prices about two or three times as high were being paid in French Togoland and in the Ivory Coast,[1] producers were beginning to show signs of restiveness.

---

[1] Towards the end of 1950 and the beginning of 1951 the price received by producers of copra in the French colonies was about £87 per ton against £40 in the Gold Coast; for palm kernels the figures were about £70 against £21.

CHAPTER 23

THE PRICE POLICIES OF THE MARKETING BOARDS (II)

The price policies of the marketing boards were described in Chapter 22; the principal implications and results of these policies are examined in this chapter.

I. DESTABILIZATION OF INCOMES OF PRODUCERS AND OF INTER-SEASONAL PRICES

In 1948–9 the Gold Coast Cocoa Marketing Board made the trifling 'loss' of £100,000 which was a fraction of 1% of its accumulated surpluses or of its annual turnover. Following this very small draft on its reserves the Board reduced the producer prices by 30% and in the following year made the huge surplus of £18 m. This was only one instance of the insistence of the marketing boards on the accumulation of surpluses.

The desire to secure surpluses, coupled with a disregard of the difference between changes in producer *prices* and in producer *incomes*, have brought about a destabilization of incomes[1] of cocoa producers and probably also of groundnut producers. As a result of the price policies of the Cocoa Boards the incomes of cocoa producers have not only been greatly reduced but they have fluctuated more violently over these years than if the crops had been paid for at full market value.

This can be seen from Table 24, in which actual incomes refer to producer prices multiplied by tonnages purchased, and potential incomes refer to annual incomes plus the annual surpluses. The figures are shown both in absolute terms and as percentages of 1947–8, the first year of the operation of the Cocoa Boards. It will be seen that the actual fluctuations were far greater than they would have been if the total net proceeds had been paid out. In short, the payment of world prices to cocoa producers would have secured a greater stability of producers' incomes at a much higher level.

It is not possible to prepare a similar table for the other major crops. The other boards have not been in existence for a sufficiently long period for construction of such a series. Moreover, prices have been kept at low absolute levels, and such price policies have rendered easy the

---

[1] Strictly speaking destabilization of proceeds. Where producers incurred any fixed costs the fluctuations in their incomes must have been even more marked than the variations in proceeds. In this section reference to incomes refers to sales proceeds. The conclusions apply *a fortiori* to incomes.

maintenance of comparatively stable levels. But a tendency towards destabilization of incomes is discernible for groundnuts and for cotton. The exportable crop of groundnuts fell almost by one-half between 1948–9 and 1949–50 (from 323,000 to 188,000 tons) and declined further (to about 143,000 tons) in 1950–1. Yet the producer price was increased only very slightly between the first two seasons and was left unchanged between the next two, with the result that money incomes of producers were far less in 1949–50 and in 1950–1 than they had been in 1948–9; real incomes declined even further, as the price of consumer goods rose appreciably over this period.[1] This policy was pursued in spite of the fact that in all three years the Board had very large surpluses and that it received a very high price for the 1950–1 crop. The policy of the Cotton Board and the experience of cotton producers have been similar. The production of palm oil and palm kernels does not vary greatly from season to season, and thus income fluctuations and price fluctuations are closely correlated.

Table 24. *Actual and potential combined money incomes of cocoa producers in the Gold Coast and Nigeria, 1947–51*

Year	Actual		Potential	
	£ m.	As percentage of 1947–8	£ m.	As percentage of 1947–8
1947–8	20·0	100	53·4	100
1948–9	46·4	232	47·1	88
1949–50	31·3	157	56·2	105
1950–1	47·3	237	78·6	147

Moreover, quite apart from this destabilization of incomes, inter-seasonal producer prices have also been destabilized in recent years. The reduction in the producer price of cocoa in the Gold Coast in 1949 was the second largest reduction in price from one season to the next, at least since 1922, which is the first year of the regular series of prices quoted in the Nowell Report. The increase in the following year was the largest on record. In 1951 the producer price of groundnuts was raised by about 70 %.[2] Much the same applies, though to a lesser

[1] The United Africa Company compiles and publishes an index of the wholesale prices of imported commodities (August 1948 = 100) for five trading centres in Nigeria and the Gold Coast. It is based on the Company's records of sales. The Kano index increased by 23 % between August 1948 and November 1950.

[2] The 1951–2 crop was exceptionally large (exportable supplies were a record), with the result that the rise in incomes was proportionately much greater even than the increase in producer prices.

extent, to the policies of the other boards. Thus between seasons the price policies of the boards have not achieved stability in any significant sense and indeed their policies have had, if anything, the reverse effect.

On the other hand, the annually fixed minimum producer prices and maximum profit margins for licensed buying agents have secured stable prices within each season in contrast with the frequent daily or weekly variations in producer prices before the war. While the evils of the frequent intra-seasonal price fluctuations have almost certainly been exaggerated by critics of the pre-war marketing system, they undoubtedly had unsettling effects, and their elimination has probably proved beneficial.

The abolition of the frequent price changes has been widely welcomed in West Africa. These have often been ascribed to the malice of European firms, and these accusations (to which a high degree of concentration lends superficial plausibility) have increased the political tension.

Unfortunately, even in West African conditions, where in the production and marketing of some of the most important crops several months elapse between the end of one season and the beginning of the next season, it is difficult, without a carefully devised scheme, to achieve intra-seasonal stability without other, much more far-reaching, results.

2. THE RELATIVE POSITION OF THE WEST AFRICAN PRODUCERS AND RIVAL SUPPLIERS

The effects of statutory marketing on the position of West African producers relative to producers of similar crops elsewhere is a matter of some interest. This section shows some of the effects of the price policies of the marketing boards on the position of the West African producers relative to producers of similar crops in other territories.

Table 25 compares the increase in producer prices of groundnuts and oil-palm produce between the mid-1930's and recent years with the changes in f.o.b. prices of identical or very similar products from other sterling area sources; it is confined to groundnuts and oil-palm produce, as it is only for these products that a regular series of price quotations is available for bulk supplies from sterling sources over this period.[1]

The figures show clearly the deterioration of the position of the West African producers compared with that of their competitors. Those for groundnuts and palm kernels are particularly telling as they refer to identical commodities; the market values of Indian and West African groundnuts and of Malayan and Nigerian palm kernels are practically

---

[1] It appears from incomplete but reliable information that the conclusions suggested by the table would be confirmed by using the New York prices of cocoa and converting the figures into sterling.

Table 25. *Changes in commodity prices, 1935–7, 1948, 1949, 1950 and 1951*

		1935–7	1948	1949	1950	1951
c	Nigerian groundnuts (producer prices):					
	£ per ton	6·9	17·9	20·4	21·2	30·1
	As percentage of 1935–7	100	259	295	307	436
c	Gambia groundnuts (ex scale Bathurst):					
	£ per ton	10·9	22·8	22·8	23·2	29·5
	As percentage of 1935–7	100	210	210	213	271
f	Indian groundnuts (c.i.f. Europe, less freight rate):					
	£ per ton	12·8	62·7	63·0	69·7	93·0
	As percentage of 1935–7	100	489	492	545	727
c	Nigerian palm kernels (producer prices):					
	£ per ton	8·1	19·7	25·1	25·1	31·0
	As percentage of 1935–7	100	242	309	309	383
f	Malayan palm kernels (c.i.f. Europe, less freight rate):					
	£ per ton	7·8	49·0	46·8	58·5	73·0
	As percentage of 1935–7	100	628	600	750	936
c	Nigerian palm oil (producer prices): Weighted average of grades 1–3 [a]					
	£ per ton	12·0	31·2	40·0	40·0	52·0
	As percentage of 1935–7	100	260	333	333	433
c	Grade 2 [a]					
	£ per ton	12·0	23·1	37·1	37·1	43·0
	As percentage of 1935–7	100	192	309	309	358
f	Malayan palm oil (c.i.f. U.K., less freight rate):					
	£ per ton	18·4	84·4	86·4	75·4	104·5
	As percentage of 1935–7	100	459	470	410	568

[a] See explanatory notes.

Note

The letter '*c*' denotes a product controlled by one or other of the West African marketing boards, and the letter '*f*' a free or uncontrolled product. This table is of some significance, and as the sources of the data are not easily accessible in every case, detailed explanatory notes are presented at the end of the chapter.

identical. It will be noted that the price received by Malayan producers of palm kernels has risen over ninefold between the mid-1930's and 1951, while the producer price in West Africa has less than quadrupled. For earlier years the discrepancy is even wider.[1]

It will also be seen that up to the end of 1950 the prices received by groundnut producers in the Gambia were about double the level of the mid-1930's. In the first Annual Report of the Gambia Oilseeds Board the producer price for 1950 is referred to as lucrative; over the same period the prices of imported textiles had quadrupled.

3. THE TERMS OF TRADE OF WEST AFRICAN PRODUCERS UNDER STATUTORY MARKETING

Throughout the period of statutory marketing the West African producers have had to sell their crops at prices controlled far below open-market levels. But they have had to purchase the imported consumer goods on which they spend their incomes at open-market prices, which were governed by general forces of supply and demand, and which were rising substantially almost without interruption throughout this period. As a result the terms of trade of the producers were depressed far below what they would have been without statutory marketing and well below those of their principal competitors. Indeed, with the important exception of the cocoa growers, the terms of trade of the producers were as late as 1950 less favourable than they had been in the mid-1930's, and this may have applied even in 1951.

The general conclusion is reasonably clear from the fact that producer prices of groundnuts and of oil-palm produce were in 1950 about three times the level of the mid-1930's, while the prices of the general range of imported goods destined for purchase by Africans had risen more. This is suggested even by two officially compiled indices of Nigeria import prices (available for only a few years) which substantially understate the general rise in import prices, and understate much more the rise in up-country prices of imported commodities.[2]

---

[1] The comparison between the relative price changes of Malayan and Nigerian palm oil, though instructive, are of slightly less interest because of the difference in the quality of the products and the changes in the relative importance over this period of different grades in Nigerian exports of palm oil (the relevance of which is discussed in the note at the end of this chapter). Palm oil is also less important among Nigerian exports, and much less important among West African exports, than groundnuts or palm kernels.

[2] These indices are reproduced in Appendix 2, which also presents indices of the producer prices of export crops year by year from the mid-1930's to 1951, and indices of the landed costs of the principal classes of cotton piece goods for the corresponding period. A few other matters bearing on the terms of trade of producers and on their computation are also considered there.

But while the general conclusion is clear, the presentation of detailed information on this topic raises certain difficulties. These arise from the fact that while indices of producer prices can be computed comparatively easily, the corresponding information on retail prices of imported merchandise is not available. It is difficult to secure for two reasons: first, the absence of a comprehensive index of import prices and, secondly, the changes in the relation of import prices to retail prices. This second factor is very important for the present discussion, since in West Africa practically throughout this period retail prices of most types of imported merchandise increased over pre-war levels proportionately much more than did c.i.f. values.[1]

These difficulties can be partially overcome, or rather by-passed, by a method which has been used at various times to express changes in the terms of trade—by relating producer prices to the prices of imported cotton piece goods, much the most important class of imported merchandise purchased by the West African producers.[2]

Over the whole period of statutory marketing (1940–51) annual imports of cotton piece goods averaged 31 % of all imports in Nigeria (simple arithmetic mean of annual percentages) and 21 % in the Gold Coast; over the five years 1947–51 the corresponding figures are 28 and 20 %. These percentages would be raised considerably if substantial classes of imports are excluded which are not trade goods in the accepted sense of the term.[3] But even without this adjustment, imports of cotton piece goods over this period were on the average about eight times the imports of any other single class of merchandise destined for purchase by the local population.[4] Cotton piece goods figure particularly

[1] The proportionately greater rise in retail prices was due to several reasons, of which the divergence between the open-market prices and the formally or informally controlled prices of so-called short-supply merchandise was the most important (cf. Appendix 2).

[2] This method has often been used for this purpose; cf. for instance, United Africa Company, *Statistical and Economic Review*, September 1948, where it is explicitly used to measure the terms of trade of cocoa producers over the war and early post-war years by means of a less elaborate calculation than that employed here.

[3] Such as imports by government departments, imports of certain types of capital goods and of raw materials, imports by the mining companies and so forth.

[4] Both in Nigeria and in the Gold Coast artificial silk piece goods were over this period quantitatively the next most important imported consumer good; in both colonies imports of this commodity averaged (simple arithmetic mean of annual percentages) 3 % over the period 1940–51; when weighted by annual values of imports the Nigeria percentage is raised to 4·7, very largely as a result of exceptionally heavy imports of this commodity in 1951. The proportionate changes in the unit import prices of artificial silk piece goods and cotton piece goods were very similar over this period, so that their growing importance in recent years serves to support rather than to invalidate the use of cotton piece goods for our purpose.

Imports of petroleum products were, over the period as a whole, proportionately

prominently in the purchases of the rural population; certain other types of imported merchandise of some importance, such as cigarettes, sugar, flour, motor fuel, fuel oil and cement and corrugated iron sheets, are bought relatively more by the urban population.

There is, however, an obvious disadvantage in the use of the prices of cotton piece goods in conjunction with producer prices as an index of producers' terms of trade. Although cotton piece goods are much the most important type of merchandise bought by the West African producers, they are still only one class; and since the outbreak of war import prices of cotton piece goods have risen appreciably more than those of all other merchandise imports. But this disadvantage is not so serious as it appears at first. Over this period retail prices rose proportionately much more than import prices or landed costs; and it is highly probable that, at least until 1950, an index of the landed costs of cotton piece goods does not significantly overstate the rise since the war in the retail prices of imported merchandise bought by the African farmer, and the index of producers' terms of trade does not present an unduly pessimistic picture.[1]

Apart from its value as an indicator of the terms of trade of producers in a more comprehensive sense, an index based on the prices of cotton piece goods is of interest for another reason. In West Africa this class of merchandise is the principal inducement-good for stimulating production, including the maintenance and extension of the acreage under export crops.[2] Thus the relation of producer prices to the prices of imported cotton piece goods is of considerable interest in its own right. Table 26 shows indices (1935–7 = 100) of the ratios between the producer prices of the principal export crops and the landed costs[3] of cotton piece goods. The figures shown here refer to all cotton piece

more important than those of artificial silk piece goods, particularly during the war years. A large part of these imports were, of course, not destined for purchase by the African population.

The present composition of the import trade is summarized in Tables 3 and 4, Chapter 4 above.

[1] This is considered further in Appendix 2. But it may be repeated here that even on the basis of the Colonial Office index of import prices, the terms of trade of producers, other than cocoa growers, were in 1950 still less favourable than they had been in the mid-1930's.

[2] Their significance in this role has been frequently and explicitly recognized since the outbreak of war. But this, of course, was no new discovery. It was recognized by Alhassan dan Tata in the early days of the groundnut industry (cf. Chapter 2 above).

[3] Landed costs refer to c.i.f. values plus duty. This basis of calculation slightly understates the rise in the true landed costs over this period, as it omits landing charges and storage costs which have risen greatly (more than in proportion to c.i.f. values) because of increases in wages and the congestion at ports.

goods; the more detailed calculations in Appendix 2 present supporting figures of the producers' terms of trade in terms of all imported cotton piece goods, printed or bleached; these are distinctions of some relevance as the producers of different crops do not purchase the same type of textiles. The figures are given for 1943, when they were at their lowest point; for 1945, the first year after the war; for 1947, which was the last year in which the West African Produce Control Board handled all these products; and for 1950 and 1951, the last two years for which the data are available.

Table 26. *Indices of the terms of trade of West African producers in terms of imported cotton piece goods* (1935–7 = 100)

Year	Gold Coast cocoa	Nigerian cocoa	Nigerian groundnuts	Nigerian palm kernels	Nigerian palm oil
1935–7	100	100	100	100	100
1943	24	25	47	35	32
1945	45	48	67	43	39
1947	87	82	67	56	56
1950	126	134	75	76	76
1951	123	152	88	77	72

There was a very marked deterioration in the terms of trade of producers and a large fall in the volume of imports during the war and the early post-war years. Until about 1945–6 the producer prices of the principal crops were at about the level of the mid-1930's, while the prices of imported textiles had doubled or trebled. There has been a great improvement since 1947, but in terms of imported merchandise generally, producers' terms of trade (other than those of cocoa producers) were as recently as 1949 and 1950 less favourable than they had been in the mid-1930's; and in terms of cotton piece goods this still applied in 1951. The producers have thus been denied the opportunity of re-covering from these setbacks, or from sharing in the prosperity of other primary producers.[1]

---

[1] These arguments are not impaired by the fact that in recent years the volume of imports of most consumer goods into West Africa has been appreciably larger than in the mid-1930's. There are various reasons for this. The terms of trade of the cocoa producers have improved considerably over this period (although, of course, much less than those of their competitors elsewhere), and this has influenced the volume of imports, especially into the Gold Coast. There has also been an increase in the volume of some export products, chiefly as a result of the increase in the number of producers for export as these economies emerge from the subsistence stage; and there has also been a rapid growth in the export of timber and of hides and skins, which are not subject to marketing boards. In addition, the higher rate of imports was

The purpose of this discussion of the changes in producers' terms of trade should be clearly understood. It is intended to show some of the results of statutory marketing; it is not intended in any way to provide a guide to policy. Attempts to stabilize the terms of trade of producers still encounter the conceptual problems and difficulties mentioned in Chapter 20 above. In particular, stabilization of the terms of trade does not offer a safeguard against loss of contact with the trend of prices, nor against adverse effects on output through the maintenance of prices below market levels.

4. THE LEVEL OF INCOME AND THE VOLUME OF IMPORTS

As a result of the constriction of money incomes by the marketing boards, the effective pull exercised by West African producers to obtain imports from overseas suppliers has diminished relative to that of competing producing territories. This has tended to diminish the West African share in total colonial imports relative to the share in total colonial exports. This is shown in Table 27. The corresponding proportions for pre-war years are also shown.

Too great emphasis should not be placed on this table. Invisible exports and imports are excluded from the trade returns from which the figures are derived. The figures are also affected by stock changes and by the inclusion of supplies destined for the armed forces and for public authorities generally. Although the trade of Hong Kong is excluded, there are other entrepôt centres, notably Singapore and Aden, which are included, and this somewhat blurs the picture. But one conclusion emerges quite clearly from the table (and is reinforced by information from other sources), that the physical volume of supplies of merchandise was not the factor limiting imports into West Africa. Available supplies were drawn into areas where the level of money incomes was less severely constricted.[1] This conclusion (which is only one of several

certainly affected by the large accumulated arrears of demand stored up during and after the war. It also reflected the effects of governmental investment and of fairly heavy investment (including investment deferred in earlier years) by merchant firms.

From the information presented in Tables 21 and 23 and in Appendix 1 it would be easy to show producers' potential terms of trade, that is, what these would have been in the absence of the various levies. This would require only simple multiplication of the actual terms of trade by the ratio of net sales proceeds per ton to producer prices, and by the ratio of net commercial values per ton to producer prices. But to present these would amount only to ringing the changes on the same set of figures.

[1] The effect of unrestricted money incomes on the level of supplies probably operates in two directions. First, directly; the higher incomes and the larger purchasing power act as an inducement to merchants to import larger supplies. Secondly, the administration in pressing its claims on the British authorities for a larger allocation of supplies (or for foreign exchange), is influenced by the level of demand (usually

pieces of evidence on this subject) disposes of the suggestion that the constriction of money incomes was necessitated by a shortage of imports, by the refusal of the United Kingdom to supply these (or the foreign exchange necessary for their purchase) to West Africa.[1]

Table 27. *Share of British West Africa (all four colonies) in total exports and imports of all British colonies* [(a)]

Year	West African exports		West African imports		Column (2) as percentage of column (4)
	£ m.	Percentage of total exports from British colonies	£ m.	Percentage of total imports into all British colonies	
	(1)	(2)	(3)	(4)	(5)
1936	30	18·8	21	15·9	118
1937	39	18·1	29	16·7	108
1938	24	15·2	18	12·3	124
1947	91	22·3	61	13·7	163
1948	124	22·7	77	14·0	162
1949	138	23·2	110	17·6	132
1950	174	17·2	116	14·2	121
1951	232	16·4	159	13·6	121

[(a)] Excluding Hong Kong.

Source: *The Colonial Empire 1950–1*, Cmd. 8243; *The Colonial Empire 1951–2*, Cmd. 8553.

The constriction of the incomes of producers was, however, the major factor in the large export surpluses of the West African colonies in recent years, since the process of restricting incomes below the sales proceeds of exports has served to reduce overall money demand for goods and services generally, including imports.[2] The accumulated unspent surpluses represent differences between the sales proceeds of exports received by the boards and the sums made available by them to producers for the purchase of imports (whether by the producers themselves, or by sellers of locally produced goods and services on which

referred to as expected requirements), and this of course depends substantially on the level of incomes. Where these are unrestricted, the administration is more likely to fear the political repercussions of the shortages of supplies.

[1] The suggestion that deflation of producer incomes was required by the shortage of imports has serious implications, which are considered in Chapter 24, § 6.

[2] This applies only to that part of the surpluses of the boards which was not spent either by the local governments (to which some loans have been made by the boards out of their reserves), or by the boards, or by another agency such as the Regional Production Development Boards. The unspent surpluses are, in fact, the great bulk of the total, and the discussion in the text is confined to these.

the producers have spent their incomes). They are thus the money equivalent of real resources lent by the West African producers, through the agency of the boards, to the outside world, primarily to the United Kingdom, as the unspent surpluses of the boards are held in sterling securities or in British bank deposits. The information in Table 27 on the share of West Africa in total British colonial exports and imports suggests that the support given to the economy of the United Kingdom by the West African colonies through the accumulation of export surpluses, and therefore of sterling balances, was relatively greater than that provided by the rest of the Colonial Empire, no doubt chiefly as a result of the constriction of producer incomes.[1]

5. LONG-TERM EFFECTS OF THE PAYMENT OF PRICES BELOW COMMERCIAL LEVELS

There are certain other results of the price policies of the statutory marketing organizations which are less obvious than those already discussed, but which may be more fundamental in their long-run effects on the West African economies.

The prolonged payment of producer prices far below commercial values cannot fail to affect the ability and the incentive to produce and to maintain or increase capacity. High prices are the prime incentive to expand production and to maintain, improve and extend productive capacity.

This is particularly obvious and important in territories where over large areas transport costs for bulky commodities are heavy, and where large sections of the population have not as yet emerged from subsistence production. In such countries the extension of capacity is necessarily to a large extent a function of price, since the production of crops for the market is not profitable, or even feasible, in outlying areas, unless the price covers transport costs and still yields a worthwhile return. The supply of individual products is particularly responsive to prices when producers can shift between different activities, occupations and crops. This they can very generally do, especially when changes in productive capacity (as distinct from changes in current production), including transfers of productive capacity from one use to another, are also considered. This applies also to tree crops, in the production of which there may be considerable delay before a decision to alter capacity is reflected in actual capacity, or in current production.[2]

---

[1] This is apart from the effects of sales to the Ministry of Food at prices below market values. The surpluses of the boards and the export surpluses do not (and cannot) take account of these.

[2] This matter is considered in greater detail in Appendix 3 which analyses the principal factors affecting the responsiveness of supply to changes in price.

Thus both the general progress from a subsistence economy to a market economy, and the production of particular crops (especially long-period supply), are greatly affected by the prices received by producers; and prolonged payment of prices below market levels will tend to affect them adversely. This is implicitly but clearly recognized in the practice of governments the world over (including that of the West African Governments), of offering higher prices for crops the output of which they wish to encourage.

This does not mean that the absolute level of output will necessarily be lower, but only that it will be lower than it would be if prices were higher. As is well known, the effects of a functional or causal relationship may be swamped by the operation of other factors, of which the general growth of the economy is likely to be particularly important in countries emerging from the stage of subsistence production. When establishing a functional relationship it is necessary for that purpose to disregard other variables.[1]

Thus reference to specific statistical verification of this general reasoning is of limited significance. But it is perhaps worth recalling the contrast, shown in Table 11 (Chapter 15, above), between the comparative stability over the last 15 years or so of exports of the principal crops controlled by statutory marketing, and the rapid expansion, especially in recent years, of exports of hides and skins and timber. The payment of comparatively low producer prices until about 1950 or 1951 was almost certainly one of the factors retarding the growth of exports subject to statutory marketing.

The policy of paying producers less than market prices has been pursued unilaterally in West Africa. For about ten years the principal competitors of the West African producers have been receiving prices far nearer commercial values, and this both enables and induces them to extend capacity, which tends adversely to affect the long-period competitive position of the West African producers. There is, therefore, an important covert risk in the policy of underpayment which, on the surface, appears to be one based purely on caution and security.[2]

---

[1] It is argued in Appendix 3 below, that although simple statistical verification of the relationship between price and supply is rarely possible, the emergence of the large tropical peasant industries (including the staple export products of West Africa), clearly confirms the general relationship, as these industries have arisen in response to profitable incentives.

[2] It may be objected that this is irrelevant because no significant adverse effect on supply can result from the payment of producer prices below market values, since the accumulated funds will be used either to support producer prices at a later date, or else will be spent as development expenditure with probably favourable results. These considerations, though relevant, do not invalidate the general conclusion; they are discussed in Chapter 24, §§ 1 and 9 respectively.

In spite of the difficulties of empirical verification just mentioned, it may be asked whether the discrepant experience of producers in West Africa and elsewhere has affected in statistically demonstrable form the relative importance of West Africa and other leading suppliers of these products. Unfortunately, the problems of statistical demonstration of a functional relationship are particularly serious in this field, since the volume of exports from different sources is affected by so many factors other than the prices received by producers. Thus exports of cocoa from French West Africa are now appreciably higher than they were in the 1930's, while exports from the Gold Coast are lower. But the latter have been affected by swollen shoot disease; while the growth of exports from French West Africa reflects to some extent the rapid progress of the early stages of an emerging economy. The contraction of ground-nut exports from India since the war almost certainly reflects a higher level of internal consumption, and the same seems to apply to French West Africa, partly connected with the development of mechanized local processing. Exports of oil-palm produce from Malaya and Sumatra, the only pre-war suppliers of any importance outside Africa, were negligible during and immediately after the Japanese war, but they have expanded again rapidly in recent years. Exports of these products from the Belgian Congo have risen substantially since the 1930's, but this is to a large extent due to long-term factors. It is also relevant that in these countries there is little internal consumption of palm oil, while this is considerable in Nigeria. As local consumption there has increased in recent years, this has tended to reduce the volume of exports.

In considering long-term effects, notably the effects of prices on long-period supply, changes in capacity are more important than changes in current production or exports. Unfortunately on this point significant empirical evidence is unobtainable, since in most of the territories concerned there are no data even of the acreages under these crops, much less of changes in these acreages. But it appears (both from the figures of exports and from other information) that over the period covered by statutory marketing there has been no substantial increase of the acreage under cocoa in the Gold Coast or Nigeria, and there may well have been a decrease when the effects of swollen shoot and the ban on cocoa-planting in Ashanti are taken into account. In several other countries, especially in Latin America, there has been substantial planting of cocoa since the war.

The significance of the structure of prices as a system of incentives and directives has been neglected in West Africa since the inception of statutory marketing. This neglect may be due to several reasons. First, there has been a general tendency in recent years (in West Africa as elsewhere) to disparage the causal influence of prices, partly to justify policies (pursued for various reasons) disregarding this influence. Again, the possible effects of higher prices on production have been considered, if at all, only by reference to producers already cultivating the crop, without regard to the extension of capacity and of production in out-lying areas or by shifts from other activities or crops, that is, through the activities of prospective rather than actual producers. Moreover, the disregard of the effects of prices has been fostered by the view that the African does not respond to incentives provided by prices, and/or that he works to a predetermined standard of living, an opinion which is incompatible with the most obvious facts of the West African economies.[1] The prices received by producers of the same or similar crops elsewhere seem to have received practically no attention.[2]

The neglect of the relation between price and supply may also be connected with the fact that the relation operates partly through changes in capacity, as well as through changes in current production. This makes it particularly likely that the effects of price changes are obscured by the operation of other forces, so that the causal relationship, though effective, is not easily discernible.

6. SOME RESULTS OF THE CENTRALIZATION OF SAVING

The heavy accumulation of surpluses by the boards almost certainly raises total savings in these communitites in which the level of capital is very low. Compulsory saving as an argument in support of these policies is considered at some length in the next chapter, but certain results and implications of the process can be conveniently considered here.

The period since the inception of statutory marketing has been one of exceptional prosperity for primary producers and has presented an unusual opportunity for the development of the habit of individual saving and for the growth of personal savings. This has been largely prevented by prescribing producer prices far below commercial values, while the producers have had to pay the full market value for their purchases of imported merchandise.

The activities of the boards, while raising total savings, necessarily

---

[1] Even if this were true, it would not dispose of the effects of higher prices on the extension of capacity and production in outlying areas, and on the output of particular crops through shifts of activity. Appendix 3 examines the validity of the contention that the African does not respond to price incentives and its relevance to price policy.

[2] About 1950 some attention was paid to producer prices in French West Africa because of the possibility of smuggling from British to French territories, and also because of some tension which arose in certain districts owing to the much higher prices across the French border.

diminish the flow of private saving by the severe reduction in the incomes of producers. This centralization of savings and the curtailment of private saving and investment entail disadvantages beyond the obvious and substantial adverse effect on the level of supply and on individual incentive to produce. Such a process tends to retard the growth of the habit of individual saving and investment among producers, many of whom have emerged only recently from the stage of subsistence production. This habit, although it has not yet taken firm root in these territories, has clearly been developing. This is readily observable both in Nigeria and in the Gold Coast in the great increase and improvement of building, especially house-building, for Africans. It can also be deduced from such evidence as the increase in the sales of agricultural and transport equipment by merchant firms to African customers; and from the growth of imports of many types of capital goods.

The severe obstacles to the further growth of private saving serve to prevent the development of a prosperous and independent peasantry which might have a stabilizing effect in the highly charged political atmosphere of West Africa.[1]

Obstacles in the way of private saving also hamper the development of independent local traders by reducing the availability of capital derived from their own savings, or from those of their relatives and friends. The weakness of the local traders disqualifies them from efficient participation in external trade, and thus tends to strengthen the high degree of concentration.

7. STATUTORY MARKETING AND NEW ENTRY INTO COMMERCIAL AND INDUSTRIAL ACTIVITY

The foregoing sections have dealt with the principal aspects and results of the price policies of the marketing boards. It is also necessary to take cognizance, if only briefly, of certain effects on the structure of the private sector of West African trade of the presence of statutory export monopolies irrespective of the policies pursued by them. As already mentioned, the reduction in status of the export merchants to the position of purchasing agents acts to some extent as a deterrent to entry, and is thus a factor tending to maintain a high degree of concentration in produce buying. Some substantial prospective entrants into the produce trade have withdrawn on learning of the presence of statutory monopolies in the export of the produce concerned. As merchants frequently extend their range of operations from the export trade to the import

[1] The far-reaching political implications and results of the large-scale centralization of saving and the retardation of private saving cannot be considered here, though they deserve mention.

trade (and to transport and industrial enterprises), these activities are also affected. The close control by statutory organizations over the principal cash crops is likely also to act as a deterrent to prospective entrants into local processing of these products. This is an obvious corollary of their extensive powers.

These effects of statutory marketing on new entry into commercial and industrial activities in the remaining private sector of the economy (and thus on the growth of the economy generally), and on the degree of concentration in the private sector, are largely inherent in the presence of statutory export monopolies. But they have been reinforced by the price policies produced which have reduced the capital available to African traders by making private savings by producers or traders very difficult; and they have also been reinforced until recently by a rather unfavourable attitude of the Nigerian authorities towards private processing of products controlled by marketing boards.[1]

8. WIDER IMPLICATIONS OF THE POLICIES AND POWERS OF THE BOARDS

The official statements announcing the decision to continue statutory marketing after the war emphasized that over a number of years the proposed boards would not be making profits or accumulating surpluses. The second Cocoa White Paper stated specifically and explicitly that the surpluses and deficits of the proposed boards would balance substantially. It also suggested that the proposed boards were analogous to the British agricultural marketing boards, whose aim is to secure the best return for their constituents.

Hitherto there has been no attempt to balance surpluses and deficits. On the contrary, prices and incomes have been controlled and de-stabilized in order to increase year after year the already very large surpluses, and this process of accumulating surpluses is freely referred to in the boards' reports as evidence of the success of their operations. Moreover, some of the funds have already been used for what are essentially general purposes. Nor do the boards bear any recognizable resemblance to the British agricultural marketing boards.

The powers and the funds of the boards present a great opportunity to politicians to entrench their position, extend their control and increase their power. It is not unlikely that African political parties gaining power will use the machinery and the funds of the boards to further the general political aims of the parties, and that they will neither abolish the system nor greatly moderate the boards' policies. This presumption is strengthened by the expressed views of influential spokesmen

[1] Cf. Appendix 4.

of the Convention Peoples' Party in the Gold Coast. These suggest that the local politicians are likely to favour a system which facilitates the retention of an appreciable proportion of their incomes from the producers, whether directly by the boards, or indirectly by making it politically easier to increase export duties.

If in the future the African political parties in power wish to use the funds openly for general purposes, the British Government and the local administrations will either have to consent to large-scale breaches of formal undertakings given at the time of the establishment of the boards, or incur the odium of objecting to the desires of African governments (chosen by an electorate which includes many people who are not producers of export crops). In the Gold Coast this dilemma is already in evidence. Meanwhile the original purposes envisaged for the boards are likely to become progressively more remote; and the interests of those who control these organizations are likely to become even further removed from the obvious direct interests of the West African producers.

The West African boards largely prescribe the level of money incomes and the standard of living over wide areas of British West Africa. By determining the producer prices of the principal cash crops they largely direct production and thus the activities of the peasant producers. They have centralized the supply of saving; and they are in a position to make individual saving by the peasant producers almost impossible. They closely control the industries subject to them. In addition to their powers derived from the ordinances, the possession of their very large funds places them in a dominant strategic position in the economies in which they function.

For good or evil the boards must be seen as instruments for the socialization of saving and for a large measure of government control and socialization of peasant production in West Africa. Suggestions that they are devised for price stabilization or that they are individual commercial organizations only obscure their nature and function. This fundamental aspect of statutory marketing and of the policies and operations of the boards raises political and social issues of the widest significance. Adequate discussion of these would clearly be impossible in this study. Indeed, even an attempt would be inappropriate, since not only have socialization of saving and socialization of peasant production not been advanced in support of the policies of the boards, but they are also tasks which are plainly outside the scope of organizations established to promote the interests of West African producers by means of price stabilization.

NOTE TO CHAPTER 23

Information underlying Table 25

This note presents the sources and method of calculation used for Table 25.

For West African products the prices shown in Table 25 are producer prices, that is, prices paid at port of shipment or at railway stations; for the comparable products from other sources they are c.i.f. prices less freight, i.e. broadly f.o.b. prices after payment of export duties and port charges. There are several appreciable cost items between producer prices and these f.o.b. prices, of which transport, landing charges and export duties are the most important. These largely explain the pre-war differences in the absolute levels of prices between comparable commodities; thus Indian groundnut prices refer to f.o.b. price, while the Nigerian prices to the Kano prices and the Gambia prices to the Bathurst quotation. For palm oil the difference in the absolute levels between the Malayan and Nigerian prices before the war reflect differences in quality as well.

The absolute level of pre-war prices shown here for comparable products are, however, very close where the West African producer prices are at port of shipment and where there are no significant quality differences. Thus the pre-war prices shown here for Gambia groundnuts (ex scale Bathurst) are very close to the prices for Indian groundnuts (c.i.f. Europe less freight); and similarly for Nigerian palm kernels (Lagos) and Malayan palm kernels (c.i.f. Liverpool less freight).

This method of presentation had to be adopted because for Malayan and Indian products only the c.i.f. prices and freight rates were available in the form of a consistent series. The comparability of the figures for the purpose of the argument is not affected by these differences in absolute levels, as only the proportionate changes over this period are relevant.

The comparisons would be slightly affected if the cost items between the producer prices and f.o.b. prices had changed in markedly different proportions in the different territories over these years. It is most unlikely that the differences in the relative movements of these items in India and Malaya compared with West Africa could have been so great as to affect the results significantly. In Malaya the only cost item of importance between the producer price and the f.o.b. price is the export duty. This was actually remitted in 1948–9 to assist the oil-palm industry, and the figures shown here understate the relative improvement of producer prices in Malaya compared to those in Nigeria. And it is most improbable that the comparison with India would be significantly affected if a series of producer prices were available instead of f.o.b. prices.

The Nigerian groundnut prices are the officially recorded Kano prices converted from a seasonal to a calendar-year basis on the assumption that 60 % of the season's crop is marketed before the end of the calendar year.

For Nigerian palm kernels the pre-war prices are the Lagos prices recorded by the Produce Inspection Branch of the Department of Agriculture. For recent years they are the gazetted producer prices, less the small gazetted deductable allowance for middleman's commission. This is necessary to ensure comparability with the pre-war figures, and is the procedure adopted in the Produce Inspection records kept up to date in the Department of Marketing and Exports.

Although the Gambia is not covered by this study, groundnut prices in that colony are shown here as they were accessible and are illuminating. Up to 1949 they are the official prices as reproduced in the *Annual Review for 1949 of Oilseeds, Oils, Oil Cakes and other Commodities*, a well-known reference book of oilseed markets issued by Messrs Frank Fehr and Company. For 1950 and 1951 they are the official gazetted producer prices; in the Gambia the groundnut season practically coincides with the calendar year.

The prices for Indian groundnuts for 1935–7, 1948 and 1949 are from Messrs Frank Fehr's review; for 1950 and 1951 they have been kindly supplied by the buying department of Unilever Ltd. The freight deducted is the conference rate from India to north continent ports. The pre-war prices of Malayan palm oil and palm kernels are the annual Liverpool prices, less freight from Singapore to Liverpool. For recent years they are the prices secured by the largest shippers of these products. For palm oil they are f.o.b.; for palm kernels they have been converted to f.o.b. by deducting freight at conference rates from Singapore to Europe. For palm kernels the 1948 prices refer to the second half of the year, as shipping to Europe was not available for the first half.

For Nigerian palm oil the pre-war prices are the Lagos prices for grade 2 oil as recorded by the Produce Inspection Branch. This is the most suitable consistently compiled pre-war series for this product, but its use presents a difficulty. In recent years the differentials paid by the Marketing Board for different grades of oil have been greatly widened and the proportionate discount of grade 2 oil below grade 1 is far wider than before the war. Moreover, in recent years the proportion of grade 1 oil has been much higher than before the war. Comparison in terms of the prices of grade 2 oil would understate the rise in the producer prices compared to pre-war; while a comparison of the producer prices shown in Table 19 (which is a weighted average of all grades) with the prices of grade 2 oil for 1935–7 would overstate the rise. To meet this difficulty two sets of prices are shown for recent years, and compared with the pre-war price of grade 2 oil, one for the weighted average price for different grades and the other for grade 2 oil. When comparing the pre-war price of grade 2 oil with the average price of different grades in recent years (mostly grade 1 oil), it should be noted that the preparation of grade 1 oil requires more effort and work.

CHAPTER 24

THE ARGUMENTS IN SUPPORT OF THE PRICE
POLICIES OF THE MARKETING BOARDS[1]

It was suggested at the end of the preceding chapter that the boards and their policies are best seen as instruments for a large measure of socialization of peasant agriculture in West Africa. This aspect of their operations does not seem to have been explicitly recognized, and it has certainly not been advanced in support of their policies. But as already stated it would be inappropriate to examine this issue here. On the other hand, it is legitimate, and indeed necessary, to examine the arguments generally advanced in support of the policies of the boards, whether by their own spokesmen or by influential supporters of these statutory monopolies.[2]

The retention over a number of years of a large part of the sales proceeds from producers and the accumulation of surpluses on the scale indicated in the preceding chapters in clear contrast to specific formal official undertakings would require detailed and logical explanation and justification. Although there are certain discernible recurrent themes in the pronouncements of their spokesmen, the statements and notices issued on behalf of the boards and the memoranda circulated by their chairmen, the boards do not seem to have presented a systematic or coherent exposition of the reasons underlying their austere price policies.

---

[1] A dilemma arose in the presentation of this chapter. A discussion in which the arguments advanced in support of the price policies of the boards are examined one by one may give the impression of being coloured by hostile bias. On the other hand, a discussion largely in general terms may be thought to be irrelevant to the boards' policies. The former of these two alternatives has been accepted, and the individual arguments are examined *seriatim* and in specific terms, even though this may result in an unintentional appearance of hostility. Unfortunately and unavoidably the discussion appears the more controversial the more specific it is, and the stranger and more unorthodox are the arguments which it has to meet. Only those arguments are considered the sources of which can easily be verified. Examination of these arguments and of their implications is the sole topic of this chapter. The reader not interested in this subject will lose little by passing on to Chapter 25.

[2] These, however, often reflect widely held views and characteristic trends of opinion which must be remembered in fairness to those proposing them (cf. § 13 below).

The necessity for price stabilization (a term used as identical with income stabilization) has been the most general line of argument advanced in support of the withholding of up to two-thirds of the proceeds available for distribution. This need for stability is stated in purely general terms, and no specific indication is given of what is intended by price stabilization. Yet, as has already been argued, this aim becomes meaningless for practical purposes unless definite and specific objectives are stated. As the future course of prices is uncertain it can always be suggested that the larger the surpluses the stronger will be the position of the boards to face a future decline in market prices. If the boards' estimates of prices prove to be incorrectly pessimistic, this again after the event provides an argument for an austere policy, since the growth of reserves is demonstrably available for future stabilization. As there is no stated finite period over which stable prices are to be achieved, the accumulation of increasing reserves can always provide its own perpetual superficial justification. *Per contra*, since any draft on past accumulations to sustain previous producer prices demonstrably reduces the boards' ability to stabilize prices in the future, there is a ready-made argument against raising or maintaining producer prices when proceeds are expected to fall.

If producer prices are kept below commercial values for a number of years a wide discrepancy may develop between market prices and producer prices. As it is politically very difficult to maintain this discrepancy indefinitely, even if it were intended to do so, the eventual adjustment may take the form of sharp discontinuous changes which destroy even the appearance of stability.

Thus general references to the need for price stability are of little value either as a guide to policy or a satisfactory explanation of past policies. This, indeed, is a corollary of the undefined and unspecified nature of the concept which seems to be so rarely appreciated.

It is often suggested, explicitly or by implication, that whatever the defects of stabilization as criterion of policy, the producers are unlikely to be much affected in the long run, since what has been withheld will be returned to them in some form or another. This argument neglects certain important relevant considerations.

First, the price policies pursued up to 1952 suggest that some of the boards are unlikely to permit any large-scale drafts on their reserves for the maintenance of producer prices on falling markets. The Gold Coast Cocoa Marketing Board, much the most important of the boards, severely reduced the producer price following an almost infinitesimal draft on its reserves, the only draft which has occurred so far.[1] Secondly, even if the funds were disbursed the producers who benefit would be a very different body of persons from those at whose expense the funds have been accumulated. Thirdly, the maintenance of producer prices below commercial values over a number of years cannot fail adversely to affect the improvement and expansion of capacity and thus of output, as well as the relative competitive position of the West African territories as suppliers of tropical produce. This adverse effect on output reduces the surpluses which are available for distribution. There is thus on this score a net loss which can never be restored to producers even if there were a general distribution of reserves. Fourthly, certain types of expenditure out of surpluses benefit the producers only slightly if at all. In particular, a substantial part of the funds have already been used for what is essentially general government expenditure, and it is probable that over a period of years the large accumulated funds will present an irresistible temptation to governments and politicians to be used for general and political purposes. This presumption is strengthened by the powers of direction over the funds of the Cocoa Marketing Board recently assumed by the Gold Coast government. Fifthly, the adverse results of the unsuccessful sales of the West African Produce Control Board, and of the Groundnut, Oil Palm Produce and Cotton Boards do not swell the reserve funds and are not even returnable in theory; and the same applies to the proceeds of the heavy export duties, some recent increases in which have probably been encouraged by the accumulation of surpluses by the boards. Lastly, the funds of the boards have already depreciated in real terms.

We now turn to the illustration of the general discussion by referring in more detail to the operations of the Nigeria Groundnut Marketing Board, the two Cocoa Marketing Boards and the Nigeria Cotton Marketing Board in the following sections.

2. THE PRICE POLICY OF THE NIGERIA GROUNDNUT MARKETING BOARD IN 1950–1

Since 1949 the Nigeria Groundnut Marketing Board has had a contract with the Ministry of Food for the sale of the entire exportable crop to the Ministry. The contract stipulates guaranteed minimum prices with actual prices to be negotiated annually.[2] The price secured for the 1948–9 crop was £55 c. and f. per ton, which yielded a surplus of about £19 per ton on the producer price of £19. 4s. 0d. In 1949–50 the

---

[1] This is discussed in § 3 below. A somewhat similar episode in the price policy of the Nigeria Groundnut Marketing Board is instanced in § 2.

[2] Since the end of 1951 the prices paid have been based on independently assessed market values (cf. Chapter 22 above).

producer price had been raised to £21. 4s. 0d. before it was settled that the price paid by the Ministry would be reduced by £2 per ton. This still would have left the Board with a surplus of about £13 per ton.[1] It was, however, decided to reduce the producer price for the next season in view of the reduction in sales proceeds. At first it was officially suggested that the producer price should also be reduced by £2; but it was subsequently decided to reduce it by £1. 4s. 0d. to £20 a ton. This was announced in February 1950.

In assessing this decision the following considerations seem relevant. The reduced price payable by the Ministry of Food still secured the Board a margin of about £13 a ton on the former producer price of £21. 4s. 0d.; and even the lowest guaranteed minimum contract price up to the end of 1952 would have still yielded a surplus on that producer price. Even the price of £21. 4s. 0d. was only about three times the level of the mid-1930's; in northern Nigeria the prices of the most important classes of imported consumer goods, especially textiles, had risen appreciably more. Producers in other soft-currency territories received much higher prices (both because their sales proceeds were higher and also because they were not subject to such deductions). Lastly, the 1949–50 crop was very poor, barely one-half that of 1948–9, so that there was thus a heavy fall in incomes. In the face of these considerations it was decided to reduce the producer price because the selling price was being slightly reduced. This suggests that although the Groundnut Board had already accumulated surpluses of about £10 m., the maintenance of the size of the surplus margin per ton was deemed more important than the maintenance of producer prices even at their previously low level. This decision both destabilized and constricted the incomes of producers who were already hard hit both by the price policy and the unfavourable harvest.

After some pressure by the mercantile community it was decided in October 1950 to restore the producer price to £21. 4s. 0d., the extremely low level of the previous season. This revision was made after world prices had risen substantially, which made it certain that the margin of the Board on the 1950–1 crop would be of the order of £30 per ton on that producer price, and after groundnut prices in French West Africa had risen so far above the Nigerian producer price that substantial illicit exports were certain to occur. Moreover, by October it was known that the crop had again failed. The prices of imported goods, especially textiles, had also risen appreciably. In the face of these considerations the suggestions for a restoration of the producer price to the very low level of 1949–50 were still strongly resisted by spokesmen of the Board.

[1] Other costs had risen somewhat between the two seasons.

In an official public notice published in the *Nigeria Gazette* (Public Notice No. 36 of 1950) the Groundnut Marketing Board adduced some of its reasons for the reduction in producer prices. The principal reason stated was the wisdom of anticipating an expected decline in world prices. This was thought necessary in spite of the contract with the Ministry of Food which for two further seasons guaranteed minimum prices assuring substantial profit margins to the Board at the then current producer prices, and the fact that the open-market prices were well above the contract prices with the Ministry, which made it certain that more than minimum prices could be expected for subsequent crops. To quote:

World prices for oils and oilseeds have evidently reached their peak and are now declining. Under its three-year selling agreement with the Ministry of Food the Board is receiving £53 per ton for the 1949–50 production of groundnuts and benniseed, which is £2 per ton less than it received for 1948–49 production. It may be regarded as practically certain that, by the time the Board's selling agreement with the Ministry of Food expires with the close of the 1951–52 season, the prices obtainable overseas for groundnuts and benniseed will have fallen much further. The level of selling prices by that time may be well below the minimum price guaranteed under the Agreement for the 1951–52 season and, unless the Board is then in a position to support the producer prices from funds reserved for the price stabilisation, a steep and sudden decline in the prices payable to the producer would be inevitable. In these circumstances a reduction by £1. 4. 0. per ton in the railway line price of Kano groundnuts with similar reductions for Rivers Areas groundnuts and for benniseed was regarded by the Board as a step called for by prudence and good sense.

At about the same time, in March 1950, the Nigeria Groundnut Marketing Board published a memorandum entitled *Minimum Prices for Groundnuts at Gazetted Buying Stations in the Kano Area*. Although this document dealt largely with transport subsidies, uniform prices and related matters, it also referred to wider issues of price policy, and suggested (pp. 17 and 20) that *producer* prices had reached their peak and that next season's price should be reduced to £19. 4s. 0d., i.e. by £2, the full amount of the reduction in the price received from the Ministry of Food.

In Public Notice No. 36 and other statements the need for increasing the reserves to a very large absolute figure was constantly emphasized. An implicit corollary of this was that the smaller the crop the greater must be the surplus margin per ton to enable this figure to be reached, and this is borne out by the low producer prices fixed for the last two years of short crops. Indeed, in official discussions with merchant representatives in the course of 1950 spokesmen of the Board and of the Department of Marketing and Exports (the executive of the Board) expressly stated that in its price policy the Board was not concerned with compensating the producer for a poor crop, as the Board was concerned with stabilizing prices and was not to act as a 'charitable fund'. It was not stated that this stabilization implied the maintenance of prices at less than one-half of the commercial level. And the practical result of the policy was the maintenance of the margin of the Board, at a rate of 65 % of the producer price, at a time when the harvest was exceptionally poor and producer incomes were very low.[1]

3. THE PRICE POLICIES OF THE COCOA MARKETING BOARDS, 1947–50

As has already been shown, the price policy of the Cocoa Marketing Boards has actually served to destabilize producer incomes. This was largely the result of the steep reduction in the producer price in the Gold Coast in 1949 following the very slight draft on reserves in the season 1948–9, when realized prices fell for a few months below the equivalent of producer prices. Following this minute draft on reserves (which in the aggregate amounted to less than 1 % of the accumulated surplus, and less than 1 % of the total proceeds for the season), the Board cut the producer price from 65s. to 45s. a load of 60 lb., or by over 30 %. This was decided in spite of the very large reserves of the Board, which were about £36 m. In Nigeria the reduction was from £120 to £100 per ton. There the Board had actually made a surplus on the year's operation, largely because it had fixed a slightly lower producer price than that ruling in the Gold Coast. By the beginning of the 1949–50 season prices had risen well above the levels ruling early in 1949, but both Boards decided to abide by their decisions taken earlier in the year, and realized very large surpluses which raised their accumulated surpluses far above the levels previously contemplated. For 1950–1 they again prescribed prices well below expected proceeds. Both Boards secured large surpluses, despite heavy increases in export duties.

The rapid accumulation in recent years of huge surpluses, even at the cost of destabilizing incomes, must be viewed in the light of formal pronouncements made by the Cocoa Boards themselves before the 1948–9 season. Thus the Nigerian Board stated that: 'By the end of the 1948–9 season the funds of the Board will have reached such substantial proportions that without further large additions these funds will be sufficient to provide an adequate measure of price stabilization and also to finance various agricultural and other schemes for the benefit of the

[1] Shortly afterwards the price agreed with the Ministry of Food for the season's crop was substantially raised, with the result that the *margin* of the Board rose to about £27 per ton or 129 % of the producer price.

cocoa farmer, the details of which will be published shortly. In fixing prices for the coming season, therefore, the Board formed the view that the price which the producer should receive should be related closely to world market prices so far as they can be foreseen.'[1] At that time its funds were about £17 m. The Gold Coast Cocoa Marketing Board in January 1948 issued a press statement that it envisaged a stabilization fund of £16 m. At the end of the 1947–8 crop year its reserves stood at £37 m. At the end of the 1949–50 season the reserves of the Gold Coast Board were about £53 m. and those of the Nigerian Board about £25 m. But although events have been far more favourable for the boards than they had hoped and planned for, this has not been allowed to influence their price policy. In 1950–1 the Gold Coast Board had a surplus of over £20 m. and the Nigerian Board of over £11 m.[2]

Recently the Gold Coast Cocoa Marketing Board has begun to sub-divide its total accumulated surplus into various reserves and to argue that only that part of total funds which is christened 'stabilization reserve' is available for price stabilization. It is implied that part of the reserves, called 'general reserve', and another part called 'general trading reserve', are not really available for this purpose. The Annual Report of the Board for 1949–50 suggests that of these reserves, which were then well over £50 m., only £30 m. represent the stabilization reserve, and only that sum is available for the future maintenance of the producer price. It is also argued there that this stabilization reserve should be raised to £50 m., whereas a year or two earlier total reserves of £16 m. were envisaged. It is of course clear that by subdividing the accumulated funds and referring to a part of these only as stabilization reserves, they can always be made to appear insufficient for this parti-cular purpose.

These examples illustrate the self-inflating nature of the accumulation of surpluses over a period of rising prices. It should not however be regarded merely as an example of arbitrary or short-sighted action on the part of the Cocoa Boards (or of any other board); it should be seen in part at any rate as an illustration or corollary of some of the con-ceptual problems of stabilization discussed in Chapter 20, § 5.

---

[1] Government Notice No. 1333 of 1948.

[2] These surpluses were struck after the payment of export duties by the two Boards of £13 m. and £4½ m. respectively.

The Annual Report of the Gold Coast Cocoa Board for 1950–51 does not even state what was the actual producer price for that year; it was £131, or about one-half of the f.o.b. proceeds per ton. On the other hand the Report states: 'Once again, in view of the increase in the world price of cocoa and the consequent in-crease in the price to the producer, the originally proposed amount for the stabiliza-tion reserve [that is only part of total reserves] of £50 million is considered inadequate, and the present aim is to build up the fund to £60 million.'

4. THE MARGINS OF THE COTTON MARKETING BOARD AND THE LEVEL OF PRODUCER PRICES, 1949–51

The price policy of the Cotton Marketing Board provides instructive examples of the same general tendency. When this Board was established the producer price of seed cotton[1] was $4d$. per lb. With that price the f.o.b. cost of cotton lint was about $15\frac{3}{4}d$. per lb. The expectation was that the Cotton Board would secure a price for the 1949–50 crop of about $17\frac{1}{4}d$. per lb. of lint f.o.b. Lagos, resulting in a surplus of $1\frac{1}{2}d$. per lb. lint with a producer price of $4d$. per lb. of seed cotton, which was the price fixed for the 1949–50 season. It was officially stated that this price was universally regarded as a very good price. It was, in fact, well below the price received by producers of similar growths even in hard-currency areas converted at the official rate of exchange. It was about three times the average price ruling in northern Nigeria in the mid-1930's while the cost of imports bought by producers had risen appreciably more.

A few months later a contract was signed with the Raw Cotton Commission which assured a better price to the Board than had been expected. For 1949–50 a price was agreed which was equivalent to $18\frac{3}{4}d$. lb. of lint f.o.b. Lagos, which yielded a margin precisely double that on which the previous calculations of the Board had been based. Nevertheless, the producer price was not reconsidered. The contract with the Raw Cotton Commission stipulated that for the next two seasons prices would be fixed after annual negotiations but would not vary by more than 15 % in either direction from the preceding year's price. It also stipulated that prices would be adjusted in the event of the devaluation of sterling.

Shortly afterwards sterling was devalued, and the price received by the Board was increased to the equivalent of $26\frac{1}{4}d$. per lb. f.o.b. Lagos. Costs also turned out lower than expected, with the result that a margin of $13d$. per lb. accrued to the Board, or about eight times the level expected earlier in the year. In aggregate terms it secured just over £900,000 in one season, which was about equal to total payments to producers. Nevertheless, the producer price for the following season (1950–1) remained unchanged.

For that season's crop the Board received far more than the maximum price (adjusted for devaluation) stipulated in its contract with the Raw Cotton Commission. The stipulated maximum price (as adjusted) would have been about $31d$. c. and f., or just over $30d$. f.o.b. In view of the very large increase in commodity prices, the Commission made an *ex*

---

[1] Seed cotton is the unginned product which includes both cotton lint and cotton seed; lint is about one-third of the total weight of seed cotton.

gratia adjustment in the price and raised it to 35¼*d.* c. and f., or about 34½*d.* f.o.b. This secured a surplus margin of about 21*d.* per lb., which was about 160% of the lint equivalent of the producer price. This margin was about ten or twelve times the level orginally envisaged in 1949 when the producer price, which was still in force in 1950–1, was fixed.[1]

5. COMBATING INFLATION AS AN ARGUMENT FOR THE ACCUMULATION OF SURPLUSES

The alleged responsibility of the boards for the welfare of the economies as a whole is one of the principal reasons advanced to justify the underpayment of producers. In practice this has been interpreted as requiring the boards to combat inflation by preventing a rise in money incomes. This supports a policy of keeping producer prices low, thus reinforcing the arguments based on the desire to build up stabilization reserves. As generally presented, the argument is insubstantial. It also carries explosive political implications, and it requires extended consideration.

The need to combat inflation is introduced in almost every discussion explaining or accounting for the price decisions of the marketing boards. Only a few examples can be quoted here. The argument was advanced in support of the proposed reduction of producer prices of groundnuts in 1950:

> The level of producer prices in relation to the general economic situation in Nigeria was a further consideration taken into account by the Board. The Board considered that the relatively high prices payable for export produce must be regarded as an important contributory cause of the present inflationary tendencies and that a moderate reduction in these prices would, without causing hardship, have the beneficial effect of helping to keep these tendencies in check.[2]

The second Annual Report of the Nigeria Cocoa Marketing Board remarks of its producer price policy for 1948–9 that 'the main restraining influence was the need to avoid or at least limit the inflationary effects' of an increase in producer prices.

There is, however, no mention of the need to combat inflation in the official documents relating to the establishment of the boards. No

---

[1] The first Annual Report of the Nigeria Cotton Board states that the purpose of the policy (which has kept the producer price at around one-third to two-fifths of the commercial value of the product), is really to secure the highest price to the producer. 'These reserves are the best guarantee of the Board's ability to carry out its main objects of giving maximum prices to the producer....' Possibly 'maximum' is an error for 'minimum', but this is not suggested by the context.

[2] Nigeria Public Notice No. 36 of 1950, p. 2. In the discussions on the proposed reduction it was also said that a higher price would confer no real benefit on producers and would merely accentuate inflation.

suggestion of this type of function can be found in the Cocoa White Papers, the *Statement on the Future Marketing of Nigerian Oils, Oilseeds and Cotton*, or the ordinances establishing the boards. The composition of the boards and of their executives also gives no indication of the very wide responsibilities which the boards claim for themselves.

The second Cocoa White Paper expressly mentions the British agricultural marketing boards as providing a precedent for the statutory organizations envisaged for West Africa. The agricultural marketing boards of this country are representative of producer interests, and it has never been intended or suggested that their functions included the discharge of broad economic responsibilities, in particular the regulation of the flow of money incomes. The White Paper clearly stated that it had in mind an organization intended to benefit the cocoa industry and not one which would assume the functions of Government.[1] The framing and execution of an anti-inflationary policy must rest with the official monetary authorities. In West Africa this is the task of the Financial Secretary or Minister of Finance and not of the marketing boards.

The suggestion that a policy of disinflation should be pursued by the marketing boards implies that these organizations, established to protect and promote the interests of the producers of export crops largely by means of short-period price stabilization, should be used to restrict consumption by substantial curtailment of the income of one section of the community only, namely, their own constituents who are asked to bear the burden of deflation.

Moreover, the boards' interpretation of the task of combating inflation has consisted simply of resisting any increase in producer prices on the grounds that it is inflationary, disturbing to the economy as a whole, and self-defeating in real as opposed to monetary terms. Proper diagnosis and treatment of inflation are, however, somewhat more complex than seems to be believed by the boards.

Inflation is used in West Africa as an omnibus term covering many different types of price increases. But the rise in prices may be due to many different causes. Thus it may be brought about by a refusal of the buyers of a country's exports to make available an equivalent amount of imports or foreign exchange for the purchase of imports. In such

---

[1] Thus according to Cmd. 6950: 'It is to be borne in mind that such a proposal is neither revolutionary nor without precedent. Statutory marketing organisations exist in other countries, including the United Kingdom. It may be true that, in some more advanced communities, direct Government operation of marketing schemes is hardly required; and were a producer-operated scheme feasible in West Africa, it would perhaps offer a solution of present difficulties. It is considered, however, that it would be impracticable to expect the African cocoa-farmer to operate such a scheme unaided at present.' It could not have been contemplated that the cocoa farmers should decide and implement the country's monetary and fiscal policies.

circumstances the rise in prices within the country is the result of a substantial export surplus or, more precisely, of compulsory unrequited exports or compulsory export of capital. Or a rise in prices may be the result of a world-wide depreciation in the value of money reflected also in the higher cost of imports. Or it may flow from a rise in the level of money incomes and prices in territories for the products of which world demand has increased; in this instance it would be the result of an improvement in the terms of trade. Again, the increase in prices may be due to a crop failure, or to a comparative decrease in the market supply of foodstuffs owing to higher consumption by producers. These kinds of general price increase differ both in their causes and in the treatment they require. It is merely confusing to lump them together as inflation, or to attempt to treat them all in the same way.

6. THE SHORTAGE OF IMPORTS AS AN ARGUMENT FOR THE ACCUMULATION OF SURPLUSES

In the general discussion of the inflationary effect of higher producer prices two topics tend to receive emphasis. First, it is argued that no additional supplies of imported merchandise were obtainable, and that in those circumstances the retail prices of imported merchandise would simply rise proportionately to the increase in producer prices. Secondly, it is argued that the rise in producer prices brings about a proportionate increase in the prices of local foodstuffs. These two arguments are sometimes used separately and sometimes in conjunction. The implication is that an increase in producer prices dissipates itself in the form of higher prices of the commodities on which producers spend their incomes, leaving them no better off than before, while causing hardship to the other sections of the population. These arguments are invalid, and they also have dangerous implications.

It is clear from the information presented in Chapter 23, § 4, on the share of the West African colonies in colonial exports and imports respectively, that the limitation on imports into West Africa was not caused by the shortage of available supplies alone. The rapid increase in the volume of imports in 1949 and 1951 when producer prices were much higher than they had been in 1948 and 1950 suggests the same conclusion. This is confirmed by simple observation of the trading situation. In 1949 and 1950 both the Gold Coast and Nigeria were actually overstocked with textiles, the prices of which were below the controlled prices in the Gold Coast.[1] In a number of instances importers were cutting their commitments as they had difficulty in disposing of their stocks. Throughout 1950 the principal importers were anxiously trying

[1] At the time there was no price control of textiles in Nigeria.

to assess the prospective producer prices to avoid excessive stocks. To maintain that the volume of imports in recent years was independent of the level of incomes and purchasing power is to reveal radical ignorance of the contents of the official trade statistics and of trading developments.

These considerations dispose of the arguments that the volume of merchandise imports throughout the period 1947–50 was unaffected by the level of prices paid to producers. The boards themselves did not really believe this, since their spokesmen frequently stated that an early announcement of producer prices was desirable to enable merchants to place orders in accordance with the requirements of the economy. But the weakness of the argument goes deeper than mere ignorance of the trading situation. Those who maintain that over this period the level of imports (including supplies from the United Kingdom and from other soft currency sources) was fixed, raise a very serious accusation against the British authorities without realizing it. Their argument implies that the incomes of the producers had to be reduced below the sale proceeds of the exports produced by them; that although the producers had made available to the United Kingdom the real resources represented by these proceeds, the British authorities refused them an equivalent amount of real resources in return. It says, in fact, that the external purchasing power of the population of these territories had to be depressed below their foreign exchange earnings, as the British authorities would not allow the British economy to supply more goods to West Africa, nor would they allocate foreign exchange required for their purchase; and that the standard of living of the British people, the level of investment in the United Kindgom and the volume of exports to destinations other than West Africa were being subsidized and supported at the expense of the West African people. The argument implies that such a policy was operative over the whole range of consumer goods over the years 1947–50. The evidence quoted in the preceding paragraph, notably the response of the volume of imports to changes in producer prices, conclusively refutes these suggestions of deliberate exploitation.

The accumulation of surpluses by the retention from producers of part of the sales proceeds does, of course, bring about just this reduction in the demand for imports both of consumer goods and of capital goods; they thus give plausibility to the view that an exploitative policy is in fact pursued. This is the clear implication of the premise that producer prices should not be raised because at any time the volume of merchandise available to West Africa is fixed.[1]

[1] It may well be true that if the rise in payments to farmers is unexpected an appreciable time-lag may occur before increased imports can arrive, and if local stocks

The absence in most other sterling area countries of institutions analogous to the West African marketing boards immediately refutes the suggestion that their policies are necessitated by the shortage of supplies,[1] since if it is thought necessary to constrict producer incomes in order to deflate demand it still needs to be explained why this policy is confined to producers in a small group of territories, thus singling out these producers to make sacrifices not demanded of other sterling area countries, or indeed of the population of soft-currency areas generally.

7. THE PRICES RECEIVED BY PRODUCERS OF EXPORT CROPS AND THE TERMS OF TRADE OF THE POPULATION

It is not possible to accept the contention that the rise in the prices paid to producers on export crops would result in a proportionate increase in local food prices and is therefore undesirable. It does not follow that food prices would rise proportionately or even nearly proportionately; and even if they did rise it does not follow that this would be undesirable.

At least until 1950 the officially collected statistics of market prices of foodstuffs were extremely defective; and there was no consistent series of internal food prices. To obtain more nearly reliable and consistent information, I approached the authorities in Nigeria and in the Gold Coast for information on the costs of providing food in certain institutions, notably prisons and hospitals. A fair amount of information on the daily average *per caput* cost of feeding African prisoners and patients was put at my disposal. The figures in general indicate a substantial increase in the prices at which food was bought as compared with prices in 1939, but do not suggest any clear or close relation to changes in producer prices for export crops. Thus even in the Gold Coast, where outside the mining areas the economy is dominated by cocoa production, the data do not show a clear correlation between the price of cocoa and the cost of purchased food. Thus the costs of feeding African inmates in the hospitals and prisons of Accra and Kumasi rose sharply from

---

are inadequate temporary shortage may occur; but the possibility of this temporary lag cannot justify the withholding from producers year after year of so large a proportion of the proceeds due to them. In fact, producer prices were generally announced well in advance (and can always be so announced), and this reduces the likelihood of such a lag.

[1] Even in countries where stabilization schemes operate the policies pursued are not so austere as in West Africa. In Great Britain (though not in other member countries of the sterling area) the level of taxation is much higher than in West Africa, and at first sight this might be thought to provide an analogy with the withholding operations of the marketing boards. This view is superficial because the tax proceeds are again expended on the purchase of goods and services.

1948–9 to 1949–50, despite the drastic reduction in the producer prices of cocoa. In fact between 1945–6 and 1948–9 the average cost of feeding African prisoners in the Gold Coast rose only very gradually by about 15 %; over the same period producer prices for cocoa rose by about 350 %.[1] On the other hand, there was a sharp *rise* in feeding costs in the following year, the sharpest annual increase recorded in the figures; yet in the season 1949–50 producer prices were cut by 30 %, which was the sharpest *reduction* in cocoa prices since before the war. The costs of other institutions showed similar tendencies.

In Port Harcourt, in the heart of the Nigerian palm belt, the cost of feeding African prisoners remained nearly stable between 1945 and 1949 and rose slightly in 1950. The cost rose by about one-sixth between 1945 and 1950. Over the same span of years producer prices for palm kernels were almost trebled and for palm oil almost quadrupled. Again, feeding costs of prisoners rose much less sharply here than producer prices. On the other hand, in the groundnut areas of northern Nigeria feeding costs of prisoners rose in appreciably greater proportion than groundnut producer prices either from 1939 to 1950 or from 1945 to 1950.

In short, there was no close connexion between changes in producer prices and changes in prices of foodstuffs as reflected in the costs of feeding at government institutions; and at any rate until 1950 these figures were more reliable and consistent than the market prices collected more or less casually by inspectors of the Departments of Labour or of Agriculture.

The prices of local foodstuffs may rise independently of changes in the producer price of export crops. They may rise if the season's supplies are short as a result of unfavourable weather conditions. They may rise as a result of a change in the consumption habits of the population. They may rise if the producers and their families themselves consume more of their produce than before; this may happen for a variety of reasons, such as substitution of local produce for imported merchandise or an increase in the number of dependents. They may rise in response to an increase in total demand, which again can come about for various reasons; an increase in the volume of export crops without any increase in producer price per unit is likely to increase the demand for local foodstuffs. It is therefore an obvious misconception to focus attention on the producer prices of export crops as the sole causal influence on the prices of local foodstuffs.

---

[1] Readers may be surprised by the magnitude of the change in producer prices. In 1945–6 the producer price was still almost at the very low wartime levels, while 1948–9 was the one season when it was accidentally and temporarily raised to the world level. Over the four seasons 1945–6 to 1948–9 the average surplus of the Cocoa Board was about two-thirds of the producer price.

A rise in producer prices of export crops will not raise internal prices substantially if producers spend a large proportion of an increase in their incomes on imported commodities, and if imports, especially flour, sugar and rice[1] (the principal imported foodstuffs on which increased incomes are spent in West Africa), are freely available. This, indeed, was the position before the war when changes in the incomes of producers were fairly promptly reflected in the volume of imports. Any time-lags were temporary, and there was no large accumulation of sterling balances following an increase in the prosperity of the industry, nor violent changes in the internal price level, either or both of which would have followed if the population had not wished to spend its increased income on imports.

This issue is thus closely linked with the dangerous suggestion that imports cannot be made available to West Africa in exchange for the vital products which she supplies to this country. The implications of this argument are particularly serious when it concerns the import of food. West Africa exports very large quantities of foodstuffs to the United Kingdom and to the United States, while her imports are very small; and the producers of these exports are very much poorer than the inhabitants of the United Kingdom whose standards of consumption they are asked, on this argument, to subsidize.[2]

But if the local population spend part of an increase in their incomes in the first instance on local products, the prices of these are likely to rise even if imported supplies are available. They are more likely to rise substantially if imports are not available readily, chiefly because the population are then perforce more likely to spend their incomes on locally produced goods and services. If imports equal to the value of exports are readily made available, there is no reason to expect heavy increases in the prices of local foodstuffs, still less that these should be proportionate to the increases in the prices received by producers of export crops. As has already been suggested, even in recent years, when certain imports on which higher incomes are readily spent were substantially restricted, the prices of local foodstuffs did not vary proportionately with producer prices. But even if local food prices rose simultaneously with, and proportionately to, producer prices, producers would be no better off than before only if they spent all their income on local foodstuffs, which is obviously not the case. Moreover, for good reasons, substantial increases in the prices of local foodstuffs may be necessary and desirable even in the absence of inflationary tendencies in the territories concerned. The rate of exchange between the West

[1] Or the foreign exchange to purchase these.

[2] Imports of sugar into Nigeria are at an annual rate of 10,000–15,000 tons against about 1½ m. tons into the United Kingdom.

African pound and other major currencies is fixed. This means that a world-wide depreciation in the value of money must be largely reflected in a rise in local prices in that section of the economy which is some way removed from the subsistence stage. When the rate of exchange is fixed an improvement in the terms of trade of the population postulates a rise in local prices and incomes relatively to the rise in import prices,[1] since only then will the population be able to purchase more imports with the income of a day's work. Thus in the circumstances higher prices of local foodstuffs may be simply part of the process of readjustment of the structure of incomes and prices to a higher level.[2]

In certain instances substantial increases in prices may also be necessary to serve as an inducement to higher production by improving the position of the rural population relatively to that of the urban population (which may have adverse effects on the latter). But such changes, though they may be both necessary and desirable, may raise political difficulties; in West Africa, especially in Nigeria, the urban population, professional men, journalists, clerks and wage-earners, are much the most vocal section of public opinion, and they are politically more influential than the producers of export crops. The difficulties of the necessary adjustment are likely to be enhanced by the delay in the necessary adaptation to changed market conditions.

8. INCREASED FOOD PRODUCTION AS AN ARGUMENT FOR THE PAYMENT OF LOW PRICES FOR EXPORT PRODUCE

Another line of argument closely connected with that examined in the preceding section suggests that modest prices paid to producers for export crops are desirable, as this helps to induce farmers to cultivate food crops rather than export crops. Once again this is an argument open to the objection that it assumes that no further imports of food are possible. There is no need to repeat the criticisms of this dangerous view which has already been examined in earlier sections of this chapter.

---

[1] The technical reader will notice that this disregards the effects of differences in the rate of progress in the production of imports and of export crops. This does not affect the argument.

[2] This seems to be entirely neglected in discussions on producer prices. An example of this neglect and of its implications for producer price policy can be seen from the following extract from an official gazette notice by the Oil Palm Produce Marketing Board, later reproduced in its Annual Report for 1950: 'The Board takes note of the continued rise in the cost of living in Nigeria and of the fact that under such conditions the benefits of price increases tend to be entirely illusory.' On this argument, the terms of trade of the producers of export crops must be depressed whenever import prices are rising; and the argument also seems to suggest that maintenance, let alone improvement, in the terms of trade of producers would be impossible unless import prices are constant or actually falling.

But the suggestion that food production should be increased by depressing the producer prices of export crops is open to criticism on wider grounds. It is a strangely inverted argument; organizations established to promote the interests of the producers of export crops do so by depressing their incomes and so driving them into producing food for their own subsistence. In fact, the farmers produce export crops because by this means they can secure a higher standard of living. A compulsory reversal of this amounts to a reduction of their standard of living. It is well known that abandonment of subsistence production and entry into a specialized exchange economy are among the first essentials of a higher standard of living. Specialization and the division of labour are the key to higher production and a better standard of living, in West Africa as elsewhere; and it is by no means clear that it is desirable to press producers of export crops to grow more food, i.e. to revert to subsistence production. In outlying districts and regions such a reversion to subsistence production, or failure to emerge from it, is the certain result of lower producer prices.

Moreover, while depression of the standard is certain, increased production of food is not. The alternatives to export crops also include production of kola nuts, petty trading, casual wage-earning, and an increased drift to the towns. Lower producer prices of export crops may also result in dismissal of migrant labour and thus in a net reduction in agricultural output without any increase in food production.

9. COMPULSORY SAVING AS AN ARGUMENT FOR THE CONSTRICTION OF INCOMES OF PRODUCERS

In view of the low level of capital in these territories the need to finance large-scale development for raising the volume of production and the standard of living is frequently advanced as a reason for the establishment of the marketing boards, as well as for the price policies they have pursued. This argument, plausible at first, on examination turns out to be unfounded.

The boards themselves have claimed that price stabilization was their primary task and the major claim on their resources. Thus the first Annual Report of the Nigeria Oil Palm Produce Marketing Board observes: 'Price stabilisation must always constitute the primary claim on the Board's actual and prospective resources after the initial requirements of working capital have been met.' There is no reference to development in the Annual Reports of the Gold Coast Cocoa Marketing Board,[1] nor are any of its reserves allocated for the purpose, except

---

[1] At least up to the end of 1951.

a contingent reserve for possible commitments in connexion with the combating of swollen shoot disease (at about one-seventh of its total reserves as at September 1950). In Nigeria the amounts set aside by the Cocoa Marketing Board for development are a small part (about one-tenth) of its funds. More substantial amounts have been allocated for this purpose by the Groundnut and Oil Palm Produce Boards, but even here the allocations are a minor part of the funds withheld from producers.

There may be a case for compulsory saving in countries where the level of capital is as low as in West Africa, especially in Nigeria. But against the possible benefits important offsetting factors need to be considered.

First, if the process of compulsory saving takes the form of paying to producers prices below commercial values, paradoxical policies may result. Thus the Nigeria Cotton Marketing Board wishes to encourage the growth of the cotton industry and, with this aim in view, is financing a Cotton Development Team. As we have seen over the period reviewed in this study the Board paid the producer's appreciably less than one-half of the local equivalent of market prices. It is not quite consistent for the Board to pay the producer less than half the market price and at the same time to send round a development team (financed ultimately by the producer) to ascertain the best means of encouraging the production of the crop. The paradox is heightened when it is noted that until quite recently the production of cotton was officially encouraged by exempting cotton from export duty to secure a slightly higher price to the producer.

Secondly, the return to be obtained from centralized saving depends on the use to which the funds are put, which in West Africa is still largely conjectural. The great bulk of these allocations to reserves is thus far unspent and has only been allocated with a view to future expenditure at an indefinite date, by which time a further depreciation of the real value may well have occurred. Nor is there any assurance that suitable projects and personnel will be available for the expenditure of these funds. Again, experience in West Africa and elsewhere suggests that the eventual expenditure may well take a form unlikely to benefit producers greatly, much less to offset the adverse effects on supply of lower producer prices. For instance, it is possible that at some future date a substantial part of the accumulated surpluses will be spent rather rapidly in a deliberate attempt to run down sterling balances or for other quasi-political reasons. Further, in the expenditure of centralized savings preference is often shown for projects which can be specifically associated with a political party or an official organization or particular persons sponsoring these; and even allowing for possible indirect advantages, the economic return on this type of expenditure is often very low.[1] The funds may also come to be spent as part of general government expenditure largely unconnected with the development of the producing region.[2]

Even if the funds are spent with care and with the best intention to promote the welfare of the producing districts, they may still prove a costly form of development expenditure. With the admittedly very important exception of the provision of basic services and the subsidization of research, centralized investment may well yield a smaller real return than would the same volume of investment by individual producers. The latter are in a better position to assess differences in their individual circumstances and costs (including access to alternatives) than is possible under centralized schemes which are generally standardized and tend to override such differences. The circumstances of individual producers do in fact differ greatly, and there is a substantial saving in resources if these differences are taken fully into account. This is possible only when decisions are taken by the individual producer.[3]

These considerations are not necessarily an argument against government investment even on a large scale in basic services. But they need to be borne in mind when assessing the merits of centralized compulsory saving especially when pursued in a manner and on a scale which obstructs private saving and retards the growth of the saving habit. And they are specially relevant when the savings are accumulated by paying the producers of cash crops prices well below commercial values. In West Africa the benefits of compulsory saving, or rather of the eventual disbursement of the funds, are contingent, uncertain and delayed; but the adverse effects of the low prices on the maintenance and extension

[1] The Nigeria Cocoa and Cotton Boards joined with the Colonial Development Corporation in the formation of a substantial project (Nigerian Fibre Industries Limited), principally for the local production of sacks. The terse account of the progress of this venture in the second Annual Report of the Colonial Development Corporation (p. 54) concludes as follows: 'Corporation considers present scheme could not be commercially viable in foreseeable future; recommended Marketing Boards to seek independent advice if not in agreement with Corporation views: Marketing Boards are obtaining second opinion; their decision awaited.'

[2] This can also come about indirectly. The accumulated compulsory savings may be spent for the development of the particular producing region but the expenditure out of general funds may be correspondingly reduced. This is a familiar device to defeat the purpose of earmarking funds.

[3] There is a tendency in contemporary economic literature to regard economic development as largely confined to industrialization and/or to officially or quasi-officially sponsored projects of various kinds; and to exclude the growth of cash crops and the establishment of small-scale plantations and peasant holdings as a form of development. This widespread and official attitude (which in part has political roots) is superficial, since this type of activity has been and still is a principal instrument of economic growth.

of capacity, and on individual saving and effort, have operated for well over ten years.

Even if compulsory saving for development is thought on balance to be beneficial or necessary, the retention by the marketing boards of a substantial part of the sales proceeds of export crops is a device of doubtful equity and efficiency for this purpose. Such a major decision of national economic policy should be taken and implemented by the governments in their capacity as fiscal and monetary authorities and as organs acting for the community as a whole, rather than by organizations established to promote the interests of the producers of export crops by means of price stabilization. Through a budget surplus the government could raise the funds just as easily as can the marketing boards. Under such a policy compulsory saving would be integrated with the rest of the tax structure,[1] and its burden borne by all taxpayers, instead of being concentrated on certain particularly productive and efficient sections of the community on whom it bears harshly, while others escape the burden altogether. Under the present system the incidence of the burden is confined to the producers of export crops; and among these it varies from product to product and year to year, so that it is haphazardly discriminatory.

10. SUBSIDIARY ARGUMENTS IN SUPPORT OF THE PRICE POLICIES OF THE MARKETING BOARDS

The arguments so far examined have been officially and repeatedly advanced in support of the policy of the accumulation of large surpluses. But reference must be made to certain subsidiary arguments put forward by supporters of this policy. These arguments do not appear to have been officially endorsed, but their manner of presentation suggests that their supporters have close contacts with the marketing boards and their spokesmen.

A special correspondent of *The Times*, writing in that newspaper in July 1951,[2] claimed on behalf of the marketing boards that their policies were the only possible method of taxation of these producers. In the words of the writer: 'No one has yet devised a satisfactory method of collecting income tax from peasants scattered throughout the bush.' This overlooks the heavy export taxes which are levied on their produce, and the import duties paid by the peasants on the merchandise they buy. Moreover, when they were established most specific assurances were

---

[1] By this is meant a process which would go beyond the simple device of raising export duties to direct part of the surpluses of the boards to the government, which still leaves the burden on these producers.

[2] *The Times*, 20 July 1951.

given that the marketing boards would not be used as a system of taxation.

The special correspondent also argued on behalf of the policy of restricting producer prices that it has helped 'to control the rise of a *kulak* class among Nigerian peasant farmers with incomes out of proportion to the rest of the population'. This is a somewhat peculiar way of supporting the policy, since it amounts to saying that by depressing producer prices the boards are, in fact, helping to prevent the standard of living of the peasant from rising. It would seem to be difficult to make a graver accusation against officially controlled organizations which were established to serve the interests of their constituents. Among many producers subject to the marketing boards there is little sign of the emergence of a *kulak* class. For instance, the great majority of groundnut producers have little more than one acre under the crop; at present prices the sale of the whole of the produce would give a cash income of about £5 per year.

More recently it has been suggested that in view of the congestion of the West African ports, especially Takoradi, and of the West African railways, no more consumer goods could be imported or transported; and that in these circumstances the compression of incomes by the marketing boards is desirable. This argument is again unacceptable on several grounds. First, the tonnage of exports much exceeds the tonnage of imports, so that there must be a considerable amount of unused railway capacity for inward freights, while at the ports a small proportional reduction in exports would, if really necessary, reduce congestion sufficiently to permit the entry of a large proportional increase in imports. That imports do in fact increase when prices to producers are raised is shown by the trade statistics. When prices paid to cocoa producers were raised in 1948–9 and 1950–1, the volume of imports rose sharply; when they were reduced in 1949–50, stocks of imported goods were left unsold in local merchants' hands. Secondly, if it is thought necessary to restrict consumption in order to prevent inflation, this should be done by means of taxation imposed by the government on the whole community in accordance with ability to pay, and not by the arbitrary withholding of income from a section of the community by administrative bodies ostensibly set up to promote the interests of that section.[1] In the form in which it is usually advanced

[1] The congestion of the West African ports and railways as a limiting factor on the volume of imports was adduced by Dr D. Seers of the Oxford University Institute of Statistics in a letter in *The Times* of 12 January 1953 in support of the price policies of the marketing boards and of the restriction of producers' incomes. The argument of the text seems to deal adequately with this contention. But if Dr Seers's statement about the effects of port congestion had indeed been correct, they would have con-

this argument seems to contradict another argument in support of the boards' price policies, namely, that additional imports are not available. The supply of imports and the capacity of the boards can both be limiting factors at the same time. It is an altogether far-fetched suggestion that the strain on West African port capacity has been a factor influencing the price policy of the boards.

II. INAPPROPRIATENESS OF DETAILED EXAMINATION OF THE REASONS FOR THE BOARDS' POLICIES

Thus the policies of the marketing boards cannot be explained satisfactorily in terms of the arguments usually advanced, which are more nearly in the nature of retrospective rationalization of the policies, rather than effective supporting arguments. They were not mentioned among the functions of the marketing boards at the time of their establishment (indeed most of the arguments examined are contrary to the aims of statutory marketing as laid down in the Cocoa White Papers), nor were most of them advanced at the time when the policies were adopted. The absence of any clear idea of the meaning of stabilization, and the failure to distinguish this aim from other aims of policy, has served to encourage such retrospective rationalization, since in these circumstances practically any decision can be justified by reference to one or other of different and often conflicting aims of policy. In the absence of satisfactory official arguments in support of the policies it is tempting to look for other explanations.

However, such a discussion would not be appropriate here, as it would necessarily involve a considerable speculative element. The various possible and plausible motives and reasons for these policies include such influences and considerations as expectation of an early fall in prices (and the failure of this to come about resulted in the emergence of large surpluses); failure to appreciate the very limited value of undefined stabilization as a guide to policy (particularly at times of fairly continuous rise in prices, which brings it about that however large the

stituted a devastating indictment of government policy. That it should be impossible, seven years after the end of the war, to permit a rise in the standard of living of a part of the Commonwealth a great deal poorer than Britain, on the ground that port facilities were inadequate to handle the imports the people had earned enough to pay for, would inevitably have looked like either ineptitude or a breach of trust. The expenditure of a sum equal to a fraction of the amounts withheld from producers by the marketing boards would have sufficed to make any additions to the capacity of the ports necessary to enable them to handle more imports. Dr Seers's letter was answered along these lines by Professor F. W. Paish and the present writer in *The Times* of 23 January 1953.

reserves they always appear insufficient); an inclination to place the interests of the organizations above those of their constituents;[1] regard for the interests of the British economy; concern with the social and political repercussions of rising prices, especially as these affect the urban population, which is politically much more influential than the peasant producers;[2] a general inclination to follow an easy course and take *ad hoc* decisions of a kind likely to strengthen the organization or to increase its prestige;[3] belief in the irrelevance of market prices (which have come to be seen as largely arbitrary quantities determined by speculators and a handful of dealers in the world's market, and as such arbitrary magnitudes to be disregarded with impunity and indeed with benefit); a feeling that those who have recently had a sharp rise in money incomes (frequently only of money incomes and not of real incomes) are better able to bear additional taxation than are others with higher incomes; belief in the desirability of the socialization of saving (both for its own sake and as an instrument to raise the level of saving), and in closer governmental control over the economy as a whole, and over peasant producers in particular. All these factors may have played a part. Even though I have had full access to the files of the boards, including the confidential minutes of their meetings, an attempt to assess the relative

[1] As is well known, administrators of large-scale organizations are often more concerned with the strength, growth and progress of the organizations than with the interests of their members whom they supposedly represent. This fate generally overtakes an organization supposedly acting on behalf of very large numbers of people who themselves do not participate in its administration. Though the organization purports to be a means to further the welfare of the producers, or of the shareholders, or of some other amorphous body whom they represent, its perpetuation and expansion become ends in themselves. After a period the administrators tend to regard their constituents or members as being opposed to themselves or to the organization, and they consider that funds paid out to them are lost or dissipated. This is particularly likely to happen when the administrators have statutory monopoly powers while their constituents are not only unorganized, but are also illiterate and not vocal.

Without entering the field of speculation, the statements of the boards suggest that such influences may have affected their policies. The growth of reserves is habitually identified in the boards' statements as evidence of profit and success, though it is merely a measure of the extent to which proceeds have been withheld from producers; substantial surpluses have been accumulated at times of very unsuccessful sales. Drafts on reserves are described as a loss to be avoided whenever possible and monies paid to producers are said to be paid *away*. Over the period reviewed here the policies pursued were in harmony with these statements.

[2] This factor, however, would be connected with a possible concern for the interests of the British economy, since the so-called inflationary tendencies would be greatly reduced by increased imports to which the income accruing from their exports entitles the West African colonies.

[3] Which in this case amounts to an accumulation of surpluses, either to increase the reserves of the board or to acquire funds for allocation to various official or semi-official purposes.

importance of these factors would be partly speculative and out of place here.

I feel, however, that the access I have had to the official files does place me under an obligation to attempt to qualify a matter of some political importance. It has been forcefully put to me, both in West Africa and in this country, that the boards have been subjected to and have complied with pressure from the United Kingdom Government. Higher producer prices imply a higher demand for imports, which in turn means either an increased allocation of foreign exchange to West Africa or increased supplies of exports from the United Kingdom, thus reducing the volume of resources available for use in this country or in the production of British exports. The superficial plausibility of this explanation is confirmed by the constant preoccupation in West Africa with the shortage of commodities (whether real or alleged), and the emphasis on the need to constrict incomes in view of the shortage of imports; these arguments imply considerable regard for the interests of the United Kingdom.

It should therefore be stated explicitly that there is no evidence whatever in official documents that the marketing boards have been influenced by official pressure designed to minimize West African demands on sterling area resources and foreign exchange reserves. Quite possibly pressure in this direction would not have been necessary (even if thought desirable), since the policies of the marketing boards have forestalled the need for it. But while these policies were no doubt welcome to the British authorities by reducing the claims on the British economy, there is much evidence to suggest that the British authorities were prepared to make available additional resources to West Africa, and that accordingly the restriction of incomes was not required by a shortage of imports.

Thus the widespread belief that the British authorities have influenced the marketing boards or their price policies is unfounded. But when statutory monopolies operate in colonial territories such suspicions are not easy to allay. The motives of a firm in a monopolistic situation cannot be unambiguously determined; nor is this necessary for an assessment of the effects of its actions on its customers. Similarly, it is not possible for the marketing boards, who have extensive monopoly powers, to establish to the satisfaction of those who do not have access to their files that their policies and decisions have not been influenced by consideration for the interests of the United Kingdom, which were favoured by low producer prices; and at times this may well produce political suspicion and mistrust when a country stands in a fiduciary relationship towards the territories which are politically dependent on it.

It is often claimed as an advantage of certain arrangements such as bulk sales or long-term contracts that they remove from the commercial sphere the economic relationships between a country and its colonies. Precisely because of the fiduciary relationship between a country and its colonies there are obvious advantages in the removal of economic relationships from the sphere of governmental decisions and political pressure, or even the suspicion of such pressure.[1]

[1] This has now come to be recognized in the marketing arrangements of Nigerian products which are sold to the Ministry of Food on the basis of open-market prices (cf. Chapter 22, § 2, above).

PART 6

THE ECONOMICS OF MARKETING REFORM

CHAPTER 25

THE ECONOMICS OF MARKETING REFORM:
MEASURES AND PROPOSALS (I)

Apart from the establishment of the marketing boards there have in recent years been other official measures, as well as numerous proposals for others, designed to alter the structure of the marketing of West African produce. This part of the study reviews certain measures and recommendations which stem from influential opinions on marketing reform in West Africa and elsewhere. Some of the proposals bear on the import trade and internal trade, as well as on the export trade, with reference to which they are usually advanced.

I. PROPOSALS FOR COMPULSORY REDUCTION IN THE NUMBER OF INTERMEDIARIES

In Chapter 2 it has been shown that the very large number of intermediaries in West African trade is to be explained in terms of underlying economic factors. In particular, it reflects the low level of capital and certain other productive resources and a comparative superabundance of unskilled labour in relation to the opportunities open to it. In these conditions the multiplicity of traders (both in the sense of a large number of traders at any given stage of distribution and of a large number of successive stages) is economic in the use of available resources.

These considerations are generally overlooked by the critics of the alleged wastefulness of the system. Compulsory reduction in the number of traders is often proposed in the belief that it will eliminate waste and reduce distributive margins. It is believed or implied that such a course would reduce prices to consumers or raise them to producers, and that some of the resources set free could be turned to more productive employment, notably to the production of more food.

As a general rule the services of an intermediary will be used only if the cost of his services to his customers (i.e. his margin) is less than the value set on them by the customers, whose capital, time and labour he saves. These services include bulking, blending, holding and distributing stocks, breaking bulk, and the establishment of market contacts. The intermediary will become redundant and will be by-passed if he is superfluous or if his charges are excessive.

This general consideration clearly applies in West Africa, where, no doubt as a result of the low level of incomes and of the comparative lack of other more productive occupations, Africans will spend much time and effort to secure price advantages in selling their produce or in purchasing merchandise. Producers are particularly sensitive to price differences. In the Eastern Provinces of Nigeria, for example, women selling palm oil might walk or cycle several miles to secure another penny or twopence on the sale of a beer bottle of palm oil or another shilling on the sale of a four-gallon tin. In these circumstances a redundant intermediary would certainly be by-passed. The presence of the large number of intermediaries indicates that the charges for their services are economic, in that their customers prefer to use these services rather than perform them for themselves. The reason for this preference is basically that the performance of even elementary marketing services requires a certain minimum of capital and skill, as well as the more substantial expenditure of effort and time, and that there are economies when one intermediary performs similar services for several customers.

A redundant intermediary is thus likely to be by-passed even if he deals only with producers and consumers. But if there is more than one intermediary in the chain of distribution (as there generally is, especially in conditions of allegedly excessive numbers of intermediaries) each middleman buys from and/or sells to another middleman. As a middleman makes his living by securing a trading margin he will certainly by-pass a redundant intermediary whose services are not worth their price, since by doing so he can either buy at a lower cost or sell at a higher price, thereby increasing his own margin.

Certain possible qualifications and objections to the general argument in the preceding paragraph have to be considered. It is argued that Africans are not aware of price differentials and may therefore rely on traders whose services are unnecessary because they are not aware of cheaper available alternatives. This is unlikely to be of any quantitative importance in West Africa. Small-scale trading is highly competitive, and those offering cheaper alternatives are active in making their terms known to prospective customers. This spreading of information is most obvious where numerous itinerant traders operate, but it is also evident in the behaviour of traders generally. Africans, especially producers and traders, are well informed about the alternatives open to them. The low level of incomes forces customers to seek out the best prices. If, at a particular time, the producer himself is unable to devote much of his time to exploring the market, the task is indirectly performed for him at small margins by the large numbers of people available for this purpose because of their generally restricted economic opportunities. Moreover, even if customers were inadequately informed about the available alternatives, a compulsory reduction in the number of traders would not improve their position. Besides reducing the range of alternatives, it would also reduce the number of agencies disseminating market information.

It is sometimes contended that the producer is not free to use the most advantageous method or channel for marketing his produce because he is forced to use the services of a particular intermediary to whom he is financially indebted. However, where the producer has a choice among a number of would-be lenders he will choose to borrow where the terms are most advantageous to himself. The terms of loans may be a combination of interest payments and of the obligation to sell the produce to the lender on favourable terms to the latter; thus what in isolation appears to be a forced sale at a low price may simply represent an indirect payment of interest on the loan. Compulsory reduction in the number of trader-lenders is likely to reduce the number of sources of funds, to make the terms of loans more onerous, and to weaken the position of the borrower. Moreover, any attempt to prevent traders from lending to producers on condition that the crop is sold to them would certainly not improve the net position of the borrower; the latter might secure an apparently better price on the sale of his produce, but only by being required to make correspondingly higher direct interest payments to the lender.[1]

There is another objection to the view that redundant or inefficient intermediaries would be by-passed by their customers, which is generally of greater importance than those discussed above. Institutional arrangements may deny customers the right to use certain channels or methods of marketing. Thus the pressure of trade interests may be applied to prevent manufacturers or producers from dealing direct with petty retailers, individual consumers, groups of consumers or large institutional buyers. For example, in some West African towns market women and their associations have successfully stopped fishermen from retailing their own catches. Again, import licensing necessarily restricts direct importing to those in receipt of licences, and debars customers from relying on other traders or from extending their own activities. The economic effects of some of these institutional barriers are discussed elsewhere in this study, and need not be considered here because the position of customers in the postulated conditions will obviously not be improved by a compulsory reduction in the number of traders.

The analysis of this section suggests that there is no foundation for

---

[1] It is often held that much of the borrowing by farmers in West Africa and elsewhere in the colonies is to finance occasional extravagant consumption, and that it would be in the interests of the population to restrict the possibility of borrowing for such purposes. This, however, is an entirely different issue from that discussed in the text.

the view that gross distributive margins could be reduced by the simple device of a compulsory limitation of the numbers engaged in trade, or by the compulsory reduction in the number of successive stages in the distributive process.[1] Indeed, the reverse is likely to be true. Restriction on entry or limitation on numbers is likely to endow each privileged trader with a measure of protection and tends to facilitate the formation of price agreements and market-sharing arrangements by the traders at the expense of their consumer and producer customers. The compulsory reduction in the number of stages in distribution is likely to result in the adoption of uneconomic trading methods and in the absorption in this activity of unnecessarily large quantities of scarce resources.

The recent Report of the Nigerian Livestock Mission is typical of influential opinions which regard the presence of numerous intermediaries as a sign of inefficiency. It expresses uncompromisingly the view that the large number of intermediaries is responsible for the wide margins between the prices received by the producer and the prices paid by the ultimate consumer, and that the activities of these intermediaries only add to costs which could be reduced by curtailing their numbers. The following quotations illustrate the view that each successive middleman simply extracts part of the ultimate value of the produce handled without adding to this value, and that therefore the multiplication of such stages merely adds to the toll taken by intermediaries from the producer and/or consumer:

...There are, therefore, two, three and sometimes more intermediaries interposed between the seller and ultimate purchaser, with each intermediary in the agency chain retaining for himself as much as may be possible of the sum of money advanced to him, and each, on occasion, trading with part of that money, acquiring textiles and other consumer goods on which a side profit is taken when ultimately these goods go to form part of the price that is paid to the seller.[2]

Briefly, the costs imposed on the livestock industry by a system of sale that is operated through a multiplicity of impecunious dealers and middlemen, leave the producer as a reward for his risk and labour with something approaching only one-third of the price paid by the consumer in the South, and impose upon the consumers everywhere a wholly unjustifiably high price for meat.

...The handling of almost the entire trade by a host of redundant dealers and middlemen, the frequent handlings of stock—that represent for Nigeria economic wastage on a prodigious scale and in large measure accounts for the unjustifiably wide gap between the prices received by the producer and those paid by the consumer.[3]

---

[1] This conclusion is of general validity and applies to West Africa with fewer qualifications than may be necessary elsewhere.

[2] P. 118.   [3] *Report of the Nigerian Livestock Mission*, pp. 87 and 95.

The report fails to ask the obvious and relevant question why these intermediaries are not being by-passed, since it is open to the producers, to each of the intermediaries, and to the final buyers to eliminate some of the stage by more direct dealing.

2. ZONING PROPOSALS

The view that competition among traders or processors is wasteful and raises costs to the detriment of customers, inspires proposals for compulsory zoning. The proposals envisage the creation by official action of local monopolies for the purchase of produce in certain defined regions or zones. It is argued that compulsory concentration of supplies conduces to efficiency by securing a larger throughput and by the avoidance of duplicated facilities. It is sometimes added that the system facilitates official control over the activities of the traders, notably over their use of weights and measures. This is supposed to remove abuses which are alleged to exist to the disadvantage of producers where numerous buyers compete.

There are several examples of systems of zonal monopolies in the purchase of produce in East Africa; such arrangements are also proposed for the Nigerian livestock trade in the Report of the Nigerian Livestock Mission, and are also often advanced for other staple West African exports.

It is doubtful whether substantial savings in cost would in fact result from the adoption of such a system in produce buying. The nature of buying establishments does not suggest the possibility of any scope for real savings. In West Africa the buying 'establishments' of middlemen are generally simple and often temporary. Fixed capital investment in these buying points is very small, and even a proliferation of them would not add greatly to the costs of buying. If there were significant economies in the operation of fewer and larger buying points, the interests of traders and the responsiveness of producers to higher prices[1] would promote a trading structure comprising a few large establishments without the need for compulsion. The action of traders and producers would tend to bring about a situation in which the possibilities of economies are appropriately balanced with producers' valuations of marketing convenience and range of alternatives. Thus even in processing, where *prima facie* there might be more substantial economies of scale than there are in trading, there would seem to be no need for the

[1] If there were substantial economies traders operating on a larger scale would be able to offer higher prices for produce. In practice they would be prepared to pay the higher prices to attract supplies, even though their current rate of purchases might temporarily be below the rate at which the full economies are secured. They would be prepared to absorb the costs of growth if substantial economies were in prospect.

compulsory elimination of alternatives which is a corollary of a system of zonal monopolies.

The establishment and supervision of zonal monopolies raise problems of their own. These tend to negative the superficial attractiveness which such systems present because of their ostensible tidiness, orderliness and amenability to official control. The absence of the spur of actual or potential competition and the costs and inconvenience of supervision[1] are likely to offset any small economies that may result from compulsory zoning. A system of zonal purchasing monopolies would also imply either local monopolies in the sale of imported merchandise, or a duplication of facilities for the purchase of produce and for the sale of merchandise, which would offset or more than offset the theoretical saving in resources. In any event, there would be a reduction in the facilities available to the population which is likely to impose inconvenience and possibly hardship on some producers (and consumers). It would also greatly increase the feeling of dependence of customers on whichever firm is selected as the zonal monopolist.

As a corollary of a zoning system it would be necessary for the Government to attempt to control the level of costs and profits of the zonal monopolists. The necessary calculations would pose difficult problems of assessment and allocation of costs and revenues; for the calculations would often have to refer to a small part of the interrelated activities of large organizations engaged in a great variety of geographically dispersed and dissimilar lines of business. In practice even in the simplest cases official allowances for costs and profits tend to be wide of the mark; the official calculation of transport differentials in groundnut purchasing in northern Nigeria is a case in point.[2] The allowances tend to be generous; indeed, they could not err on the side of underestimate since the desired services would then not be provided. Of course, unlike the over-generous allowances in northern Nigeria, under a system of zonal monopolies any additional profits or savings in cost would not be passed on to customers, but would be retained by the monopolist.[3]

---

[1] Two kinds of supervision would be involved. The zonal monopolist would have to be regulated by the authorities in an attempt to prevent the abuse of monopoly power; and the local clerks and employees of the monopolist would have to be supervised much more closely by responsible officers to prevent their clerks from exploiting the producers who, *ex hypothesi*, cannot remove their custom if they are dissatisfied with their treatment.

[2] Cf. Chapter 18 above, where it is shown that in recent years intermediaries in the groundnut trade have frequently competed away a substantial part of their allowances for transporting the product which were based on officially calculated transport costs.

[3] An extensive system of zonal monopolies is in force in the purchasing and ginning of cotton in Uganda. The costs and remuneration of the ginners have for years been

In determining permitted margins or prices the authorities would be faced with the almost impossible task of distinguishing between genuine reductions in cost and those savings in cost which might be secured by depriving customers of valuable services, or of access to more numerous stores for which they (or some of them) would be prepared to pay. There is a danger that government officials concerned with such schemes might too readily accept any measure designed to reduce costs in an effort to justify the continuation of the arrangements. On the other hand, there is the opposite danger that the monopolist might be encouraged to provide unnecessarily elaborate services; he can recover his greater costs because producers have no less elaborate and cheaper alternatives open to them, and regard for technical efficiency as opposed to economic efficiency may dispose supervisory officials favourably towards uneconomic improvements.

The establishment of a system of zonal monopolies imposes on the government the task of selecting the individual monopolists. In West Africa the choice is likely to raise considerable political difficulties. It may seem that some aspects of the problem could be solved by auctioning monopoly rights from time to time to firms who offer to perform the services at the lowest margins. For political reasons such an attempt to avoid partiality would be impracticable; and the procedure would be impracticable for other reasons as well. First, it would be difficult to ensure that the monopolist renders satisfactory service. Secondly, costs of operations would depend upon the number and dispersion of areas in which the applicant has been successful. As this cannot be known in advance, many suitable applicants might be reluctant to bid. Thirdly, it would be difficult to secure competitive bidding where the applicants are few in number and are aware of the high stakes involved. Fourthly, auctioning may lead to an economically and politically dangerous degree of concentration.

calculated on various formulae based on official estimates of costs and on reasonable returns. As is well known the system secured large profits to the licence holders which were reflected in the high capital value of licensed ginneries.

Similar influences seem to be at work in Nigeria, though their results are not so easily measureable. Reference has already been made to the comparatively easy profits of trading in the Middle Belt of Nigeria and to the absence of overpayments in groundnut purchasing in that region. The employees of the buying agents seem also to have benefited from the absence of competition. A European district officer recently stationed in the Benue region informed me that the African clerk in charge of the groundnut and benniseed buying post of one of the two European firms in that area (between whom there are informal zoning arrangements) had recently retired a rich man, with property worth about £10,000. His official remuneration had been of the order of £200 a year. The district officer added that he had never noticed a similar instance in Bornu (where he had been stationed before) where the clerks were exposed to much competition.

3. PRODUCER-CONTROLLED ZONAL MONOPOLIES

It may seem that many of the difficulties enumerated in the preceding section could be avoided if producer-controlled organizations were appointed as the zonal monopolists.[1] Where a producers' agency is the zonal monopolist it may appear as if the interests of the producers and the interests of the trader (monopolist) are identical. However, in practice the harmony of interests is not easily established or maintained. Those managing the monopoly are likely to regard their organization as an end in itself, with interests possibly different from, or even antagonistic to, those of the majority of producers. The divergence of interest and outlook between the administrators of large organizations and their unorganized and often uninformed constituents is a conspicuous feature of modern economic organization in large-scale public and private enterprises.

It is remarkable that this dichotomy of interests is so frequently disregarded in proposals for marketing reform, particularly in immature societies. In such societies detailed and democratic control by producers over the administrators of the organizations supposed to be acting on their behalf is likely to be feeble, and not an effective check on the formulation of policy and economy of operations. Where such organizations are endowed with statutory monopoly powers a further check is removed in that dissatisfied constituents cannot transfer their custom elsewhere. At the same time new entrants cannot expose the possible inefficiency of the organization, or the feasibility of other more attractive price and marketing policies.

Moreover, it is not correct to assume or to imply that the interests of all producers of a particular product are necessarily the same. The interests of the producer-constituents of the marketing organizations are likely to differ in many matters. These include the determination of different prices for different grades of the same product, the question whether each producer should bear his own transport costs or whether these costs should be averaged, the distribution of representation on the governing body, and the timing of payments to producers. The specific policies adopted by an organization are certain to affect some of its constituents less favourably than others; those who feel that their interests are adversely affected relatively to those of their fellow-producers are unable to seek better treatment elsewhere.

These considerations suggest that the objections to the establishment of zonal monopolies listed in § 3 above apply largely also to producer-controlled monopolies. These organizations are open to a further objec-

---

[1] Producer-controlled marketing monopolies are frequently advocated for a variety of reasons—not only to secure the alleged economies of zonal purchasing organizations.

tion where they control a large share of the market supply of the product. Here the monopolist-buyer is also a monopolist-seller, and there is an obvious possibility that consumers may be exploited. This risk is present even when the organization sells the bulk of its supplies to overseas buyers, since it may have a measure of market control.[1] But in practice it is greatest when consumption is largely local and when the organization would have complete monopoly of supply.[2] This danger is often overlooked because the divergence of interests between different sections of the population is not recognized. The danger that the monopoly powers will be used to the detriment of consumers is obvious where the actual producer-constituents are in effective control of their organization. But it is likely to be present even where the policy of the organization is effectively directed by its permanent administrators. The latter may wish to justify the organization to their producer-constituents by selling at high prices; moreover, if costs are inflated the administrators would have a direct incentive to take advantage of the selling monopoly to charge high prices.

Proposals for the establishment of zonal monopolies, especially producer-controlled monopolies, are sometimes advanced in order to redress alleged inequalities of bargaining power. It is implied that producers, being more numerous and individually less wealthy than merchants, suffer from an inherent weakness which causes them to sell their produce at lower prices than are warranted by market conditions. It is therefore advocated that their bargaining power should be increased by collective action, or, alternatively, that the right to buy should be confined to a single organization specifically charged with the duty of safeguarding producer interests, or to one which is officially supervised and controlled for that purpose.

Such proposals overlook several important considerations. Where several buyers act independently their competition will ensure that producers receive prices in line with market conditions, even though producers are far more numerous than traders and operate on a far smaller individual scale. In West African conditions even a small number of buyers appears to be sufficient to ensure that producers receive such prices.[3] Even if there are a few buyers, they may still have to pay prices not much out of line with commercial values (as governed by the prices they themselves secure), as long as entry of new buyers is

---

[1] In many cases the organization may have little or no market control in those overseas markets in which its supply is a small part of the total. Here it has effective monopoly power as a buyer but not as a seller.

[2] Such a situation is envisaged in the proposals of the Nigerian Livestock Mission.

[3] This again is borne out by the operation of competition in the purchase of groundnuts in Nigeria discussed in Chapter 18, above.

easy; in such conditions any attempt to depress producer prices would be upset by the competing offers of new buyers. In other words, bargaining power, that is, the ability of sellers to secure the full market value for their produce, depends primarily on access to independent alternatives and not on differences in wealth between sellers and buyers.

Moreover, even if there are only a few buyers and the possibility of new entry is limited, it does not follow that the position of the actual producers would be improved by the establishment of producer-controlled or other zonal buying monopolies. As has already been shown, the disadvantages inherent in monopoly buying are not automatically or necessarily removed by changing the organization of the monopoly, or by providing for its official supervision and control. An additional disadvantage of statutory monopolies is that the moderating influence of the possibility of new entrants is eliminated. It would seem preferable to strengthen the position of producers by endeavouring to widen the alternatives open to them, rather than by restricting them still further. The development of communications and the removal of barriers to new entry are two examples of possible improvements in this direction.

4. COMPULSORY CENTRALIZATION OF MARKETS

Another type of proposal inspired by the desire to protect the producer from exploitation by traders envisages the compulsory centralization of market transactions. The underlying contention is that producers, who are otherwise allegedly at the mercy of one trader or of a few traders in some regions, would secure better terms by being forced to deal in a market where there are more buyers and therefore more competition. This proposal is in one sense the opposite of the proposals for zoning. It extols the virtues of competition, and advocates that a special type of competition (i.e. the presence of more buyers in one place) should be promoted by denying to producers access to other opportunities of selling their produce.[1] On the other hand, zoning proposals extol the virtues of monopoly, at least to the extent of preferring it to the type of competition which would allegedly otherwise take place.

A proposal along these lines has been put forward by Mr J. Mars in his contribution to a recent study of the Nigerian economy.[2] It is one

---

[1] Occasional attempts to introduce such a system in cocoa buying in Abeokuta Province of south-western Nigeria have not been rigorously enforced. No reliable information is available about its operation. Somewhat similar arrangements seem also to operate in the marketing of certain crops in East Africa. The system of scheduled markets in cotton buying in northern Nigeria was instituted for different reasons, and despite superficial resemblances is not suitable for discussion here.

[2] *Mining, Commerce and Finance in Nigeria*, edited by Miss Margery Perham.

of his suggestions that the outlying trading stations of the European firms should be compulsorily closed. He argues that there is a large element of local monopoly in their operations, and that compulsory centralization could increase the extent of competition:

It has been pointed out that the tendency towards oligopsony and eventual monopsony is absolutely inevitable in the produce business of Nigeria if up-country stations of exporting firms remain open. If all such up-country stations were compulsorily closed down, the tendency towards monopsony would be much weakened if not eradicated.[1]

It is not clear whether it is proposed to close down all trading points outside the ports or only those outside the larger commercial centres. The former suggestion would bring the economy to a standstill. If the latter course is intended, the proposal would mean that producers and small-scale rural traders, who even now may have to make journeys of fifty miles or more to a trading station in some areas, would in the future have to undertake journeys of several hundred miles to obtain supplies or to dispose of their produce. The idea that competition is fostered by reducing the alternatives open to producers and consumers is here driven almost to its logical but absurd conclusion. To be consistent the author of the proposal should have advocated compulsory cessation of export produce buying in West Africa so that producers would be forced to take their produce to overseas terminal markets where the largest numbers of buyers are concentrated.[2]

Exaggerated emphasis on the dangers of local buying monopolies in any area neglects the fact that such buyers, while appearing to have no competitors, nevertheless have to set their buying prices in competition with other buyers elsewhere; they cannot depress them so much that

---

[1] *Mining, Commerce and Finance in Nigeria*, vol. 2, p. 131. The terms 'oligopsony' and 'monopsony' mean oligopoly and monopoly in buying. These concepts are discussed in Chapter 6, § 3, and Chapter 7, §§ 1 and 2, above.

[2] The proposal for compulsory centralization criticized in the text is only one among several suggestions intended to promote competition by compulsory standardization, i.e. by reducing the number of alternatives open to customers. Such proposals rest upon a misconception of the nature of competition and of competitive forces. From the narrow definition of perfect competition in static economic analysis it is inferred that competition prevails only where the customers can choose from among a number of *identical* alternatives, that is, from among alternatives which are identical as regards quality, place and time of supply. In fact, where *demand* is not identical or uniform, competition is not promoted by forcing demand into a common mould by denying to suppliers the opportunity of adapting their product or service to the varying requirements and unstandardized demands of customers. Geographical differences are generally significant in bringing about unstandardized demands, and they are particularly important in West Africa. In such circumstances competition tends to take the form of making available to customers a range of alternatives adjusted to individual circumstances of demand.

producers would be better off by taking their produce to other more distant buyers. Accordingly, where producers are able to get their produce to other markets without great cost in time, effort or money, the prices they receive locally for their produce cannot be far below those obtaining in the more important market centres. In West Africa producers are sensitive to price differences of which knowledge spreads quickly, and they are generally prepared to cover long distances to secure attractive prices. On the other hand, where producers are not in a position to undertake long journeys the compulsory closure of out-stations would cause otherwise avoidable loss and hardship. It would either deprive them of markets altogether or require them to undertake costly journeys to distant markets. This reasoning is borne out by the fact that buyers in outlying areas are voluntarily supported by sufficient producers to keep them in business.

5. PROPOSALS FOR COMPULSORY DIRECTION OF PRODUCE

Another type of proposal for marketing reform requires the compulsory direction of produce along officially determined routes or to officially determined destinations. Such proposals are often put forward in the belief that, without regulation, produce tends to travel uneconomic distances or in unprofitable directions with consequent losses to producers and consumers.[1] These ideas seem to underlie some of the discussion and one of the major recommendations of the Nigerian Livestock Mission.

The principal recommendation urges the establishment of a large abattoir in Kano for the slaughter and processing of cattle which at present pass through Kano and the surrounding area on their way south. This abattoir is to be granted the sole right to purchase cattle in Kano and an undefined area around it. The Livestock Mission Report regards it as self-evident that this would be a more economical way of disposing of the cattle than the present method of sending them southwards on the hoof.

This [monopoly right of purchase] we believe should, *in the first instance,* be restricted to an area centred round Kano, of a size convenient for such purposes as the purchase of supplies and the administration of the scheme. All cattle at present sold in Kano for slaughter at the public slaughter slabs, all cattle passing through the prescribed area en route for the south, all cattle brought into Kano for transport from Kano to the south, must be sold to the Board [to be sent up to control the abattoir and marketing arrangements].

---

[1] The discussion in this section is not concerned with regulation of produce routes introduced solely for purposes of veterinary control.

We have given the most careful consideration to the possibility of omitting from compulsory sale to the Board these 35,000 cattle railed annually to Lagos. We are satisfied, however, that there cannot be two channels of sale available in Kano, the Board and the sale yard, and although the Board will not require the 35,000 cattle railed annually to Lagos for their initial abattoir purposes, they must control those supplied as to price, quality, transport and ultimate sale in Lagos.[1]

As the advantage of the proposed abattoir and of the policy of sending southwards meat rather than cattle is so confidently assumed, it is surprising that the Report should insist that owners of livestock in a large area should be forced to sell their cattle to the proposed marketing authority and should have no alternative method of sale. It is implied that left to themselves many producers would continue to use uneconomic methods and routes for disposing of their produce. Again, as in the proposals for the compulsory reduction in numbers of traders, the crucial question is not asked why producers would persist in employing methods of marketing which are supposed to reduce their returns unnecessarily. Once again it is tacitly assumed (as in many other proposals for marketing reform) that producers are so ignorant of their own interests that they cannot be relied on to sell simple unprocessed produce as advantageously as is possible.[2]

The proposals of the livestock mission envisage a substantial investment of resources in improved processing and transport facilities. But their proposals imply that without compulsion producers and traders would not adapt their methods to the additional alternatives which would then be open to them. This assumption is contrary to the observed responsiveness of producers in West Africa to changing and emerging

---

[1] *Report of the Nigerian Livestock Mission*, p. 141 (author's italics).

[2] This assumption is at the root of the opinion in the report that the physical condition of large numbers of cattle passing through Jebba 'is so deplorable that they should be compulsorily detained or slaughtered almost immediately' (*Report*, p. 88). It needs to be asked why these cattle are being driven on if they are fit only for immediate slaughter. The answer lies in the absence of a suitable market for meat in the poor and sparsely populated areas round Jebba and Ilorin; any deterioration in the condition of the animals through further trekking is more than offset by the greater value of the meat in the south. Compulsory slaughter of these cattle, not on account of any specific complaint, but simply because of their generally poor physical condition, would be exceedingly wasteful. It would also be inequitable, and the owners could justly claim compensation on the basis of the selling value of the beasts in the south. In point of fact, deterioration in the condition of these animals from further trekking is not certain, since pasture in the south-west is generally better than in the areas from which the cattle come. From the context it seems clear that the proposal in the report was inspired by the alleged wastefulness of the cattle treks rather than by humanitarian regard for the cattle. Diseased animals are already compulsorily detained by the veterinary services.

opportunities which enable them to secure better returns for their productive efforts.

Even if such investment were the best way of dealing with the specific problems investigated by the mission, it would not follow that from the point of view of the Nigerian economy as a whole this use of scarce resources would be the most advantageous possible.[1] The productivity of the necessary capital may well be greater elsewhere; there is at least a presumption that this is so, because private firms and traders participating in the cattle trade and with access to funds have not yet thought fit to embark on the installation of expensive and specialized equipment even on a tentative and experimental basis. This suggests caution in the implementation of proposals for substantial official capital investment and the granting of powers to direct producers in the disposal of their output.

6. PROPOSALS FOR ELIMINATION OF ABUSES IN MARKETING

The alleged prevalence of abuses practised chiefly by middlemen has often served as a justification for measures of marketing reform. Reforms have been urged on the grounds that official control or supervision over transactions is required to protect producers against the use of false weights and measures and other similar malpractices which are said to deprive them of part of the commercial value of their produce. This type of argument has been invoked in support of such proposals as the establishment of zonal monopolies, centralized scheduled markets, and compulsory official grading and inspection. Whilst a high level of morality in commercial affairs is obviously desirable on general grounds, it seems nevertheless questionable whether this cause is best served by official supervision and compulsory standardization, especially in backward areas.

In West Africa there is generally much actual or potential competition among the intermediaries who deal directly with producers. Where there is competition among middlemen their gross profit margins and their earnings are closely determined by the level of rewards obtainable in small-scale trading and in similar occupations. Earnings, whether from fair trading or improper practices, could not remain for long above this level; competition among the existing traders or from new entrants would reduce margins. Competition forces buyers to pass on the equivalent of illicit gains to the producer; for example, if the weights used are debased, under competitive conditions buyers would be forced to offer correspondingly higher prices per debased unit in their search

---

[1] This limitation is probably inevitable in recommendations which are directed solely at problems in particular sections of an economy.

for business.[1] From the producer's point of view the result is the same as if he had received payment for full weight at a lower price per unit.

In general it does not matter much whether producers themselves are familiar with or ignorant of standard weights and measures. The individual producer is concerned with sales of specific lots of produce, and he will endeavour to obtain price offers for such lots from itinerant traders and/or from traders at one or more trading centres. Even though ignorant of weights the producer is able to judge which is the most favourable offer.

The conclusion is not substantially affected in circumstances in which the producer does not receive several offers simultaneously for the same lot of produce; his knowledge of his trading opportunities is widened by his contact with different traders and the treatment and terms offered by each. The ability to make such comparisons and the competition of buyers tend to ensure that producers receive competitive prices for their produce irrespective of apparent abuses. The ultimate incidence of the alleged abuses tends to be neither on the producers nor on the ultimate buyers of the produce; paradoxically, the illicit gains to middlemen from the use of false weights (for example) are more apparent than real.

On the other hand, the producer is liable to exploitation where he has no choice of buyers and is forced to deal with a sole buyer or a concerted group of buyers, whose monopoly position is protected from competition by obstacles to new entry.[2] Here again the question of abuses is largely irrelevant; for by one means or another the monopolist will continue to pay an effective price just sufficient to elicit the supply he desires. It is of little consequence whether this effective price is expressed in terms of standard or of debased weights.

Measures to eliminate specific abuses are likely to be costly and may themselves contain strong possibilities of abuse to the detriment of producers. Most of them postulate the establishment and maintenance of expensive control, supervisory and inspecting staff. The administrative costs can be reduced by requiring all transactions to take place at a limited number of centres at which the necessary supervisory services are provided. But here the costs are merely transferred to the producer or the smaller trader who has to travel longer distances to market. Moreover, the inspecting staff generally consists of large numbers of petty officials with extensive powers over the activities of traders and

[1] A trader 'inventing' a new type of abuse may secure temporary abnormal gains until his competitors and/or customers become familiar with the new practice. This is obviously unlikely to be significant in an activity such as small-scale trading which is technically simple and into which entry is easy.

[2] If there is only one buyer, but new entry is easy, the buyer would have to pay a price of approximately the same level as would prevail if more buyers were actually operating.

producers. They are therefore in the position to abuse their powers for their own profit. Such abuses, however, differ greatly from abuses in competitive markets in that their fruits will not be competed away in favour of producers. And the backwardness of the producers tends to deprive them of the opportunity of obtaining redress from higher authority.[1]

Even in the absence of such measures (whether on account of costs, administrative difficulty or for other reasons) the producer is still protected if there is competition among buyers. But these measures alone are of little value in the absence of competition, without the prescription of minimum prices and the institution of controls to ensure that payment of these prices is not avoided by various sharp practices. This seems to be the only case where the prescription and enforcement of terms and conditions of sale may serve to protect producers. Even in such circumstances the costs of establishing, maintaining and enforcing these arrangements (including the costs falling on the producers and traders) must be weighed against the value of the protection to the producer. In particular, it may be more economical and effective to secure this result by facilitating new entry and competition, and by the spreading of market information by such methods as the local notification of prices ruling in the principal markets.[2]

7. UNIFORM PRICE SYSTEMS

In recent years there has been a tendency in West Africa to introduce systems of uniform prices to be paid to producers irrespective of their distance from the ports, and this tendency has increased since the establishment of statutory marketing. Although not strictly a measure for marketing reform, this practice is frequently advocated as an improvement in the transport and distribution of export produce. Its implications and results may usefully be considered in this context.

In the purchase of cocoa in the Gold Coast a uniform price payable at all railway stations was introduced in 1942. In Nigeria the railway has for years past charged uniform freight rates for groundnuts throughout almost the entire northern area. The statutory minimum prices payable at outlying road stations are heavily subsidized by the Groundnut

---

[1] Experience in the operation of compulsory inspection and grading of Nigerian export produce is discussed in the following chapter.

[2] Greater uniformity in price quotations will tend to make price comparisons easier and expose the profitability of particular markets, thus facilitating new entry. This is not likely to be a major advantage of compulsory standardization of the terms of transactions in backward areas. On the other hand, greater standardization of the terms of transactions tends to facilitate the establishment and maintenance of agreements among buyers.

Marketing Board. In 1950 the Northern Regional Administration advanced proposals for a uniform producer price for groundnuts at both rail and road stations throughout practically all northern Nigeria. In the purchase of cotton uniform minimum prices are payable throughout the northern area. In southern Nigeria there has in recent years been increasing pressure for a uniform producer price for cocoa irrespective of distance from the ports.

Uniform price systems are attractive because superficially they appear to treat producers equally and equitably. Advocates of such systems claim that it is unfair that certain producers should receive lower prices merely because they happen to be farther away from the ports, and they suggest that the 'burden of transportation' should be borne equally by all producers, near or far. It is also contended that uniform prices encourage production by benefiting marginal producers. Moreover, uniform price systems sometimes appear to be preferable on administrative grounds—there are fewer prices to worry about. However, the arguments are not convincing.

Production in distant areas requires more transport (i.e. the use of additional scarce resources) to move the crops to the ports or to the markets; it does not seem inequitable, and it certainly promotes the husbanding of scarce resources, to require that the additional costs should be borne by the producers who cause the additional resources to be used and who benefit directly from their use.

The suggestion that uniform prices stimulate marginal production overlooks the distinction between intensive and extensive margins. Producers near the ports or centres of communication can expand their output of the crops by more intensive effort, by more costly methods of production, or by diversion of effort and resources from other productive activities. Uniform price systems reduce the returns to nearby producers (or prevent the returns from being raised), and so discourage these types of marginal adjustment in response to market conditions. Such systems may encourage the extension of cultivation in distant areas, but only by making expansion of cultivation less attractive in more favourably placed regions. Moreover, of course, the increased transport costs represent an additional reduction of incomes to producers as a whole.

The enthusiasm for uniform price systems may be less pronounced if it is realized that they result in the use of greater amounts of scarce resources to yield a given total output of the crop, and that they bring about a penalization of some producers for the benefit of others. These considerations are relevant in West Africa, which is poor in capital equipment, especially in transport, and where producers, even those favourably placed near the main markets, are generally poor. If it is intended to develop outlying areas, this can be done much more efficiently by direct subsidy or grant rather than covertly and wastefully.

The administrative convenience of uniform prices is also more apparent than real. If the transportation of the crop to the ports is undertaken in the first instance by buyers, they naturally would have to be reimbursed for transport charges incurred. The marketing authority would therefore have to deal with countless claims, and would have to institute burdensome systems of checking, filing and repayment.[1] These costs of administration are additional to the extra demands on transport resulting from uniform price systems. In the final analysis these costs amount to a reduction in the incomes of producers as a whole.[2]

There has been a tendency on the part of the authorities to suggest that the establishment in some instances of uniform price systems, in conjunction with the introduction of marketing boards, has resulted in the abolition of certain costs which previously had to be borne by the producers. This is claimed, for example, in the first Annual Report of the Gold Coast Marketing Board:

> Transport is paid from all railway stations and from Senchi Ferry; thus increases in this respect do not affect the farmer. Export duty, handling charges, lighterage and insurance are similarly undertaken and variations in these charges are unknown. Costs of several of the above items have been increased during the year, e.g. export duty and railway freight, handling charges, bags and finance. Under the old commercial method of purchasing for export the costs of a number of these items were added together and the total deducted from the f.o.b. price. Thus, in the event of the cost of such items being increased, a corresponding reduction would be made in the price per load paid to producers.[3]

This passage is obviously misleading in suggesting that these costs no longer affect the farmer or indeed are no longer incurred. They are incurred much as before, though they may be obscured by the method of payment and/or by the surpluses of the boards. Statements such as that just quoted can serve only to retard further the slow progress of economic education in West Africa.[4]

---

[1] These difficulties are already evident in the administration of the subsidy payments in groundnut buying intended to maintain the prices at certain outlying stations at uneconomic levels.

[2] The costs of dealing with buyers' claims can be avoided if the authority takes over the purchases at these buying points, but this alternative is likely to be even more costly than the one it can theoretically replace.

[3] *Annual Report of the Gold Coast Cocoa Marketing Board for 1947–8*, p. 5.

[4] Indeed, real costs are likely to be higher than before, since the surpluses of the boards encourage the institution of transport subsidies, flat-rate price systems and similar devices.

CHAPTER 26

THE ECONOMICS OF MARKETING REFORM:
MEASURES AND PROPOSALS (II)

For some years past the establishment of systems of produce grading and the imposition of minimum standards have been widely regarded as being essential for the improvement of marketing methods for colonial produce. In recent years these ideas have gained acceptance in West Africa.

1. ESTABLISHMENT AND GROWTH OF COMPULSORY PRODUCE INSPECTION IN NIGERIA

In West Africa there is an extensive system of compulsory inspection, and in certain cases compulsory grading, of export produce. The system is prominent in Nigeria, where it covers almost the whole range of export produce, and where those administering the system have wide powers of licensing, search and inspection. The discussion here will be confined to Nigeria, although the analysis would apply to similar but less advanced systems elsewhere. In Nigeria all exports except minerals, hides and skins, timber and bananas are subject to compulsory official inspection; exports of cocoa and palm oil are also subject to compulsory grading. In essence the system amounts to the prescription of minimum export standards; only produce inspected and rated above the minimum may be exported or bought for export. Compulsory grading is superimposed on the minimum standards and establishes grade differentials according to certain standards officially laid down; payments to producers are linked with these grades.

The Nigerian produce inspection arrangements were started in the 1920's; they were extended in scope during the wartime control of the West African Produce Control Board, and have since then been further strengthened by the operations of the marketing boards. In the purchase of all commodities controlled by the boards, members of the produce inspection staff check the quality of the produce and the standard weight at the point of purchase by the licensed buying agents or those acting on their behalf. The weight is checked again by check-weighing a substantial sample at the port of shipment. There is in addition compulsory inspection to check the exportable quality of some produce not controlled by the marketing boards, notably rubber, chillies and ginger.

Until 1948 produce inspection was the task of the Department of Agriculture. It was then taken over by the Department of Marketing and Exports. In 1951 a separate Produce Inspection Service was established under the control of a statutory Produce Inspection Board. The inspecting staff numbers several hundred.

Wide extensions of the scope and functions of the already extensive official produce inspection are envisaged under the present system. Powers granted to the Produce Inspection Board and to members of the Produce Inspection Service include the prescription and licensing of places and premises where sales may take place and the licensing of individual sellers and buyers; inspection and grading of produce and the prohibition of export of uninspected or substandard produce; the prescription of the minimum requirements for storage facilities and the licensing and registration of such facilities and buildings; prescription of fees payable for inspection and grading services; prescription of markets and inspection stations; and prescription of containers to be used for export produce. There is also a provision granting extensive general powers of licensing to members of the Produce Inspection Service, but it is impossible to ascertain from the ordinance who is to be licensed and for what purposes.[1]

To enforce these powers, members of the inspection services (including junior examiners) have powers of entry, search and seizure without individual warrants; they also have the power to direct persons to convey produce to a designated place for examination, and to require any person to furnish them with any information they deem necessary. It is specifically provided that produce already examined may be re-examined at the discretion of the examiner, and apparently this is possible as often as the examiner desires. Aggrieved persons may appeal against the decisions of the examiner to the Director of Marketing and Exports, and from the Director to the Produce Inspection Board, of which he is the Chairman.

2. SOME RESULTS OF THE POWERS OF THE INSPECTORATE IN NIGERIA

These powers are extensive and detailed even by European standards. In West Africa they put the smaller local traders and the employees of the smaller and politically less influential licensed buying agents at the mercy of the African produce inspector or examiner. In many parts of Nigeria petty tyranny and corruption in the operation of produce inspection were widespread and oppressive even before the recent

---

[1] The width and scope of the powers can only be appreciated by a study of the Produce Inspection Ordinance, No 24 of 1950. Lengthy quotations would be required to reproduce its flavour or to illustrate the great powers it confers on all members of the Produce Inspection Service.

extension of the powers of the inspectorate. On extended visits to Nigeria in 1949 and 1950 it was found that in many places there was a recognized scale of (illicit) fees payable to examiners to have the produce inspected and passed. Those who refused to pay were made to wait for such long periods that their produce deteriorated and fell below standard;[1] or they were forced to sell their produce uninspected to another intermediary at below its commercial value; or they were liable to have their produce down-graded by the examiners. Wherever possible the traders or clerks tried to placate the examiners by paying the recognized bribes; and, indeed, they were apt to complain only when the bribes exacted exceeded the level regarded as reasonable. It was universally recognized that complaints to officials would be useless as formal proof would be difficult to secure. Moreover, a successful denunciation of one examiner followed by his conviction would be noted by his successor, possibly to the serious disadvantage of the protestant.[2]

It would seem that only very compelling reasons would justify such drastic powers in conditions in which they are so widely abused. Analysis fails to reveal any such reasons. The underlying justification for the system of compulsory produce inspection is in fact not at all clear.

3. THE ARGUMENTS IN SUPPORT OF COMPULSORY PRODUCE INSPECTION

Before the war export produce which was subject to compulsory inspection was shipped by firms of standing (and the same is true of shippers of chillies, rubber and ginger[3] today). They could be expected

---

[1] A producer or buyer can never compel an examiner to inspect his produce; the examiner can always state that he is engaged elsewhere.

[2] These products are subject to compulsory inspection. The other products for which minimum exportable standards are prescribed are handled by the marketing boards.

[3] It may be asked how the information in this paragraph has been obtained, since formal proof is admittedly difficult. It was a common subject of discussion throughout southern Nigeria amongst traders, their commission buyers and clerks. In many places several individuals interrogated gave identical figures as the scale of bribes current in the area. The prevalence of the practice was admitted as a matter of course by a prominent European official of the Department of Marketing and Exports who thought that the great majority of the African examiners abused their position. Finally, the following specific piece of evidence is informative. In a Nigerian town a European trader was in 1950 buying rubber, securing larger quantities than did the well-known large firms active in the area. He explained that he actually paid less than these firms, but, unlike his competitors, he was prepared to buy uninspected rubber at well below the prevailing price for inspected rubber. He then had the rubber inspected; and although part of his purchases were rejected, on balance he obtained his exportable supplies at a very reasonable price. He said that he gained

to ship according to the grades and requirements of the world produce markets. Where a premium was obtainable for better quality they were quite ready to pay a correspondingly higher price in Nigeria for the better grade of produce, or for the material from which it could be secured through suitable blending. If they were prepared to purchase inferior quality produce as well this was because the inferior grade was readily saleable abroad.

When compulsory inspection and minimum standards were introduced it was argued that competition among the merchant firms induced their executives to accept all produce offered to them irrespective of quality, and that this process resulted in a constant undermining of the quality of Nigerian export produce appearing on world markets. The reasoning is not easy to follow, since it would appear that intense competition forces merchants to adjust the prices they pay for different qualities more precisely in accordance with market valuations. They will buy only if they can sell abroad; and the more intense the competition and the finer the margins on which they work, the more closely the shippers will have to adjust their buying prices to market requirements. It is thus difficult to accept the view that intense competition would lead to a constant deterioration in quality in the absence of compulsory produce inspection; it will, indeed, lead to increasing vigilance in seeking out supplies acceptable in world markets, and this would obviously be to the advantage of producers.

Moreover, it was not correct to argue that the system was required to protect overseas buyers against dishonest or irresponsible shippers. The shippers were firms of substance almost always well known to the buyers; and for a shipment defective in quality or under weight an adjustment would be made, while disagreement was referred to arbitration in accordance with the standard practice in produce markets. The inclusion (accidentally or otherwise) of produce inferior to that specified in the contract would be rectified between the parties, and if persistently practised might have injured the goodwill of the particular shipper. But it could not have damaged the reputation of Nigerian produce as such.

Overseas buyers often complained about the quality of Nigerian export produce, but the complaints were rarely coupled with any suggestion of differential payments for different grades. Frequently they amounted to no more than the suggestion that a better quality of product would be highly acceptable at the same price.

this advantage because he was a European and was thus not liable to the same degree of extortion by the produce examiners as were African traders. Many of the latter were thus anxious to sell to him, or to others willing to buy uninspected rubber, in preference to facing the expense and uncertainty of compulsory inspection.

4. THE VOLUNTARY TIMBER INSPECTION SCHEME
IN NIGERIA

In those export trades in which many of the shippers are small firms which are not well known nor represented abroad, difficulties arise when supplies on arrival are found to be below contract specification in quantity or in quality. As consignments are normally shipped under a letter of credit, the importer has difficulty in obtaining redress because the exporter has by then received most of the contract price. Moreover, as the exporter is not represented abroad disputes cannot be referred to arbitration. In these circumstances the additional risks of the importer may seriously retard the development of the export trade. In such cases, however, it is in the interests of both importers and exporters to devise methods to provide safeguards to traders. They are thus likely to support firms of cargo supervisors who can inspect consignments before they are accepted. Where the establishment of such agencies is difficult or delayed, a voluntary inspection scheme by the government may provide the necessary service.

The problem and the two types of solution are illustrated by recent developments in the Nigerian export trade in logs. In recent years this has been the only branch of the export trade in which African shippers have been prominent. With the influx of many new shippers after the war there was a considerable increase in consignments of logs which on arrival were seriously below specified weight or quality, and overseas importers were increasingly reluctant to place contracts with the smaller exporters. Eventually one of the smaller merchant firms undertook to act as cargo superintendents. The services it provided were not regarded as sufficiently extensive, and in 1949 the Nigerian authorities devised a simple and practical scheme which proved an immediate success. It provides for voluntary inspection; the exporter on application can have his consignment inspected during the loading of the timber on the ship;[1] an official certificate of quality and quantity is issued, which is presented by the exporter to the bank with which the letter of credit is arranged. The actual amount paid out to the shipper under the credit depends on the contents of the certificate, a procedure which effectively safeguards the overseas importer against loss. The scheme has been widely publicized in the principal overseas markets for Nigerian timber, and importers now generally insist on this inspection certificate before arranging a letter of credit.

[1] Inspection at this stage is necessary since timber does not cross a wharf but is either rafted alongside the ship or shipped from lighters. Inspection must thus take place in a form which prevents substitution between the time of inspection and the time of shipment.

The scheme is voluntary and serves to protect the interests of the trade without investing the inspectors with compulsory powers and without introducing arbitrary grading or quality standards. Yet it fulfils all the essential requirements, since unless the overseas importer neglects to take advantage of this simple facility he is effectively safeguarded against loss and need have no reluctance in placing an order with a shipper unknown to him.

5. THE FUNCTIONS OF PRODUCE INSPECTION UNDER THE MARKETING BOARDS

In the purchase of produce by licensed buying agents on behalf of the marketing boards produce inspection has important functions additional to the checking of minimum standards. The inspection service relieves the boards of the necessity of examining the produce at the point at which they take it over from the buying agents. (The fact that the boards check-weigh and check-test consignments at ports merely suggests that they do not regard the inspection service as fully reliable.) The government inspection service performs for the boards what commercial buyers elsewhere perform for themselves, or pay others to undertake on their behalf.

Even here the serious adverse effects of up-country inspection suggest that thought should be given to possible simplification or modification of the present procedure. In the majority of instances it is possible to identify separate consignments of produce bought by the different licensed buying agents up to the point of bulking, or even up to the point of ultimate discharge abroad. In such cases licensed buying agents responsible for faulty purchases can be identified and penalized if this is thought necessary. There may be certain difficulties in assessing the responsibility of buying agents for defective parcels, but such difficulties (which are mainly in the nature of administrative inconvenience) must be weighed against the advantages of the removal of the burden of the present system on African traders and producers.

6. ECONOMIC LOSS THROUGH THE IMPOSITION OF ARBITRARY MINIMUM STANDARDS FOR EXPORT PRODUCE

The minimum exportable quality prescribed under the system of compulsory inspection and grading is always higher than the lowest qualities that are acceptable on the world markets. The prohibition of the export of inferior but commercially marketable qualities of produce means an unamibiguous loss to the producers and to the economy as a whole. This proposition is not always appreciated, and it is often argued that all production or export ought to be confined to high grade and quality, and that, as a corollary, the absence of lower grades among shipments is wholly beneficial. It can readily be shown that this argument is misconceived. If it were correct it should be in the interests of the motor-car industry and of the British economy to restrict the output of the industry to Rolls Royces or similar high grades of motor-cars. Inferior products would disappear and the quality of output and exports would be greatly raised. Yet nobody would argue that technically inferior but cheaper cars should not be exported when there is a very large and profitable demand for them in world markets. Similarly, there is no case for refusing to allow the export of inferior grades of cocoa or other produce for which there is a demand at a lower price, simply because they do not conform to certain prescribed technical standards.

It is generally forgotten that the ban on the export of so-called sub-standard produce (which is produced but cannot be exported because of the rigid standards imposed by authority) results in a loss to the producers and to the economy, and further that time and resources expended on raising the quality of sub-standard produce to the exportable level are likely to be more costly than the resulting increases in true commercial value and sales proceeds. In fact, the stress on minimum standards, and the obvious pride in the improvement of quality, represent an instance of the familiar confusion of technical and economic efficiency. Thus the satisfaction of the Nigeria Cocoa Marketing Board is misplaced when it claims that it no longer buys and exports cocoa of grades 3 and 4; or when it prevented the shipment of deteriorated stocks of cocoa for which there was a ready demand; or when it notes that its policies have caused a scarcity of grade 3 cocoa in the world's markets;[1] or when it emphasizes the large increase in the proportion of grade 1 cocoa in total shipments; or when it opposes the establishment of a cocoa butter factory in Nigeria on the grounds that it would purchase inferior grades of cocoa, the production of which it considers undesirable. The

---

[1] A monopolist may refuse to deal in lower grade produce as a device for restricting supplies reaching the market. This does not appear to have been the motive of the boards in their refusal to allow the export of certain low grades of produce. Yet this is a distinct possibility which must be borne in mind, particularly in considering the policies of a statutory organization with monopoly powers of purchase and sale. This inherently restrictive device is the more insidious because it can be spuriously argued that the raising of standards is in the interests of the consumers.

The Nigerian Livestock Mission expressed disapproval of the sale of certain kinds of offal, such as guts, hides and lungs, which in some western countries are not usually regarded as edible. The sale of these foods in West Africa is deplored as being 'a very unsatisfactory position from the consumer point of view' (*Report of the Nigerian Livestock Mission*, p. 109). These remarks ignore the obvious fact that consumers willingly buy these products, and that their withdrawal from sale would merely force consumers to consume less meat. The proposed livestock monopoly could use this device to increase its revenues by restricting total supplies.

loss to producers is particularly obvious because their competitors else-where are not penalized in this way; they can supply the market for the so-called inferior grades (including the supply of cocoa beans for the manufacture of cocoa butter) from which Nigerian producers are arbitrarily barred. The extent of the loss cannot be assessed, since it is impossible to measure the volume of frustrated production or export resulting from the imposition of arbitrary minimum standards, or to measure the additional labour expended in efforts to raise quality to the minimum standards. Naturally, farmers refrain from producing or harvesting or processing sub-standard produce for which there is no market because of the regulations. However, the ban on the export of deteriorated but marketable stocks, the refusal to buy cocoa of grades 3 and 4, and the opposition to the manufacture of cocoa butter suggest that appreciable quantities of cocoa and appreciable sums of money were involved.

Recent experience in the marketing of Nigerian chillies provides an example of the wasteful results of arbitrary quality standards. One of the smaller shippers was prevented from exporting a consignment which, according to the produce inspector, was below minimum exportable quality. After protracted argument extending over several months he was allowed to ship the chillies, which were readily accepted by the consignee in spite of the deterioration caused by the delay.[1] In Nigeria the Department of Co-operation has also been affected by this procedure. On the recommendation of a commercial firm the department insisted on very high standards for the chillies produced by certain co-operative marketing societies on the understanding that the particular firm would export the product. However, the chillies did not reach these exacting standards. Fortunately the standard was relaxed, and another shipper readily accepted them at the *same* price and was able to dispose of them successfully overseas.

The large firms do not seem to have opposed compulsory produce inspection and grading and on occasions have even supported it. There seem to be several reasons for this *prima facie* unexpected attitude. Possibly the firms may not have appreciated fully the implications of the system. Moreover, though the firms are at a disadvantage in that the system has certain adverse effects on total supplies of produce, most of the costs, particularly the more obvious costs, are borne by the producers and the small-scale buyers. There are even certain advantages in the system to the large firms. The responsibilities and the work of the local executives are to some extent diminished and administration and control

---

[1] It is understood that this consignment, which was shipped to the United Kingdom, was subsequently re-exported to the United States (for dollars) after a further delay, and was still found to be satisfactory.

facilitated; these are important considerations in view of the size and complexity of the large firms, and the problem of efficient control by overseas head offices. The system tends also to work to the detriment of the smaller (but reputable) produce buyers and shippers in whose operations the ability to take quick advantage of special market opportunities has always been important. Thus the absence of opposition by the large firms to compulsory inspection and grading is not altogether surprising, but this is no evidence that the system does not operate in the manner analysed here.

7. SOME RESULTS OF COMPULSORY GRADING

The Nigeria Cocoa Marketing Board and the Nigeria Oil Palm Produce Marketing Board prescribe widely different producer prices for the different grades of cocoa and palm oil they purchase. In cocoa the grade depends on the maximum permitted percentage of insufficiently fermented beans in a sample; in palm oil it depends on the percentage of free fatty acid in the oil. In both cases the price differentials paid bear little relation to the price differentials on different grades in world markets and in the sales proceeds.

For cocoa the world market does not generally distinguish between grades 1 and 2; very slight premia of the order of £1 a ton occasionally emerge, whereas the Board's buying prices for the two grades have in recent years differed by £5 a ton. In the export of palm oil the Oil Palm Produce Marketing Board distinguishes between five grades in its producer prices. Each grade covers a range of degrees of free fatty acid content. Thus grade 1 includes oil with free fatty acid content from 0 to 9%, and grade 2 from 9 to 18%, and so on by steps of 9%. There are substantial differences in the buying prices for different grades far in excess of differences ruling in markets or stipulated in the contract of the Board with the Ministry of Food. Within each grade, however, no allowance is made for varying degrees of free fatty acid content, while in market contracts (as well as in the contracts between the Ministry of Food and other suppliers) the price paid makes allowance for small differences (of 1%) in free fatty acid content.[1]

The practice of prescribing grades and price differentials which do not conform with commercial values reinforces some of the adverse effects of the imposition of arbitrary minimum standards for exports. It induces additional expenditures of effort and resources which would not have been necessary if only commercial differences were paid, and

[1] Compulsory grading is also in force for Nigerian cotton. The price differentials paid by the Cotton Marketing Board do not seem to be so widely divorced from commercial values as those paid for cocoa and palm oil. No separate issues of principle are raised by this operation of compulsory grading.

the improvement in quality, which is not recognized by buyers, is therefore apparent rather than real. This means that some producers incur expenditures in raising quality which are in excess of the additional income received by the boards from selling higher grades of produce. If the boards are considered as the collective interests of producers, the results are patently uneconomic; if, however, the boards are considered by others or by their executives as something apart from the producers, then this policy might still be favoured, since the extra exertions and expenditures of the producers would not affect the boards, whereas the higher receipts would obviously raise their proceeds and surpluses.

It is conceivable that arbitrary wide-grade differentials may result in some loss of production, somewhat analogous to the loss brought about by arbitrary minimum exportable standards. Some producers may find that the price paid for the lowest grade is not sufficient to cover its cost of production, and that the extra costs of qualifying for the higher grades (and therefore better prices) are beyond their reach for technical or economic reasons. These discriminate against producers of the lower grades, on the sales of which the boards secure wider surplus margins. There is thus an arbitrary redistribution of income among different classes of producers.

8. SOME ARGUMENTS IN FAVOUR OF COMPULSORY MINIMUM STANDARDS AND OF ARBITRARY PREMIUM PAYMENTS

Some arguments, said to be specially relevant to West African conditions, are often advanced in support of the policy of compulsory minimum standards and of the payment of arbitrary premia for superior quality.

It is often argued that in the long run the improvement in the quality of West African produce will strengthen the position of these territories in adverse market conditions. The contention is that without an improvement in quality West African produce will lose its markets in slump conditions. In so far as the standards imposed are not in accordance with the assessments of the consumers as reflected in market price differentials, the concept of 'improvement of quality' is meaningless from the commercial point of view, which alone governs the selling prospects of the produce. Thus the argument is invalid. Improvement in quality is irrelevant if not in accordance with market assessment.

No West African cocoa or palm produce was left unsold even in the trough of the depression. Prices fell heavily for these products generally, with the result that in outlying areas some producers stopped marketing, but this fall in prices affected all grades and sources of supply.

Over the last few decades the export of palm oil from West Africa has been approximately stationary, while exports of plantation palm oil from Sumatra, Malaya and the Belgian Congo increased rapidly. There has also been a substantial increase in the exports of palm kernels from West Africa. These data are sometimes instanced in support of the argument that the production of West African palm oil has stagnated because, as a result of its low quality, Nigerian palm oil was being squeezed out of the world market; and that wide grade differentials in the purchase of palm oil would serve to improve quality and thus re-establish the position of West African palm oil in world markets which, in turn, would result in increased production.

These views and arguments reflect several misconceptions. First, they confuse production and export. Although exports have been stationary, there has been a rapid increase in internal consumption of palm oil over the last few decades, and a marked increase in *production*. Secondly, there is no evidence that overseas buyers were unwilling to purchase West African palm oil at the prices ruling in the 1930's which reflected quality differences as assessed by the market, chiefly on the basis of free fatty acid content. For reasons already stated grade differentials based on arbitrary standards and not related to market valuation can only harm the market prospects and the level of production of West African oil.

It is also argued sometimes that compulsory grading protects the producer against underpayment by middlemen. A little reflection will show that when buying is competitive this protection is unnecessary, while in the absence of competition compulsory grading will not assist the producer.

9. SUMMARY OF THE CONSEQUENCES OF COMPULSORY MINIMUM STANDARDS AND OF GRADING DIVORCED FROM COMMERCIAL VALUES

The analysis of the preceding sections suggests that compulsory produce inspection, the enforcement of minimum standards in the export trades and the establishment of wide grade differentials in producer prices entail serious disadvantages. These include widespread oppression and extortion by junior members of the produce inspection service through their very extensive, and in practice unchallengeable, powers over African traders and indirectly over producers; loss of production and export of readily marketable produce with detrimental effects on the producers and on the economy as a whole; and uneconomic stimulation of expenditure and effort on largely illusory improvement of quality. Moreover, the system requires for its administration a large staff of European and African personnel. All these disadvantages are likely to be substantially enhanced with the extension of the scope and powers of the Produce Inspection Service in Nigeria under the newly established statutory Produce Inspection Board.

10. UNDERLYING SIMILARITY OF THE DIFFERENT TYPES OF MARKETING REFORM REVIEWED

A conclusion of general interest emerges from the discussion and analysis in this chapter and Chapter 25. The various proposals and measures for the reform of marketing here reviewed are very different. Nevertheless, they have an important result in common, and they are indeed designed to bring about this result in different ways. They would all limit the range of alternatives open to producers and their customers. It is not surprising that measures which restrict the producers' range of choice in fact are not likely to improve their economic position.[1] A better way of raising producer incomes would seem to be a widening of the range of alternatives open to producers; this has the major additional advantage that gains to the producers are not achieved at the expense of the community. Government action promoting this aim would include removal of barriers to the entry and movement of traders and supplies, measures to prevent restrictive activities of traders, improvement in the means of communication used by producers and traders, and the general stimulation of competition.

Several of the actual or proposed measures reviewed in these chapters serve not only to reduce the number of alternatives open to the population, but also specifically to increase its dependence on particular traders or groups of traders, especially on purchasers of their produce. This applies to such measures as the compulsory reduction in the number of traders, to zonal monopolies and to the system of scheduled markets.[2] This greater dependence is likely to increase the inclination of the population to ascribe adverse market changes to the malice of the traders, and this in turn conduces to political tension.

The arguments in favour of several of the measures of reform discussed in this part imply that producers or consumers are unable to make sensible choices between different alternatives; and that, left to themselves, many of them are likely to follow courses of action which would adversely affect their own interests to a significant extent. This implied lack of discrimination on the part of colonial producers and consumers in matters which affect their incomes directly is difficult to reconcile with other assessments, frequently held by the same observers or officials, of the abilities of these people to decide upon difficult and remote political issues.

---

[1] Producer-controlled selling monopolies may improve the position of producers by exploiting their monopoly situation. This type of 'market reform' is obviously directly at the expense of consumers.

[2] Compulsory produce inspection also increases the dependence of sellers, but primarily on the inspectors and examiners rather than on the buyers.

PART 7

INTERNAL TRADE

CHAPTER 27

PRINCIPAL FEATURES OF INTERNAL TRADE

I. SCOPE OF THIS CHAPTER

The information available on the important topic of internal trade is of uneven quality and some of it is fragmentary. There are various reasons for this comparative paucity of information. Internal trade does not pass international boundaries at which its composition and volume are recorded for customs purposes, and it is not centred on a few ports where trade statistics could be recorded for purposes other than customs control. Moreover, this trade represents a section of the economy which has no direct contact with European traders or Western methods. Its organization is often closely connected with local customs and with the family and tribal system; this makes for additional difficulties in the collection of information. Lastly, unlike external trade, it has not, until recently, presented serious economic and political problems to administrators, and they have not been particularly concerned with it.

Internal trade plays a large part in the West African economies. The bulk of the population depend upon supplies of locally produced food which is a main item in urban budgets. The functioning of internal trade greatly affects the level of food production. Farmers will not produce for sale unless a surplus output is profitable. The state of communications, the flow of internal trade and the enterprise of traders are the principal influences affecting marketability of local produce. If internal trade is restricted by communications or by economic or institutional obstacles to the flow of commodities, consumers have to pay higher prices which are not reflected in any higher return to the farmer and therefore do not act as an incentive to expand supplies. Internal trade is thus a topic which needs to be considered, but the information available does not justify detailed treatment. This chapter, therefore, indicates the principal features of internal trade in West Africa and illustrates these with examples drawn from certain branches of the trade selected in accordance with their importance and/or the availability of reliable information.

2. QUANTITATIVE IMPORTANCE OF INTERNAL TRADE

There is a large internal trade in many important products in West Africa, especially in Nigeria, and much scattered information to show its importance.

There is the presence of a large urban population. Since approximately 30 % of the population of Nigeria lives in towns with 5000 or more inhabitants, it is reasonable to infer that there is a substantial internal trade in foodstuffs. Although the urban population includes many farmers and cultivators, it is so large that it could not be sustained without the importation of the surpluses of food produced in other centres or regions. Again, both in Nigeria and in the Gold Coast there are many communities of northern origin in the south and communities of southerners in the north. Most of these migrant communities have retained their preference for the foodstuffs of their home districts, and large quantities of these are brought to them over long distances by rail, road and river transport. Moreover, the wide range of foodstuffs, partly from neighbouring areas and partly from more distant sources, displayed in the food markets of most fair-sized towns, confirms the existence of a large internal trade.

Both in Nigeria and in the Gold Coast scattered information is available in the form of agricultural surveys which suggest that farmers sell appreciable portions of their output of local produce, and also that farmers themselves often buy significant quantities of locally grown produce.

Lastly, there is some quantitative information on one or two substantial branches of internal trade of which the information relating to the trade in kola nuts is briefly summarized in § 3 below.

Railway returns suggest that internal trade in foodstuffs is not only extensive but is also growing rapidly. The Annual Reports of the Nigerian Railway show freight traffic under various clauses. One of these is termed Agricultural Products and refers almost exclusively to local foodstuffs, since export produce is classified separately. In 1938–9 this traffic totalled 50,000 tons, whereas in 1948–9 it exceeded 100,000 tons. As lorry traffic and petrol consumption had increased between the two years, the increase cannot be attributed to diversion from road to rail transport.

The bulk of internal trade is in local foodstuffs, including kola nuts. In Nigeria there is also a substantial trade in locally grown tobacco, cotton and palm wine as well as in the products of simple handicrafts, especially woven cloth, leather products and earthenware. Some imported articles are converted locally into other products which are sold within the territories. For instance, cigarette and kerosene tins and salt and flour bags are converted into simple oil lamps and tunics.

3. THE KOLA TRADE

In 1950 expenditure on kola nuts in Nigeria certainly exceeded £5 m. at retail prices, and may have been much higher.[1] There is sufficient reliable information to show both the extent and rapid growth of the trade.

The chewing of kola is widespread in Nigeria and in many areas almost universal. It gratifies a habit and acts as a stimulant; its role in these respects may be likened to the combined functions of a cigarette, a cup of coffee and a piece of chewing gum. The kola nut is also of considerable nutritive value, and can sustain life for some time even if no other foods are eaten; it thus serves as a slab of chocolate or a vitamin tablet, and for this reason it is widely used on caravan routes and is consumed in large quantities over the vast areas of French West Africa. Throughout Nigeria it is also used as a gift on family, social and cere- monial occasions. Emirs, chiefs and headmen are presented with kola nuts on anniversaries and other festive occasions; presents of nuts are exchanged on Moslem festivals; and Hausa women are often presented with kola nuts on the birth of a child. The nuts also serve as a cosmetic, since the tint produced on the lips and teeth by chewing red kola nuts is sometimes esteemed by the Hausa. In parts of Nigeria they are used as a dye stabilizer, the liquid expressed from crushed nuts is mixed with certain dyes and is then diluted with water; in some uses the resulting solution acts as an effective mordant.

The fruit is grown on small plantations of one or two acres each. Production is confined to the south, most of the acreage being in the Western Provinces and in the vicinity of Lagos. There is some produc- tion in the east, which appears to be increasing. Most of the consump- tion is in the Hausa areas of northern Nigeria and the neighbouring French territories and Kano is the centre of the trade. Though it is said that twenty years ago kola consumption in the south was very small, today it seems to be increasing; kola nuts can be seen everywhere in the markets, even in areas where there are few Hausa, and they are a principal article sold by street vendors. The bulk of the output is sent northwards over long distances. As most of the kola traffic to the north is by rail, the volume of this part of the trade can be estimated from railway statistics. Table 28 illustrates its growth. The difference between railings and imports represents that part of the output of the Western Provinces and the vicinity of Lagos which is sent to the north.[2] These

---

[1] Even £5 m. is about double the value of Nigerian cotton exports.

[2] When the difference is negative, this indicates that in that year the imports retained in the south exceed the contribution of local production to the northward flow of kolas.

figures understate both the importance of the industry and its rate of growth, as they exclude the substantial trade and consumption in the south, as well as the nuts carried northwards by other means of transport.

Table 28. *Railings and imports of kola nuts, Nigeria, 1920–48*
(thousand tons)

Year	Railings	Imports	Excess of railings over imports
1920	7·1	7·6	−0·5
1925	9·6	7·0	2·6
1930	11·8	4·8	7·0
1940	26·0	—	26·0
1948	47·4	0·2	47·2

The rise and growth of the kola industry are a remarkable example of native enterprise. They also point to considerable spontaneous organizing ability, since the marketing and distribution of kola nuts are not simple. On a smaller scale the growth of the industry resembles that of the West African cocoa industry or that of the native section of the Far Eastern rubber industry. A period of profitable prices has called into being a major industry with hardly any official assistance; and the maintenance of law and order and the development of essential communications have contributed towards its growth. Progress has not been without difficulties, and wide price fluctuations have at times caused dissatisfaction. But the difficulties have been small when set against the substantial contribution of the industry to the welfare of producers and consumers.

4. LONG-DISTANCE TRADE IN CERTAIN COMMODITIES

The internal trade in certain commodities is conducted over long distances, and partly, though not solely, for that reason it involves complex activities. These in turn often require a considerable degree of organization which may, however, be informal.[1]

There is much long-distance trade in staple foodstuffs, part of which supplies the migrant communities who often reside far from their districts of origin. Certain branches of this long-distance trade present interesting features, and the information available is sufficient to warrant

---

[1] Some branches of this trade might perhaps be more accurately described as overland trade rather than internal trade, as it crosses the frontiers. But in its personnel, organization and management, this trade differs radically from the overseas external trade and is properly considered under the general heading of internal trade.

brief discussion. This applies particularly to the trade in kola nuts, cattle and dried fish.

In Nigeria kola nuts are produced largely by Yoruba farmers. The nuts are marketed in the first instance by their wives, who take them in baskets or calabashes to the nearest roadside market. They are usually collected by Yoruba traders and taken to a larger market, frequently on the railway line. At that point they are generally bought by Hausa traders or by Hausa agents of principals in the north.

Special care is needed in the packing and transport of kola nuts, as the fruit is liable to attack by insects which quickly spoil its quality and reduce its value. For long-distance journeys the nuts are packed in bundles (sometimes known as *blies*) lined with wet leaves. They are sent northwards in special wagons, each of which is generally accompanied by an agent or employee either of the consigner or of the consignee, who periodically opens the baskets, turns the leaves over and sprinkles them with water.

At Kano or at other railway stations the kola trains are met by scores of Hausa traders who receive the consignments, and who often form a market in which dealings take place on the arrival of the nuts. The bundles or baskets are then loaded on lorries, camels or donkeys, and are sent either into the town or to smaller towns or villages where they are consumed or purchased for further resale and possibly for despatch across the frontier into French territory. An appreciable proportion of the kola nuts sent northward eventually reaches French Niger, or the French Sudan or the Chad. In the aggregate they are an appreciable unrecorded export.

The trade in livestock is conducted over even longer distances than the trade in kola nuts. Cattle, which provide the bulk of the meat supply of West Africa, are bred and reared in the extensive and sparsely populated areas of northern Nigeria, the Northern Territories of the Gold Coast and the French West African colonies, while most of the consumption is in the prosperous and populous towns and villages of the south.

The principal cattle-breeding areas of northern Nigeria and the neighbouring French territories are about a thousand miles or more distant from the principal consuming centres in the south. Much of the supply of livestock imported into the Gold Coast is derived from even more distant sources, such as the Niger bend round Timbuctoo, the Chad or the French Cameroons, which may be 1200 miles or more from the coastal towns. The reason for this wide separation of the producing and consuming areas are partly climatic and partly economic. Cattle-rearing requires extensive areas (particularly in West Africa where pasture is sparse), and these are likely to be distant from the densely populated regions.

Most of the cattle are bred and reared by nomadic Fulani herdsmen. The animals are purchased from the owners in the first instance by Hausa merchants (or traders belonging to other Moslem tribes of these regions) and are driven southwards by drovers who may be the agents of these traders or who may be accompanied by their agents. In most of the large towns they are then purchased by or consigned to Hausa traders. Finally, they are sold to butchers who may be Hausa or southerners. Many of the cattle are sold off at smaller places on their way to the south; conversely, they may be joined by other cattle bought on the way.

The direction of the flow of the cattle trade is exactly the reverse of that of the trade in kola nuts. The same trader often deals in both commodities, sending kolas northwards and cattle to the south. The wholesale trade in both kola nuts and cattle is predominantly in Hausa hands.

There is a fairly elaborate credit system in the trade from the earliest purchase to the ultimate sale. The trader or his local agent periodically visits the herds and gives advances on individual animals when these are still quite young. A pound or so may be advanced on a small calf when only a few months old. The following year another pound or two may be paid on it, according to its appearance or growth, and this may continue until the animal is ready to be taken away. Credit is fairly general up to the point of sale to the butcher and in some cases to the sale to the consumer.

There is also a substantial long-distance trade in dried fish and dried meat. The former especially presents several interesting aspects. Most of the supply of dried fish consumed in the southern towns is derived from distant up-country sources. In Nigeria much of it comes from the rivers of northern or north-eastern Nigeria which flow into Lake Chad. These are about 800–1000 miles from the coastal towns. In the Gold Coast some of the dried fish consumed on the coast comes from the French territories to the north, principally from the region of Mopti and Timbuctoo about a thousand miles from Accra. Some of this fish is obtained from the Cape Verde Islands, whence it is transported to the French colonies around the Upper Niger and re-consigned to the Gold Coast.

It may seem strange that fish should be sent from inland areas on the edge of the desert to the sea ports and riverine towns of the south a thousand miles away. The explanation is that sun-drying is not possible in the high humidity of the south, while the dry atmosphere inland is suitable for the process which enables fish to keep for weeks.[1]

---

[1] The dried fish supply of southern Nigeria is derived partly from the arid semi-desert regions of the Bornu-Lake Chad area, and partly from arctic waters north of the North Cape. Norwegian stockfish (sun-dried cod or haddock) is fished in the Arctic Sea, sun dried and shipped in large quantities to Nigeria, where it is consumed

An appreciable long-distance trade in sun-dried meat has grown up in recent years between north-eastern Nigeria and the Western Provinces. In Ibadan many people now use sun-dried meat as a substantial ingredient in their stew, and hunks of dried meat are carried about for occasional snacks during the day. The meat is produced chiefly in the general area of Nguru and Hadejia, that is, around one of the northern railheads of the Nigerian Railway. The trade, which is largely in the hands of Yoruba merchants who consign the meat from Nguru to the south-west, appears to have considerable possibilities, since even at present sheep and goats are still cheap in many parts of the north.

Much of the internal trade, especially at the retail stage, is on a very small scale; for instance, it is usual to see children peddling kolas a nut at a time. But some of the traders conducting long-distance trade operate on a large scale and are men of wealth and influence. In Accra in the Gold Coast there is a cattle trader operating on a large scale who began life as a migrant farm labourer. He administers a large business and imports cattle from as far as Duala in the French Cameroons, Lake Chad in French Equatorial Africa and Timbuctoo in the Niger bend. His secondary interests include grain dealing and the operation of a transport enterprise serving places as distant as Khartoum. Although he cannot sign his name, he recently gave a deposit of £50,000 on a government contract.[1]

For some African merchants internal trade has proved a training ground for dealing in export crops. Thus, Alhassan dan Tata, the largest groundnut buyer for the United Africa Company, who operates on a very large scale indeed, began his trading career as a cattle dealer.

5. RECENT CRITICISMS OF THE ORGANIZATION OF INTERNAL TRADE

In recent years some aspects of internal trade have been subject to much ill-informed criticism. For instance, the large number of intermediaries and the long distances covered by certain types of trade, especially cattle, have been severely criticized by the Nigerian Livestock Mission.

The Mission criticizes especially the long trek from the producing to

mainly in the Eastern Provinces a few degrees north of the Equator. The population of these districts has repeatedly shown its strong preference for this source of supply, as has been found out to their cost by importers who tried alternative sources.

The consignment of large quantities of dried fish from the arctic regions of Norway and from the semi-desert of the western Sudan to the ports of Nigeria and the Gold Coast is perhaps a not uninteresting example of the operation of the 'invisible hand' which it is at present so fashionable to ridicule.

[1] I was unable to verify this detail. I received it from a well-informed senior officer of the Gold Coast Department of Animal Health.

the consuming areas and the number of stages between the first purchase and ultimate retail sale. These do indeed superficially appear to be wasteful, but they are largely the result of underlying economic conditions, especially those discussed in Chapter 2 above. In the livestock trade the marketing methods clearly reflect the long distances between the producing regions and the centre of consumption, the poor communications (especially in the sparsely populated north), the low level of capital, the small scale of production and of individual purchases, and the comparative abundance of unskilled labour. If each small trader were to attempt to accompany his few cattle in their journey to the larger markets, the cost in time and in herdsmen's wages would exceed the profit of the intermediary who collects a comparatively small number of cattle from each smaller dealer and resells them in larger quantities.

The absence of standardized units in the conduct of trade and the great diversity of weights and measures have also at times attracted unfavourable comment. Transactions are usually by volume and not by weight. For instance, the market prices of foodstuffs in Nigeria (collected by the Labour Department or the Department of Agriculture) are quoted in bundles, heaps, *oloruka*, cigarette tins, *mudu*, or in single pieces, such as one yam. 'Bundles' may refer to bundles of three or five yams of widely varying weight; even where prices are quoted in what appears to be a unit of weight, this is deceptive as the value of the unit varies. Thus a *mudu* of beans or of gari in Minna is supposed to weigh 1 lb. 13 oz. and in Jos 2 lb. 13 oz.; the weight of a *mudu* of guinea corn is again different. This represents only a small proportion of the many different units in which the prices are calculated and expressed.

In the fish trade transactions are almost invariably by volume. In Nigeria the typical unit is known as the place, which is simply a heap of fish generally selling for 1*s*. or 2*s*. In the kola trade, transactions appear to be more standardized, until it is realized that units which appear to be identical in fact vary greatly in weight. Thus, wholesale transactions are in *blies*; but a *bly* in Nigeria may contain from 1¼ to 3 cwt. and from 3000 to 10,000 nuts.

These diversities and variations, while disturbing to observers, and aggravating to those who wish to collect statistics of prices, do not seem to inconvenience those participating in trade. For instance, they do not seem to have materially affected the rapid progress of the kola trade. In general, the customers of the traders seem to be well aware of what they buy. Apparent anomalies in prices, such as substantial differences in the prices of the same weight of fish, usually reflect differences in quality and size; large fish, for example, are worth more than small fish of an equal weight and quality, as there is a much higher loss from bone and waste in small fish.

6. PRICE DISCREPANCIES AND PRICE FLUCTUATIONS

There is very little reliable information on prices in internal trade. The absence of standardized weights is the most important of several obvious difficulties in the collection of reliable statistics. But while the obstacles are serious and evident, it would seem that the collection and presentation of prices of local produce is unsatisfactory, especially in Nigeria. Prices are quoted of allegedly identical quantities of foodstuffs showing differences of 500 or even 1000 % in localities only a few miles or a few score miles away from each other on motorable roads. The prices seem to be recorded as they are received without much inquiry whether these discrepancies are apparent or real, which would be a matter of much interest.[1] In the Gold Coast the collection of these data seems more critical and systematic, but there too the figures are doubtfully reliable, and the quoted prices show wide discrepancies for identical products in different towns easily accessible to each other.[2]

But while there are few reliable price statistics, there is much evidence of wide seasonal fluctuations in prices, especially of kola nuts and of the staple foodstuffs of northern Nigeria and the Northern Territories of the Gold Coast. There exist several series of monthly prices of kola nuts at Agege and Kano markets in Nigeria, some collected on their own initiative by individual officers, others collected officially by the Department of Agriculture. They all suggest that the prices in the months immediately before the harvest are about four to six times the level ruling after the harvest.

There is also available an interesting set of figures relating to one particular market in the Northern Territories of the Gold Coast. Some enterprising officers of the Department of Agriculture have over a number of years collected monthly prices of staple foodstuffs in the fairly important market of Bawku. The figures are reproduced here (Table 29) exactly as they have been collected. They relate to local units—the number of cigarette tins of millet and guinea corn and the number of

---

[1] For instance, in February 1934 a special inquiry was held into local prices. The price of yams for that month is shown as 6d. per cwt. in Ilorin, 2s. 3d. in Oyo and 14s. 3d. in Warri. In 1950 the Department of Agriculture was again engaged in collecting market prices, this time a series of monthly prices at different places. The price of yams for 1950 is shown by the Department as 8s. 8d. per cwt. in Ogbomosho and as 48s. in Ondo. This was only one example among many, and there is no evidence that these prices have ever been queried.

[2] Both in Nigeria and in the Gold Coast the movements in the prices of foodstuffs collected and quoted by the Departments of Statistics, Agriculture and Labour are often difficult to reconcile with changes in the cost of feeding inmates of government institutions. Not only the extent but the direction of the movements are often different.

pounds of groundnuts obtainable for 3*d.*, the nearest approach to standardized units obtainable.

In Table 29, (*a*) refers to late millet, (*b*) to guinea corn and (*c*) to groundnuts; and the figures show the number of units obtainable for 3*d.*; they are thus the *inverse* of prices. The three products are harvested between August and December. The figures have been collected fairly regularly, but the information is not available for 1944–5, and there are a few other gaps. These figures, although informally collected and presented, show the wide seasonal variations in prices, which just before the harvest are generally between two and eight times as great as the levels ruling immediately after.

Table 29. *Data bearing on the prices of* (*a*) *late millet,* (*b*) *guinea corn and* (*c*) *groundnuts in Bawku market in certain months, 1941–9*

	Nov.	Dec.	Jan.	May	June	July
1941–2: (*a*)	9	12	9	4	3	3¼
(*b*)	14	16	9	6	4½	5
(*c*)	3½	5	—	—	2	2
1942–3: (*a*)	6	7	6	4½	4½	5
(*b*)	6½	11	8½	6¼	5	6
(*c*)	6	6	5½	3	3	3
1943–4: (*a*)	6	6	5	4	3	3
(*b*)	9	7½	7½	4¼	3¼	4
(*c*)	5¾	5¼	4½	3	2¼	3½
1945–6: (*a*)	3½	4	3½	1½	1¼	1¼
(*b*)	5	5	4¼	1½	1¼	1¾
(*c*)	4½	4	2½	1½	1	½
1946–7: (*a*)	2½	3½	2¾	2	2¼	2
(*b*)	3¾	4½	3½	2½	2½	2¼
(*c*)	2¾	2½	1¾	1	¾	½
1947–8: (*a*)	—	—	3½	3¼	—	2¼
(*b*)	—	—	3¾	4	—	3
(*c*)	—	—	2	1	—	1
1948–9: (*a*)	3	3¾	2¼	1¼	1	1¼
(*b*)	4	3½	3	1¾	1	1¾
(*c*)	1	2	½	¼	¼	¼

Wide fluctuations in prices are often erroneously attributed to the activities of speculators; such complaints are levelled particularly against the activities of Lebanese corn traders in the few areas in which they operate. Wide seasonal variations in the prices of foodstuffs are universal in backward agricultural communities, where markets are narrow, and where neither producers, consumers, nor dealers command adequate storage facilities or capital reserves. The so-called speculators buy up the surplus after the harvest, and hold it profitably until the period of comparative scarcity. In their absence the price would fall to even lower levels after the harvest, which would stimulate consumption and waste at that period, and aggravate the dearth before the next harvest, so that price fluctuations would be even wider.

The data bearing on the prices of foodstuffs in Bawku refer to an area in which there are no substantial grain traders; they suggest empirically what is obvious on general grounds, that these fluctuations are not caused by the activities of traders and speculators.

Though some of the available price statistics are unreliable and exaggerate inter-regional price differences, prices for the same product may differ considerably between nearby areas. The discrepancies may persist, for instance, because of high cost of transport or imperfect market intelligence, though this latter is unlikely to be of major importance. From the information available it is not possible to assess the prevalence or extent of the local price discrepancies.

7. RESTRICTIVE TENDENCIES IN INTERNAL TRADE

The emergence and persistence of price differences may be due to organized restrictions, which may take the form of barriers to the flow of goods and/or the movement or entry of traders into a particular district or trade. There is some evidence of organized restriction and of the erection of barriers to entry in some branches of internal trade.

In the livestock trade restrictive measures are at times attempted by small groups of large-scale cattle dealers, and these tendencies seem to be promoted by the hierarchical outlook and social structure of the Hausa. The privileges of the Hausa chiefs sometimes combine the traditional rights belonging to the leaders of the community with powers to restrict competition of a more modern flavour. Even in the south, the Hausa communities generally have their recognized chief or leader who is often entitled to regulate the number of cattle the local Hausa traders are permitted to sell and the prices at which they can be sold.[1] The chief is often a cattle trader or a former cattle trader, and he is in a position to use his status in the community to regulate the market to suit his interest.

In some areas in the south the meat traders are also largely Hausa. The communal solidarity among the Hausa makes it easier to form sellers' rings to prevent price competition. It is said that in some markets if a newcomer enters the meat trade and does not conform to the prescribed prices, one of the Hausa traders quietly takes up a position

---

[1] This appears to be the position in the principal cattle market in Ibadan, where the local Hausa chief, who is also a substantial cattle trader, seems to have the right to regulate the number of cattle which can be offered for sale.

o

close to the newcomer and sells at a specially low price to drive him out of business. Whilst such measures may be effective over a limited area and for a short period, it is doubtful whether they are likely to raise prices effectively for any length of time when entry into the market is free. In particular, it is unlikely that organized price maintenance greatly affects prices in places where the right to sell in markets is not confined to permanent stall-holders but is also open to other sellers on payment of small daily fees or without payment of fees. The gradual entry of Ibo and Yoruba into the retail meat trade is likely to weaken communal solidarity among traders and thus to reduce the effectiveness of price rings.

In recent years there have also been instances of organized barriers to entry in the fish trade and in the trade in staple foodstuffs. Fish sellers in southern Nigeria at times endeavour to prevent fishermen and their wives from taking their catches to the towns and selling them there; in some cases physical violence seems to have been employed. Local sellers of foodstuffs also try occasionally to prevent farmers from selling their own produce in the towns.

8. OFFICAL ATTITUDES TOWARDS RESTRICTIVE TENDENCIES

The official attitude towards the restrictive practices described above is somewhat ambiguous and tends to vary. They are occasionally consciously combated by individual administrators. At times, sellers of foodstuffs spread rumours that it is illegal for farmers to bring their produce into the towns; and these rumours may be reinforced by threats of intimidation. Administrators have at times instructed the headmen to announce that these rumours were untrue and that farmers were free to bring their crops to the town. But more often administrative action tends, though possibly quite unwittingly, to promote and assist restrictive tendencies.

Thus the inter-regional flow of commodities is frequently discouraged by district officers or native authorities, partly with the laudable but parochial motive of reserving the supply for their own areas, or from the misguided belief that such movement is the result of harmful and therefore undesirable speculation.

At times restrictions on the flow of trade and/or the movement and activities of migrant traders are intended to satisfy or placate a vocal or influential section (often connected with a local chief or political leader) at the expense of the people at large.

An instructive example occurred recently in Kumasi, where the migrant Gao wholesale food merchants were removed by the authorities from the main market and its vicinity, and relegated to an area about two miles away. This action was brought about by the pressure of local trading interests, though the alleged malpractices of these traders[1] were advanced as the ostensible reason.

Entry into petty retail food distribution is occasionally obstructed by arrangements in the markets. Market women's unions are ubiquitous in southern Nigeria and in the Gold Coast. In the Lagos area practically all fish sellers in the principal markets belong to one or other of the fish market women's unions. In southern Nigeria these unions are often well organized and influential, and enjoy a fair measure of recognition from the authorities. Thus, stalls in many markets in the larger towns seem to be reserved for their members. The unions also tend to press for the exclusion of casual sellers (usually hawkers admitted to the markets on the payment of a daily fee). In many towns there are several open markets to which all sellers (not only stallholders) are admitted. For various reasons the authorities often insist that those open markets should be far from the principal central markets. The principal reasons for this seem to be pressure from the market women's unions, though the interest of the authorities in the tidy appearance of the markets, and a desire to protect the revenue derived from the renting of stalls may also play a part.

9. COMPARATIVE INEFFECTIVENESS OF THESE TENDENCIES

The market sellers do not appear, generally, to find it easy to organize effective price maintenance. Visits to fish markets, for instance, suggest that organized price maintenance would be largely ineffective, even in this trade in which sellers are comparatively highly organized. There are crowds of customers milling round the large number of sellers, all of whom sell by volume, usually after some bargaining. In these conditions organized price maintenance is practically impossible. The whole mechanism of price fixing is somewhat informal.[2] But while organized price maintenance is rarely effective, the restriction of the right to sell in the markets to stall-holders, and especially to members of market women's unions, tends to increase the margins of intermediaries and thus to raise the prices paid by the consumer, and/or to reduce the prices received by the fishermen.

It does not appear that price rings and organized restriction on entry

---

[1] For example, they were alleged to have seduced many young Ashanti women of Kumasi. However, it is plain that this was not the real objection to their activities.

[2] There is often nominal and ineffective price maintenance, which is freely evaded. For instance, in Sekondi I asked a fish seller the price of a small heap of three fish and was told that the price was 6d., but that I could have the fish for 4d.

are major influences on the prices of local produce.[1] Effective price rings seem to be most easily organized where there are few traders and where they are of the same race or tribe; the activities of the Hausa cattle traders are an example of this. But even these restrictive practices do not seem materially to affect the market situation unless supported by administrative action through restriction on entry and movement. Where there are many traders, and/or no administrative bar to the flow of trade, there seems to be little or no effective price maintenance. It will be recognized that this conclusion is very similar to that reached in the discussion of monopolistic influences in the internal trade of West Africa.

10. EXPATRIATE ENTERPRISE AND INTERNAL TRADE

The sharp fluctuations in prices within seasons and between seasons, as well as some of the price discrepancies between different places, result from the narrowness of markets, the poverty of communications and the inadequacy of storage facilities. The persistence of these differences and fluctuations in turn reflect the low level of capital and organization of those participating in the trade in local produce. The expatriate merchant firms realise that large profits could be made in internal trade, but for political reasons they are barred from it. In the early 1930's the United Africa Company attempted to enter this trade in Nigeria, but this extension of its activities aroused such fierce opposition from local trading interests that the administration asked the company to refrain, and since about 1932 it has not traded in local produce.[2] This episode illustrates the divergence between the sectional interests of certain African groups (the traders in local produce) and the interests of the African population as a whole, since the population generally would undoubtedly benefit from the smoother flow of internal trade which would tend to be brought about by the participation of European firms.

[1] In West Africa increases in the prices of local foodstuffs in recent years have often been attributed to the activities of sellers' rings, often called 'mammy' rings. There is little reliable evidence, and no conclusive evidence, to support this view. The activities of sellers' rings could not have been a major factor in the general rise in prices, which has resulted from the operation of much more powerful influences.

[2] If this bar is regarded as a result of restrictive pressures by the local traders rather than as an instance of the general tendency to curtail the activities of expatriate traders, it provides an important exception to the conclusion of the preceding section on the comparative ineffectiveness of restrictive measures in internal trade.

APPENDICES

APPENDIX 1

STATISTICS OF STATUTORY MARKETING OF WEST AFRICAN EXPORTS

This appendix presents the detailed statistics of the operation of statutory marketing underlying the discussion in Chapters 22 and 23. The operations of the West African Produce Control Board are also dealt with. There has been a large measure of continuity in producer price policy over the whole period of statutory marketing, and this is a relevant fact in assessing the effects of the policies of the marketing boards. As the statistics are shown year by year, the operations of the West African Produce Control Board and those of the present marketing boards are kept distinct. The summary of the information presented and the outline of its bases were given in Chapters 22 and 23; the following tables and notes present the statistics and their sources in detail.

Table 30. *Statistics relating to the marketing of Gold Coast cocoa, 1939–51*

(Prices in £ per ton)

Year	(1) Producer price	(2) Export duty	(3) Surplus of marketing organization	(4) Net sales proceeds (a) i.e. (1) + (2) + (3)	(5) Gross Proceeds (f.o.b.)	(6) Sale price to M.O.F. (c. and f. U.K.)	(7) New York spot price (converted at official rates of exchange)	(8) Tonnages purchased (up to 1946-7, or shipped from 1947-8) (000's tons)
1939–40	14·4	2·1	0·8	17·3	22·8	32·5	29·4	181
1940–41	11·5	2·1	5·7	19·3	24·3	31·5	37·4	237
1941–42	13·4	2·1	–0·8	14·7	19·6	31·5	50·0	251
1942–43	11·6	2·1	6·0	19·7	24·9	30·5	49·8	207
1943–44	13·0	2·1	9·3	24·4	30·5	35·0	49·8	196
1944–45	22·4	2·1	5·8	30·3	36·7	35·7	49·8	229
1945–46	27·0	2·1	5·0	34·1	40·8	45·5	49·8	209
1946–47	51·3	2·1	49·5	102·9	108·3	111·7	155·0	192
1947–48	74·7	2·8	116·0	193·5	201·0	207·0	238·0	206
1948–49	121·3	6·1	–0·5	126·9	138·0	142·0	139·0	275
1949–50	84·0	12·2	68·3	164·5	178·4	(b)	(b)	253
1950–51	130·7	51·1	72·7	254·5	270·0	(b)	(b)	262

(a) F.o.b. sale proceeds, less expenses other than export duty; i.e. amounts available to be shared between the government, the marketing organization and the producer. The differences between columns 4 and 5 represent the marketing expenses other than export duty between the point where the producer price applies and f.o.b.

(b) Private purchase of cocoa restored in 1949.

Table 31. *Statistics relating to the marketing of Nigerian cocoa, 1939–51*

(Prices in £ per ton)

Year	(1) Producer price	(2) Export duty	(3) Surplus of marketing organization	(4) Net sales proceeds [a] i.e. (1)+(2)+(3)	(5) Gross proceeds (f.o.b.)	(6) Sale price to M.O.F. (c. and f. U.K.)	(7) New York spot price (converted at official rates of exchange)	(8) Tonnages purchased (000's tons)
1939–40	17·0	1·3	0·8	19·1	22·7	31·5	29·4	82
1940–41	14·0	1·3	5·7	21·0	23·9	30·5	37·4	101
1941–42	15·0	2·2	−0·8	16·4	19·4	30·5	50·0	99
1942–43	13·0	2·2	6·7	21·9	24·9	29·5	49·8	111
1943–44	13·0	2·2	12·1	27·3	30·7	34·0	49·8	71
1944–45	23·0	2·2	7·9	33·1	37·1	34·3	49·8	86
1945–46	27·5	2·2	7·0	36·7	40·7	44·5	49·8	103
1946–47	50·0	2·2	52·6	104·8	110·0	110·7	155·0	111
1947–48	62·5	4·3	125·0	191·8	195·0	201·0	238·0	74
1948–49	120·0	6·0	3·0	129·0	138·0	142·0	139·0	109
1949–50	100·0	6·0	64·0	170·0	181·0	(b)	(b)	100
1950–51	120·0	40·0	95·0	255·0	267·0	(b)	(b)	110

[a] F.o.b. sale proceeds, less expenses other than export duty; i.e. amount available to be shared locally between the government, the marketing organization and the producer; cf. note [a] to Table 30.   [b] Private purchase of cocoa restored in 1949.

Table 32. Levies on producers of Gold Coast and Nigerian cocoa, 1939–51

Year	Gold Coast							Nigeria						
	(1) Export duty	(2) Surplus	(3) Total levies, i.e. (1)+(2)	(4) Producer price	(5) Export duty	(6) Surplus	(7) Total levies, i.e. (5)+(6)	(8) Export duty	(9) Surplus	(10) Total levies, i.e. (8)+(9)	(11) Producer price	(12) Export duty	(13) Surplus	(14) Total levies
	As percentage of producer price, i.e. percentage of (1) in Table 30			As percentage of sales proceeds, i.e. percentage of (4) in Table 30				As percentage of producer price, i.e. percentage of (1) in Table 31			As percentage of sales proceeds, i.e. percentage of (4) in Table 31			
1939–40	15	6	20	83	12	5	17	8	5	12	89	7	4	11
1940–41	18	50	68	60	11	30	40	9	41	50	67	6	27	33
1941–42	16	−6	10	91	14	−5	9	15	−5	9	91	13	−5	9
1942–43	18	52	70	59	11	30	41	17	52	68	59	10	31	41
1943–44	16	72	88	53	9	38	47	17	93	110	48	8	44	52
1944–45	9	26	35	74	7	19	26	10	34	44	69	7	24	31
1945–46	8	19	26	79	6	15	21	8	25	33	75	6	19	25
1946–47	4	96	101	50	2	48	50	4	105	110	48	2	50	52
1947–48	4	155	159	39	1	60	61	7	200	207	33	2	65	67
1948–49	5	−0·4	5	96	5	−0·4	4	5	3	8	93	5	2	7
1949–50	15	81	96	51	7	42	49	6	64	70	59	4	38	41
1950–51	39	56	95	51	20	29	49	33	79	112	47	16	37	53

398

Notes (Tables 30–32)

1. In the Gold Coast the officially announced statutory producer prices referred to prices payable at port of shipment up to 1942–3 and to prices payable at railway buying stations from 1943 to 1944. In this table (in column 1) for consistency they are shown on a comparable basis throughout as prices at railway buying stations; for the four seasons 1939–40 to 1942–3 a deduction of 30s. a ton has been made from the official port of shipment price to allow for the cost of transport from buying stations to port of shipment. This deduction has been estimated on the basis of official figures of transport charges for subsequent seasons.

2. In Nigeria the statutory prices refer to gazetted minima at port of shipment. Those shown here refer to grade 1 cocoa. Over most of this period more than half of the crop purchased was of grade 2 or of lower grade, and for these lower prices were paid. Thus the surplus of the marketing organizations expressed as a percentage of producer prices was greater than is shown in the tables.

3. For the period covered by the West African Produce Control Board or its predecessor the Cocoa Control Board most of the figures have been extracted or calculated from a paper given by Mr E. Melville, of the Colonial Office, to the Cocoa Conference of 1948; these data were supplemented by information published in the Appendices of the two Cocoa White Papers. From 1947 they have been calculated from the Annual Reports of the Marketing Boards.

There are slight differences in the surpluses of the Cocoa Boards shown here and in Table 19 in Chapter 22. These arise from the inclusion of interest on the funds of the Boards in the calculation of their surpluses in Table 19 and their exclusion here. The reasons for this omission are given in Chapter 22.

4. As well as the levies on producers represented by the surpluses and the export duties there have also been differences between the proceeds secured at market prices or, more precisely, sale proceeds realizable in certain directions. This discrepancy was far less important in cocoa marketing than in the sale of other products, and was, moreover, almost entirely confined to the operations of the West African Produce Control Board. But it was not altogether insignificant. It has been computed as follows.

Both the New York price and the price paid by the Ministry of Food c. and f. United Kingdom are available over this period; the latter has been made available from the records of the Colonial Office. Over the seasons during which the New York price was controlled, the difference between that price and the buying price of the Ministry of Food was multiplied by the tonnage imported into the United Kingdom in the corresponding calendar year (for instance, 1941 for the season 1940–1). Over the seasons when the New York price was not controlled (1940–1, 1946–8) one-third of the difference was taken and multiplied by the tonnage imported into the United Kingdom in recognition of the consideration that if more had been sold in New York the price there would have been less. The resulting total is about

£12½ m. Total cocoa purchases by the statutory marketing organizations from 1939 to 1951 totalled 3·8 m. tons. This results in a figure of £3·4 per ton over the period as a whole, which has been rounded off to £3 in the tables of Chapter 22. For reasons stated in Chapter 22, § 2, the item is shown in the tables only for the period of operations of the West African Produce Control Board.

This computation is arbitrary, but is more likely to understate than over-state this item, especially in view of the fact that the New York price has been converted into sterling at the official rate of exchange; and also because in outside markets much higher prices ruled when the New York price was controlled. But because there is this element of arbitrariness, which is absent in the calculation of the contribution to buyers in the marketing of the other export products, the figures are not shown year by year (as they are for the other products reviewed in this appendix), but are presented as aggregates and averages in Tables 21–23.

5. Between 1940 and 1944 some 230,000 tons of cocoa were destroyed in the Gold Coast and Nigeria as they could not be shipped. This does not affect the calculation of the surpluses or of the under-realization, either in total or as rates per ton. The surpluses are shown as totals earned by the marketing organizations and as rates per ton purchased, and the amount destroyed is included in purchases. Under-realization is computed on the basis of amounts shipped and purchased, and is also unaffected. Rates of export duty are not affected either. But the calculation of total export duties over the period is affected, as no export duty was payable on tonnage destroyed. The required adjustment of £0·5 m. has been made before pre-senting in Table 23 the aggregate payments of export duties.

6. The prices paid by the Ministry of Food for West African produce have been made available for this inquiry from the records of the Colonial Office. The figures can also be calculated from the trade returns, since the Ministry of Food bought on c. and f. terms, and was sole importer over the relevant periods. The New York prices of cocoa have been made available by the United Africa Company, and are derived from *Commodities 1950*, a well-known book of reference of the cocoa industry, published by Bache and Co., New York.

Table 33. *Statistics relating to the marketing of Nigerian groundnuts, 1942–51*

(Prices in £ per ton)

Year	(1) Producer price (at railway stations in Kano area)	(2) Export duty	(3) Surplus of marketing organization	(4) Net sales proceeds,[a] i.e. (1) + (2) + (3)	(5) Under-realization[b] i.e. (8) − (7)	(6) Net commercial values, i.e. (4) + (5)	(7) Sale price to M.O.F. (c. and f. U.K.)	(8) Price of Indian groundnuts c. and f. U.K. up to 1947–8, c.i.f. Europe 1948–9 to 1950–1	(9) Tonnage purchased (000's tons)
1942–43	6·5	0·5	—	7·0	17·5	24·5	18·4	35·9	108
1943–44	9·0	0·5	—	9·5	14·2	23·7	21·4	35·6	194
1944–45	12·0	0·5	—	12·5	9·0	21·5	24·0	33·0	228
1945–46	12·0	0·5	—	12·5	9·7	22·2	24·5	34·2	301
1946–47	16·0	0·9	—	16·9	31·9	48·8	29·0	60·9	323
1947–48	16·0	2·6	12·7	31·3	17·3	48·6	45·0	62·3	336
1948–49	19·2	3·3	19·0	41·5	13·1	54·6	55·0	68·1	323
1949–50	21·2	3·3	13·0	37·5	18·0	55·5	53·0	71·0	188
1950–51	21·2	6·4	22·0	49·6	17·0	66·6	70·0	87·0	143

[a] F.o.b. proceeds less expenses to f.o.b. other than export duty; i.e. the amount available to be shared locally between the government, the marketing organization and the producer.

[b] Column 5 is the difference between the figures in columns 8 and 7. Column 6 is in no way comparable with column 7. The former shows the amounts which would have been available to be shared *locally* between the three parties, and is net of expenses other than export duty; column 7 is gross of all expenses to c. and f. U.K.

Table 34. *Levies on producers of Nigerian groundnuts, 1942–51*

Year	(1) Export duty	(2) Surplus	(3) Under-realization	(4) Total levies, i.e. (1)+(2)+(3)	(5) Producer price	(6) Export duty	(7) Surplus	(8) Duty and surplus, i.e. (6)+(7)	(9) Producer price	(10) Export duty	(11) Surplus	(12) Under-realization	(13) Total levies, i.e. (10)+(11)+(12)
	As percentage of producer price, i.e. percentage of (1) in Table 33				As percentage of sales proceeds, i.e. percentage of (4) in Table 33				As percentage of commercial values, i.e. percentage of (6) in Table 33				
1942–43	8	—	269	277	93	7	—	7	27	2	—	71	73
1943–44	6	—	158	163	95	5	—	5	38	2	—	60	62
1944–45	4	—	75	79	96	4	—	4	56	2	—	42	44
1945–46	4	—	81	85	96	4	—	4	54	2	—	44	46
1946–47	6	—	199	205	95	5	—	5	33	2	—	65	67
1947–48	16	79	108	204	51	8	41	49	33	5	26	36	67
1948–49	17	99	68	184	46	8	46	54	35	6	35	24	65
1949–50	16	61	85	162	57	9	35	43	38	6	23	32	62
1950–51	30	104	80	214	43	13	44	57	32	10	33	26	68

Notes (Tables 33 and 34)

1. The series in these tables begin with the crop year 1942–3, when the marketing of groundnuts was taken over by the West African Produce Control Board. From the outbreak of war until 1942 the merchant firms shipped the crop to the Ministry of Food, which paid prices broadly in accord with world prices. Details of these arrangements are discussed in Chapter 19.

2. Up to 1947 the Ministry of Food paid prices to the West African Produce Control Board calculated to cover exactly the latter's buying prices and other expenses, and thus no surpluses were accumulated. The Nigeria Groundnut Marketing Board took over from the West African Produce Control Board in 1949.

3. Column 8 of Table 33 shows the prices paid by the Ministry of Food for Indian groundnuts up to 1948, and the price of Indian groundnuts c.i.f. Europe thereafter. As shown in Table 18 the Ministry of Food bought large quantities of Indian groundnuts until 1946 and appreciable quantities until 1948. After 1948 exports of Indian groundnuts to the United Kingdom fell to negligible quantities, chiefly because of the revival of the European market. The prices shown here for the early post-war years are far below those paid for Indian and French West African groundnuts in various markets of western Europe at the time. From 1948 there was again a large market in vegetable oils and oilseeds in western Europe, and the c.i.f. quotations shown here are reliable indices of commercial values.

Table 35. *Statistics relating to the marketing of Nigerian palm kernels, 1942–51*

(Prices in £ per ton)

Year	(1) Producer price	(2) Export duty	(3) Surplus of marketing organization	(4) Net sales proceeds,(a) i.e. (1) + (2) + (3)	(5) Under-realization, i.e. (8) − (7)(b)	(6) Net commercial values,(b) i.e. (4) + (5)	(7) Sale price to M.O.F. (c. and f. U.K.)	(8) Estimated price to M.O.F. of similar items up to 1947, c.i.f. market values 1948–51 (see notes)	(9) Tonnage purchased (000's tons)
1942	5·8	0·5	—	6·3	13·7	20·0	13·3	27	345
1943	6·8	0·5	—	7·3	11·5	18·8	15·5	27	331
1944	9·1	0·5	—	9·6	7·9	17·5	17·1	25	314
1945	9·1	0·5	—	9·6	7·9	17·5	17·1	25	293
1946	11·1	0·5	—	11·6	15·2	26·8	19·8	35	277
1947	16·3	1·1	7·7	25·1	19·2	44·3	33·8	53	316
1948	20·3	2·4	7·8	30·5	16·7	47·2	39·3	56	327
1949	26·0	2·2	12·0	40·2	3·0	43·2	50·0	53	376
1950	26·0	2·9	7·5	36·4	18·5	54·9	46·5	65	381
1951	32·0	5·3	14·2	51·5	15·0	66·5	65·0	80	330

(a) F.o.b. proceeds less expenses to f.o.b. other than export duty; i.e. the amount available to be shared *locally* between the government, the marketing organization and the producer.

(b) Column 5 is the difference between the figures in columns 8 and 7. Column 6 is in no way comparable with column 7. The former shows the amounts which would have been available to be shared *locally* between the three parties, and is net of expenses other than export duty; column 7 is gross of all expenses to c. and f. U.K.

Table 36. *Levies on producers of Nigerian palm kernels, 1942–51*

Year	(1) Export duty	(2) Surplus	(3) Under-realization	(4) Total levies, i.e. (1) + (2) + (3)	(5) Producer price	(6) Export duty	(7) Surplus	(8) Duty and surplus, i.e. (6) + (7)	(9) Producer price	(10) Export duty	(11) Surplus	(12) Under-realization	(13) Total levies, i.e. (10) + (11) + (12) + (13)
	As percentage of producer price, i.e. percentage of (1) in Table 35				As percentage of sales proceeds, i.e. percentage of (4) in Table 35				As percentage of commercial values, i.e. percentage of (6) in Table 35				
1942	9	—	236	245	92	8	—	8	29	3	—	69	71
1943	7	—	169	176	93	7	—	7	36	3	—	61	64
1944	5	—	87	92	95	5	—	5	52	3	—	45	48
1945	5	—	87	92	95	5	—	5	52	3	—	45	48
1946	5	—	137	141	96	4	—	4	41	2	—	57	59
1947	7	47	118	172	65	4	31	35	37	2	17	43	63
1948	12	38	82	133	67	8	26	33	43	5	17	35	57
1949	8	46	12	66	65	5	30	35	60	5	28	7	40
1950	11	29	71	111	71	8	21	29	47	5	14	34	53
1951	17	44	47	108	62	10	28	38	48	8	21	23	52

Notes (*Tables 35 and 36*)

1. Until 1949 producer prices were changed at various times during the year. The prices shown here are simple averages of the official monthly prices. The same applies to the prices paid for Nigerian palm kernels by the Ministry of Food.

2. Until February 1947 the Ministry of Food paid prices to the West African Produce Control Board calculated to cover exactly the latter's buying prices and other expenses, and thus no surpluses were accumulated.

3. The series in columns 5, 6 and 8 of Table 35 necessarily contain some element of estimate. The Ministry of Food did not regularly purchase large quantities of palm kernels from sources other than West African, and it has thus not been possible to make a direct comparison between prices paid for the same product from different sources such as was possible with prices of Indian and Nigerian groundnuts. An approximate estimate has been made on the following basis. Groundnuts and palm kernels are close but imperfect substitutes in oilseed crushing and their values are therefore related. The relationship is not constant, but tends to vary with the absolute level of prices. Since 1939 the Ministry of Food has bought the West African output both of groundnuts and of palm kernels on c. and f. terms. The discount of palm-kernel prices below those of groundnuts was of the general order of one-quarter up to 1946 and about one-eighth from 1947. These discounts have been applied to the prices paid by the Ministry of Food for Indian groundnuts for these years to arrive at the estimated values of palm kernels to the Ministry. This method is free from the objection that it uses the prices paid for marginal quantities for assessing the value of bulk supplies. From 1948 the prices in column 8 of Table 35 are those of Malayan palm kernels c.i.f. Europe.

Table 37. *Statistics relating to the marketing of Nigerian palm oil, 1943–51*

(Prices in £ per ton)

Year	(1) Producer price	(2) Export duty	(3) Surplus of marketing organization	(4) Net sales proceeds, (a) i.e. (1) + (2) + (3)	(5) Under-realization, (b) i.e. (8) − (7)	(6) Net commercial values, i.e. (4) + (5)	(7) Sale price to M.O.F. (c. and f. U.K.)	(8) Price paid by M.O.F. for Congo palm oil less 10% (see notes)	(9) Tonnage purchased (000's tons)
1943	9·4	0·6	—	10·0	12·2	22·2	20·0	32·2	135
1944	11·5	0·6	—	12·1	8·9	21·0	23·0	31·9	125
1945	11·5	0·6	—	12·1	8·9	21·0	23·0	31·9	114
1946	17·0	0·6	7·9	17·6	10·1	27·7	27·5	37·6	101
1947	24·8	0·6	22·8	33·3	22·1	55·4	43·5	65·6	126
1948	31·2	2·5	15·6	56·5	8·8	65·3	70·0	78·8	139
1949	40·0	4·1	13·0	59·7	12·6	72·3	75·0	87·6	161
1950	40·0	4·5	17·8	57·5	8·1	65·6	70·5	78·6	159
1951	52·0	7·8		77·6	46·0	123·6	94·0	140·0	143

(a) F.o.b. proceeds less expenses to f.o.b. other than export duty; i.e. the amount available to be shared locally between the government, the marketing organization and the producer.

(b) Column 5 is the difference between the figures in columns 8 and 7. Column 6 is in no way comparable with column 7. The former shows the amounts which would have been available to be shared *locally* between the three parties, and is net of expenses other than export duty; column 7 is gross of all expenses to c. and f. U.K.

Table 38. *Levies on producers of Nigerian palm oil, 1943–51*

Year	(1) Export duty	(2) Surplus	(3) Under-realization	(4) Total levies, i.e. (1) + (2) + (3)	(5) Producer price	(6) Export duty	(7) Surplus	(8) Duty and surplus, i.e. (6) + (7)	(9) Producer price	(10) Export duty	(11) Surplus	(12) Under-realization	(13) Total levies, i.e. (10) + (11) + (12)
	As percentage of producer price, i.e. percentage of (1) in Table 37				As percentage of sales proceeds, i.e. percentage in (4) in Table 37				As percentage of commercial values, i.e. percentage of (6) in Table 37				
1943	6	—	130	136	94	6	—	6	42	3	—	55	58
1944	5	—	77	83	95	5	—	5	55	3	—	42	45
1945	5	—	77	83	95	5	—	5	55	3	—	42	45
1946	4	—	59	63	97	3	—	3	61	2	—	36	49
1947	2	32	89	123	74	2	24	26	45	1	14	40	55
1948	8	73	28	109	55	4	40	45	48	4	35	13	52
1949	10	39	32	81	67	7	26	33	55	6	22	17	45
1950	11	33	20	64	70	8	23	30	61	7	20	12	39
1951	15	34	88	138	67	10	23	33	42	6	14	37	58

Notes (Tables 37 and 38)

1. These series begin with 1943, the year in which the West African Produce Control Board became responsible for the marketing of palm oil.

2. Up to 1948 the producer price refers to that of grade 1 oil (up to 9 % free fatty acid). From 1946 the West African Produce Control Board and its successor, the Oil Palm Produce Marketing Board, paid appreciably lower prices for lower quality oil, though the Ministry of Food until recently paid identical prices for all soft oils (oil up to 23½ % free fatty acid) which cover the great bulk of Nigerian palm-oil exports. The actual producer prices at port of shipment were thus somewhat lower than indicated in column 4. From 1949 the producer price is the weighted average of grades 1–3 as shown in Table 19.

3. Throughout these years appreciable quantities of plantation oil were bought by the Ministry of Food. A consecutive series is available of the prices paid for Congo oil. Congo oil is of better quality than Nigerian soft trade oil, and 10 % has been deducted from the price of the former to allow for this difference. This deduction is reasonable for the period as a whole. Two points are relevant in this connexion. First, Congo oil is liable to duty at 10 % in the United Kingdom, while Nigerian oil is imported free of duty. Thus the effective price paid by the Ministry for Congo oil (c. and f. value plus import duty) is 10 % higher than the series of prices on which column 8 is based. As this duty has been ignored in the calculation, the entries in column 8 are understated to that extent. Secondly, in the 1930's the Liverpool price for first quality Nigerian trade oil was practically identical with that of estate oil with only a few shillings difference per ton for differences in free fatty acid content. For these reasons the deduction of 10 % from the c. and f. value of Congo plantation oil before payment of import duty seems reasonable to arrive at an equivalent commercial value for Nigerian oil bought by the Ministry of Food.

APPENDIX 2

THE TERMS OF TRADE OF PRODUCERS OF EXPORT CROPS

1. CALCULATION OF THE TERMS OF TRADE OF PRODUCERS

This appendix is confined to the presentation in some detail of the information underlying the discussion of the terms of trade of producers in Chapter 23, above. Close measurement of changes in the terms of trade of producers of export crops raises much greater difficulties than measurement of changes in the terms of trade in the conventional sense, since the former relate producer prices to the retail prices of imported merchandise and not to c.i.f. values. Ideally, therefore, calculation of the terms of trade of producers would require a series of indices of producer prices and of retail prices in the producing areas. Series of the former can be calculated comparatively easily, and are presented in the tables at the end of this appendix. But there is no index of retail prices over this period in West Africa; indeed, even a reasonably comprehensive index of import prices before 1948 is not available.

The compilation of a consistent and meaningful index of import prices would be difficult, in view of the very great changes in the quantity, quality, composition and sources of imports in the years between 1939 and 1950, including the eclipse over most of this period of some important sources of supply. The familiar conceptual and statistical difficulties are aggravated by the effects of quantitative restrictions over a wide range of imports, with the result that import prices often refer to commodities not freely available at these prices, and at times available only in very small quantities.

Even if it were available, a comprehensive index of import prices would not suffice for the calculation of changes of producer terms of trade. For several reasons, the retail prices of most types of merchandise in West Africa rose between 1939 and 1950 proportionately much more than did import prices. There were various reasons for this. The rates of import duties were increased on many commodities; bottlenecks in communications served to widen the gap between import prices and the relevant internal prices; and quantitatively the most important factor, the retail prices of the so-called short-supply commodities (that is commodities for which demand exceeded available supplies at prices equal to landed costs plus normal distributive expenses and profits) increased proportionately far more than did import prices. Over most of this period a large proportion of all merchandise imports, including all commodities subjected to specific licensing, were short-supply goods in this sense. For these commodities, effective retail prices were far above landed costs and distributive expenses.[1] Thus, increases in import prices, and even increases in landed costs understate the proportionate rise in retail prices.

For a few war and post-war years there are available two series of officially computed indices of Nigerian import prices. One of these is an unpublished series prepared in the Colonial Office (1939 = 100); the other is a Nigerian series (1937-8 = 100) reproduced in the Nigerian *Digest of Statistics*, 1950. The compilation of this latter series was suspended in 1950; the former is still computed. As will be seen from Table 42, where the two series are reproduced, they are very close for the years for which they overlap, and their value and limitations are very similar. It is therefore sufficient to discuss the Colonial Office index of the method of compilation of which details are available.

The index is based on twenty items, weighted according to their relative importance in Nigerian imports in 1939. The commodities include several items not purchased normally by African producers of export crops, such as whisky, cement, fuel oil, and motor vehicles; the prices of these have risen much less over this period than the prices of the general range of merchandise. The index refers to c.i.f. values and not to landed costs or to retail prices, and this is particularly significant as it includes several short-supply commodities. It greatly understates the rise in both the landed costs and retail prices of imported merchandise destined for consumption by Africans. Both the Colonial Office index and the Nigerian index refer to Nigeria only.

As indicated in Chapter 23, an index of producers' terms of trade in terms of the *landed costs* of cotton piece goods is of considerable interest in West African conditions, both in its own right and also as providing, at least up to 1950, a reasonably close approximation to a comprehensive index calculated on the basis of the *retail prices* of imported goods bought by producers.

Indices of the landed costs of imported cotton piece goods have been calculated for both Nigeria and the Gold Coast. The base period adopted is the average of the three calendar years 1935 to 1937, the last complete three-year period before the war, which was a period of fair but not

---

[1] This discrepancy was a prominent feature of West African merchandise trade throughout the war and early post-war years, and is described in many official reports. It was present even as late as 1950. For instance, in January 1950 the wholesale list price of a case of a standard brand of cigarettes in Kano was nominally £63; the effective open-market price ranged from £82 to £88. Only the preferred wholesale customers of the large firms were able to secure the cigarettes at the nominal price, and even they were always rationed and often subjected to conditional sales.

abnormal prosperity in West Africa. The following procedure was adopted in computing the indices.[1]

From the trade returns and reports the annual c.i.f. values plus import duty per square yard of cotton piece goods have been calculated for all cotton piece goods, for printed cotton piece goods alone, and for bleached cotton piece goods alone. These unit values, referred to as landed costs,[2] have been calculated separately, because while the producers of cocoa and oil-palm produce buy principally printed cotton piece goods, the groundnut producers buy mostly bleached or unbleached cotton piece goods.[3]

[1] Miss P. Ady has suggested (*Journal of the Royal Statistical Society*, 1954, Part I) that this base period was one of altogether exceptional prosperity in West Africa; and that its adoption presents a misleading picture both of the pre-war situation and, by implication, of the position of producers under statutory marketing. The period was chosen as it covered the last complete three calendar years before the outbreak of war, with the exception of 1938, which was not only the most depressed year on record for West Africa, but one in which the import trade of the Gold Coast was disorganized by the hold-up and boycott of imported merchandise. In fact, the choice of an earlier period up to 1933 would have been more favourable to the producers. Only the years 1934–5 and 1938–9 would have resulted in significantly less favourable base periods. The use of producer prices in these calculations (instead of f.o.b. values) has also brought it about that the very low up-country prices of groundnuts in the autumn of 1937 are fully included in the calculations of the base period, while they were not fully reflected in f.o.b. values until somewhat later.

The effects of statutory marketing on the terms of trade of producers through the retention of a large part of sales proceeds at a time of rising prices of imports are unambiguous. Disputes over the choice of the base period, and similar issues, can only obscure the essential points.

Various matters bearing on the computation of the terms of trade of producers are referred to in a paper by the present writer, 'Statistics of Statutory Marketing in West Africa, 1939–51', and in the discussion of the paper, published in the *Journal of the Royal Statistical Society*, 1954, Part I.

[2] This definition and method of calculation of landed costs omits a few minor items and this tends slightly to understate the rise in true landed costs since the outbreak of war; cf. Chapter 23, § 3, above.

[3] Printed cotton piece goods and bleached cotton piece goods are the most important types of imported cotton piece goods in West Africa. But there are also substantial imports of unbleached and dyed cotton piece goods, and the relative importance of the different categories tends to vary. The landed costs of these are included in those calculations which refer to all imported cotton piece goods, and these calculations therefore both allow for and reflect changes in the relative importance of different classes of cotton piece goods in consumer expenditure. Because of the inclusion of these other classes, indices of the landed costs of all cotton piece goods may move differently from the indices of the landed costs of printed or bleached cotton piece goods, and they may also lie outside these indices; and the same applies to the indices of the terms of trade of producers expressed in terms of all cotton piece goods, in terms of bleached cotton piece goods and in terms of printed cotton piece goods. As will be seen from the diagrams and from the tables in the note at the end of this appendix, such erratic movements occur in a few years, but they do not significantly affect the

The average landed costs per yard (i.e. the c.i.f. value plus duty) have been transformed into index number series; in each case the average landed costs for the three years 1935–7 have been taken as the base (1935–7 = 100). The prices received by West African producers have similarly been collected and converted into index number series, with the average producer prices for 1935 to 1937 taken as 100. Finally, series of index numbers showing changes in producers' terms of trade have been calculated (in terms of cotton piece goods). This has been done by dividing the producer price index by the corresponding import price (landed cost) index and expressing the new series on a percentage basis with 1935–7 again as 100.

Table 39. *Indices of landed costs of cotton piece goods (1936–7 = 100) and of the c.i.f. values of 20 Nigerian imports (1939 = 100)*

Year	(a) Index of the landed costs of all cotton piece goods (1935–7 = 100)	(b) Colonial Office index of c.i.f. values of 20 Nigerian imports (1939 = 100)	(a) as percentage of (b)
1939	101	100	101
1943	247	222	111
1945	258	223	116
1949	381	329	116
1950	407	312	130
1951	496	352	141

The series are reproduced in the note to this appendix. In conjunction with the indices of producer prices they are the bases of the diagrams in the next section.

For those years for which the Colonial Office index is available, it is instructive to compare its movement with that of the index of the landed costs of cotton piece goods.[1] As is to be expected, the index of the landed costs of cotton piece goods rose more. The series are shown in Table 39.

For two distinct reasons the Colonial Office index rose much less over general picture. The reader may readily form his own assessment of the relevance or significance of this factor, since indices of the terms of trade of producers are shown separately in terms of both printed and bleached cotton piece goods, as well as in terms of all cotton piece goods.

[1] In the Colonial Office index 1939 = 100 and in the series of the landed costs of cotton piece goods 1935–7 = 100. This difference does not signify for our purpose, since Nigerian import prices in 1939 were very close to those of 1935–7. The index of the landed costs of cotton piece goods with the years 1935–7 as 100 stood at 101 in 1939.

this period than the general level of retail prices of merchandise bought by the producers. First, the basis of the Colonial Office index includes a number of commodities the prices of which were relatively stable and which are not purchased by the producers. Secondly, increases in up-country retail prices were proportionately far greater than increases in c.i.f. values, or even in landed costs. For these reasons it is probable that the index of the landed costs of cotton piece goods (which also rose less than their retail prices) actually provides a better indication of the increases in the retail prices of the general range of imported merchandise bought by producers than does the Colonial Office index. It is clear that at least until 1950 landed costs of cotton piece goods did not rise significantly more than the general level of retail prices of imported merchandise bought by the producer. Accordingly, the use of landed costs of cotton piece goods does not present a seriously misleading picture of the course of the terms of trade of producers over this period.[1]

As the tables in the note to this appendix reproduce the Colonial Office index and the Nigerian index, besides presenting series of indices of producer prices, the reader can easily use these series in preference to indices expressed in terms of cotton piece goods, if this is thought desirable.

It will be seen that even on the basis of these series there has been little or no improvement in real terms in the position of the West African producers compared to the mid-1930's, with the exception in recent

[1] This is confirmed by some detailed information on import prices submitted by the United Africa Company to the Aiken Watson Commission in the Gold Coast in 1948. This showed that the rise in the landed costs of the principal classes of merchandise handled by that firm was much greater than that shown by the Colonial Office index. The data submitted suggest that compared to 1939 the landed cost of textiles increased in about the same proportion as the average of the principal consumer goods purchased by Africans; this was due partly to the temporary eclipse of low cost suppliers of cheap hardware. The table below, reproduced from the report of the Commission, is based on that information.

Index numbers of landed costs, including duty of certain classes of commodities imported into the Gold Coast, 1939 and 1948 (weighted according to 1939 quantities)

	1939	1948
Textiles	100	314
Haberdashery	100	292
Tobacco	100	155
Drinks[a]	100	167
Hardware	100	445
Provisions	100	352
Sundry	100	283

[a] Much of this is for consumption by non-Africans.
Source: Colonial No. 231, 1948.

years of the position of the cocoa producers.[1] It is not suggested that this result is a necessary consequence of statutory marketing. But it is a corollary of the payment of producer prices below commercial values (whether as a result of the accumulation of surpluses and/or of sales at prices below commercial values), over a period of rising prices of imported merchandise bought by the producers.

Chart 3. Indices of terms of trade of Gold Coast cocoa producers in terms of bleached, printed and all imported cotton piece goods (1935–7 = 100).

2. DIAGRAMS OF THE TERMS OF TRADE OF PRODUCERS

This section presents diagrams of the course of the terms of trade of producers in terms of cotton piece goods.

Chart 3 well reflects the severe deterioration in the terms of trade during the war. The index reached its lowest point in 1943. In that year the index in terms of all imported cotton piece goods was less

[1] As already indicated, this conclusion is not significantly affected by the fact that in the Colonial Office series 1939 = 100 (cf. § 1, above).

than one-quarter of the base period; on that basis producers would have had to produce about four times as much cocoa to secure a given volume of imports. However, as retail prices had risen much more than landed costs at that time the true proportion was certainly significantly larger. It will be seen that the terms of trade continued below the level

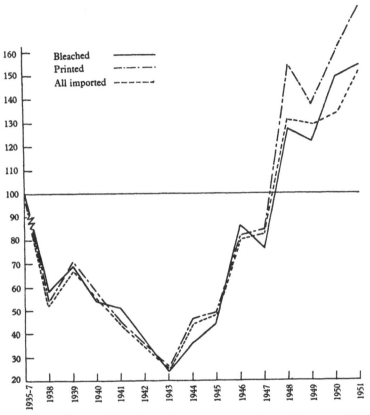

Chart 4. Indices of terms of trade of Nigerian cocoa producers in terms of bleached, printed and all imported cotton piece goods (1935-7 = 100).

of the base period until well after the war. Indeed, they did not rise above it until 1948 and they fell again in the following year as a result of the drastic cut in producer prices in that year. By 1950 they were appreciably above the level of the base period.[1]

Chart 4 reflects much the same experience as Chart 3. The only

[1] Charts 3 and 4 include calculations in terms of imports of bleached cotton piece goods. In fact this class of cotton piece goods figures little in the cocoa producing areas. The calculations have been included for the sake of completeness and consistency.

difference of significance is the absence of the serious recession of the index in 1949; this difference is accounted for by the much smaller proportionate reduction in producer prices in Nigeria in the 1949–50 season compared with the reduction in the Gold Coast.

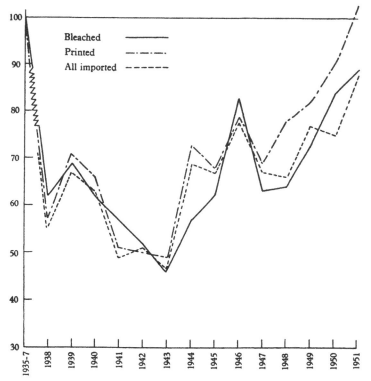

Chart 5. Indices of terms of trade of Nigerian groundnut producers in terms of bleached, printed and all imported cotton piece goods (1935–7 = 100).

Chart 5 largely explains itself, and reflects a situation very different from that implied by the widely held views about the prosperity of Nigerian oilseed producers. During the war the producers' terms of trade were far below those of the mid-1930's and even below the very depressed level of 1938, which was a year of severe depression for producers of oilseeds. Around 1942–3 the index of the terms of trade was under one-half of the level of the base period.

The recent experience of these producers is, however, much more interesting and significant. The producers' terms of trade (in terms of cotton piece goods) have remained consistently below the level of the base period. They had reached only about 80 % of this level in 1950.

Chart 6 conforms closely to the pattern of Chart 5. The war-time decline in the producers' terms of trade was somewhat greater for palm kernels than for groundnuts. This probably reflects the relatively greater urgency of the demand for groundnuts during 1942–4. After the war the terms of trade of palm kernel producers improved somewhat further than those of groundnut producers, but had not in 1950 reached the level of the base period. In that year the terms of trade were about 80–85 % of those in the base period.

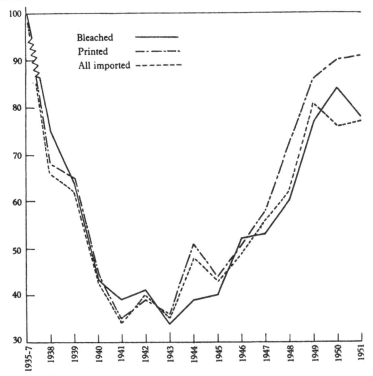

Chart 6. Indices of terms of trade of Nigerian palm kernel producers in terms of bleached, printed and all imported cotton piece goods (1935–7 = 100).

The course of the terms of trade of palm oil producers (Chart 7) is very similar to that of the palm kernel producers, which is in accordance with expectations, since producer prices for the two products are prescribed by the same authorities, they are produced in the same area and usually by the same producers or their close relatives.[1]

[1] The information presented suggests at first sight that the experience of the palm-oil producers in recent years has been more unfavourable than that of the producers of palm kernels. This is almost certainly an apparent discrepancy only, which arises

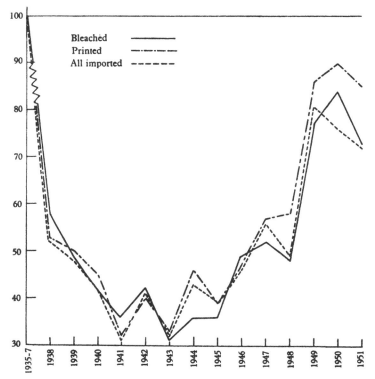

Chart 7. Indices of terms of trade of Nigerian palm oil producers in terms of bleached, printed and all imported cotton piece goods (1935–7 = 100). [Palm oil grade 2, Lagos.]

3. THE TERMS OF TRADE AND THE INCOME OF PRODUCERS

Changes in producers' terms of trade (however measured) do not of course necessarily reflect changes in real incomes, which are also affected by the changes in output by producer. But over this period there has certainly been no substantial increase in the output per producer in any of the major export crops, at least not in output for export. Total exports of cocoa and of oil-palm produce have been approximately stationary. Exports of groundnuts have increased compared to the mid-1930's, though the secular increase in exports seems to have been appreciably less pronounced since then. Nigeria and the Gold Coast are, however,

from the necessity of relying on the price of grade 2 oil for the construction of the underlying series. For reasons explained in the note to Chapter 23 this procedure somewhat understates the rise in the producer prices of palm oil. The underestimate is of the general order of 10 %; this can be seen from Table 26 above. The use of this grade for the series was unavoidable as no figures are available of the proportions of different grades bought before the establishment of the present Marketing Board.

still in the stage in which the exchange economy is emerging from the subsistence economy—this is particularly true for northern Nigeria. It is almost certain that the number of groundnut producers for export had increased over this period and is still increasing.

Thus on the whole, export production per producer over this period has certainly not increased and may have declined. This can also be inferred from the fact that with the probable exception of the extraction of palm oil there has been little or no change in the methods of production.

NOTE TO APPENDIX 2

Tables of index numbers used in the calculation of producer terms of trade

1. The import prices (including duties) underlying the indices of prices of cotton piece goods have been derived from the official trade returns and trade reports. There are substantial imports of cotton piece goods other than the two classes shown here; this explains why the index for all cotton piece goods occasionally lies outside the range of the two classes shown here.

2. The underlying producer prices of cocoa in the Gold Coast refer to prices at railway buying stations. These are available from various official sources for the entire period under review. These prices refer, however, to crop years and have been converted to a calendar year basis to render them comparable with the import price series. In the conversion from crop year to calendar year basis it has been assumed that 80 % of each crop was purchased by the end of December.

3. The producer prices of Nigerian cocoa forming the basis of the index number series refer to producer prices at port of shipment for grade 1 cocoa. This is available from official sources season by season since 1939–40. For the earlier years export values calculated from the trade returns have been taken, with a deduction of £4. 17s. 6d. per ton to allow for export duty and other charges. For conversion from crop year to calendar year basis, it has been assumed that 60 % of the crop was purchased by the end of December.

4. The producer prices of groundnuts and oil-palm produce are the same as those used in Table 25. For groundnuts the seasonal prices have been converted to an annual basis on the assumption that 60 % of the crop is purchased by the end of the calendar year.

5. The conversion from crop year to calendar year necessarily involves a degree of estimate; any error in one year is automatically compensated for in the following year, so that, except in small details, the results over a period of years are not affected.

Table 40. *Indices of the landed costs of bleached, printed and all imported cotton piece goods and those of producer prices of cocoa, groundnuts and oil palm products in Nigeria* (*1935–7* = *100*)

Year	Cotton piece goods			Producer Prices			
	Bleached	Printed	All	Cocoa	Ground-nuts	Palm oil	Palm kernels
1935–7	100	100	100	100	100	100	100
1938	91	99	102	53	56	53	68
1939	99	96	101	68	68	48	63
1940	127	120	126	69	79	53	54
1941	137	154	160	70	78	50	54
1942	170	175	174	63	88	71	69
1943	254	239	247	61	116	79	87
1944	274	213	226	99	156	97	108
1945	282	257	258	125	174	101	112
1946	251	263	268	215	208	124	132
1947	370	336	345	283	232	192	194
1948	404	330	390	512	259	192	242
1949	402	358	381	491	295	309	309
1950	366	343	407	547	307	309	309
1951	490	422	496	755	436	358	383

Table 41. *Indices of Nigerian import prices*

Year	Colonial Office index	Nigerian index
1937–8	—	100
1939	100	—
1940	134	—
1941	146	—
1942	166	—
1943	222	—
1944	—	230
1945	223	216
1946	—	240
1947	—	280
1948	—	292
1949	329	318
1950	312	—
1951	352	—

P

Table 42. *Indices of terms of trade of Nigerian cocoa producers in terms of bleached, printed and all imported cotton piece goods* (1935–7 = 100)

Year	In terms of bleached cotton piece goods	In terms of printed cotton piece goods	In terms of all cotton piece goods
1935–7	100	100	100
1938	58	54	52
1939	69	71	67
1940	54	58	55
1941	51	45	44
1942	37	36	36
1943	24	26	25
1944	36	46	44
1945	44	49	48
1946	86	82	80
1947	76	84	82
1948	127	155	131
1949	122	137	129
1950	149	159	134
1951	154	179	152

Table 43. *Indices of terms of trade of Nigerian groundnut producers in terms of bleached, printed and all imported cotton piece goods* (1935–7 = 100)

Year	In terms of bleached cotton piece goods	In terms of printed cotton piece goods	In terms of all cotton piece goods
1935–7	100	100	100
1938	62	57	55
1939	69	71	67
1940	62	66	63
1941	57	51	49
1942	52	50	51
1943	46	49	47
1944	57	73	69
1945	62	68	67
1946	83	79	78
1947	63	69	67
1948	64	78	66
1949	73	82	77
1950	84	90	75
1951	89	103	88

Table 44. *Indices of terms of trade of Nigerian palm kernel producers in terms of bleached, printed and all imported cotton piece goods* ($1935-7 = 100$)

Year	In terms of bleached cotton piece goods	In terms of printed cotton piece goods	In terms of all cotton piece goods
1935–7	100	100	100
1938	75	68	66
1939	64	65	62
1940	43	45	43
1941	39	35	34
1942	41	39	40
1943	34	36	35
1944	39	51	48
1945	40	44	43
1946	52	50	49
1947	53	58	56
1948	60	73	62
1949	77	86	81
1950	84	90	76
1951	78	91	77

Table 45. *Indices of terms of trade of Nigerian palm oil producers in terms of bleached, printed and all imported cotton piece goods* ($1935-7 = 100$)

Year	In terms of bleached cotton piece goods	In terms of printed cotton piece goods	In terms of all cotton piece goods
1935–7	100	100	100
1938	58	53	52
1939	49	50	48
1940	42	45	42
1941	36	32	31
1942	42	40	41
1943	31	33	32
1944	36	46	43
1945	36	39	39
1946	49	47	46
1947	52	57	56
1948	48	58	49
1949	77	86	81
1950	84	90	76
1951	73	85	72

Table 46. *Indices of landed costs of bleached, printed and all imported cotton piece goods and those of producer prices of cocoa in the Gold Coast (1935–7 = 100)*

Year	Cotton piece goods			Cocoa
	Bleached	Printed	All	
1935–7	100	100	100	100
1938	103	99	112	66
1939	91	96	111	66
1940	125	120	140	55
1941	153	133	157	59
1942	187	160	178	55
1943	241	199	240	58
1944	273	205	253	93
1945	281	218	264	119
1946	305	258	293	211
1947	385	342	364	318
1948	397	337	413	509
1949	390	331	414	416
1950	371	333	435	549
1951	509	412	541	664

Table 47. *Indices of terms of trade of Gold Coast cocoa producers in terms of bleached, printed and all cotton piece goods (1935–7 = 100)*

Year	In terms of bleached cotton piece goods	In terms of printed cotton piece goods	In terms of all cotton piece goods
1935–7	100	100	100
1938	64	67	59
1939	73	69	59
1940	44	46	39
1941	39	44	38
1942	29	34	31
1943	24	29	24
1944	34	45	37
1945	42	55	45
1946	69	82	72
1947	83	93	87
1948	128	151	123
1949	107	126	100
1950	148	165	126
1951	130	161	123

APPENDIX 3

THE RESPONSIVENESS OF SUPPLY TO THE
PRICES RECEIVED BY PRODUCERS

The response of producers to the prices received by them is a subject frequently discussed in West Africa, chiefly, though not solely, in connexion with the price policies of the marketing boards. This topic bears on widest issues of economic policy in underdeveloped countries.

1. THE RESPONSE OF PRODUCTION TO PRICE

Various arguments have been advanced, explicitly or by implication, against the view that producer prices influence incentive, and thus the level of production in West Africa. Notably, it is said that the African does not respond to financial incentives, and in fact is likely to produce less and not more in response to a higher price.

It should be recognized that even if the producers already engaged in the cultivation of a particular crop responded to higher prices by producing less, this need not result in a reduction in supply, because prospective producers who previously had not cultivated the crop may do so as a result of the higher price. The entry of new producers is certain to be a major factor in the response of supply to price whenever extension of production in outlying regions or shifts between crops and activities are possible. This practically always applies; and it does so with particular force in extensive territories with poor communications which are still partly in the stage of subsistence production. Higher prices for cash crops will facilitate and promote their cultivation in areas where previously this was not feasible.

If the output of crops produced by the native peasantry did not respond to prices it would be impossible to explain the rapid growth of the large tropical peasant export industries, such as the Nigerian groundnut industry, the Gold Coast and Nigerian cocoa industry, the Uganda cotton industry and several others. From their emergence and growth it is clear that the supply of these products does respond to price.

Nor is it possible to accept the view that the individual African producer already cultivating the crop responds to a higher price by curtailing production. This argument implies that the African has a predetermined level of consumption and therefore wants no more than a certain real income. Since this opinion is usually advanced to justify the freezing of a given level of producer incomes,[1] the clear implication

[1] Thus in justifying the exceedingly low producer prices paid by the West African Produce Control Board, it used to be argued officially that higher prices would not

is that African wants have become sated at one particular point in history. If this were true it is difficult to see how the growing market for all kinds of imported merchandise could have arisen. The most casual observation of African habits, let alone African economic development (e.g. the growth of imports both in volume and variety), exposes the shallowness of such views.[1]

There is a particularly strong presumption that higher prices for individual commodities or groups of commodities tend to increase the rate of production and to conduce to the improvement and extension of capacity of these commodities. There can be little doubt that, like other human beings, the African, once having entered the market economy, will tend to concentrate his activities on those products which are relatively more profitable. These responses reinforce the effects on output of the entry of producers previously not engaged in the cultivation of the particular crop or crops.

These considerations are not really in dispute. Their validity is recognized in the practice of governments the world over, including that of the West African Governments, in offering higher prices for the products the output of which they wish to encourage.[2] Several senior officers of the agricultural service in West Africa told me that whenever they wished to encourage the production of a particular crop in an area they would tell the farmers that they could expect better prices. One of the deputy directors of agriculture in Nigeria, who spent years in the north, said that he was in no doubt that both the groundnut and cotton grower responded readily to the incentive of higher prices. He emphasized this particularly with reference to the cotton grower, who could be expected promptly to increase his acreage in response to higher prices, other things remaining equal.

stimulate production. Similar arguments have been advanced in support of some of the decisions of the marketing boards. No one has as yet had the temerity to advocate the reduction of producer prices below their previous level in order to secure higher output of much needed export produce.

[1] Even if it were true, as it manifestly is not, that Africans respond to higher prices for particular products by producing less, this would not be an argument for the payment of low prices. First, it is not obviously in the interests of the African producers that they be forced to produce more by paying them less per unit, and that they should be deprived of the leisure they would otherwise enjoy when prices are high. Secondly, if the wants of African producers are rigidly limited there is little point in considering public expenditure for development of production, since if such expenditure is effective, production would be curtailed even more.

[2] Until a year or two ago Nigerian cotton was exempt from export duty to secure a higher price to the producer for this crop the output of which the Government wished to encourage. For similar reasons high prices were at times offered by the West African authorities for various local foodstuffs.

There are various technical difficulties in the way of detailed and specific empirical verification of these general propositions. To begin with, the response is likely to be more marked in the extension of capacity than in current production, with the result that the effect may be delayed. Further, there is the familiar difficulty of establishing causal relationships in economics because of the impossibility of eliminating the disturbing influence of other factors. Thus a higher price may conduce to a higher level of production, yet an increase in price may be followed by a reduced output if the innumerable other influences bearing on the situation have not remained constant. But these and other difficulties in the way of specific empirical proof do not detract from the validity of the proposition established from simple general reasoning and confirmed by historical evidence. In general there is no doubt that a higher price tends to induce both the establishment, improvement and extension of productive capacity, as well as a higher rate of production with existing capacity. The establishment and growth of the large tropical peasant industries is conclusive evidence.

It is also argued occasionally that producer prices in West Africa in recent years have risen so high as to represent the maximum incentive to production. This is clearly incorrect when the extension of production in outlying areas or possible shifts between activities and crops are considered. A price which may be sufficient to secure a higher rate of production from a given capacity may still be insufficient to ensure an extension of productive capacity. Moreover, as we have seen, producer prices have not risen so greatly in real terms. There can be no question of present prices representing maximum inducement even for current production, much less for extension and improvement of capacity.

While it is often argued in West Africa that the African is not influenced by normal economic incentives, and thus that the withholding of a large part of the market price will not affect his behaviour, the converse argument is also often put forward in support of the same policy. An instance of this is a suggestion (already discussed in Chapter 24) that high producer prices of export crops would diminish food production. There is no need to enlarge on what was there said on this subject, except perhaps to point out that it clearly assumes that the African is responsive to economic incentive and is influenced by the relative profitability of different crops in his decision on what to produce.

2. THE PRESENCE OF STABILIZATION FUNDS AS AN INCENTIVE TO PRODUCE

It is also often suggested that any diminution of the inducement to produce through lower prices would be offset by the presence of accumulated funds; in particular, that the substantial stabilization reserves assure a large measure of stability to farmers which serves as an important incentive for the maintenance and extension of capacity.

The contention is clearly largely, or wholly, irrelevant to the position and reactions of potential producers, that is, people outside the extensive margin of cultivation, or who are engaged in some other activity (including the cultivation of another crop), but who might be attracted by higher prices into the production of the particular crop.

In practice the responses of cultivators already engaged in the production of the crop is also unaffected by the presence of the accumulated funds. The great majority of producers, especially in Nigeria, are ignorant of the existence of these funds and of the promises of future price stability. In June 1950 I visited the village of Garko only about forty miles south-east of Kano on a good road. The prices for the forthcoming groundnut season, which was due to begin in November, had been announced in March. I asked two prosperous-looking cultivators, one of whom was a man of some authority in the village, what they thought of next season's price. They said that they did not know what the price would be in the forthcoming season, and they felt it was hardly fair to ask what would happen in the future. This instance is by no means exceptional.

Even those producers who may be aware of the presence of so-called stabilization funds are likely to be dubious of their value in the light of past experience. No indication has been given of the period over which prices are to be stabilized, nor of the limits of the accumulated funds. The policies so far pursued would lead any thoughtful producer to discount heavily the prospects of his receiving directly any substantial part of these reserves. Contemporary discussions and developments in the Gold Coast are likely to confirm these doubts.

It is, moreover, doubtful whether stability of prices would present a substantial incentive to the great bulk of the West African producers. The staple exports are produced by small-scale enterprises using little capital and relying on the cultivator's own labour or on that of his family or hiring daily paid or seasonal labour. Present effort is conditioned by immediately past experience and current prospects. These producers are not likely to be influenced greatly by the promise of stable prices for several years ahead. In deciding on improvements and extensions they are more likely to respond to the simple incentive of high prices for their produce, of a liberal supply of consumer goods and the availability of funds for improving their methods.

APPENDIX 4

THE EFFECTS OF STATUTORY MARKETING ON THE PROCESSORS OF EXPORT PRODUCTS

I. THE CONTROL OF PROCESSORS UNDER STATUTORY MARKETING

In view of the low level of capital[1] and technical skill in West Africa, and the heavy pressure of unskilled labour for employment in Nigeria, a measure of local processing of export produce, if economic, would substantially benefit these countries. Accordingly, the effects of statutory marketing on processors is a matter of some significance.

The need for controlling the exports of processed produce under statutory marketing stems essentially from the discrepancy between market price and the local price; and the wider the difference the more acute are likely to be the problems which arise. Unless the processors are allowed to retain the fortuitous profits arising from the discrepancy between local prices and world prices, it is inevitable that the boards should either have the sole right to export the processed products, or that they should have the power to impose a special levy on private exporters, designed to appropriate the advantage resulting from the possibility of purchasing produce at the low price.

The legislation establishing the statutory export monopolies has, accordingly, confined to the boards the right to export processed products; in addition, the boards are empowered to authorize private firms to export on conditions laid down by themselves, particularly the imposition of such special levies. Another corollary of this system would however be the payment of rebates or refunds at times when the price paid by the board exceeds the market price. But no announcement has as yet been made on this subject.

The power of the boards over the processors is so extensive that the survival of a processing enterprise depends largely on their goodwill. This is obvious from the powers of the boards to stipulate that processors using mechanical methods should buy their own material from the board concerned. The boards have also extensive licensing powers over such enterprises, and this is likely to have deterrent effects on the establishment of new ones. This is enhanced by the unfavourable

---

[1] It should not be inferred from the references to the low level of capital that a substantial influx of capital would necessarily yield a high real return. The real return on capital in West Africa is high, but only when it is suitably managed and combined with other resources (cf. Chapter 1, § 3, above).

attitude of the authorities in Nigeria[1] towards processors in such
matters as the granting of immigration permits for expatriate personnel, the allocation of supplies, and the calculation of export duties
on processed products.[2] In one or two instances the authorities stated
in official communications to actual or prospective processors that they
did not favour the establishment of private expatriate processing enterprises for the export products under the authority of the boards.

2. THE EXPERIENCE OF THE PROCESSORS OF GROUNDNUTS UNDER STATUTORY MARKETING

Groundnut milling (the mechanized processing of groundnuts to yield
groundnut oil and cake) is the most important processing activity subject to a marketing board. Although still comparatively small, this
industry has grown considerably since its inception in 1941; exports of
groundnut oil from Nigeria in 1951 were 10,000 tons. This processing
activity has thus shown some promise of viability in spite of great
difficulties caused by severe restrictions on its activities, especially over
the period covered by the West African Produce Control Board. It is in
this industry that the difficulties have become most manifest of efficient
and equitable computation of the levies on the exports of processed
products postulated by the separation of local prices from market prices.

The first enterprise in this industry was established in 1942, a few
months before the marketing of groundnuts was taken over by the West
African Produce Control Board. From 1943 to 1947 there was a ban
on local expression, with quantitatively negligible exceptions for processing for the armed forces; and the local movement of groundnuts
and of groundnut oil was also banned, except with the consent of the
authorities, which was refused for the products of mechanized processing. The legality of some of these restrictions was doubtful, as they
were not based on general legislation, but were simply communicated
by the authorities to the processors. As late as 1947 applications to

---

[1] The description and analysis of the effects of statutory marketing on the position
of local processing applies to Nigeria only, and only up to 1952. There were signs in
that year that there might be changes in policy. The attitude of the Gold Coast Cocoa
Marketing Board to this activity has been much more favourable than that of the
Nigerian boards and authorities. But in the Gold Coast local processing of cocoa is
less important than the processing of groundnuts and oil-palm produce in Nigeria.

[2] The export duty is levied on an *ad valorem* basis on the processed products which
amounts to the levying of duy on the processing activity, as well as on the raw material
content of the exports. This has been important in groundnut milling, where the
export duty on oil and cake is appreciably heavier than on the unprocessed product.
This necessarily encourages the export of the latter, and discourages the production
and export of the former.

crush a few hundred tons for export from the Northern Provinces to the south, or to the other West African colonies or to the Ministry of Food were all refused.

The reason for these restrictions and prohibitions was said to be the need to export to the United Kingdom every ton of groundnuts in an unprocessed form. In assessing these measures it is relevant that the amount which the local processor wished to use was far less than 1 % of the entire exports; that the price for groundnuts and groundnut oil in Lagos was about four times the price paid at that time by the Ministry of Food; that some of the oil was actually intended for the Ministry of Food and the rest for consumption in West Africa; and that from 1946 there were increasing difficulties of evacuating groundnuts from Kano, where large stocks were accumulating and where in due course appreciable quantities suffered insect damage as a result of excessively long storage.

Since its establishment in 1949 the Nigeria Groundnut Marketing Board has exported all unprocessed groundnuts. In the first year or two of its operation some oil and cake was exported by the processors on their own account, but subject to levies by the Board, while a further quantity was taken over from the processors and exported by the Board on its own account. Gradually the latter method became more important.

The Groundnut Marketing Board and its executive have consistently taken up the position that export licences could be granted only if on each shipment processors would surrender an amount of money sufficient to secure for the Board the same profit as it would have secured if it had exported the groundnuts itself. It was argued that by the adoption of this method statutory marketing would not affect the prospects of the processors either way, that it neither penalized nor subsidized them, and that it thus provided a test of the viability of processing. It was also suggested that levies at lower rates would deprive the Board of funds which would otherwise accrue to it, and would thus amount to a subsidization of uneconomic processing at the expense of producers.

At first sight this reasoning is attractive; but in the circumstances of statutory marketing in Nigeria, and especially under the marketing arrangements for groundnuts, this method did not prove neutral in its effects on processors. Some of the difficulties which have arisen under this system are of interest, since in different guises they are likely to arise frequently in attempts to find a *modus vivendi* for processors of raw materials subject to this kind of control.

3. DIFFICULTIES OF COMPUTING APPROPRIATE LEVIES ON EXPORTING PROCESSORS

Statutory marketing of groundnuts has affected both the costs and the selling prospects of processors, independently of the imposition of the levies. The costs of processors were raised by the insistence that they should purchase their raw material through the Board at prices appreciably higher than the statutory producer price. They have also had to comply with many more formalities than would be necessary in the absence of such a system, and this tends to raise costs, especially in small or medium-sized organizations. The selling prospects of processors have been already affected by statutory marketing on several counts. It has restricted their room for manoeuvre, in such matters as taking advantage of favourable opportunities on fluctuating markets or securing shipping at special charter rates and so forth. Moreover, they cannot enter into long forward contracts on the open market since the price of their raw material is subject to wide and discontinuous fluctuations against which they cannot hedge in terminal markets.

The level and burden of the levies was increased by the operation of the export duty which affected adversely the net proceeds derived from the sale of oil and cake (whether sold by the Board or by the processors) compared with the sale proceeds of unprocessed groundnuts.[1] This in turn resulted in the imposition of heavier levies to make the net margin secured by the Board from the exports of oil and cake more nearly comparable to the surplus it retained on its sales of groundnuts.

Again, the marketing arrangements (in both the marketing of groundnuts and of the processed products) introduced arbitrary elements, which tended to affect processors adversely, into the calculation of the levies. This resulted partly from the marketing arrangements of the Board and partly from the purchasing arrangements of the Ministry of Food.

The Board itself sold part of the exports of oil and cake, as well as all exports of groundnuts. This meant that the results of the selling policies of the Board necessarily influenced the computation of the levy, since it was the aim to secure as nearly as was possible the same margin on the export of the processed products as accrued to the Board from the export of groundnuts (although the operation of the export duty ensured that this aim could not be completely realized). But the processors who were subject to the levy (the actual level of which was thus affected by the results of the Board's sales) had no influence over its selling policy. A substantial arbitrary element was introduced into the calculations of the levy because the selling transactions took place between official bodies.

---

[1] This is the inevitable result of calculating duty on an *ad valorem* basis, and thus levying it on the processing activity as well as on the raw material content.

This was aggravated because the relative prices offered by the Ministry of Food for groundnuts and groundnut oil were affected by the crushing fees agreed between the Ministry and the crushing firms in the United Kingdom on the basis of the latter's costs. Such calculations involve arbitrary elements, since they are substantially affected by such factors as the period over which capital is to be amortized and by the allocation of overhead costs among various activities of a firm. The arbitrary elements are likely to be marked where the firms engage in a variety of activities, as do the large crushers in the United Kingdom, where much the most important processor of oilseeds is Unilever, whose range of activities is widespread and diverse.

The wide powers of the Groundnut Marketing Board, their method of exercise and particularly the computation of the levies, have resulted in lengthy arguments between the Board and its executive and some of the processors.[1] Eventually the latter became processing agents acting for the boards on a cost-plus basis. While such an arrangement is not necessarily unprofitable to the processors, it is unlikely to attract as much new enterprise as would otherwise be the case; nor perhaps is it likely to attract enterprise of the same kind.

4. GENERAL CONCLUSION ON THE POSITION OF PROCESSORS UNDER STATUTORY MARKETING

Some of the difficulties of the processors in Nigeria and certain events in their relations with the authorities were no doubt the outcome of circumstances peculiar to the country and to the period; and they were to some extent influenced by the political climate, by chance occurrences and by the interaction of personalities. But in a large measure they are

---

[1] Many of these arguments centred around the question of the exact rate of the levy to be imposed on the processed products. The Board and its executive often argued that it would be a breach of trust towards the producers if the board failed to secure the full margin of profit on the unprocessed groundnuts, or a levy on the processed products yielding an equal sum. For reasons already stated (of which the operation of the export duty is the most obvious in its effects) this cannot be attained without penalizing the processors.

Although the amounts at issue were only a few thousand pounds (and at times even less), the Board and its executive argued that (in the interests of the producers) the Board could not afford to forego these sums; and that as far as possible it would impose levies to secure the full margin it could realise on the export of unprocessed groundnuts. The reasoning of the authorities is not easy to reconcile with the results of the selling transactions with the Ministry of Food, or with the allocation of large sums to the Regional Production Development Board as outright subsidy for development from funds compulsorily withheld from the groundnut producers.

deeply rooted in a form of marketing which involves an export monopoly and a substantial discrepancy between market prices and producer prices. The arbitrary elements in the computation of the levies, the uncertainty over possible refunds, the additional costs of processors and the restrictions on their marketing opportunities, the extension of the power of the boards over processors far beyond those necessary for price stabilization, are all likely to emerge under such a system.

APPENDIX 5

A NOTE ON CONDITIONAL SALES

I. EMERGENCE OF CONDITIONAL SALES

Reference has been made repeatedly in this study to conditional sales. This note considers these in somewhat greater detail. Conditional sales were widespread during the war and still affect certain sections of the West African import trade. Moreover, they may again become more extensive.

In essence the operation of conditional sales is simple. A commodity for which the demand exceeds supply at the controlled price is made available at that price to those buyers only who undertake to purchase another commodity or range of commodities, which otherwise they would not buy, at least not at the price which they now have to pay. As is well known, conditional sales can be used to defeat the operation of price control. The Adshead Commission of Enquiry into Conditional Sales found in Nigeria in 1948 that in quite remote areas such unexpected articles as table-tennis sets, roulette machines and tulip bulbs had been forced on to the buyers (whether resellers or consumers) of the controlled commodities. Where the importers or wholesale sellers are familiar with market prices they can skim off the bulk, or even the whole, of the apparently large profits of the resellers by charging appropriately high prices for the commodities sold alongside with the controlled commodities so as to leave the resellers with only a normal or minimum profit on the transaction as a whole. Thus the conditional sellers[1] secure part or all of the abnormal profits inherent in the situation, and also escape the odium of black-market transactions, since they appear to sell at controlled prices while their buyers resell at open-market or black-market prices.

It has been shown that in West Africa conditional sales may at times become virtually unavoidable. As has already been stated, rationing and price control are practically impossible at the stage of petty retail sales, and in the vast majority of cases consumers buy at open-market prices. When, in such circumstances, merchant firms sell at controlled prices they present their customers with a cash gift in the form of an effortless and riskless profit. This results in an immediate inflation o the demand as large numbers of traders, including many *ad hoc* intermediaries, wish to have these easy profits. The firms are thus compelled

---

[1] It seems difficult to avoid this awkward expression.

to ration the commodity severely.[1] In these circumstances, conditional sales represent a form of rationing which has much to commend it, especially to the firms and their executives. In view of the absence of effective price control and rationing at the consumer stage, it may be argued that conditional sales are simply a convenient way of circumventing unwise measures imposed partly under political pressure.

In 1950 there were few commodities in Nigeria the prices of which were officially controlled; they included stockfish and petroleum products, while the prices of certain other commodities, notably flour, salt, sugar, cigarettes and certain brands of bicycles, were controlled by informal agreements between the authorities and the merchants. In the Gold Coast the range of price control was then far wider and comprised the bulk of imported merchandise in considerable detail. Over a wide range, however, the difference between the open-market price and the controlled price was negligible, and for many commodities the open-market price was actually below the controlled price, so that price control was redundant. In Sierra Leone, on the other hand, price control covered a wide range of merchandise and controlled prices were fixed well below open-market levels.

2. EXTENT OF CONDITIONAL SALES

The extent of conditional sales is closely related to the range of the so-called short supply merchandise, for which the demand exceeds supply at controlled prices. It is thus not surprising that in 1949–50 conditional sales were relatively much more widespread in Sierra Leone than in Nigeria or the Gold Coast. Detailed figures shown to me by Levantine, Indian and African traders in Freetown suggested that certain sellers had calculated with some accuracy the profits which would be made on controlled commodities by resellers and had judiciously skimmed these off by means of conditional sales, leaving resellers with just sufficient inducement to conclude the transaction.[2] Sugar, flour and cotton cards (equipment used in cleaning cotton) were the controlled commodities used as a lever in these transactions, while textiles of unpopular design and tinned fish of doubtful quality were sold alongside the controlled commodities. In one instance deteriorated onions figured in a conditional sale.

---

[1] A measure of rationing is implicit in any system of price control, where price control is not redundant. With the inflation of the demand the severity of rationing (measured by the extent to which expressed demands are met) is increased.

[2] The following are two examples among several shown to me independently by a number of traders in Freetown. In 1949 sugar was a principal short supply line. At the controlled price of 57s. 1d. per bag of 100 lb., demand exceeded supply; supply

In the Gold Coast, where price control was largely redundant, conditional sales were less widespread. They were, however, by no means unknown, especially in the sale of sugar, flour and a few high-grade textile prints. Tins of a well-known beverage of which stocks were temporarily heavy, were often sold together with these commodities.

Somewhat surprisingly, there were still instances of conditional sales in Nigeria in spite of the very restricted range of statutory price control. Conditional sales were frequent in the marketing of stockfish and not uncommon in the sale of sugar, locally manufactured cigarettes, certain brands of bicycles and of indigo dyes, commodities which at the time were not subject to statutory price control.

3. SPECIAL REASONS FOR THE PREVALENCE OF CONDITIONAL SALES

As has been shown, conditional sales were found even outside the range of statutory price control. There are various reasons for this unexpected extension of their field of operation.

The principal reason is the reluctance of the sellers to incur unpopularity by raising the prices of certain commodities much above the landed cost for fear either of adverse political repercussions or of administrative reaction in the form of reimposition of price control. It is possible to appear to sell at prices well below open-market levels and thus to impress certain sections of public opinion, and yet to secure abnormal profits by means of conditional sales.

Secondly, the open-market price fluctuates often from week to week and even from day to day. The firms quite understandably do not wish to change their own prices in accordance with these ephemeral fluctuations, and in some instances cannot do so openly if their selling prices are prescribed by the suppliers. Yet whenever the open-market price rises

and demand balanced with a price around 80s. per bag. A provision trader received 45 bags from one of the importers, invoiced at 57s. 1d. These he sold at 80s. making a gross profit of over £50. He had, however, also to take 15 cases of tinned fruit at £3 a case. These had to be destroyed as unfit for human consumption. Thus the true profit was around £6. 10s. or about one-eighth of the apparent profit. Cotton cards were another short supply line in 1949. The controlled price was £12. 4s. a case; the open-market price was about £18. A trader was allocated seven cases by one of the importing firms at the controlled price. He also had to take twenty pieces of real Madras of an unfashionable design at 30s. a piece, as well as three cases of tinned fish at 98s. 6d. a case. The cotton cards he re-sold at £18 a case at a total gross profit of over £40. The real Madras was re-sold at 18s. a piece and the fish was unfit for human consumption; the trader was therefore left with a net profit of £14. It may be thought that some of the purchases represent poor judgement on the part of the buyer, but on the whole this is improbable, and would not account for purchases of defective tinned provisions.

above the fixed selling price there is inevitably a rush for the commodity. This forces the firms to resort to some form of rationing. Moreover, they do not wish to present resellers with windfall profits; so they reduce these profits by means of clear-cut conditional sales, or allocate the commodity to their customers more or less in proportion to their purchases over a previous period. This method is closely analogous to the restriction of sales of certain formally unrationed commodities to registered customers, a practice prevalent in Great Britain which it is often difficult to distinguish from conditional sales.

Thirdly, conditional sales are frequently used by the local executives of the importing houses to conceal from their own head offices (or in some cases from local headquarters) errors of indenting and buying policy. Head offices are apt to blame the executives on the coast when sales of certain lines are slow or, worse still, when losses are incurred. To avoid unpleasant exchanges, such commodities are quietly disposed of by means of conditional sales without the knowledge of the principals in the United Kingdom or even of the merchandise departments at local headquarters. This course amounts to subsidization of the sales of one commodity by surrendering part of the profits on another commodity, and has the interesting result of obscuring from the firms themselves the true relative market position of the different commodities, which may tend to perpetuate the mistake that it serves to conceal.

To some extent the prevalence of conditional sales is related to the local system of trading by which the principal customers of the firms are themselves general traders who expect to secure an allocation of a wide range of merchandise from the firms. At the same time the firms, for good reasons, do not wish to change their own selling prices too frequently. In these circumstances it is hard to avoid a measure of unofficial action in confining certain commodities to established customers more or less according to their general purchases. But the extent of conditional sales is wider than would be suggested by these considerations alone and they have, since the war, come to be regarded as a fairly regular aspect of local trading methods.

In the absence of fiscal measures designed to equate supply and demand by means of variations in taxation, especially indirect taxation, it is quite probable that conditional sales may increase again in the course of the next few years when the combined effect of rearmament and of higher produce prices will come to be felt. Both the firms and their executives may find conditional sales the easiest, the most advantageous and possibly the only method for dealing with the resulting situation.

4. EFFECTS OF CONDITIONAL SALES

The adverse effects of conditional sales are sometimes exaggerated. It might even be argued that the economic effects are small since effective price control is impossible at the retail level; and further, that the incidence of conditional sales does not materially affect the course of events, since beyond the stage of first sale the prices charged and the volume of sales are the same as if there had been no conditional sale; the price of the controlled commodity rises to the open-market level, while the other commodity or commodities also realize their true market value.

Although this reasoning is not without substance, there are important disadvantages in the use of conditional sales for equating supply and demand. First, conditional sales tend to mask the true relation between the values of different commodities, and thus to perpetuate mistakes in indenting and to draw unsuitable supplies into the country. Secondly, they are apt to unsettle the market for the commodities sold alongside the controlled commodities; the former may be forced on the market in larger quantities over short periods than would normally be the case if they were held by sellers more concerned with the market for that particular commodity. Specialized traders frequently complain with some justification that the market for the commodities they sell is temporarily upset by these conditional sales. This influence is temporary but may nevertheless be disturbing. Again, by perpetuating mistakes of indenting policy and by obscuring the true market position, conditional sales may prolong the period over which the demand for the controlled commodity exceeds the supply at controlled price. In the tense atmosphere of West Africa such excesses of demand over supply result in suspicion, agitation and allegations of favouritism and profiteering.

APPENDIX 6

THE STOCKFISH AGREEMENT

In the 1930's and from 1946 to 1951 the bulk of Norwegian stockfish imported into Nigeria was covered by an agreement between the National Association of Norwegian Stockfish Exporters, a statutory organization whose members alone had the right to export stockfish, and a group of West African import merchants.[1] The existence of the agreement and its broad outline were widely known and were the subject of frequent complaint in West Africa.[2] The agreement was abandoned in 1951. Its operation presented some features of interest of special relevance to a study of marketing arrangements in a trade in which there is a comparatively high degree of concentration both among suppliers and distributors.

It may be thought that the existence of the agreement did not affect the average price paid by the West African consumer, since total available imports were determined by the size of the catch and the export allocation of the Norwegian cartel. Although there is some truth in this contention, it is not wholly correct. First, in the absence of the agreement competition among West African importers would probably have raised the price offered to the cartel without raising the selling price to consumers. At the higher price a larger share of the catch would have been allocated by the cartel to the West African market. Moreover, the total supply might have been stimulated by the higher price. In either case the larger supplies in West Africa would tend to bring about somewhat lower prices to the consumer. Secondly, the existence of the agreement and the concentration of supplies might conceivably have made it easier for the importers to arrange the regional distribution of supplies in such a way that the average price received was higher than it would have been if the same total quantity had been sold by a larger number of independent firms.

The motives of the Norwegian cartel in entering into successive annual agreements after the war were not quite clear, since it appeared probable that the Norwegian sellers could have improved their earnings in the absence of an agreement.[3] The quantities made available to the West African market were well below pre-war levels and were expected to

---

[1] The main provisions of the agreement are outlined in Chapter 10, § 2, above.

[2] And occasionally in Great Britain. It even became the subject of parliamentary questions.

[3] Throughout the currency of the agreement this was also the opinion of a substantial minority of the members of the cartel.

remain so for some years. Demand much exceeded supply at the controlled (and at the agreement) price, and it was unlikely to decline. Thus the market was assured for a considerable period at prices not less favourable than the price stipulated in the annual agreements. The agreement did not serve to promote the long-run security of the Norwegian cartel, since it did not extend over a long period, and there was no provision either for its automatic renewal or for minimum prices for future agreements. Indeed, by confining so large a proportion of their sales to a small number of distributors acting in concert, the Norwegian exporters retarded the development of other independent distributors, and in this way increased and prolonged their dependence on the favoured firms. As their financial and trading position was perceptibly improved by the agreement, the bargaining strength of the favoured importers was further enhanced, and this did not increase the long-run security of the Norwegian exporters.

The cartel may have favoured the agreement in the belief that the importers who were signatories of the agreement were the only distributors capable of handling its products in the required volume, and that therefore the retention of their goodwill was indispensable even at some sacrifice.[1] The cartel may have feared that its product would be boycotted by the favoured distributors unless it entered into an agreement which in effect largely excluded its competitors. If this had been the motive, it would have been based on erroneous premises. Other importers of substance could have handled a large part of the available supplies, though probably not the entire supply. Moreover, it does not seem likely that the importers favoured by the agreement would have refrained for long from participating in a lucrative trade in which their competitors were active and from dealing in a product for which the demand was insistent. The exporters may have felt that in such circumstances the dissatisfied importers might have sought alternative sources of supply or might have attempted to develop acceptable substitutes. These, however, were unlikely contingencies. The production of stockfish of the Norwegian type is highly localised because of the climatic conditions necessary in its preparation. The presumption that acceptable substitutes or sources are not available is greatly strengthened by recent experience; stockfish was very scarce in Nigeria for a number of years, and the trade was very profitable, yet no successful alternatives

---

[1] A representative of the National Association of Norwegian Stockfish Exporters visited Nigeria in 1950. This was apparently the first occasion on which a representative of the Association visited this important market. He was surprised to find several substantial merchants, and at least one large firm, outside the group of firms with which his Association had a supply agreement. He appeared to be under the impression that apart from that group there were only small African importers.

have been developed either by the parties to the agreement or by other importers.

There is a possibility that the exporters might have been embarrassed by a temporary reluctance or refusal of the favoured importers to handle the product if the agreement were discontinued. If this consideration were sufficient to persuade the cartel of the wisdom of an otherwise unprofitable agreement it would have indicated such a hopeless dependence on the selected importers as is hardly credible in spite of the high degree of concentration in West African trade. On the whole it is more likely that the cartel or its officials may not have been fully aware of the market situation or of its implications. Possibly the agreement was renewed almost as a matter of routine (but for changes in certain of its terms), since it was first concluded in the 1930's, despite gradual but cumulative changes in the market situation, and in the number and standing of firms in the West African import trade. The regular renewal of an accustomed agreement is likely to be attractive and congenial to cartel administrators.

Even assuming that the agreement was advantageous to the export cartel, it would seem that the agreed price in recent years must have been extremely profitable to the importers. This may have been the result of a possible failure of the exporters to appreciate that the control of retail prices was imperfect, and that at least until 1950 the open-market price was much above the nominal controlled price.

It is not possible to assess the extent (if any) to which the importers in the agreement exerted pressure upon the Norwegian exporters. Once again it is not possible to distinguish the results of fear engendered by the possibilities inherent in a high degree of concentration from the results of pressure and implied threats. The significant conclusion is that the Norwegian cartel followed a course which is explicable only by the presence of a high degree of concentration and of concerted action in the West African import trade. The restrictive stockfish agreement cannot be understood without the presence of a dominant group of importers; the proximate reasons for the actions of the cartel, the wisdom of its decision, and the presence or absence of any pressure from the importers are of little significance for the effects of the agreement on West African trade.

It would seem that the provisions against the resale of stockfish to West Africa were not fully effective or enforceable. There is evidence of some shipments from Norway to other destinations having been transshipped in Denmark and Holland and consigned to West Africa. Nevertheless, the share of the favoured group of importers was sufficiently large for these firms necessarily to influence the market. As a corollary they could benefit themselves at all times by keeping the market short, as long as they could prevent others from expanding supply. There were frequent accusations in West Africa that the market was being kept shorter than it need be. Given the large share of the trade in a few concerted hands, it is impossible conclusively to refute the charge that supplies are curtailed deliberately, or through a measure of inertia, or through failure or unwillingness to pay higher prices to suppliers. Such charges appear more serious, as well as more plausible, in a situation in which conclusive and convincing refutation is inherently impossible.

In assessing the history and the effects of the stockfish agreement it must be remembered that throughout its currency the Norwegian exporters were members of a statutory cartel. If exports had not been confined to the members of a statutory association, it is most unlikely that the agreement could have remained substantially effective for such a comparatively long period, as it covered a largely unprocessed product, shipped by a multiplicity of exporters. This strong general presumption is confirmed in this case by the repeated opposition of some exporters to the periodic renewal of the agreement.

INDEX

For Product Safety Concerns and Information please contact our EU representative GPSR@taylorandfrancis.com Taylor & Francis Verlag GmbH, Kaufingerstraße 24, 80331 München, Germany

Printed and bound by CPI Group (UK) Ltd, Croydon, CR0 4YY

08/05/2025

01864501-0001